# 175 Best Mini Pie Recipes

## sweet to savory

## Julie Anne Hession

Robert ROSE

175 Best Mini Pie Recipes
Text copyright © 2013 Julie Anne Hession
Photographs copyright © 2013 Robert Rose Inc.
Cover and text design copyright © 2013 Robert Rose Inc.

*For complete cataloguing information, see page 321.*

**Disclaimer**

The recipes in this book have been carefully tested by our kitchen and our tasters. To the best of our knowledge, they are safe and nutritious for ordinary use and users. For those people with food or other allergies, or who have special food requirements or health issues, please read the suggested contents of each recipe carefully and determine whether or not they may create a problem for you. All recipes are used at the risk of the consumer.

We cannot be responsible for any hazards, loss or damage that may occur as a result of any recipe use.

For those with special needs, allergies, requirements or health problems, in the event of any doubt, please contact your medical adviser prior to the use of any recipe.

Design and Production: Kevin Cockburn/PageWave Graphics Inc.
Editor: Judith Finlayson
Copyeditor: Gillian Watts
Recipe Tester: Audrey King
Proofreader: Gillian Watts
Indexer: Gillian Watts
Technique Photographer: David Shaughnessy
Techniques Food Stylist: Anne Fisher
Techniques Prop Stylist: Helena Dunn
Techniques Hand Model: Shannon Knopke
Cover and Recipe Photographer: Colin Erricson
Associate Photographer: Matt Johannsson
Food Styling: Kathryn Robertson
Prop Styling: Charlene Erricson

Cover image: Southern Fried Peach Pies (page 112), Lemon Meringue Tartlets (page 60) and Campfire S'mores Pies (page 178)

We acknowledge the financial support of the Government of Canada through the Book Publishing Industry Development Program (BPIDP) for our publishing activities.

Published by Robert Rose Inc.
120 Eglinton Avenue East, Suite 800, Toronto, Ontario, Canada  M4P 1E2
Tel: (416) 322-6552  Fax: (416) 322-6936
www.robertrose.ca

Printed and bound in USA

1 2 3 4 5 6 7 8 9 CKV 21 20 19 18 17 16 15 14 13

# Contents

*For Eric, my "sweetie pie."*

# Acknowledgments

I want to thank everyone who supported me on this book, whether you worked directly on the manuscript, helped to inspire a recipe or simply encouraged me with your enthusiasm for pies!

To Bob Dees, thank you for taking a chance on a first-time cookbook author, for working with me to come up with the perfect subject matter and for introducing me to butter tarts. I'm not sure how I survived without them.

Judith Finlayson, you have been such a pleasure to work with throughout the editing process. I truly felt like this was a collaborative effort, and I have learned so much from you.

Thank you to Marian Jarkovich for your support on the marketing and production side.

Thanks to Kevin Cockburn for your outstanding work on book design as well as to Joseph Gisini and the team at PageWave Graphics. Colin Erricson, thank you for the lovely food photography, and Charlene Erricson, thank you for your prop styling.

Thank you to Kathryn Robertson and the styling team for making my recipes look beautiful and delectable. Audrey King, thank you so much for your meticulous recipe testing. Gillian Watts, thank you for your hard work on the index and copy editing; your feedback was extremely insightful.

Thank you, Camilla Saulsbury, for making the introduction. As one of the most talented recipe developers and cookbook authors I know, your stamp of approval was the ultimate form of flattery.

Thank you to Brandi Farra at Brandi Marketing for creating my beautiful website and videos.

Thank you to friends and family who helped to inspire specific recipes in this book, including Beth, Emily, Laurie and Lily, Bob and Kathie, and Sara.

Thank you to my mom for allowing me to help in the kitchen at a young age, experiment with recipes and play "restaurant" on a regular basis. Thanks to my dad for encouraging me to find what I love to do and turn it into my profession and for having a fast metabolism that allows you to enjoy that second piece of pie. Thank you to my brother, Jay, for being my very first sous-chef and for being my most willing taste-tester as I learned how to bake.

Thank you to my wonderful husband, Eric, for always being so supportive of all my culinary endeavors. Thank you for tolerating the constant film of flour that coated our kitchen while I tested recipes and for enthusiastically eating pie every day for three months.

# Introduction

*Good things come in small packages.*
*— Old proverb*

There is something truly satisfying about creating a pie from scratch. Perhaps it's because baking pies is perceived to be difficult — ignore that pesky rumor that making a flaky pie crust is next to impossible; it is not — or because baking the ultimate comfort food conjures up pleasant childhood memories. One of my earliest recollections is standing on a three-legged stool next to my mother as she rolled out dough and eased it into a ceramic dish. She routinely passed me the scraps, which I coated with cinnamon sugar and twisted into shapes for baking. I haven't stopped baking since.

Or perhaps people just love pie. Whether it's that mile-high slice of lemon meringue in a pastry case or the homemade versions that lead you to try "just a small slice" of each from the Thanksgiving table, a piece of well-made pie is hard to resist.

That said, pie is certainly not without flaws. It can be messy and it doesn't keep well. And sometimes a whole piece is just too much. You really want only a bite or two, a small but satisfying taste of delicious filling encased in a warm, flaky crust.

Have you ever wondered why cupcakes are so popular? I know they are delicious, but I believe there is more to it. Eating things that you can hold in your hand is fun. It is also convenient. It means you can take your treat with you to work or to the park or you can eat it while you are walking down the street.

And best of all, it's yours. A cupcake isn't a slice from a cake that you have to share with other people. It's your own personal treat, and you get to eat the whole thing, all by yourself. In other words, it's a very private pleasure.

Why, I wondered, couldn't you transfer the benefits of cupcakes to luscious, lip-smacking pies? In this book, *175 Best Mini Pie Recipes,* that is exactly what I've done. Like cupcakes, mini pies can be created in both sweet and savory versions. They are portable. They are also individually sized and fun to eat. They are convenient to pack, store, freeze and reheat, making them an ideal treat, whether you have a family that appreciates freshly baked pocket pies as they head out the door or you are a single person who wants a cost-effective and easy dinner-for-one that can be baked at a moment's notice.

Not only were the recipes in this book fun to create, the process encouraged me to think outside the box, challenging me to come up with brand-new fillings for pies or to reimagine some of the old classics.

I encourage you to play around with the recipes, mixing different types of crusts with different types of fillings. Make some of these recipes, and what might once have seemed daunting will soon seem — well, easy as pie. Get used to the various shapes and sizes, and try as many as possible. You might be surprised and find a new favorite!

Happy baking!

*— Julie Anne Hession*

# Creating Perfect Mini Pies

I'm sure you have heard people with all levels of culinary skills, from celebrity chefs on TV to your less experienced friends or family members, claim that they are "not bakers." I always find this statement amusing, because as I see it, if you can follow a recipe, then you can also bake. This applies not only to seemingly more approachable categories such as "one-bowl" muffins, cupcakes and cookies, but also to the slightly more intimidating world of pies and tarts.

Is creating an enviably light and flaky pie crust beyond your reach? Would baking a batch of Double Strawberry Pie Pops (page 170) for your child's birthday require hours upon hours of labor? Does making a hot, hearty portable breakfast you can hand to your family as they walk out the door mean you need to set your alarm for three a.m.?

It's not. It wouldn't. It doesn't.

The following is a list of tips and techniques that will put you well on your way to making perfect mini pies.

## Proper Measuring

Accurately measuring your ingredients is a mandatory step on the road to successfully baked and impressively delicious mini pies. The ratio of dry ingredients to wet ingredients in pie and tart crusts makes the difference between a flaky, crisp shell and an overly dense and doughy shell. A common mistake of inexperienced bakers is not measuring the ingredients properly.

Dry ingredients, particularly flour, should be measured using the popular "scoop-and-level" (sometimes called scoop-and-sweep) method. Do not use the measuring cup or spoon as a scoop.

Instead, use a large spoon to transfer dry ingredients to the appropriate vessel (measuring cup or spoon), then level off the top with a flat edge such as a knife blade or offset spatula. When you use the measuring cup as a scoop, the ingredients become compacted rather than aerated and fluffed, which is preferable for baking. In addition, when dry ingredients are compacted, you may end up with a larger quantity than is ideal for the recipe. Brown sugar is an exception to this rule — it is always measured "firmly packed" into the measuring cup or spoon.

Measure liquid ingredients by using a clear glass or plastic measuring cup with the quantities marked by lines on the side. Set the cup on a level surface before adding the liquid. Hold the cup at eye level to make sure you have an accurate read.

### No More Sticky Cups

For sticky liquids such as honey, corn syrup or maple syrup, coat the measuring cup with a thin layer of oil or nonstick baking spray before measuring. They will slide right out of the cup!

## Working with Dough

### Mixing

There are two basic ways to mix a pie crust: by hand or with a food processor. While purists might argue that a pie crust should be made without the help of an electric gadget, it is tough to argue with the convenience of using a powerful kitchen appliance. In this book, all the pie crusts spend at least a little time in the food processor (or, in a couple of cases, an electric mixer), and many of them remain there from start to finish. However, I have provided alternative instructions for those who do not own these appliances.

A food processor is beneficial in that its sharp metal blade is able to cut through hard ingredients, such as cold butter or shortening, quickly and efficiently after they have been added to the dry ingredients. This creates the desired pea-sized bits in a matter of seconds. When you cut in butter by hand, you risk warming the ingredients too much. This will affect the overall flakiness of the crust.

When adding cold liquid, such as ice water or buttermilk, incorporate it by pulsing the food processor until the dough just begins to come together, or transfer the dough to a large bowl and work in the liquid by hand.

Both methods produce flaky crusts so long as the butter is not over-blended — a danger of using the food processor. However, in my opinion, adding the liquid by hand produces slightly flakier results, presumably because this method allows more control over how much the dough is manipulated. For some recipes I suggest using the "bowl method," while others keep the ingredients in the food processor. Decide for yourself which approach you prefer.

**Using a pastry blender**

If you don't have a food processor or stand mixer (which is used here for making Shortcut Puff Pastry and Pizza/Calzone Dough) you can mix the fat into the dough by hand. For this method, it is best to use a pastry cutter made from either wire or, preferably, sturdy metal blades. After combining the dry ingredients in a large bowl, sprinkle the cubed fat (butter, cream cheese, shortening or vegan butter) overtop of the mixture. Using the pastry cutter, work the fat into the flour by repeatedly pressing down and turning the blades. As with the food processor, the fat should be cut only until it is the size of small peas. Once that has been achieved, add the liquid to the mixture as specified by the recipe, stirring with a fork to combine, until the dough begins to hold together in moist clumps.

**Chilling**

If there is one consistent theme to working with pie and pastry dough, it is "keep it cold." Throughout the baking process, from mixing the ingredients until your pies are placed in the oven, you will find that you must chill the dough multiple times along the way.

Chilled dough is more consistently flaky and tender. When the fat you add to the flour (whether it's butter or shortening) is cold, it retains its shape. This creates layers of fat between the dry ingredients, which, when heated, release moisture, creating flaky, crispy layers. Fats that are warm (and soft) when added to flour simply get blended into the dry ingredients, creating dense, tough crusts.

Keeping all your ingredients cold — fats, liquids, flour and even the filling, if possible — helps to ensure successful results. When baking, your refrigerator and freezer are your best friends.

**Rolling**

When rolling out dough, the goal is to shape it into an even, smooth surface without overworking the gluten. Gluten is a protein found in foods made from wheat. It gives dough elasticity, helping to maintain its shape. Overworked gluten creates dough that doesn't hold its shape, which can be a huge source of frustration when creating filled pies.

When rolling out dough, you may find it easier to divide the batch in half and to roll and cut each half separately.

Combine the scraps and reroll to obtain the correct yield.

Depending on how long the dough has been chilling, it may be a good idea to let it sit at room temperature for 10 minutes to soften, only slightly, before you roll it out. Ensure that your work surface is clean and cool, preferably cold. Have on hand a measuring cup filled with all-purpose flour (or an acceptable gluten-free substitute) for dusting the work surface.

## Keep It Cold

Remember our theme? Cold. If at any time during the rolling or shaping process you find that the dough has become warm and too sticky, return it to the refrigerator or freezer for 15 to 20 minutes to firm up.

After you have lightly dusted your work area with flour, roll out the dough evenly by pushing firmly away from you, starting in the center of the dough. To create an even thickness, rotate the dough a one-eighth turn with every roll. This process might seem a bit fussy at first, but as the dough lengthens it will produce a smooth, uniform surface from which you can easily cut shapes. You can also flip over the dough throughout the process, dusting with flour as necessary, to keep it even.

## Keep a Measuring Tape or Ruler Handy!

Time after time when making pies, I've found myself running into the garage or my upstairs office in search of a measuring tape or ruler. I finally had the sense to purchase one for using in the kitchen. A measuring tape comes in handy for almost every recipe, whether you are sizing cutters or rolling out dough to a specified size and shape.

Try to work the dough as little as possible when rerolling scraps, which is necessary to maximize yield. If the dough seems too springy or elastic, let it rest in the refrigerator for 15 minutes before continuing the rolling process. This should relax the gluten, making it easier to roll.

## Shaping and cutting

Part of the fun of making mini pies is the variety of shapes you can use. From three-bite pie pops on a stick to savory hand pies stuffed with a hearty filling, you can find a shape to fit almost any occasion. After the dough has been rolled out, most of the shapes come together easily with the help of round cutters or suitable substitutes.

It's a good idea to have round cutters in a variety of sizes when making these little pies. The round metal cookie or biscuit cutters used in these recipes range from 3 to 6 inches (7.5 to 15 cm). Some kitchen supply stores carry sets of round cutters, but you can also purchase them through an online supplier such as Ateco or Copper Gifts. If you don't have specialized cutters, get creative with what you have on hand in the kitchen! The rims of drinking glasses, lids or small bowls all make great substitutes. Purposed cutters can be washed in the dishwasher, but make sure they are fully dry before returning to their tin.

# Types of Mini Pies

The following mini-pie shapes are what you can make from this collection of recipes.

## Hand pies

Hand pies are the most common of all pie shapes in this book. Formed by placing filling on circles of dough, then folding one side over to make a half-moon shape, they are neat and easy to hold and they travel well. Hand pies also have the benefit of size flexibility, from small circles containing only a spoonful of filling to large circles that hold enough for a meal. All the recipes specify a certain yield, but feel free to tailor the size to fit your needs. There are various types of hand pies in this book, including fried pies, calzones, samosas, turnovers and empanadas.

## Pie pops

Given the popularity of cake pops, it was only a matter of time before pie pops hit the baking scene. Pie pops are made by filling two small circles of dough (about 3 inches/7.5 cm in diameter) and attaching them to a wooden or paper lollipop stick. Not only are these a great starter shape to work with (because of their small size), but making them is also a fun activity to enjoy with children.

## Pocket pies

Inspired by Pop-Tarts, a favorite childhood breakfast treat, pocket pies are similar to pie pops in that they are composed of two equal-sized pieces of dough pressed around a filling. The pocket pies in this book are either rectangular or circular, but you can certainly get creative with the shape. For instance, you can make heart- or pumpkin-shaped pocket pies if you have access to an array of cookie cutters.

## Tartlets

Tartlets are formed by carefully fitting rounds of dough into standard muffin cups. Depending on the filling, the bottom crust will either come up to the top of the cup or reach only halfway up the sides. After the round has been placed in the cup, there will usually be some dough overlap, causing wrinkling; pressing the dough against the sides of the cup will alleviate this problem. If

the dough tears at all during the shaping process, you can patch it by pressing with your fingers.

### Lovely Lattice

You may want to add a lattice crust to your fruit-filled tartlets, because a pie with a lattice top is always a showstopper. Shiny fruit filling peeking through golden brown crisscross strips of pastry creates, perhaps, the ultimate statement pie. While the process of making a lattice crust might seem immensely labor-intensive and complicated, it's really quite simple, even for a mini pie — really, I promise! For information on how to make a lattice crust, see the step-by-step photos on pages 36 and 37 and the detailed instructions on page 122.

## Mini pot pies

Like tartlets, mini pot pies are shaped in a standard muffin cup. The bottom crust comes all the way up the sides of the cup, and it is filled to the top with the filling, which can be savory or sweet. A top crust is brushed with egg wash and pressed onto the bottom crust, covering the filling. Pot pies can be made from either puff pastry or pie dough.

## Mini galettes

Galettes, also called crostata, are free-form tarts. My mini versions are about the diameter of an English muffin. Galettes are formed by placing filling in the center of a round of dough, leaving a border. The border is folded up over the filling, leaving the center exposed. This book features examples of both sweet and savory galettes.

# Fillings

The pies in this book are filled with both sweet and savory fillings. They range from simple fruit fillings that highlight ingredients such as fresh berries or apples, pears and stone fruits to entrees from around the world, for vegetarians and meat-eaters alike. Some fillings are completely enclosed by crusts; others are nestled in tartlet shells with no top crust. Whatever filling you choose, here are some key tips to remember for flawlessly filling your mini pies.

### Keep cool

No surprise here. As with every other step, you will produce the best pies when you fill them with cool, or even cold, ingredients. When a perfectly chilled crust comes in contact with a piping hot filling, the heat softens the fat in the dough and reduces the possibility that you will produce a flaky crust. In many cases you can make your filling in advance and refrigerate it overnight. In fact, many custard-type fillings will not be thick enough to fill the pies unless they are chilled. All the recipes take this into consideration.

### Less is more

Overfilling your pies is one of the best ways to ensure that your filling will burst through the crust, making a sticky mess on the baking sheet. Most pies in this book use between 2 tbsp (30 mL) and 1/4 cup (60 mL) filling — not a large amount. The dough should fold neatly over the filling without much stretching. While it may appear that you can fit more in, many of the fillings bubble up or expand during the baking process. For best results, restrain yourself from adding that extra spoonful!

### Seal and vent

The following steps are very important when fillings are completely enclosed by crust (for example, in hand pies and pie pops). Once the dough is folded over the filling, the edges must be joined and tightly sealed, first by pressing them together with your fingers, then by pinching them together with the tines of a fork. Brushing egg wash over the surface also helps to bind the edges together. This is the first step to ensure that your filling does not escape.

The second step is to cut small slits in the top of the crust just prior to baking. These slits act as air vents, letting steam escape so it doesn't force itself between the joined edges, which breaks the seal and allows filling to escape. Don't worry if the filling bubbles up through the vents. It just provides a sneak peek of the special treat inside! (Venting is not necessary for fried, puff pastry or phyllo pies.)

### Leftovers

With some of the recipes in this book, you will end up with excess filling after using up all of your dough (this is usually indicated in the Tips). In such cases, you can either choose to make a second batch or half-batch of dough or simply enjoy the filling on its own.

## Egg Washes

The purpose of the egg wash is twofold. First, it creates a beautiful sheen and a crisp coat on finished baked pies. Second, it acts as a binding agent for the separate pieces of pie dough, so they adhere to each other throughout the baking process and don't allow any of that precious filling to escape.

There are several different versions of egg wash, most of which can be used interchangeably. For this book, all the recipes were tested using one whole large egg mixed with 1 tbsp (15 mL) water, which lends a light golden color and an attractive sheen.

Other options for creating an egg wash include one whisked egg or egg yolk on its own; egg yolk mixed with cream or milk; plain cream (still considered an egg wash despite the absence of egg); and plain water, which is used in vegan recipes. Feel free to experiment with some or all of these washes to determine your personal favorite.

## Chilling . . . Again

Once the pies are filled, it is best to refrigerate or, preferably, freeze them for at least 30 minutes before transferring them to the oven or fryer. This helps them to hold their shape while baking or frying. While the pies are chilling, you can be preheating your oven.

## Baking Pies

One of the many great things about mini pies is that they have a shorter baking time than larger ones, meaning that a warm fruit-filled tartlet will be yours to enjoy much sooner than if you were baking one full-sized pie. The pies in this book tend to take anywhere from 15 to 45 minutes to bake, depending on size and filling.

## Finishing and Decorating

Once the pies have finished baking, you have the option of adding a little bit of extra pizzazz in the form of a glaze or a dusting of confectioners' (icing)

sugar — or you can simply leave them as they are. A wide range of glaze variations is offered in the recipes. However, treat these as guidelines. You should feel free to mix and match them, based on your favorite flavor combinations.

Glazes should be at room temperature when applied to pies. You can drizzle them from a fork in a decorative zigzag motion or you can spoon a smooth coat of glaze over the entire top crust. Before glazing or dusting with confectioners' sugar, place the pies on a wire rack set over parchment or waxed paper for easy clean-up.

## Storing, Freezing and Reheating

As mentioned in the Introduction, one of the benefits of many mini pies is that they can be made in advance and then frozen, ready to bake at a moment's notice. Once sealed in an air-tight container, tightly wrapped in their tins or enclosed in a zip-top bag, the pies can be frozen for one week or more, all the way up to one month, depending on the recipe (see "Make Ahead" for each recipe).

Once you're ready to bake the pies, simply transfer them from the freezer to a parchment-lined baking sheet and then directly into a preheated oven — no thawing necessary. One at a time, two at a time, ten at a time — you can have freshly baked pies morning, noon and night!

# Dough

# Blind Baking

When pies contain fillings that have a short baking time or that require no extra baking, the shells are filled with weights and either partially or fully baked before being filled. This process is known as blind baking. For step-by-step photographs of the process, see page 33.

When a recipe calls for blind baking the shells, follow the recipe instructions for rolling, cutting and shaping the dough. While the pastry is chilling in the muffin tins, cut squares of parchment paper or aluminum foil large enough to line insides of muffin cups, allowing for a 1-inch (2.5 cm) overhang. You will need one square for each pie shell. If using foil squares, lightly butter one side to prevent sticking.

When you're ready to bake, remove tins from the freezer. (Unfilled shells can remain in the freezer for up to 2 hours, uncovered, or up to 1 week, in the tin, tightly wrapped in plastic.) Using the tines of a fork, prick bottoms of crusts 2 or 3 times. Press one square of parchment or foil (butter side down) into each pie shell. Weight lining with pie weights or dried beans, filling almost to top edge of shell. Repeat with remaining shells.

Place prepared tins in center of preheated oven and bake just until edges start to brown, as specified by the recipe. Remove tins from oven and carefully remove liners and weights. (The easiest way to do this is to lift the four corners of the liner, cupping the weights so they don't fall out.) Discard liners.

**To partially bake pie shells:** After discarding the liners, add the filling and complete the baking process according to recipe instructions.

**To fully bake pie shells:** Follow the instructions above, but after discarding the liners, return the unfilled shells to the oven and follow the recipe instructions, baking until the bottoms are light golden brown.

## Pie Weights

Pie weights are marble-sized ceramic or metal balls that are used for blind baking pies and tarts. They help to keep the sides of the crust from slumping while it bakes. Pie weights can be found in kitchen supply stores or even in the baking aisle of many grocery stores. Because they are reusable, pie weights are a good investment, but if you do not have any you can substitute for them with dried beans or lentils or dry rice.

# Flaky Pie Dough

*Although this recipe requires one extra step, incorporating the buttermilk by hand rather than with a food processor ensures that you work the dough as little as possible, yielding a tender and flaky crust.*

## Tips

For the coldest butter and shortening, cut it into cubes and freeze for 30 minutes before using.

If you don't have buttermilk, substitute ⅔ cup (150 mL) cold milk mixed with 1 tsp (5 mL) white or cider vinegar and set aside at room temperature for 5 minutes.

● **Food processor**

| | | |
|---|---|---|
| 3 cups | all-purpose flour | 750 mL |
| 1 tbsp | granulated sugar | 15 mL |
| 1 tsp | salt | 5 mL |
| 9 tbsp | cold unsalted butter, cubed | 135 mL |
| 9 tbsp | cold shortening, cubed | 135 mL |
| ⅔ cup | cold buttermilk (approx.), divided (see Tips, left) | 150 mL |

1. In food processor fitted with the metal blade, pulse flour, sugar and salt to combine. (If you don't have a food processor, see the instructions for using a pastry blender on page 8.)

2. Scatter butter and shortening pieces over flour mixture and pulse several times, until pieces are the size of peas. Transfer to a medium bowl.

3. Add ⅓ cup (75 mL) buttermilk, stirring with a fork to combine. Add more buttermilk 1 tbsp (15 mL) at a time, stirring after each addition, just until dough begins to hold together in moist clumps (you might not need all the buttermilk).

4. Shape dough into a ball. Flatten into a disk and wrap tightly in plastic. Refrigerate for at least 1 hour (see Make Ahead, below).

## Variation

*Herbed Flaky Pie Dough:* Add 3 tbsp (45 mL) chopped mixed fresh herbs, such as parsley, thyme, sage, rosemary or oregano, to food processor along with the flour.

## Make Ahead

This dough can be made ahead and refrigerated for up to two days or frozen for up to one month. If frozen, thaw overnight in the refrigerator before using.

# All-Butter Pie Dough

**Makes about
1¾ lbs (875 g)
dough
Enough for 12 to
24 pies, depending
on size**

*My favorite pie crust is
one made with only butter
(as opposed to a blend of
butter and shortening).
Butter crusts seem to deliver
the richest flavor and the
crispest texture. Large bits
of butter left in the dough
during the blending process
ensure plenty of flaky layers
when baking.*

## Tips

Although the water mixture
can be added to the dough
using the food processor,
stirring it in by hand helps to
achieve the flakiest dough.
You should still be able to see
bits of butter in the dough
when you roll it out.

9 oz (275 g) butter = 1 cup
plus 2 tbsp (280 mL)

● **Food processor**

| | | |
|---|---|---|
| 3 cups | all-purpose flour | 750 mL |
| 1 tbsp | granulated sugar | 15 mL |
| ½ tsp | salt | 2 mL |
| 9 oz | cold unsalted butter, cubed (see Tips, left) | 275 g |
| ¾ cup | ice water | 175 mL |
| 2 tsp | cider vinegar | 10 mL |

1. In food processor fitted with the metal blade, pulse flour, sugar and salt to combine. (If you don't have a food processor, see the instructions for using a pastry blender on page 8.)

2. Scatter butter over flour mixture and pulse several times, until butter is the size of peas. Transfer to a bowl.

3. In a small bowl, stir together ice water and vinegar.

4. Add half of the water mixture to flour mixture, stirring with a fork to combine. Add more of the water mixture 1 tbsp (15 mL) at a time, just until dough begins to hold together in moist clumps (you might not need all the mixture).

5. Shape dough into a ball, then transfer to a large piece of plastic wrap and flatten into a disk. Wrap tightly in plastic. Refrigerate for at least 1 hour (see Make Ahead, below).

## Make Ahead

This dough can be made ahead and refrigerated for up to two days or frozen for up to one month. If frozen, thaw overnight in the refrigerator before using.

# Sweet Tart Dough

**Makes about
1¾ lbs (875 g)
dough
Enough for 16 to
24 pies, depending
on size**

*This crust, which is basically
a shortbread crust, is known
in France as* pâte sablée. *It is
sweeter and less flaky than
traditional pie crust. The
texture is similar to that of a
sugar cookie, and it can be
crumbly and more difficult
to roll out than regular pie
crust. In a pinch, simply
press the dough into the
mold with your fingers.*

## Tips

If you don't have a food
processor, see the instructions
for using a pastry blender on
page 8. Use a fork to stir the
egg mixture into the dough
in Step 3.

A neater alternative to
transferring the dough to
plastic wrap (Step 4) is to
transfer it to a large bowl to
form it into a ball.

● **Food processor**

| | | |
|---|---|---|
| 2 | large egg yolks | 2 |
| 3 tbsp | cold heavy or whipping (35%) cream | 45 mL |
| 2½ cups | all-purpose flour | 625 mL |
| ¾ cup | confectioners' (icing) sugar, sifted | 175 mL |
| ½ tsp | salt | 2 mL |
| 8 oz | cold unsalted butter, cubed | 250 g |

1. In a small bowl, whisk together egg yolks and cream. Set aside.

2. In food processor fitted with the metal blade, pulse flour, sugar and salt to combine. Scatter butter overtop and pulse until mixture resembles coarse meal.

3. While pulsing, slowly add reserved egg mixture through the feed tube, continuing to pulse until mixture starts to come together in clumps.

4. Transfer dough to a large piece of plastic wrap and shape into a ball. Flatten into a disk and wrap tightly in plastic. Refrigerate for at least 1 hour (see Make Ahead, below).

## Variation

*Chocolate Sweet Tart Dough:* Substitute ¼ cup (60 mL) unsweetened cocoa powder for ¼ cup (60 mL) of the flour.

## Make Ahead

This dough can be made ahead and refrigerated for up to two days or frozen for up to one month. If frozen, thaw overnight in the refrigerator before using.

# Whole Wheat Pie Dough

**Makes about 1¾ lbs (875 g) dough**
**Enough for 12 to 24 pies, depending on size**

*Whole wheat pastry flour yields a tender crust that is hearty and nutty in flavor. It is more nutritious than its white counterpart, containing more fiber, iron and potassium. This crust works equally well for savory pies and fresh fruit fillings.*

## Tips

Whole wheat pastry flour is a low-protein flour made from whole grains. This is the preferred whole wheat flour for baking, as it is softer and finer than regular whole wheat flour. A good substitution is to blend equal parts all-purpose flour and regular whole wheat flour.

Look for whole wheat pastry flour in the bulk section of natural and specialty food markets or in the baking aisle of well-stocked supermarkets.

Once opened, it is best to store whole wheat pastry flour in a cool, dry place, tightly sealed in a container. Freeze for extended shelf life.

● **Food processor**

| | | |
|---|---|---|
| 2 cups | whole wheat pastry flour (see Tips, left) | 500 mL |
| 1 cup | all-purpose flour | 250 mL |
| 1 tbsp | granulated sugar | 15 mL |
| ½ tsp | salt | 2 mL |
| 8 oz | cold unsalted butter, cubed | 250 g |
| 2 | large egg yolks | 2 |
| 2 tsp | cider vinegar | 10 mL |
| ½ cup | ice water | 125 mL |

1. In food processor fitted with the metal blade, pulse whole wheat and all-purpose flours, sugar and salt to combine. (If you don't have a food processor, see the instructions for using a pastry blender on page 8.)

2. Scatter butter overtop and pulse several times, until pieces are the size of peas.

3. In a small bowl, whisk together egg yolks, vinegar and ice water.

4. Drizzle half the water mixture over dough and pulse 4 to 5 times to combine. Add more of the mixture 1 tbsp (15 mL) at a time, pulsing after each addition, just until dough begins to hold together in moist clumps (you might not need all the mixture).

5. Transfer to a large piece of plastic wrap or a large bowl and shape into a ball. Flatten into a disk and wrap tightly in plastic. Refrigerate at for least 1 hour (see Make Ahead, below).

## Make Ahead

This dough can be made ahead and refrigerated for up to two days or frozen for up to one month. If frozen, thaw overnight in the refrigerator before using.

# Cornmeal Pie Dough

*To add a pleasant crunch, either white or yellow cornmeal may be used in this recipe. This crust pairs beautifully with stone fruit such as apricots, as well as with spicy savory fillings.*

## Tips

Once opened, cornmeal should be stored in an airtight container in a cool, dry place for up to six months or stored in the freezer for up to two years.

Stone-ground or coarse yellow cornmeal was used for this recipe, but you may substitute fine cornmeal for a less crunchy texture.

A neater alternative to transferring the dough to plastic wrap (Step 5) is to transfer it to a large bowl to form it into a ball.

**● Food processor**

| | | |
|---|---|---|
| 2¼ cups | all-purpose flour | 550 mL |
| ¾ cup | cornmeal (see Tips, left) | 175 mL |
| 1 tbsp | granulated sugar | 15 mL |
| 1 tsp | salt | 5 mL |
| 8 oz | cold unsalted butter, cubed | 250 g |
| 1 | large egg | 1 |
| 2 tsp | cider vinegar | 10 mL |
| ⅔ cup | ice water | 150 mL |

1. In food processor fitted with the metal blade, pulse flour, cornmeal, sugar and salt to combine. (If you don't have a food processor, see the instructions for using a pastry blender on page 8.)

2. Scatter butter overtop and pulse several times, until pieces are the size of peas.

3. In a small bowl, whisk together egg, vinegar and ice water.

4. Drizzle half the water mixture over flour and pulse 4 to 5 times to combine. Add more of the mixture 1 tbsp (15 mL) at a time, pulsing after each addition, just until dough begins to hold together in moist clumps (you might not need all the water mixture).

5. Transfer dough to a large piece of plastic wrap and shape into a ball. Flatten into a disk and wrap tightly in plastic. Refrigerate for at least 1 hour (see Make Ahead, below).

## Make Ahead

This dough can be made ahead and refrigerated for up to two days or frozen for up to one month. If frozen, thaw overnight in the refrigerator before using.

# Cream Cheese Pie Dough

**Makes about
1¾ lbs (875 g)
dough
Enough for 12 to
24 pies, depending
on size**

*This tangy dough is easy
to work with, versatile
and forgiving, so it's great
"starter" dough if you are
new to shaping crusts.
Because of its sturdy nature,
this dough is a good option
for fried pies as well as for
baked ones.*

## Tips

Opt for full-fat cream cheese
as opposed to "light" or
fat-free, as it will yield a
flakier crust.

A neater alternative to
transferring the dough to
plastic wrap (Step 4) is to
transfer it to a large bowl to
form it into a ball.

### ● Food processor

| | | |
|---|---|---|
| 3 cups | all-purpose flour | 750 mL |
| 2 tbsp | granulated sugar | 30 mL |
| 1 tsp | salt | 5 mL |
| 6 oz | cold block cream cheese, cubed (see Tips, left) | 175 g |
| 9 tbsp | cold unsalted butter, cubed | 135 mL |
| ½ cup | cold buttermilk (approx.), divided | 125 mL |

1. In food processor fitted with the metal blade, pulse flour, sugar and salt to combine. (If you don't have a food processor, see the instructions for using a pastry blender on page 8.)

2. Scatter cream cheese and butter overtop and pulse several times, until pieces are the size of peas.

3. Drizzle half the buttermilk over flour mixture and pulse 4 to 5 times to combine. Add more buttermilk 1 tbsp (15 mL) at a time, pulsing after each addition, just until dough begins to hold together in moist clumps (you might not need all the buttermilk).

4. Transfer dough to a large piece of plastic wrap and shape into a ball. Flatten into a disk and wrap tightly in plastic. Refrigerate for at least 1 hour (see Make Ahead, below).

## Make Ahead

This dough can be made ahead and refrigerated for up to two days or frozen for up to one month. If frozen, thaw overnight in the refrigerator before using.

# Dark Chocolate Pie Dough

**Makes about 1¾ lbs (875 g) dough
Enough for 16 to 24 pies, depending on size**

*This not-too-sweet chocolate crust is the perfect pairing for rich cream fillings, as well as for sour cherries or tart raspberries.*

## Tips

For best results, always sift cocoa powder before adding it to recipes, to avoid scattered clumps of bitter cocoa flavor in your crust or pie filling.

If you don't have buttermilk, substitute ½ cup (125 mL) cold milk mixed with 1 tsp (5 mL) white or cider vinegar. Set aside at room temperature for 5 minutes before using in recipe.

This dough can be a bit more crumbly than some of the others, so you may need to work it a bit more to make it pliable and easy to shape.

● **Food processor**

| | | |
|---|---|---|
| 3 cups | all-purpose flour | 750 mL |
| 6 tbsp | unsweetened cocoa powder | 90 mL |
| 6 tbsp | granulated sugar | 90 mL |
| ½ tsp | salt | 2 mL |
| 8 oz | cold unsalted butter, cubed | 250 g |
| ½ cup | cold buttermilk (see Tips, left) | 125 mL |
| 1 | large egg yolk | 1 |

1. In food processor fitted with the metal blade, pulse flour, cocoa powder, sugar and salt to combine. (If you don't have a food processor, see the instructions for using a pastry blender on page 8.)

2. Scatter butter overtop and pulse several times, until pieces are the size of peas.

3. In a small bowl, whisk together buttermilk and egg yolk.

4. Drizzle half the buttermilk mixture over flour mixture and pulse 4 to 5 times to combine. Add more of the mixture 1 tbsp (15 mL) at a time, pulsing after each addition, just until dough begins to hold together in moist clumps (you might not need all the mixture).

5. Transfer to a large piece of plastic wrap or a large bowl and shape into a ball. Flatten into a disk and wrap tightly in plastic. Refrigerate for at least 1 hour (see Make Ahead, below).

## Make Ahead

This dough can be made ahead and refrigerated for up to two days or frozen for up to one month. If frozen, thaw overnight in the refrigerator before using.

# Toasted Coconut Tartlet Dough

*The addition of lightly
toasted shredded coconut
brings a sweet tropical
twist to buttery pie crust.
This dough pairs nicely
with creamy custard and
fruit fillings.*

## Tips

To toast coconut, spread it
in an even layer in a baking
pan. Place pan in preheated
300°F (150°C) oven and toast,
stirring every 5 minutes, until
coconut is lightly golden,
about 15 to 20 minutes.

A neater alternative to
transferring the dough to
plastic wrap (Step 4) is to
transfer it to a large bowl to
form it into a ball.

● **Food processor**

| | | |
|---|---|---|
| 2 cups | all-purpose flour | 500 mL |
| 1 cup | sweetened shredded coconut, lightly toasted (see Tips, left) | 250 mL |
| 1 tbsp | granulated sugar, divided | 15 mL |
| ¹⁄₄ tsp | salt | 1 mL |
| ³⁄₄ cup | cold unsalted butter, cubed | 175 mL |
| ¹⁄₂ cup | ice water, divided | 125 mL |

1. In food processor fitted with the metal blade, pulse flour, coconut, sugar and salt to combine. (If you don't have a food processor, see the instructions for using a pastry blender on page 8.)

2. Scatter butter over flour mixture and pulse several times, until pieces are the size of small peas.

3. Add ¹⁄₄ cup (60 mL) ice water to flour mixture and pulse 4 or 5 times to combine. Add water 1 tbsp (15 mL) at a time, pulsing after each addition, just until dough begins to hold together in moist clumps (you may not use all the water).

4. Transfer to a piece of plastic wrap and shape into a ball. Flatten into a disk, wrap tightly and chill until firm, for at least 1 hour (see Make Ahead, below).

## Make Ahead

This dough can be made ahead and refrigerated for up to two days or frozen for up to one month. If frozen, thaw overnight in the refrigerator before using.

# Savory Cheese Dough

*Mixing cheese right into the crust ensures that every bite of pie is enhanced by its sharp and tangy flavor. Most hard cheeses will work well in this recipe, so feel free to substitute Parmesan, dry Monterey Jack, Gruyère or even a combination!*

## Tips

While the flavor of vegetable shortening is arguably not as good as butter's, pie crusts containing this fat tend to be extremely flaky, and they hold their shape better than all-butter crusts. It's best to use a combination of vegetable shortening and butter in crusts, as opposed to 100% shortening, so you can get at least partial benefit of butter's rich flavor.

If you don't have buttermilk, substitute ½ cup (125 mL) cold milk mixed with 1 tsp (5 mL) white or cider vinegar. Set aside at room temperature for 5 minutes before using in recipe.

● **Food processor**

| | | |
|---|---|---|
| 2½ cups | all-purpose flour | 625 mL |
| 1 tbsp | granulated sugar | 15 mL |
| ½ tsp | salt | 2 mL |
| 2 cups | shredded Cheddar cheese | 500 mL |
| ½ cup | cold unsalted butter, cubed | 125 mL |
| ¼ cup | cold shortening, cubed | 60 mL |
| ½ cup | cold buttermilk (approx.), divided (see Tips, left) | 125 mL |

1. In food processor fitted with the metal blade, pulse flour, sugar and salt to combine. (If you don't have a food processor, see the instructions for using a pastry blender on page 8.) Add cheese and pulse 5 to 6 times, until combined.

2. Scatter butter and shortening over flour mixture and pulse several times, until pieces are the size of peas.

3. Drizzle half the buttermilk over flour mixture and pulse 4 to 5 times to combine. Add more buttermilk 1 tbsp (15 mL) at a time, pulsing after each addition, just until the dough begins to hold together in moist clumps (you might not need all the buttermilk).

4. Transfer to a large piece of plastic wrap or a large bowl and shape into a ball. Flatten into a disk and wrap tightly in plastic. Refrigerate for at least 1 hour (see Make Ahead, below).

## Variations

Substitute for the Cheddar with an equal quantity of Parmesan, Monterey Jack or Gruyère cheese.

## Make Ahead

This dough can be made ahead and refrigerated for up to two days or frozen for up to one month. If frozen, thaw overnight in the refrigerator before using.

# Gluten-Free Pie Dough

**Makes about 1¾ lbs (875 g) dough**
**Enough for 12 to 24 pies, depending on size**

*You might be surprised (as I was!) to discover that this dough is one of the easiest to work with and shape. Although a few extra ingredients are involved, they each play an important part in creating a buttery, flavorful crust that works well with both sweet and savory recipes.*

## Tips

When rolling out Gluten-Free Pie Dough, be sure to dust your surface lightly with cornstarch or rice flour — not all-purpose flour, which contains gluten.

Because they can become rancid very quickly, store rice flours in an airtight container in the refrigerator or freezer after opening.

Sweet rice flour has a higher starch content than other kinds of rice flour, making it an efficient binder with a less gritty texture.

● **Food processor**

| | | |
|---|---|---|
| 1½ cups | finely ground brown rice flour (see Tips, left) | 375 mL |
| ⅔ cup | sweet rice flour (see Tips, left) | 150 mL |
| ⅔ cup | potato starch | 150 mL |
| 6 tbsp | tapioca starch | 90 mL |
| 1 tsp | xanthan gum | 5 mL |
| 1 tbsp | granulated sugar | 15 mL |
| 1 tsp | salt | 5 mL |
| 8 oz | cold unsalted butter, cubed | 250 g |
| 2 | large egg yolks | 2 |
| ½ cup | ice water | 125 mL |
| 2 tsp | cider vinegar | 10 mL |

1. In food processor fitted with the metal blade, pulse brown and sweet rice flours, potato starch, tapioca starch, xanthan gum, sugar and salt to combine. (If you don't have a food processor, see the instructions for using a pastry blender on page 8.)

2. Scatter butter overtop and pulse several times, until pieces are the size of peas.

3. In a small bowl, whisk together egg yolks, ice water and vinegar. Drizzle half the water mixture over flour and pulse 4 to 5 times to combine. Add more of the mixture 1 tbsp (15 mL) at a time, pulsing after each addition, just until dough begins to hold together in moist clumps (you might not need all the mixture).

4. Transfer to a large piece of plastic wrap or a large bowl and shape into a ball. Flatten into a disk and wrap tightly in plastic. Refrigerate for at least 1 hour (see Make Ahead, below).

## Make Ahead

This dough can be made ahead and refrigerated for up to two days or frozen for up to one month. If frozen, thaw overnight in the refrigerator before using.

# Vegan Pie Dough

*Preparing a delicious vegan pie crust can be a challenge, since traditional pastry "must-haves" such as butter cannot be used. This version, incorporating ground flax seeds and whole wheat flour, is less flaky and more hearty than a conventional crust, but it works perfectly for a fruit-filled hand pie or a rustic vegetable galette.*

## Tips

Ground flax seeds are often called flaxseed meal. They can be found in the cereal aisle or the natural foods section of your grocery store.

Numerous recipes in this book are either already vegan or they can be made vegan with just a few simple substitutions (look for "Vegan Alternative" in the variations). A common substitution is swapping vegan butter, which is usually made from vegetable oils, for unsalted butter.

● **Food processor**

| | | |
|---|---|---|
| 1½ cups | whole wheat pastry flour | 375 mL |
| 1½ cups | all-purpose flour | 375 mL |
| ¼ cup | ground flax seeds, optional (see Tips, left) | 60 mL |
| 2 tbsp | granulated sugar | 30 mL |
| ½ tsp | salt | 2 mL |
| 6 oz | cold vegan butter, cubed (12 tbsp/180 mL) | 175 g |
| ⅔ cup | cold coconut milk (approx.), divided | 150 mL |

1. In food processor fitted with the metal blade, pulse whole wheat and all-purpose flours, flax seeds (if using), sugar and salt to combine. (If you don't have a food processor, see the instructions for using a pastry blender on page 8.)

2. Scatter vegan butter overtop and pulse several times, until pieces are the size of peas.

3. Drizzle half the coconut milk over flour mixture and pulse 4 to 5 times to combine. Add more coconut milk 1 tbsp (15 mL) at a time, pulsing after each addition, just until dough begins to hold together in moist clumps (you might not need all the coconut milk).

4. Transfer to a large piece of plastic wrap or a large bowl and shape into a ball. Flatten into a disk and wrap tightly in plastic. Refrigerate for at least 1 hour (see Make Ahead, below).

## Make Ahead

This dough can be made ahead and refrigerated for up to two days or frozen for up to one month. If frozen, thaw overnight in the refrigerator before using.

# Pocket Pie Dough

**Makes enough for 12 pocket pies**

*The addition of buttermilk yields a very tender and flaky crust, making this dough perfect for creating a homemade version of Pop-Tarts, the popular store-bought breakfast treats.*

## Tips

Don't worry too much about making perfectly shaped rectangular pocket pies. Squares and circles will taste just as delicious!

You may need to add an additional tbsp (15 mL) of buttermilk, depending upon how well the dough is holding together.

If you don't have buttermilk, substitute ¼ cup (60 mL) cold milk mixed with ½ tsp (2 mL) white or cider vinegar. Set aside at room temperature for 5 minutes before using in recipe.

● **Food processor**

| | | |
|---|---|---|
| 2½ cups | all-purpose flour | 625 mL |
| 2 tbsp | granulated sugar | 30 mL |
| ½ tsp | salt | 2 mL |
| 1 cup | cold unsalted butter, cubed | 250 mL |
| 2 | large egg yolks | 2 |
| ¼ cup | cold buttermilk (approx.; see Tips, left) | 60 mL |

1. In food processor fitted with the metal blade, pulse flour, sugar and salt to combine. (If you don't have a food processor, see the instructions for using a pastry blender on page 8.)
2. Scatter butter overtop. Pulse several times, until butter is the size of peas. Transfer to a medium bowl.
3. In a small bowl, combine egg yolks and buttermilk.
4. Add half the buttermilk mixture to flour mixture, stirring with a fork to combine. Add remaining buttermilk mixture 1 tbsp (15 mL) at a time, stirring after each addition, until dough begins to hold together in moist clumps. Add 1 tbsp (15 mL) buttermilk, if necessary.
5. Transfer to a large piece of plastic wrap and gently press into a 6-inch (15 cm) square. Wrap tightly in plastic. Refrigerate for at least 1 hour (see Make Ahead, below).

## Variation

*Whole Wheat Pocket Pie Dough:* Replace half of the all-purpose flour with whole wheat flour or whole wheat pastry flour.

## Make Ahead

This dough can be made ahead and refrigerated for up to two days or frozen for up to one month. If frozen, thaw overnight in the refrigerator before using.

# Hand Pie Dough

*The small amount of baking powder in this dough allows it to puff up during the baking process, creating extra space for the bubbly sweet or savory filling. Use it for fried pies, baked pies or pie pops.*

## Tip

If you don't have buttermilk, substitute ⅔ cup (150 mL) cold milk mixed with 1 tsp (5 mL) white or cider vinegar. Set aside at room temperature for 5 minutes before using in recipe.

### Food processor

| | | |
|---|---|---|
| 3 cups | all-purpose flour | 750 mL |
| 1 tbsp | granulated sugar | 15 mL |
| 1 tsp | baking powder | 5 mL |
| ½ tsp | salt | 2 mL |
| 7 oz | cold unsalted butter, cubed | 210 g |
| ⅔ cup | cold buttermilk, divided (see Tip, left) | 150 mL |

1. In food processor fitted with the metal blade, pulse flour, sugar, baking powder and salt to combine. (If you don't have a food processor, see the instructions for using a pastry blender on page 8.)

2. Scatter butter overtop and pulse several times, until pieces are the size of peas.

3. Drizzle half the buttermilk over flour mixture and pulse 4 to 5 times to combine. Add more buttermilk 1 tbsp (15 mL) at a time, pulsing after each addition, just until dough begins to hold together in moist clumps (you might not need all the buttermilk).

4. Transfer to a large piece of plastic wrap and shape into a ball. Flatten into a disk and wrap tightly in plastic. Refrigerate for at least 1 hour (see Make Ahead, below).

## Make Ahead

This dough can be made ahead and refrigerated for up to two days or frozen for up to one month. If frozen, thaw overnight in the refrigerator before using.

# Graham Cracker Pie Dough

*When it comes to handheld pies, traditional graham cracker crusts can be a challenge. They tend to be crumbly and are likely to fall apart in mid-bite. I created this graham cracker crust to give you the flavor of graham crackers in a sturdy (and not crumbly!) cookie-like shell.*

## Tips

Look for whole wheat pastry flour in the bulk section of most natural or specialty food markets or in the baking aisle of any well-stocked grocery store.

Because it can become rancid very quickly, store whole wheat pastry flour in an airtight container in the refrigerator or freezer after opening.

● **Electric mixer**

| | | |
|---|---|---|
| 1¾ cups | all-purpose flour | 425 mL |
| 1¼ cups | whole wheat pastry flour | 300 mL |
| ½ tsp | ground cinnamon | 2 mL |
| ½ tsp | baking soda | 2 mL |
| ½ tsp | salt | 2 mL |
| ¾ cup | unsalted butter, softened | 175 mL |
| ¾ cup | packed dark brown sugar | 175 mL |
| ¼ cup | liquid honey | 60 mL |
| ¼ cup | whole milk | 60 mL |
| 1 | large egg | 1 |
| 1 tsp | vanilla extract | 5 mL |

1. In a medium bowl, whisk together all-purpose and whole wheat pastry flours, cinnamon, baking soda and salt.

2. In a bowl, using electric mixer at medium speed, beat butter until creamy, about 2 minutes. Add brown sugar, mixing until combined. Add honey, milk, egg and vanilla, stopping to scrape down sides of bowl as necessary. Add dry ingredients and mix just until combined, to avoid overmixing.

3. Transfer dough to a large piece of plastic wrap or a large bowl and shape into a flat disk. Wrap tightly in plastic and refrigerate for at least 2 hours (see Make Ahead, below).

## Make Ahead

This dough can be made ahead and refrigerated for up to two days or frozen for up to two weeks. If frozen, thaw overnight in the refrigerator before using.

# Shortcut Puff Pastry

**Makes about 2 lbs (1 kg) dough Enough for about 16 pies**

*Making traditional puff pastry is a labor-intensive and exhausting process. This method was inspired by one created by the great Julia Child. It results in a buttery, flaky pastry that is almost identical to the one that takes much more time and effort. See step-by-step photographs on pages 42 and 43.*

## Tips

Pastries made using cake flour have a lighter texture and finer crumb. If necessary, substitute ¾ cup (175 mL) minus 1½ tbsp (22 mL) sifted all-purpose flour, plus 1½ tbsp (22 mL) cornstarch.

Don't worry if the dough is tough to work with at first. It will smooth out and become more cohesive with every turn.

If the dough becomes too soft during the shaping process, wrap it tightly and chill for 30 minutes.

If you do not own a stand mixer, cut the butter into the flour mixture using a pastry blender (see page 8). Add water and mix with a fork just until dough comes together.

- Electric stand mixer fitted with paddle attachment (see Tips, left)

| | | |
|---|---|---|
| 2 ½ cups | all-purpose flour | 625 mL |
| ¾ cup | cake flour | 175 mL |
| 1 tsp | salt | 5 mL |
| 1 lb | very cold unsalted butter, cut into ½-inch (1 cm) cubes | 500 g |
| ¾ cup | ice water | 175 mL |

1. In bowl of stand mixer, beat all-purpose and cake flours and salt until combined. Scatter butter overtop and mix at low speed until butter is the size of lima beans. Add water and mix at low speed just until dough starts to come together, 10 to 15 seconds.

2. Transfer to a floured work surface and gently shape into an 8-inch (20 cm) square. Using a rolling pin, roll out into a 10- by 18-inch (25 by 45 cm) rectangle.

3. Using a knife, lightly score dough lengthwise to make three 10- by 6-inch (25 by 15 cm) sections. Using a flat cookie sheet or large spatula, carefully lift right third of dough and flip it over onto center section. Repeat with left third of the dough, as if folding a business letter. Rotate dough 90 degrees so that the long (10-inch/25 cm) side is facing you. You have now completed one turn of the dough.

4. Lightly flour work surface to prevent sticking and reroll dough into a 10- by 18-inch (25 by 45 cm) rectangle. Give the dough a second turn by scoring into thirds and flipping over the right and left thirds as you did in Step 3. Rotate dough 90 degrees so the long (10-inch/25 cm) side is facing you.

5. Repeat Step 4 twice, to make a total of four turns.

6. Wrap tightly in plastic wrap and refrigerate for 1 hour.

7. Transfer chilled dough to a lightly floured surface with the long side facing you. Give the dough two more turns. Rewrap in plastic and refrigerate for at least 1 hour (see Make Ahead, below).

## Make Ahead

Puff pastry can be refrigerated, tightly wrapped in plastic, for up to two days or frozen for up to one month. If frozen, thaw overnight in the refrigerator.

# Pizza/Calzone Dough

**Makes about 12 large or 24 small calzones**

*This yeasty dough is simple to prepare and yields a crust that is crisp on the outside and chewy on the inside. Because it is slightly more elastic than other doughs, it may not hold its shape as well when it is rolled out and filled. Fortunately, it will hold its crowd-pleasing flavor every time!*

## Tips

Bread flour has a higher gluten content than the other flours, which yields a much more elastic dough that can be kneaded and worked.

If you don't have a stand mixer, add salt, olive oil and flour to yeast mixture (Step 2) and transfer mixture to floured work surface. Knead for 6 to 8 minutes, until dough is smooth and elastic, adding additional flour if dough is too sticky.

For the crispest bottom crusts, bake the pies on a pizza stone that has been warmed in the oven during the preheating process.

● **Stand mixer, fitted with paddle attachment (see Tips, left)**

| | | |
|---|---|---|
| 2¼ tsp | instant dry yeast (1 packet) | 11 mL |
| 1½ cups | warm water (110°F/43°C) | 375 mL |
| 1 tbsp | liquid honey | 15 mL |
| 1 tsp | salt | 5 mL |
| 2 tbsp | olive oil | 30 mL |
| 4½ cups | bread flour, divided | 1.125 L |

1. In bowl of stand mixer, combine yeast, water and honey. Stir to combine and set aside to proof for 5 minutes, until foamy.

2. Add salt, olive oil and 3½ cups (875 mL) flour to bowl. Mix until dough forms a solid ball, adding remaining flour 2 tbsp (30 mL) at a time if dough is sticky.

3. Transfer to a lightly floured surface and knead for a few minutes to form a smooth and elastic ball (additional flour may be sprinkled on work surface if necessary).

4. Place dough in a lightly oiled bowl and turn to coat. Cover with plastic wrap and place in a warm, draft-free area until dough has doubled in size, 40 to 60 minutes.

5. Turn dough out onto a lightly floured surface and divide in half. If not using immediately, wrap each piece in plastic and refrigerate until ready to use (see Make Ahead, below).

## Variation

All-purpose flour may be substituted for some or all of the bread flour, yielding a chewier and less crisp crust.

## Make Ahead

The dough can be refrigerated, tightly wrapped, for one day or frozen, sealed in zip-top bags, for up to one month. If frozen, thaw in the refrigerator before using.

# Working with Dough

# About the Techniques

Because I love baking and bake all the time, making various kinds of dough and creating a wide variety of shapes from it is easy for me to do. I also find it very enjoyable. However, I recognize that when it comes to making pies of any kind, many people are intimidated. That's why we decided to include step-by-step photographs of some of the more common (making hand pies or pie pops, or blind baking tart shells) or complicated (making galettes, puff pastry or a lattice crust) techniques we use in this book. We have also included two techniques for using phyllo pastry: making traditional triangles (as for spanakopita), which are often served as appetizers, and phyllo packets, which produce lovely little mini strudels.

With the help of these photos, you will be well on your way to producing perfect mini pies, no matter what recipe you choose.

# Blind-Baking Tart Shells

Carefully fit pastry rounds into muffin cups.

Prick bottoms 2 or 3 times.

Press one square of parchment into each pie shell.

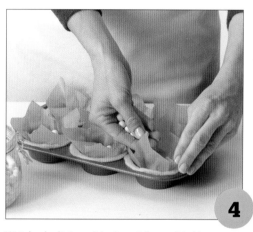

Weight the lining with pie weights or dried beans, filling almost to the top edge of the shells.

Place the prepared tins in center of preheated oven and bake as specified by the recipe.

Remove tins from oven and carefully remove liners and weights. Complete recipe accordingly.

# Making Galettes

1

Starting at the center, on a lightly floured surface, roll dough evenly, away from you.

2

When dough reaches desired thickness, cut out rounds (done with a guide such as a tart pan).

3

Place on baking sheet lined with parchment and brush edges with egg wash.

4

Place filling in center, leaving a border.

5

Fold up edges of dough over filling, leaving center exposed.

6

Pleat dough as necessary.

# Making Hand Pies

Cut out dough rounds using a cutter. Place filling in center of each round.

Brush edges with egg wash.

Fold in half, enclosing filling. Pinch edges together to seal.

Crimp with the tines of a fork.

Brush tops with egg wash.

When you are ready to bake, cut 2 or 3 slits in the top of each turnover with a sharp knife.

# Making Lattice Crust

Roll out dough for crust out to a thickness of ⅛ inch (3 mm).

Place dough on a baking sheet and cut out rounds.

Using a sharp knife or pastry cutter, cut each round into 8 strips of equal width.

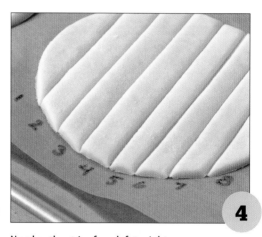

Number the strips from left to right.

Place strips 1, 3, 5 and 7 (in that order) vertically across the pie, spacing apart.

Fold back strips 3 and 7 from top of pie. Lay strip 2 horizontally across the pie.

7

Straighten strips 3 and 7.

8

Fold back strips 1 and 5 from top of pie. Lay strip 4 across pie, parallel to strip 2.

9

Straighten strips 1 and 5.

10

Fold back strips 3 and 7 from bottom of pie. Lay strip 6 across pie. Straighten strips 3 and 7.

11

Fold back strips 1 and 5 from bottom of pie. Lay strip 8 across pie. Straighten strips 1 and 5.

12

Press ends of the strips into bottom crust to adhere and brush tops of strips with egg wash.

# Making Phyllo Packets

Place 1 sheet of phyllo on a clean work surface, short side facing you.

Cover remaining sheets with damp towel to prevent drying.

Working quickly, brush sheet with melted butter.

Sprinkle with toppings, if using.

Top with a second sheet of phyllo.

Place filling on bottom center of phyllo, leaving a border at the bottom and borders on both sides.

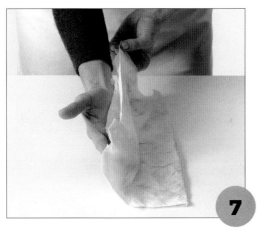

Carefully fold both sides over the filling, so they meet and overlap, covering filling completely.

Brush top surface of phyllo rectangle with melted butter.

Fold border on the bottom over filling and phyllo.

Using your fingers fold the packet onto dough, continuing to fold until you reach the end.

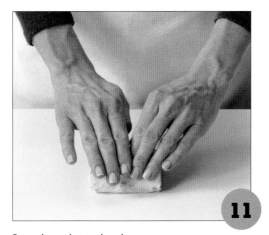

Press the end to seal packet.

Transfer packet to prepared baking sheet, seam side down.

# Making Phyllo Triangles

Place 1 sheet of phyllo on a clean work surface, short side facing you.

Cover remaining sheets with damp towel to prevent drying.

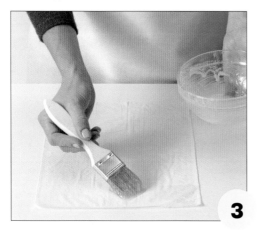

Brush sheet of phyllo with melted butter.

Fold in half lengthwise.

Brush again with butter.

Spoon filling on bottom-left side of strip, leaving a border at the bottom.

**7**

Fold bottom left corner over the filling to form a triangle.

**8**

Fold triangle at right angles to make a new triangle with additional phyllo layers.

**9**

Continue to fold triangles up the strip of phyllo to the top, as if you were folding a flag.

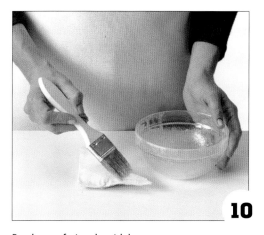

**10**

Brush top of triangle with butter.

**11**

Press end to seal.

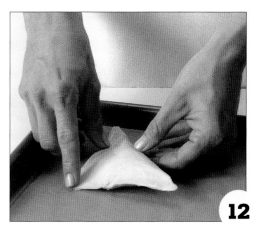

**12**

Place triangle, seam side down, on prepared baking sheet.

# Making Shortcut Puff Pastry

Mix dry ingredients with butter in a stand mixer until butter resembles lima beans.

Add water and mix until dough starts to come together, 10 to 15 seconds.

Gently shape into an 8-inch (20 cm) square.

Roll into a 10- by 18-inch (25 by 45 cm) rectangle.

Lightly score dough to make 3 sections, each 10 by 6 inches.

Lift right third of dough and flip onto center section.

Repeat with left third of dough.

Rotate dough 90 degrees.

Lightly flour work surface and reroll into a 10- by 18-inch (25 by 45 cm) rectangle.

Repeat Steps 5, 6, 7, 8 and 9 three times. (Dough will become smoother with each repeat.)

Wrap tightly in plastic wrap and refrigerate for 1 hour.

Repeat Steps 5 through 9 twice and refrigerate for at least 1 hour. (Dough will be very smooth at the end.)

# Making Pie Pops

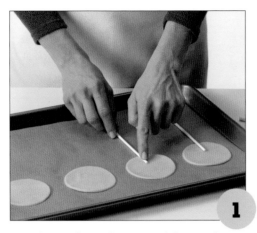

Press the top of a wooden or paper lollipop stick into the bottom inch (2.5 cm) of each small dough round.

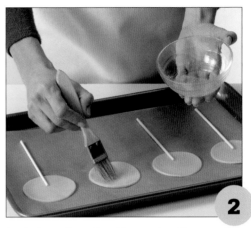

Brush the surfaces of smaller rounds with egg wash.

Place a generous 1 tbsp (15 mL) of desired filling on the center of each small round.

Top each filling with a larger dough round, pinching firmly around the edges to stick and seal.

Crimp with the tines of a fork.

Brush tops with egg wash and sprinkle with any toppings, as directed by the recipe.

# Fillings, Glazes and Toppings

# Rich Chocolate Ganache

**Makes**
**2 cups (500 mL)**

*How can a recipe so simple create a flavor so heavenly? This rich and velvety dark chocolate cream can play the part of a topping or a filling — or both if you're the ultimate chocoholic. I love it drizzled on Chocolate Raspberry Pie Pops (page 190) or Double Chocolate Peanut Butter Hand Pies (page 202).*

## Tip

The cream can also be brought to a simmer by placing it in a microwave-safe bowl and microwaving on High for 30 to 45 seconds, until small bubbles form around the edges.

| | | |
|---|---|---|
| 1 cup | heavy or whipping (35%) cream | 250 mL |
| 10 oz | bittersweet or semisweet chocolate, chopped | 300 g |
| 1 tbsp | unsalted butter, at room temperature | 15 mL |
| 1 tsp | vanilla extract | 5 mL |
| ⅛ tsp | salt | 0.5 mL |

1. In a small saucepan over medium heat, bring cream to a simmer (see Tip, left).

2. Place chocolate in a medium bowl. Add warm cream and set aside for 2 minutes. Whisk until smooth. Add butter, vanilla and salt and whisk until smooth. Use immediately or cover and refrigerate for up to 1 week.

## Variations

*Milk Chocolate Ganache:* Substitute an equal amount of milk chocolate for the bittersweet.

*White Chocolate Ganache:* Substitute an equal quantity of white chocolate for the bittersweet.

## Make Ahead

The ganache can be prepared and refrigerated, tightly covered, for up to one week.

# Lemon Curd

*We are fortunate enough to have a large Meyer lemon tree in our backyard, which yields upwards of 500 lemons every year. The need to find a use for this bumper crop is a good problem to have. This pleasantly tart lemon curd is one of my go-to solutions!*

## Tip

If the curd develops little bits of cooked or curdled egg during the heating process, simply strain it though a fine-mesh sieve after cooking to achieve a smooth texture.

| | | |
|---|---|---|
| 4 | large egg yolks | 4 |
| 2 | large eggs | 2 |
| 1¼ cups | granulated sugar | 300 mL |
| | Zest of 2 lemons | |
| ¾ cup | freshly squeezed lemon juice | 175 mL |
| ⅛ tsp | salt | 0.5 mL |
| 6 tbsp | unsalted butter, cubed | 90 mL |

1. In a medium non-reactive saucepan, whisk together egg yolks, whole eggs and sugar. Whisk in lemon zest and juice and salt.

2. Set saucepan over medium-low heat and cook, whisking constantly, until thickened, 10 to 12 minutes.

3. Remove from heat and whisk in butter until melted. Transfer to a non-reactive bowl. Cover and refrigerate until cold.

## Variations

*Lime Curd:* Substitute an equal quantity of lime zest and juice for the lemon.

*Orange Curd:* Substitute an equal quantity of orange zest and juice for the lemon.

## Make Ahead

Lemon curd can be stored for up to two weeks, refrigerated, in an airtight container.

# Vanilla Glaze

*A sugary glaze complements fillings for sweet pies of all kinds particularly well, providing a clue to the treat wrapped in the crust. Find your own favorite flavor combination from the variations listed.*

## Tip

Rewarm glaze in a saucepan over medium-low heat, whisking frequently, until pourable. You can also rewarm it by microwaving on High in 10-second bursts, stirring after each, until pourable.

| 3 cups | confectioners' (icing) sugar, sifted | 750 mL |
| 1 tsp | vanilla extract | 5 mL |
| 5 tbsp | milk (approx.), divided | 75 mL |

1. Place confectioners' sugar in a medium bowl. Add vanilla and 3 tbsp (45 mL) milk, whisking to combine.

2. Add more milk 1 tsp (5 mL) at a time, whisking after each addition, until desired consistency is achieved. (The glaze should be thick but pourable; you might not need all the milk.) Use immediately or cover tightly and refrigerate for up to 1 week. Bring to room temperature before using (see Tip, left).

## Variations

*Coconut Glaze:* Substitute 1 tsp (5 mL) coconut extract for the vanilla extract.

*Almond Glaze:* Reduce vanilla extract to $1/2$ tsp (2 mL) and add $1^1/2$ tsp (7 mL) almond extract.

*Orange Glaze:* Substitute an equal quantity of freshly squeezed orange juice for the milk.

*Lemon Glaze:* Substitute an equal quantity of freshly squeezed lemon juice for the milk.

*Cinnamon Glaze:* Add $1/2$ tsp (2 mL) ground cinnamon to the confectioners' sugar and mix well before adding the other ingredients.

*Maple Glaze:* Add 6 tbsp (90 mL) pure maple syrup to the confectioners' sugar and mix well before adding the other ingredients. Reduce the milk to 2 to 3 tbsp (30 to 45 mL) and, for an intense maple flavor, replace the vanilla extract with $1/2$ tsp (2 mL) maple extract.

*Honey Glaze:* Add 6 tbsp (90 mL) liquid honey to the confectioners' sugar and mix well before adding the other ingredients. Reduce the milk to 3 to 4 tbsp (45 to 60 mL).

*Vegan Glazes:* You can make a vegan version of Vanilla Glaze, as well as all the variations (except for Honey Glaze), by substituting an equal quantity of coconut milk for the milk.

## Make Ahead

The glaze can be prepared up to one week in advance.

# Chocolate Glaze

*Just when you thought your freshly baked mini pie could not get any better, this easy glaze comes along and drapes it in a smooth, sweet and glossy coat of chocolate. I'm all for gilding the lily, so I often add this to Southern Banana Pudding Pies (page 141) or German Chocolate Hand Pies (page 204), among others.*

## Tips

In most cases, Chocolate Glaze can be used interchangeably with Rich Chocolate Ganache (see page 46).

Rewarm glaze in a saucepan over medium-low heat, whisking frequently, until pourable. You can also rewarm it by microwaving on High in 10-second bursts, stirring after each, until pourable.

| | | |
|---|---|---|
| ⅓ cup | whole milk | 75 mL |
| ¼ cup | unsalted butter | 60 mL |
| 4 oz | bittersweet or semisweet chocolate, chopped | 125 g |
| 1 tbsp | corn syrup | 15 mL |
| 2 cups | confectioners' (icing) sugar | 500 mL |
| 1 tsp | vanilla extract | 5 mL |

1. In a medium saucepan over medium-low heat, whisk milk, butter and chocolate until melted and smooth.

2. Add corn syrup and confectioners' sugar; whisk until smooth and glossy. Whisk in vanilla. Use immediately or cover tightly and refrigerate for up to 1 week. Bring to room temperature before using.

## Make Ahead

The glaze can be prepared up to one week in advance.

# Brown Butter Icing

When I owned a bakery, we used the large walk-in refrigerator to cool this addictive icing. As a result, the walk-in was filled with the most enticing nutty aroma, and I always knew where to look for missing employees! I especially love this drizzled over Pumpkin Pecan Pies (page 224) and Oatmeal Raisin Cookie Pies (page 192).

## Tip

Keep a close eye on the butter as it cooks. It can go from being perfectly browned to burned in a matter of seconds.

| | | |
|---|---|---|
| 6 tbsp | unsalted butter | 90 mL |
| 2¼ cups | confectioners' (icing) sugar | 550 mL |
| 1 tsp | vanilla extract | 5 mL |
| 2 to 3 tbsp | whole milk | 30 to 45 mL |

1. In a small saucepan, melt butter over medium-high heat. Cook, stirring occasionally, until butter becomes brown in color and fragrant, about 8 minutes.

2. Add sugar, vanilla and 2 tbsp (30 mL) milk; whisk until smooth. If icing is too thick, add remaining 1 tbsp (15 mL) milk a little at a time, until a drizzling consistency is achieved. Set aside in saucepan to cool for 5 minutes. Use immediately or cover and refrigerate for up to 1 week (see Make Ahead, below).

## Make Ahead

The icing can be stored in the refrigerator, tightly covered, for up to one week. Rewarm in a saucepan over medium-low heat or in a microwave oven on High in 10-second bursts, stirring after each, until pourable.

# Vanilla Bean Pastry Cream

*Smooth, thick and custardy, this pastry cream sets the foundation for classic fruit tarts and plays a key role in my handheld version of Southern Banana Pudding Pies (see page 141).*

## Tips

To remove vanilla bean seeds, halve the bean lengthwise with the tip of a paring knife and place the bean, cut side up, on a work surface. Holding the knife blade perpendicular to the bean, run it down the cut side, scraping out the seeds. Instead of discarding the used vanilla bean, submerge it in the sugar jar to scent the sugar.

Although a vanilla bean will provide the most pronounced vanilla flavor, you may substitute 1 tbsp (15 mL) pure vanilla extract.

Store pastry cream in refrigerator, tightly covered, until ready to use.

| | | |
|---|---|---|
| 1½ cups | whole milk | 375 mL |
| ½ | vanilla bean, split, seeds scraped out and reserved (see Tips, left) | ½ |
| ¼ cup | cornstarch | 60 mL |
| ½ cup | granulated sugar | 125 mL |
| 4 | large egg yolks | 4 |
| ¼ tsp | salt | 1 mL |
| ½ cup | heavy or whipping (35%) cream | 125 mL |
| 2 tbsp | unsalted butter | 30 mL |

1. In a medium saucepan, combine milk and vanilla bean and seeds. Bring to a simmer over medium heat.

2. In a large bowl, whisk together cornstarch, sugar, egg yolks and salt. Gradually whisk in cream.

3. Gradually add hot milk to egg mixture, whisking constantly, until thoroughly incorporated. Transfer to the saucepan and whisk constantly over medium heat until mixture almost comes to a boil and is thick enough to coat the back of a spoon, 3 to 4 minutes. Remove from heat and whisk in butter.

4. Transfer to a heatproof bowl and cover with plastic wrap, pressing the plastic directly onto the surface. Refrigerate until cold, about 2 hours, or up to 3 days.

## Make Ahead

The pastry cream can be prepared up to three days in advance.

# Beth's Salted Caramel Sauce

*My friend Beth makes the most fantastic salted caramels, which she sends to lucky recipients during the holidays. Her generous (and addictive!) gift inspired this sweet and slightly salty sauce. You'll know that you're hooked when you find an excuse to drizzle it on just about anything.*

## Tips

If the sugar sticks to the sides of the saucepan before dissolving, wash it down with a wet pastry brush.

Pay close attention to the caramel as it starts to deepen in color. Caramel can go from perfect to burned in a matter of seconds!

| | | |
|---|---|---|
| 1 cup | granulated sugar | 250 mL |
| ¼ cup | water | 60 mL |
| 2 tbsp | corn syrup | 30 mL |
| 4 tbsp | unsalted butter, cubed | 60 mL |
| ⅔ cup | heavy or whipping (35%) cream | 150 mL |
| 1 tsp | coarse or flaked sea salt | 5 mL |

1. In a medium saucepan over medium-high heat, combine sugar, water and corn syrup. Bring to a boil, whisking constantly until sugar dissolves. Continue to boil, whisking occasionally, until deep amber in color, 5 to 6 minutes.

2. Remove pan from the heat and carefully stir in butter, cream and salt (mixture will bubble vigorously). Return to low heat and continue to whisk for 2 to 3 minutes, until caramel is smooth and thickened. Cool until warm or cover and refrigerate for up to 5 days. Rewarm before serving (see Make Ahead, below).

## Variations

Add 1 tsp (5 mL) finely grated orange zest along with the butter, cream and salt.

Add 1 tbsp (15 mL) brandy or bourbon after stirring in the butter, cream and salt.

## Make Ahead

Caramel sauce can be prepared up to five days in advance. To rewarm before serving, heat in a saucepan over low heat, stirring frequently, or rewarm on High in the microwave in 10-second bursts, stirring after each.

# Nutty Streusel Topping

*The word* streusel *comes from the German verb* streuen, *which means "to scatter or strew." Toasted nuts add crunch to this sumptuous sweet topping.*

## Tips

Although streusel is most commonly seen atop breakfast or dessert pies, it will also pair nicely with sweet and earthy vegetables, such as on Maple Orange Glazed Root Vegetable Galettes (page 298).

To blanch hazelnuts with the skins on, place in a single layer on a baking sheet. Toast in a 350°F (180°C) oven until fragrant and warmed through, about 10 minutes. Allow nuts to cool for 5 minutes, then wrap them in a cloth towel. Rub nuts briskly with the towel to remove skins.

| | | |
|---|---|---|
| ⅔ cup | packed light brown sugar | 150 mL |
| ⅔ cup | all-purpose flour | 150 mL |
| ¾ cup | sliced almonds | 175 mL |
| 1 tsp | ground cinnamon | 5 mL |
| ¼ tsp | salt | 1 mL |
| ½ cup | cold unsalted butter, cubed | 125 mL |

1. In a medium bowl, whisk together brown sugar, flour, almonds, cinnamon and salt. Using your fingers, rub in butter until clumps form.
2. Use immediately or refrigerate, covered, for up to 1 week.

## Variations

*Pecan Streusel Topping:* Substitute ¾ cup (175 mL) chopped pecans for the almonds.

*Hazelnut Streusel Topping:* Substitute ¾ cup (175 mL) chopped blanched hazelnuts for the almonds (see Tips, left).

*Walnut Streusel Topping:* Substitute ¾ cup (175 mL) chopped walnuts for the almonds.

*Macadamia Nut Streusel Topping:* Substitute ¾ cup (175 mL) chopped macadamia nuts for the almonds.

*Gluten-Free Streusel Topping:* Substitute ½ cup (125 mL) brown rice flour, 2 tbsp (30 mL) potato starch and 1 tbsp (15 mL) tapioca starch for the all-purpose flour.

## Make Ahead

Streusel can be prepared and refrigerated, tightly covered, for up to one week.

# Toasted Oat Streusel Topping

*This is a great alternative streusel topping if nut allergies are a concern. Toasted large-flake whole oats provide nutty flavor and add crunchy texture to the buttery clusters. This is great on Strawberry Rhubarb Streusel Tartlets (page 78).*

## Tip

Make sure to use old-fashioned or "whole" oats — not "quick-cooking" oats — in this topping. Quick-cooking oats are cut into small pieces before being steamed and rolled, so they will not provide the same texture as large-flake oats.

| | | |
|---|---|---|
| ⅔ cup | all-purpose flour | 150 mL |
| ⅔ cup | packed light brown sugar | 150 mL |
| ⅔ cup | large-flake (old-fashioned) rolled oats | 150 mL |
| ½ tsp | ground cinnamon | 2 mL |
| ⅛ tsp | salt | 0.5 mL |
| ½ cup | cold unsalted butter, cubed | 125 mL |

1. In a medium bowl, whisk together flour, brown sugar, oats, cinnamon and salt. Using your fingers, rub in cold butter with your fingers until clumps form.

2. Use immediately or cover and refrigerate for up to 1 week.

## Variation

*Gluten-Free Toasted Oat Streusel Topping:* Substitute gluten-free oats for the large-flake rolled oats and ½ cup (125 mL) brown rice flour, 2 tbsp (30 mL) potato starch and 1 tbsp (15 mL) tapioca starch for the all-purpose flour.

## Make Ahead

The streusel can be prepared and refrigerated, tightly covered, for up to one week.

# The Top Ten Classics

# Mom's Mini Apple Pies

**Makes 16 pies**

- **GF Friendly**
- **Vegan Friendly**

*I can't think of a dessert that is more classic than all-American apple pie. In this miniaturized variation, perfect for school lunches or football game treats, a mixture of spiced sweet and tart apples is wrapped in a flaky crust.*

## Tips

For step-by-step photographs of making hand pies, see page 35.

Instead of using Granny Smiths, other good tart apple options are Cortlands and Pippins. Golden Delicious apples can be used in place of Galas.

For easiest rolling, roll your dough, including scraps, between two sheets of plastic wrap. That way, you do not need to add flour to keep the dough from sticking to your work surface.

- 5-inch (12.5 cm) round cutter
- 2 baking sheets lined with parchment

### Filling

| | | |
|---|---|---|
| 1 tbsp | unsalted butter | 15 mL |
| 2 | Granny Smith apples, peeled and chopped | 2 |
| 1 | Gala apple, peeled and chopped | 1 |
| ¼ cup | granulated sugar | 60 mL |
| 2 tsp | freshly squeezed lemon juice | 10 mL |
| ¼ cup | packed light brown sugar | 60 mL |
| 1 tbsp | all-purpose flour | 15 mL |
| ½ tsp | ground cinnamon | 2 mL |
| ¼ tsp | ground ginger | 1 mL |
| ¼ tsp | ground allspice | 1 mL |
| ⅛ tsp | salt | 0.5 mL |

### Cinnamon Sugar

| | | |
|---|---|---|
| ½ cup | granulated sugar | 125 mL |
| ½ tsp | ground cinnamon | 2 mL |
| 1 | recipe Hand Pie Dough (page 27) | 1 |
| 1 | large egg, lightly beaten with 1 tbsp (15 mL) water | 1 |

1. *Filling:* In a medium skillet over medium heat, melt butter. Add apples, granulated sugar and lemon juice; cook, stirring, until soft, 4 to 5 minutes. Drain off liquid and transfer to a medium bowl. Add brown sugar, flour, cinnamon, ginger, allspice and salt and toss to blend. Set aside to cool completely.

2. *Cinnamon Sugar:* In a small bowl, combine sugar and cinnamon. Set aside.

3. Divide dough into halves. On a lightly floured surface, roll out one piece to a thickness of about $\frac{1}{16}$ inch (2 mm). Using cutter, cut into rounds and place on prepared baking sheets, spacing apart. Repeat with remaining dough. Reroll scraps as necessary.

4. Brush edges with egg wash. Place about 2 tbsp (30 mL) filling in center of each round. Fold in half, enclosing filling. Pinch edges together to seal, and crimp with the tines of a fork. Brush tops with egg wash and sprinkle with cinnamon sugar.

## Tips

Allow pies to rest slightly before serving so they are cool enough to hold in your hand!

A dough scraper is very useful to have when making these recipes. During the rolling process, it collects the little bits for rerolling and it cleans up the pastry board very efficiently. It also simplifies picking up the cut rounds; you just slide the scraper underneath. Even if they are sticking a bit, they will detach without tearing.

5. Place pies, on baking sheets, in freezer for 30 minutes. Meanwhile, position racks in upper and lower thirds of oven and preheat oven to 375°F (190°C).

6. Using tip of a sharp knife, cut 2 or 3 slits in top of each pie. Bake in preheated oven for 25 to 30 minutes, switching positions of baking sheets halfway through, until puffed and golden brown and filling is bubbling. Let cool (see Tips, left) on baking sheets on wire racks. Serve warm or at room temperature.

## Variations

Substitute Cream Cheese Pie Dough (page 20), Whole Wheat Pie Dough (page 18), Cornmeal Pie Dough (page 19), Flaky Pie Dough (page 15) or All-Butter Pie Dough (page 16) for the Hand Pie Dough.

*Vegan Alternative:* Substitute Vegan Pie Dough (page 25) for the Hand Pie Dough and an equal quantity of vegan butter for the unsalted butter. Replace the egg wash with water.

*Gluten-Free Alternative:* Substitute Gluten-Free Pie Dough (page 24) for the Hand Pie Dough and an equal quantity of cornstarch for the flour in the filling.

## Make Ahead

The pies can be fully assembled and frozen for up to one month. Complete Steps 1 through 4. Freeze for 30 minutes on trays, then transfer to zip-top bags and seal. Bake as directed.

# Maple-Glazed Pumpkin Pies

- - - - - - - - - - - - - - - - - - - - - - - - - - - - - - - - - -

**Makes 16 pies**

● **GF Friendly**

*When I think of autumn, maple and pumpkin are two flavors that first come to mind. In this handheld variation of classic pumpkin pie, pure maple syrup and pumpkin purée are blended in a creamy custard filling and the crust is drizzled with a sweet maple glaze.*

## Tips

Maple sugar comes from the sap of the sugar maple tree. It is the crystallized product that remains when the sap is boiled and almost all of its water has been removed. Look for it in specialty markets or natural foods stores.

Make sure to purchase canned pumpkin labeled "100% pumpkin purée" and not pumpkin pie filling, which already contains spices and sugar.

● **5-inch (12.5 cm) round cutter**
● **2 baking sheets lined with parchment**

### Filling

| | | |
|---|---|---|
| 2 | large eggs | 2 |
| ¼ cup | maple sugar (see Tips, left) | 60 mL |
| 2 tbsp | cornstarch | 30 mL |
| 1 cup | whole milk | 250 mL |
| ¾ cup | pumpkin purée (see Tips, left) | 175 mL |
| ½ cup | pure maple syrup | 125 mL |
| ¼ tsp | ground cinnamon | 1 mL |
| ¼ tsp | ground ginger | 1 mL |
| ⅛ tsp | ground allspice | 0.5 mL |
| ⅛ tsp | salt | 0.5 mL |
| | | |
| 1 | recipe Hand Pie Dough (page 27) | 1 |
| 1 | large egg, lightly beaten with 1 tbsp (15 mL) water | 1 |
| 1 | recipe Maple Glaze (Variations, page 48) | 1 |

1. *Filling:* In a medium saucepan, whisk together eggs, maple sugar and cornstarch. Slowly add milk, whisking constantly until smooth. Whisk in pumpkin, maple syrup, cinnamon, ginger, allspice and salt.

2. Place over medium-low heat and bring mixture to a simmer, whisking constantly until thickened and smooth. Remove from heat and transfer to a bowl. Set aside to cool completely.

3. Divide dough into halves. On a lightly floured surface, roll out one piece to a thickness of about ¹⁄₁₆ inch (2 mm). Using cutter, cut into rounds and place on prepared baking sheets, spacing apart. Repeat with remaining dough. Reroll scraps as necessary.

4. Brush edges with egg wash. Place about 2 to 2¹⁄₂ tbsp (30 to 37 mL) pumpkin filling in center of each round. Fold in half, enclosing filling. Pinch edges together to seal, and crimp with the tines of a fork. Brush tops with egg wash.

5. Place pies, on baking sheets, in freezer for 30 minutes. Meanwhile, position racks in upper and lower thirds of oven and preheat oven to 375°F (190°C).

## Tips

For step-by-step photographs of making hand pies, see page 35.

Wire baking racks are important to have on hand for the cooling process. After pies have finished baking, either set the muffin tin on the rack or transfer the pies from the baking sheet to the rack. This lets the air circulate around the pies, cooling them evenly.

6. Using tip of a sharp knife, cut 2 or 3 slits in top of each pie. Bake in preheated oven for 25 to 30 minutes, switching positions of baking sheets halfway through, until puffed and golden brown. Cool for 10 minutes on baking sheets set on racks, then drizzle with maple glaze. Let glaze set for at least 10 minutes. Serve warm or at room temperature.

## Variations

Substitute Cream Cheese Pie Dough (page 20), Whole Wheat Pie Dough (page 18), Flaky Pie Dough (page 15) or All-Butter Pie Dough (page 16) for the Hand Pie Dough.

*Gluten-Free Alternative:* Substitute Gluten-Free Pie Dough (page 24) for the Hand Pie Dough.

## Make Ahead

The pies can be fully assembled and frozen for up to one month. Complete Steps 1 through 4. Freeze for 30 minutes on trays, then transfer to zip-top bags and seal. Bake from frozen as directed.

# Lemon Meringue Tartlets

● **GF Friendly**

*What these three-bite treats may lack in size they certainly make up in flavor! One taste gives you a burst of tart lemon curd, buttery sweet crust and toasted fluffy meringue. These petite pies are also perfect for entertaining. Just be sure to make a double batch, as they will disappear quickly!*

## Tips

A dough scraper is very useful to have when making these recipes. During the rolling process, it collects the little bits for rerolling and it cleans up the pastry board very efficiently. It also simplifies picking up the cut rounds; you just slide the scraper underneath. Even if they are sticking a bit, they will detach without tearing.

The easiest way to remove tarts from muffin tins is to run a small, sharp knife or small offset spatula around the edges, loosening the sides. You should then be able to carefully lift out the tarts, guiding them with the knife or spatula.

● 3½- to 4-inch (8.75 to 10 cm) round cutter
● Two 12-cup muffin tins
● Parchment paper
● Pie weights or dried beans
● Electric mixer
● Kitchen torch (optional)

| | | |
|---|---|---|
| 1 | recipe Sweet Tart Dough (page 17) | 1 |
| 2 cups | Lemon Curd (page 47) | 500 mL |
| 3 | large egg whites | 3 |
| ⅓ cup | granulated sugar | 75 mL |
| ⅛ tsp | cream of tartar | 0.5 mL |

1. On a lightly floured surface, roll out dough to a thickness of ⅛ inch (3 mm). Using cutter, cut into rounds and carefully fit into muffin cups (there will be some overlap). Reroll scraps as necessary.

2. Place tins in freezer for 30 minutes. Meanwhile, preheat oven to 350°F (180°C).

3. Blind-bake shells (see page 14 and Tips, page 61) in center of preheated oven for 8 minutes. Carefully remove weights and parchment and continue to bake until shells are golden brown, 8 to 10 minutes longer. Let cool in pans on racks for 10 minutes, then carefully remove from cups and transfer to rack to cool completely.

4. When cool, spoon about 2 tbsp (30 mL) lemon curd into each shell. Set aside.

5. In a heatproof bowl set over simmering water, whisk egg whites and sugar until sugar has dissolved and mixture is very warm to the touch. Remove from heat.

6. Using electric mixer, beat egg whites at medium speed until foamy. Add cream of tartar and continue beating at medium-high speed until stiff peaks form.

7. Top each pie with about 2 tbsp (30 mL) meringue, covering surface completely and swirling decoratively. Using kitchen torch, lightly brown meringue (or place on a baking sheet under preheated broiler for 1 minute, watching carefully as the meringue can quickly burn). Serve immediately or set aside for up to 4 hours.

## Tips

For step-by-step photographs of the blind baking process, see page 33.

Expect a longer baking time (6 to 10 minutes) if you need to use 2 muffin tins because they are too large to fit on one rack.

These pies are best eaten the same day they are prepared.

## Variations

*Lime Meringue Pies:* Use Lime Curd (Variations, page 47) in place of the Lemon Curd.

Substitute Graham Cracker Pie Dough (page 28) for the Sweet Tart Dough.

*Gluten-Free Alternative:* Substitute Gluten-Free Pie Dough (page 24) for the Sweet Tart Dough.

# Cherry and Hazelnut Strudels

## Makes 12 strudels

*Strudels are flaky layered pastries, usually wrapped around sweet fruit fillings, that are traditional in Austria and Hungary. This cherry version, known as* Weichselstrudel, *is enhanced with a crunchy hazelnut cinnamon sugar sprinkled between layers of crisp phyllo dough. These strudels are equally good any time of the day, from first thing in the morning to a sweet treat before bedtime!*

## Tips

Your phyllo sheets should be about 14 by 9 inches (35 by 23 cm). You can work with rectangles that approximate this size, but if the configuration of your phyllo sheets is dramatically different, roll them out or trim them to something that roughly conforms.

When working with thawed phyllo (Step 3), be sure to keep it covered with a damp clean tea towel. Until you brush it with the melted butter, it will dry out quickly when exposed to air.

These strudels are best eaten the same day they are baked.

- Preheat oven to 350°F (180°C), positioning racks in upper and lower thirds
- Food processor
- 2 baking sheets lined with parchment
- Damp tea towel

### Hazelnut Cinnamon Sugar

| | | |
|---|---|---|
| ¾ cup | chopped blanched hazelnuts | 175 mL |
| ½ cup | granulated sugar | 125 mL |
| ½ tsp | ground cinnamon | 2 mL |

### Cherry Filling

| | | |
|---|---|---|
| 4½ cups | fresh or frozen pitted cherries (thawed if frozen) | 1.125 L |
| ¾ cup | granulated sugar | 175 mL |
| 3 tbsp | cornstarch | 45 mL |
| 1 tbsp | cherry liqueur (such as Kirsch) | 15 mL |
| ½ tsp | ground cinnamon | 2 mL |
| 24 | sheets phyllo dough, thawed (see Tips, left) | 24 |
| ¾ cup | unsalted butter, melted | 175 mL |

1. *Hazelnut Cinnamon Sugar:* In food processor fitted with the metal blade, process hazelnuts, sugar and cinnamon until finely ground.

2. *Cherry Filling:* In a medium saucepan, combine cherries, sugar, cornstarch, liqueur and cinnamon. Place over medium heat and bring to a boil, stirring frequently. Cook, stirring, until thickened, about 2 minutes. Remove from heat and set aside to cool to room temperature.

3. Place one sheet of phyllo on clean work surface, short side facing you. Working quickly, brush with melted butter and sprinkle with hazelnut cinnamon sugar. Top with a second sheet of phyllo.

4. Place ¼ cup (60 mL) cherry filling 1 inch (2.5 cm) from bottom edge of phyllo, leaving 3-inch (7.5 cm) borders on each side and about 10 inches (25 cm) at the top. Carefully fold both long sides over filling so they overlap, completely covering filling. You will now have a 3-inch (7.5 cm) by 14-inch (35 cm) rectangle.

## Tips

If using fresh cherries, here is an easy method for pitting if you don't own a cherry pitter: Place a stemmed cherry over the top of an empty beer or soda bottle. Using the end of a chopstick, push the pit through the bottom of the cherry so it lands in the bottle.

For step-by-step photographs of making phyllo packets (mini strudels), see page 38.

5. Brush top surface of phyllo rectangle with melted butter and sprinkle with more hazelnut mixture. Fold up the 1-inch (2.5 cm) bottom edge to form a little packet for the filling, then fold packet over and over until you reach other end of phyllo. Press end to seal. Transfer packet to prepared baking sheet, seam side down. Brush top with butter and sprinkle with more hazelnut mixture. Repeat with remaining phyllo sheets and filling, making 12 packets in total.

6. Bake in preheated oven for 25 to 30 minutes, switching positions of baking sheets halfway through, until phyllo is deep golden brown and crisp. Serve warm or at room temperature.

## Make Ahead

The strudels can be fully assembled and frozen for up to one month. Place in zip-top bags in one layer and freeze completely. Bake as directed (without thawing first) on parchment-lined baking sheets.

# Mississippi Mud Pies

● **GF Friendly**

*This over-the-top dense chocolate pie was named for its resemblance to the banks of the Mississippi River. Once it was associated only with Southern cuisine, but interpretations of this decadent dessert are now enjoyed around the world — proof that everyone understands the universal language of chocolate!*

## Tips

Expect a longer baking time (6 to 10 minutes) if you need to use 2 muffin tins because they are too large to fit on one rack.

The easiest way to remove tarts from muffin tins is to run a small, sharp knife or small offset spatula around the edges, loosening the sides. You should then be able to carefully lift out the tarts, guiding them with the knife or spatula.

For step-by-step photographs of the blind-baking process, see page 33.

● 4-inch (10 cm) round cutter
● Two 12-cup muffin tins
● Parchment paper
● Pie weights or dried beans

| | | |
|---|---|---|
| 1 cup | crushed chocolate wafer cookies (approx.) | 250 mL |
| 1 | recipe Dark Chocolate Pie Dough (page 21) | 1 |

### Chocolate Filling

| | | |
|---|---|---|
| 6 oz | unsalted butter, in pieces | 175 g |
| 6 oz | bittersweet chocolate, chopped | 175 g |
| 3/4 cup | granulated sugar | 175 mL |
| 2 tbsp | unsweetened cocoa powder | 30 mL |
| 4 | large eggs | 4 |
| 1 tsp | vanilla extract | 5 mL |
| 1/4 tsp | salt | 1 mL |
| 1 | recipe Rich Chocolate Ganache, warmed (page 46) | 1 |
| | Lightly sweetened whipped cream, optional | |
| | Chocolate shavings, optional | |

1. On a clean work surface, scatter $1/2$ cup (125 mL) cookie crumbs. Place half the dough on surface and roll out to $1/8$ inch (3 mm) thick, embedding cookie crumbs in dough. Using cutter, cut into rounds and carefully fit into muffin cups (there may be some overlap.) Repeat with remainder of dough, cutting and rerolling scraps and scattering additional cookie crumbs on work surface as necessary, until you have 24 shells. Freeze any leftover dough for another use.

2. Place tins in freezer for 30 minutes. Meanwhile, preheat oven to 350°F (180°C).

3. Blind-bake shells (see page 14 and Tips, left) in center of preheated oven for 12 minutes. Carefully remove weights and parchment; cool slightly. Lower oven temperature to 325°F (160°C).

4. *Chocolate Filling:* In a medium saucepan over medium-low heat, melt butter with chocolate, stirring constantly until smooth. Remove saucepan from heat and whisk in sugar and cocoa powder. Add eggs, one at a time, whisking well after each addition. Whisk in vanilla and salt.

5. Pour 2 tbsp (30 mL) filling into each shell. Bake in center of preheated oven for 15 to 18 minutes, until filling is puffed and just set. (A tester inserted in the center will not come out completely clean.) Cool completely in pans on wire racks.

6. Pour about 1 tbsp (15 mL) chocolate ganache on top of each pie, spreading to form a thin layer. Refrigerate pies until cold, about 2 hours. Carefully unmold and top with whipped cream and shaved chocolate, if using.

## Make Ahead

The pies can be fully assembled and chilled, covered, for up to two days. Top with whipped cream and shaved chocolate, if using, just before serving.

# Mini Chicken Pot Pies

• **GF Friendly**

*Chicken pot pie is the quintessential comfort food. Often it is served casserole style, featuring one large flaky crust covering enough filling for a crowd. I much prefer it served in individual portions, with the savory filling wrapped in a buttery package spiked with flavorful herbs. Take one to the office for lunch for a deliciously hearty change of pace.*

## Tips

The easiest way to remove tarts from muffin tins is to run a small, sharp knife or small offset spatula around the edges, loosening the sides. You should then be able to carefully lift out the tarts, guiding them with the knife or spatula.

If you don't own round cutters in the appropriate sizes, look for lids of the same size from prepared foods.

● Two round cutters, 3 and 4½ inches (7.5 and 11.25 cm) in diameter (see Tips, left)
● 12-cup muffin tin, lightly greased

| | | |
|---|---|---|
| 3 tbsp | unsalted butter | 45 mL |
| ½ cup | sliced leeks (white and light green parts only) | 125 mL |
| 1 | carrot, chopped | 1 |
| 1 | stalk celery, chopped | 1 |
| 1 tbsp | chopped fresh thyme leaves | 15 mL |
| ½ cup | diced peeled red potato | 125 mL |
| ¼ cup | all-purpose flour | 60 mL |
| ¼ cup | dry white wine | 60 mL |
| 1½ cups | prepared chicken stock | 375 mL |
| 2 cups | shredded roasted chicken breast | 500 mL |
| ½ cup | frozen peas | 125 mL |
| 2 tbsp | heavy or whipping (35%) cream | 30 mL |
| | Salt and freshly ground black pepper | |
| 1 | recipe Herbed Flaky Pie Dough (Variation, page 15) | 1 |
| 1 | large egg, lightly beaten with 1 tbsp (15 mL) water | 1 |

1. In a large skillet over medium-high heat, melt butter. Add leeks, carrot, celery and thyme; sauté until tender, about 5 minutes. Add potato and sauté for 3 minutes, until slightly tender.

2. Add flour to skillet and stir constantly for 1 minute. Add white wine and cook, stirring, until it almost evaporates. Add chicken stock and bring to a boil, stirring until thickened. Add chicken and peas; stir until warmed through, about 3 minutes. Stir in cream. Season to taste with salt and pepper. Remove from heat and set aside to cool completely.

3. Divide dough into two pieces, one slightly larger than the other. On a lightly floured surface, roll out larger piece of dough to a thickness of ⅛ inch (3 mm).

4. Using 4½-inch (11.25 cm) cutter, cut 12 rounds and carefully fit into muffin cups (they should stand a bit higher than edges of cups). Reroll scraps as necessary. Fill each cup with a heaping ¼ cup (60 mL) chicken filling.

## Tips

A dough scraper is very useful to have when making these recipes. During the rolling process, it collects the little bits for rerolling and it cleans up the pastry board very efficiently. It also simplifies picking up the cut rounds; you just slide the scraper underneath. Even if they are sticking a bit, they will detach without tearing.

Leftover baked pies can be stored, uncovered, in the refrigerator and reheated for 30 seconds in the microwave or for 10 minutes on a baking sheet in a 300°F (150°C) oven.

5. On a lightly floured surface, roll out smaller piece of dough to a thickness of $1/16$ inch (2 mm). Using 3-inch (7.5 cm) cutter, cut 12 rounds, rerolling scraps as necessary.

6. Brush bottoms of smaller rounds with egg wash and carefully place over filled shells, pressing edges together to seal tightly. Brush tops with egg wash.

7. Place tin in freezer for 30 minutes. Meanwhile, preheat oven to 375°F (190°C).

8. Using tip of a sharp knife, cut 3 slits in top crusts. Bake on center rack in oven for 30 to 40 minutes, until tops are golden brown and filling is bubbling through holes.

9. Cool pies in tin on rack for 10 minutes, then carefully unmold and transfer to serving plates. Serve warm.

## Variations

Substitute Whole Wheat Pie Dough (page 18), All-Butter Pie Dough (page 16) or Savory Cheese Dough (page 23) for the Herbed Flaky Pie Dough.

*Gluten-Free Alternative:* Substitute Gluten-Free Pie Dough (page 24) for the Herbed Flaky Pie Dough and rice flour for the all-purpose flour in the filling.

## Make Ahead

The pies can be fully assembled and frozen, tightly covered, for up to two weeks. Complete Steps 1 through 6, then cover tin tightly in plastic wrap and freeze. Bake from frozen as directed.

# Steak and Mushroom Guinness Stew Pasties

**Makes 12 pasties**

● **GF Friendly**

*My husband comes from an Irish family, so not long after we were married I was introduced to Guinness stew — steak and vegetables slowly simmered in a stout-based sauce. The stout helps to tenderize the beef and lends a richer flavor to the stew. Serve these for a St. Patrick's Day dinner along with some champ (Irish-style mashed potatoes with green onions) and a simple green salad.*

## Tip

Clean mushrooms either by giving them a quick rinse under water or by brushing them off with a kitchen towel or mushroom brush. Do not soak them, because they will absorb the water, which affects their texture.

● **6-inch (15 cm) round cutter**
● **2 baking sheets lined with parchment**

### Filling

| | | |
|---|---|---|
| 1 tbsp | extra-virgin olive oil | 15 mL |
| 1 lb | beef chuck or sirloin, cubed | 500 g |
| 1 tbsp | unsalted butter | 15 mL |
| ½ cup | chopped yellow onion | 125 mL |
| ½ cup | chopped carrot | 125 mL |
| ½ cup | chopped celery | 125 mL |
| 2 tsp | minced garlic | 10 mL |
| 1 tbsp | chopped fresh thyme | 15 mL |
| 6 oz | button mushrooms, sliced | 175 g |
| | Salt and freshly ground black pepper | |
| 3 tbsp | all-purpose flour | 45 mL |
| 12 oz | Guinness stout (or other stout beer) | 350 mL |
| 1 tbsp | Worcestershire sauce | 15 mL |
| 1½ cups | reduced-sodium prepared beef stock | 375 mL |
| 3 tbsp | chopped parsley | 45 mL |
| ½ cup | frozen peas | 125 mL |
| 1 | recipe Flaky Pie Dough (page 15; see Tip, page 69) | 1 |
| 1 | large egg, lightly beaten with 1 tbsp (15 mL) water | 1 |
| 1½ cups | shredded sharp (aged) Cheddar cheese, divided | 375 mL |

1. *Filling:* In a large, deep saucepan or Dutch oven, heat oil over medium-high heat. Add beef, in batches, and brown on all sides, 3 to 5 minutes per batch. Transfer to a plate lined with paper towels to drain.

2. Add butter, onion, carrot and celery to pan and sauté, stirring often, until softened, about 5 minutes. Add garlic and thyme and sauté for 1 minute. Add mushrooms and sauté until softened and browned, 4 to 5 minutes. Season to taste with salt and pepper.

This recipe may leave you
with some extra filling. If so,
enjoy the filling on its own,
served with mashed potatoes.

3. Sprinkle with flour and cook, stirring constantly, for 1 minute. Add stout, Worcestershire sauce and stock; stir, scraping browned bits from bottom of pan.

4. Bring mixture to a boil, reduce heat and return beef to pan. Stir in parsley. Cover and simmer until meat is tender, about 1 hour. Remove lid and continue to simmer until liquid has reduced and thickened, about 20 to 30 minutes. Stir in peas. Remove from heat and set aside to cool completely.

5. On a lightly floured surface, roll out dough to slightly less than $\frac{1}{8}$ inch (3 mm) thick. Using cutter, cut into rounds and place on prepared baking sheets, spacing apart. Reroll scraps as necessary.

6. Brush edges with egg wash. Place a generous $\frac{1}{4}$ cup (60 mL) filling in center of each circle. Sprinkle each with 2 tbsp (30 mL) cheese. Fold in half, enclosing filling. Pinch edges together to seal; crimp with the tines of a fork. Brush tops with egg wash.

7. Place pies, on baking sheets, in freezer for 30 minutes. Meanwhile, position racks in upper and lower thirds of oven and preheat oven to 375°F (190°C).

8. Using tip of a sharp knife, cut 3 slits in top of each pie. Bake in preheated oven for 30 to 35 minutes, switching positions of baking sheets halfway through, until pies are puffed and golden brown. Let cool on baking sheets on racks for 10 minutes before serving.

## Variations

Substitute Whole Wheat Pie Dough (page 18), Savory Cheese Dough (page 23) or All-Butter Pie Dough (page 16) for the Flaky Pie Dough.

*Gluten-Free Alternative:* Substitute Gluten-Free Pie Dough (page 24) for the Flaky Pie Dough and rice flour for the all-purpose flour in the filling.

## Make Ahead

The pies can be fully assembled and frozen for up to one month. Complete Steps 1 through 6, freeze for 30 minutes on trays, then transfer to zip-top bags and seal. Bake from frozen as directed.

# Spanakopita

*When people think of Greek food, spanakopita is likely one of the first dishes that come to mind. Serve these crisp spinach and feta phyllo pies as a flavorful vegetarian appetizer at parties — they will quickly disappear!*

## Tips

Your phyllo sheets should be about 14 by 9 inches (35 by 23 cm). You can work with rectangles that approximate this size, but if the configuration of your phyllo sheet is dramatically different, roll it out or trim it to something that roughly conforms.

When working with thawed phyllo (Step 3), be sure to keep it covered with a damp clean tea towel. Until you brush it with melted butter, it will dry out quickly when exposed to air.

For step-by-step photographs of making phyllo triangles, see page 40.

- **Preheat oven to 375°F (190°C), positioning racks in upper and lower thirds**
- **2 baking sheets lined with parchment**
- **Damp tea towel**

## Filling

| | | |
|---|---|---:|
| 1 tbsp | unsalted butter | 15 mL |
| 1 tbsp | extra-virgin olive oil | 15 mL |
| 12 oz | fresh baby spinach | 375 g |
| ½ cup | chopped green onions | 125 mL |
| 2 tbsp | chopped parsley | 30 mL |
| 1 tbsp | freshly squeezed lemon juice | 15 mL |
| 1 | large egg, lightly beaten | 1 |
| ¼ tsp | ground nutmeg | 1 mL |
| 1 tsp | salt | 5 mL |
| ½ tsp | freshly ground black pepper | 2 mL |
| 1 cup | crumbled feta cheese | 250 mL |
| 24 | sheets phyllo dough, thawed (see Tips, left) | 24 |
| ¾ cup | unsalted butter, melted | 175 mL |

1. *Filling:* In a large skillet, melt butter with olive oil over medium heat. Add spinach and cook, stirring, until wilted, about 4 minutes. Remove from heat and set aside to cool for 15 minutes.

2. Squeeze excess liquid from spinach, then transfer to a cutting board. Chop coarsely and place in a large bowl. Add green onions, parsley, lemon juice, egg, nutmeg, salt and pepper; stir to blend. Add feta and toss to blend.

3. Place one sheet of phyllo on clean work surface, short side facing you. Working quickly, brush with melted butter and fold in half lengthwise. Brush again with butter.

## Tip

The key to making perfectly crisp spanakopita is to ensure that excess liquid is removed from the spinach before filling. If your filling begins to produce liquid while you are still constructing the triangles, remove it by straining or by pressing the spoonful against the side of the bowl before placing on the pastry. This will make the difference between soggy and spectacular bites.

4. Spoon 1 heaping tbsp (20 mL) spinach filling onto bottom left side of strip, leaving about a 1-inch (2.5 cm) border at the bottom. Fold bottom left corner over the filling to form a triangle, then continue to fold triangles up the strip of phyllo to the top as if you were folding a flag. Brush top of triangle with butter, pressing end to seal. Place triangle, seam side down, on prepared baking sheet. Repeat with remaining phyllo and filling, making 24 triangles.

5. Bake in preheated oven for 18 to 20 minutes, switching positions of baking sheets halfway through, until phyllo is deep golden brown and crisp. Cool slightly and serve warm.

### Make Ahead

Spanakopita can be assembled and frozen for up to five days. Freeze pies for 30 minutes on baking sheets, then seal in zip-top bags. Bake from frozen as directed.

# Baked Masala Vegetable Samosas

- **GF Friendly**
- **Vegan Friendly**

Masala *is a term used in Asian cuisines to describe a mixture of spices. These popular Indian treats transform bland mashed potatoes into an exotic festival of flavor.*

## Tips

For the most vibrant flavors from spices such as cumin and coriander, use a spice grinder or a mortar and pestle to grind whole seeds just before adding to a recipe.

If counter space is at a premium, divide the dough in half and roll it out in two batches.

For step-by-step photographs of making hand pies, see page 35.

• 5-inch (12.5 cm) round cutter
• 2 baking sheets lined with parchment

**Filling**

| | | |
|---|---|---|
| 1 lb | russet potatoes, peeled and cut in 1-inch (2.5 cm) pieces | 500 g |
| 3 tbsp | unsalted butter, at room temperature, divided | 45 mL |
| 1 | small yellow onion, chopped | 1 |
| 1 | green chile pepper, seeded and minced | 1 |
| 1½ tsp | ground cumin | 7 mL |
| 1½ tsp | ground coriander | 7 mL |
| 1 tsp | garam masala | 5 mL |
| 1 tbsp | finely chopped mint leaves | 15 mL |
| 1 tsp | salt | 5 mL |
| ½ tsp | freshly ground black pepper | 2 mL |
| ½ cup | frozen peas, thawed | 125 mL |
| 1 | recipe Flaky Pie Dough (page 15) | 1 |
| 1 | large egg, lightly beaten with 1 tbsp (15 mL) water | 1 |

1. *Filling:* In a medium saucepan, cover potatoes with cold water. Bring to a boil over medium-high heat. Reduce heat, cover and cook until potatoes are tender, 10 to 12 minutes. Drain.

2. In a medium skillet, melt 2 tbsp (30 mL) butter over medium-high heat. Add onion and chile pepper; sauté until softened, 4 to 5 minutes. Add cumin, coriander and garam masala; sauté for 1 minute.

3. Transfer onion mixture to a large bowl and add potatoes. Using a potato masher, mash until potatoes form small to medium-sized lumps. Stir in mint, salt, pepper, peas and remaining 1 tbsp (15 mL) butter. Set aside to cool.

4. On a lightly floured surface, roll out dough to slightly thicker than $1/16$ inch (2 mm). Using cutter, cut into rounds and place on prepared baking sheets, spacing apart. Reroll scraps as necessary.

## Tips

For easiest rolling, roll your dough, including scraps, between two sheets of plastic wrap. That way, you do not need to add flour to keep the dough from sticking to your work surface.

A dough scraper is very useful to have when making these recipes. During the rolling process, it collects the little bits for rerolling and it cleans up the pastry board very efficiently. It also simplifies picking up the cut rounds; you just slide the scraper underneath. Even if they are sticking a bit, they will detach without tearing.

5. Brush edges of rounds with egg wash. Place about 2 tbsp (30 mL) filling in center of each round. Fold in half, enclosing filling. Pinch edges together to seal; crimp with the tines of a fork. Brush tops with egg wash.

6. Place pies, on baking sheets, in freezer for 30 minutes. Meanwhile, position racks in upper and lower thirds of oven and preheat oven to 375°F (190°C).

7. Using tip of a sharp knife, cut 2 or 3 slits in top of each pie. Bake in preheated oven for 25 to 30 minutes, switching positions of baking sheets halfway through, until pies are puffed and golden brown. Serve warm.

## Variations

Substitute 1 recipe All-Butter Pie Dough (page 16) or Whole Wheat Pie Dough (page 18) for the Flaky Pie Dough.

*Gluten-Free Alternative:* Substitute 1 recipe Gluten-Free Pie Dough (page 24) for the Flaky Pie Dough.

*Vegan Alternative:* Substitute 1 recipe Vegan Pie Dough (page 25) for the Flaky Pie Dough. Substitute vegan butter for the unsalted butter.

## Make Ahead

The pies can be fully assembled and frozen for up to one week. Complete Steps 1 through 5. Freeze for 30 minutes on baking trays, then transfer to zip-top bags and seal. Bake from frozen as directed.

# Ham and Cheese Quiches

**• GF Friendly**

*I remember my mom making ham and cheese quiche to serve for lunch when her bridge group played at our house. The filling was easy to assemble, so it was the ideal job for me as her young "sous-chef." Delicious warm or at room temperature, these mini versions are perfect for any breakfast, brunch or lunch occasion when you'd rather enjoy yourself than fuss over the food.*

## Tips

Quiches can be fully baked, cooled to room temperature, and frozen for up to two weeks, sealed in a zip-top bag. Reheat, without defrosting, on baking sheets at 350°F (180°C) for 15 to 20 minutes or until heated through.

For step-by-step photographs of blind-baking the shells, see page 33.

● **4-inch (10 cm) round cutter**
● **Two 12-cup muffin tins**

| | | |
|---|---|---|
| 1 | recipe Flaky Pie Dough (page 15) | 1 |
| **Filling** | | |
| 4 | large eggs | 4 |
| 1⅓ cups | half-and-half (10%) cream | 325 mL |
| 1⅓ cups | diced smoked ham | 325 mL |
| 1⅓ cups | shredded Gruyère or Swiss cheese | 325 mL |
| ⅓ cup | chopped green onions | 75 mL |
| 4 tsp | Dijon mustard | 20 mL |
| ½ tsp | salt | 2 mL |
| ¼ tsp | freshly ground black pepper | 1 mL |

1. On a lightly floured surface, roll out half the dough to a thickness of ⅛ inch (3 mm). Using cutter, cut into rounds and carefully fit into muffin cups (there will be some overlap). Repeat, rerolling scraps as necessary.

2. Place tins in freezer for at least 30 minutes. Preheat oven to 375°F (190°C).

3. Blind-bake shells (see page 14 and Tips, left) in center of preheated oven for 12 minutes. Carefully remove parchment and weights. Cool in pans on racks for 5 minutes. Lower oven temperature to 350°F (180°C).

4. *Filling:* In a large bowl, whisk together eggs, cream, ham, cheese, green onions, mustard, salt and pepper.

5. Pour or spoon filling into shells, filling almost to the top. Bake in center of preheated oven for 30 to 35 minutes, until tops are puffed and lightly browned. Cool for 10 minutes in pans set on racks, then carefully unmold. Serve warm or at room temperature.

## Variations

Substitute 1 recipe All-Butter Pie Dough (page 16) or Savory Cheese Dough (page 23) for the Flaky Pie Dough.

*Gluten-Free Alternative:* Substitute Gluten-Free Pie Dough (page 24) for the Flaky Pie Dough.

## Make Ahead

The quiches can be baked, cooled and frozen for up to two weeks.

# Berry Yummy Pies

# Fresh Strawberry Hand Pies

**Makes 16 pies**

- **GF Friendly**
- **Vegan Friendly**

*When I was little, I used to go to a pick-your-own strawberry farm with my mother. We would arrive home with enough fruit to make several strawberry pies. The already sweet berries needed only a bit of sugar and some lemon juice before being placed in the crust — their naturally perfect flavor spoke for itself. These hand pies capture that same lush summer flavor I remember so fondly.*

## Tip

Once you start using parchment paper, you will never want to go back to silicone liners or greased baking sheets. Disposable, heat-resistant and nonstick, parchment will make your pie-baking life much, much easier! Use it to line baking sheets or tart shells when blind-baking. When you have finished baking, simply throw out the used parchment. It makes for extremely easy clean-up.

- 5-inch (12.5 cm) round cutter
- 2 baking sheets lined with parchment

### Strawberry Filling

| | | |
|---|---|---|
| 2 cups | diced hulled strawberries (see Tips, page 77) | 500 mL |
| 3 tbsp | granulated sugar | 45 mL |
| 1½ tbsp | cornstarch | 22 mL |
| 1 tsp | freshly squeezed lemon juice | 5 mL |
| 1 | recipe Hand Pie Dough (page 27) | 1 |
| 1 | large egg, lightly beaten with 1 tbsp (15 mL) water | 1 |
| | Coarse sugar for sprinkling | |

1. *Strawberry Filling:* In a medium bowl, mix strawberries, sugar, cornstarch and lemon juice.

2. On a lightly floured surface, roll out dough to a thickness of about $1/16$ inch (2 mm). Using cutter, cut into rounds and place on prepared baking sheets, spacing apart. Reroll scraps as necessary.

3. Brush edges of rounds with egg wash. Place about 2 tbsp (30 mL) filling in center of each round. Fold in half, enclosing filling. Pinch edges together to seal and crimp with the tines of a fork.

4. Brush tops with egg wash and sprinkle with coarse sugar.

5. Place pies, on baking sheets, in freezer for 30 minutes. Meanwhile, position oven racks in upper and lower thirds of oven and preheat oven to 375°F (190°C).

6. Using tip of a sharp knife, cut 2 or 3 slits in top of each pie. Bake in preheated oven for 25 to 30 minutes, switching positions of baking sheets halfway through, until pies are puffed and golden brown and filling is bubbling. Let cool (see Tips, page 77). Serve warm or at room temperature.

## Tips

For step-by-step photographs of making hand pies, see page 35.

If using frozen strawberries instead of fresh, thaw them completely and drain before dicing.

Allow the pies to rest a short time before serving so they are cool enough to hold in your hand!

## Variations

Substitute Cream Cheese Pie Dough (page 20), Whole Wheat Pie Dough (page 18), Flaky Pie Dough (page 15) or All-Butter Pie Dough (page 16) for the Hand Pie Dough.

*Vegan Alternative:* Substitute Vegan Pie Dough (page 25) for the Hand Pie Dough and replace the egg wash with water.

*Gluten-Free Alternative:* Substitute Gluten-Free Pie Dough (page 24) for the Hand Pie Dough.

## Make Ahead

The pies can be fully assembled (Steps 1 through 4) and frozen for up to one month. Freeze at least 30 minutes on trays, then transfer to zip-top bags and seal. Bake as directed.

# Strawberry Rhubarb Streusel Tartlets

*The first time I tried strawberry rhubarb pie, I was apprehensive. I had heard about rhubarb's naturally sour flavor, so I was prepared to pucker my lips. What I wasn't expecting was the perfect balance of sweet and tart that resulted from combining the two fruits in a flaky shell topped with streusel. Make this in late spring or early summer, when both strawberries and rhubarb are at their peak.*

## Tip

The easiest way to remove tarts from muffin tins is to run a small, sharp knife or small offset spatula around the edges, loosening the sides. You should then be able to carefully lift out the tarts, guiding them with the knife or spatula.

- 3$\frac{1}{2}$- to 4-inch (8.75 to 10 cm) round cutter
- Two 12-cup muffin tins, lightly greased

| | | |
|---|---|---|
| 1 | recipe Flaky Pie Dough (page 15) | 1 |

**Strawberry Rhubarb Filling**

| | | |
|---|---|---|
| 2 tbsp | unsalted butter | 30 mL |
| 1$\frac{1}{2}$ cups | chopped rhubarb | 375 mL |
| $\frac{1}{2}$ cup | packed light brown sugar | 125 mL |
| 2 tsp | finely grated lemon zest | 10 mL |
| 2 tsp | freshly squeezed lemon juice | 10 mL |
| 1 tsp | vanilla extract | 5 mL |
| $\frac{1}{2}$ tsp | ground cinnamon | 2 mL |
| $\frac{1}{4}$ tsp | salt | 1 mL |
| 2 cups | chopped hulled strawberries | 500 mL |
| 3 tbsp | all-purpose flour | 45 mL |
| 1 | recipe Toasted Oat Streusel Topping (page 54) | 1 |

1. On a lightly floured work surface, roll out dough to a thickness of $\frac{1}{8}$ inch (3 mm). Using cutter, cut into rounds and carefully fit into muffin cups (there will be some overlap). Reroll scraps as necessary.

2. Place tins in freezer for 30 minutes. Preheat oven to 350°F (180°C).

3. *Strawberry Rhubarb Filling:* In a medium skillet over medium heat, melt butter. Add rhubarb, brown sugar, and lemon zest and juice; cook, stirring, until rhubarb is softened, 4 to 5 minutes. Drain excess liquid and transfer to a large bowl. Stir in vanilla, cinnamon and salt. Set aside to cool completely.

4. Add strawberries and flour to cooled rhubarb mixture; toss until well combined.

5. Place about 2 tbsp (30 mL) filling in each chilled shell and top with about 1$\frac{1}{2}$ tbsp (22 mL) streusel.

6. Bake in center of preheated oven for 30 to 35 minutes, until streusel is browned and filling is bubbly.

## Tips

Although peak rhubarb season in North America runs from about April to September, many well-stocked grocery stores carry the fruit chopped and frozen. Substitute an equal quantity of thawed frozen rhubarb for the fresh.

These pies are best eaten within one day of baking.

**7.** Cool in pans on wire racks for 15 minutes, then carefully remove from tins and transfer to racks to cool completely.

## Variations

Substitute Whole Wheat Pie Dough (page 18), All-Butter Pie Dough (page 16), Cream Cheese Pie Dough (page 20) or Toasted Coconut Tartlet Dough (page 22) for the Flaky Pie Dough.

## Make Ahead

The pies can be fully assembled (Steps 1 through 5) and frozen in their tins, tightly covered, for up to three days. Bake from frozen as directed.

# Strawberry Basil Hand Pies

**Makes 16 pies**

● **GF Friendly**

*The combination of strawberries and fresh basil in a pie might strike you as odd, but basil is a member of the mint family, which often pairs beautifully with fresh fruit in desserts. In these pies basil plays two roles: the chopped herb is tossed with juicy strawberries for the filling, while fresh whole leaves are steeped in sweet melted chocolate for a mildly seasoned sweet glaze.*

## Tips

For maximum freshness, fresh basil is best used within a few days of purchase.

For step-by-step photographs of making hand pies, see page 35.

● 5-inch (12.5 cm) round cutter
● 2 baking sheets lined with parchment paper
● Fine-mesh sieve

### White Chocolate Basil Glaze

| | | |
|---|---|---|
| ¾ cup | heavy or whipping (35%) cream | 175 mL |
| 10 | fresh basil leaves | 10 |
| 1 cup | chopped white chocolate | 250 mL |

### Strawberry Basil Filling

| | | |
|---|---|---|
| 2½ cups | diced strawberries | 625 mL |
| 2 tbsp | chopped fresh basil | 30 mL |
| ¼ cup | granulated sugar | 60 mL |
| 2 tbsp | cornstarch | 30 mL |
| 2 tsp | freshly squeezed lemon juice | 10 mL |
| 1 | recipe Hand Pie Dough (page 27) | 1 |
| 1 | large egg, lightly beaten with 1 tbsp (15 mL) water | 1 |

1. *White Chocolate Basil Glaze:* In small saucepan, bring cream to a simmer over medium heat. Add whole basil leaves, pressing with a spoon to release their flavor. Remove from heat, cover and set aside to steep for 15 minutes.

2. *Strawberry Basil Filling:* In a medium bowl, toss strawberries with chopped basil, sugar, cornstarch and lemon juice.

3. On a lightly floured surface, roll out dough to slightly thicker than $1/16$ inch (2 mm). Using cutter, cut into rounds and place on prepared baking sheets, spacing apart. Reroll scraps as necessary.

4. Brush edges of rounds with egg wash. Place about 2 to $2^1/_2$ tbsp (30 to 37 mL) filling in center of each circle. Fold circles in half, enclosing filling. Pinch together edges to seal and crimp with the tines of a fork. Brush tops with egg wash.

5. Place pies on baking sheets in freezer for 30 minutes. Position oven racks in upper and lower thirds of oven and preheat oven to 375°F (190°C).

## Tips

For easiest rolling, roll your dough, including scraps, between two sheets of plastic wrap. That way, you do not need to add flour to keep the dough from sticking to your work surface.

A dough scraper is very useful to have when making these recipes. During the rolling process, it collects the little bits for rerolling and it cleans up the pastry board very efficiently. It also simplifies picking up the cut rounds; you just slide the scraper underneath. Even if they are sticking a bit, they will detach without tearing.

6. Meanwhile, strain basil and cream mixture through sieve. Return cream to saucepan and bring to a simmer over medium heat. Add white chocolate, remove from heat, and stir until smooth.

7. Using tip of a knife, cut 2 or 3 slits in top of each pie. Bake in preheated oven for 25 to 30 minutes, switching positions of baking sheets halfway through, until pies are golden brown and filling is bubbling. Cool for 15 minutes on baking sheets set on wire racks, then drizzle with warm white chocolate mixture. Cool completely to set glaze, then serve.

## Variations

Substitute Whole Wheat Pie Dough (page 18), Flaky Pie Dough (page 15), All-Butter Pie Dough (page 16) or Cream Cheese Pie Dough (page 20) for the Hand Pie Dough.

*Gluten-Free Alternative:* Substitute one recipe Gluten-Free Pie Dough (page 24) for the Hand Pie Dough.

## Make Ahead

The pies can be fully assembled (Steps 1 through 4) and frozen for up to one month. Freeze for at least 30 minutes on trays, then transfer to zip-top bags and seal. Bake in preheated oven from frozen, as directed.

The white chocolate mixture (Steps 1 and 6) is actually a white chocolate basil ganache. It can be made one week in advance. Refrigerate, tightly covered, until ready to use.

# Wild Blueberry Almond Pocket Pies

| | | |
|---|---|---|
| **Makes** | | |
| **12 pocket pies** | | |

● **GF Friendly**

*Sourcing fresh wild blueberries that don't cost a fortune can be a challenge. Fortunately, this filling works just as well with the frozen variety, which are much easier to find and much easier on your wallet. These treats are ideal for busy mornings when breakfast needs to be packed "to go" — you can pop them straight from the freezer into the oven on an as-needed basis.*

## Tip

Once you start using parchment paper, you will never want to go back to silicone liners or greased baking sheets. Disposable, heat-resistant and nonstick, parchment will make your pie-baking life much, much easier! Use it to line baking sheets or tart shells when blind-baking. When you have finished baking, simply throw out the used parchment. It makes for extremely easy clean-up.

● 4-inch (10 cm) round cutter
● 2 baking sheets lined with parchment

### Blueberry Filling

| | | |
|---|---|---|
| 2 cups | frozen wild blueberries | 500 mL |
| 1½ cups | granulated sugar | 375 mL |
| 1 tbsp | freshly squeezed lemon juice | 15 mL |
| ¼ tsp | ground cinnamon | 1 mL |
| 1 | recipe Pocket Pie Dough (page 26) | 1 |
| 1 | large egg, lightly beaten with 1 tbsp (15 mL) water | 1 |
| 1 | recipe Almond Glaze (see Variations, page 48) | 1 |
| ½ cup | lightly toasted sliced almonds, chopped | 125 mL |

1. *Blueberry Filling:* In a medium saucepan, combine blueberries, sugar, lemon juice and cinnamon. Bring to a boil over medium-high heat, stirring to dissolve the sugar. Reduce heat and simmer until thickened, 15 to 20 minutes. Cover and refrigerate until cold.

2. Divide dough into halves. On a lightly floured surface, roll out one half to a thickness of slightly more than $1/16$ inch (2 mm). Using cutter, cut into rounds and place on prepared baking sheets, spacing apart. Reroll scraps as necessary.

3. Brush surfaces with egg wash and place about $1^1/_2$ tbsp (22 mL) cold blueberry mixture in center of each circle.

4. On a lightly floured surface, roll out remaining dough to a thickness of slightly more than $1/16$ inch (2 mm). Using cutter, cut out rounds, rerolling scraps as necessary. Place on top of blueberry filling, press edges together to seal, and crimp with the tines of a fork. Brush tops with egg wash.

5. Place pies, on baking sheets, in freezer for 30 minutes. Meanwhile, position oven racks in upper and lower thirds of oven and preheat oven to 375°F (190°C).

## Tips

If you are fortunate enough to find fresh wild blueberries, substitute an equal quantity for the frozen ones.

A dough scraper is very useful to have when making these recipes. During the rolling process, it collects the little bits for rerolling and it cleans up the pastry board very efficiently. It also simplifies picking up the cut rounds; you just slide the scraper underneath. Even if they are sticking a bit, they will detach without tearing.

6. When you're ready to bake, pierce tops several times with tip of a sharp knife or a toothpick. Bake in preheated oven for 22 to 28 minutes, switching positions of baking sheets halfway through, until pastries are puffed and golden brown. Let cool on baking sheets on wire racks for 10 minutes, then coat with almond glaze. Sprinkle with almonds and set aside for at least 10 minutes, until set.

## Variations

Substitute Flaky Pie Dough (page 15), Whole Wheat Pie Dough (page 18) or All-Butter Pie Dough (page 16) for the Pocket Pie Dough.

*Gluten-Free Alternative:* Substitute Gluten-Free Pie Dough (page 24) for the Pocket Pie Dough.

## Make Ahead

The pies can be fully assembled (Steps 1 through 4) and frozen for up to one month. Freeze for at least 30 minutes on trays, then transfer to zip-top bags and seal. Bake in preheated oven from frozen, as directed.

# Blueberry Streusel Pies

| Makes 16 pies |
|---|

● **Vegan Friendly**

---

*My family used to spend our summers in New Hampshire, where fresh blueberries grew in abundance. Every morning before going to the lake, my brother and I were tasked with picking a pint of blueberries from the bushes in our yard, which my mom would often turn into a streusel-topped crisp for dessert. This portable interpretation of that treat would have been great to take along to the lake for a picnic lunch — a little reward for our berry-picking efforts!*

## Tips

If using frozen blueberries instead of fresh, thaw and drain them completely before using in the recipe.

The easiest way to zest or finely grate lemon peel is by using a Microplane or rasp grater, available at kitchen supply stores and many supermarkets. Avoid grating the white pith of the lemon, which can taste bitter.

● 3$\frac{1}{2}$- to 4-inch (8.75 to 10 cm) round cutter
● Two 12-cup muffin tins, lightly greased

| 1 | recipe All-Butter Pie Dough (page 16) | 1 |
|---|---|---|
| **Blueberry Filling** | | |
| 2 cups | blueberries | 500 mL |
| 1 | lemon, zested and juiced | 1 |
| $\frac{1}{4}$ cup | granulated sugar | 60 mL |
| 1 tbsp | cornstarch | 15 mL |
| $\frac{1}{4}$ tsp | ground cinnamon | 1 mL |
| $\frac{1}{8}$ tsp | salt | 0.5 mL |
| 1 | recipe Nutty Streusel Topping (page 53) | 1 |

1. On a lightly floured surface, roll out dough to a thickness of $\frac{1}{8}$ inch (3 mm). Using cutter, cut into rounds and fit into muffin cups. Reroll scraps as necessary.

2. Place tins in freezer for 30 minutes. Meanwhile, preheat oven to 350°F (180°C).

3. *Blueberry Filling:* In a medium bowl, mix blueberries, lemon zest and juice, sugar, cornstarch, cinnamon and salt.

4. Place 1$\frac{1}{2}$ to 2 tbsp (22 to 30 mL) blueberry filling in each chilled shell and top with about 1$\frac{1}{2}$ tbsp (22 mL) streusel. Bake in center of preheated oven until streusel is browned and filling is bubbly, 24 to 28 minutes.

5. Cool pies in pans on wire racks for 15 minutes, then carefully remove from tins and transfer to racks to cool completely.

---

## Variations

Substitute Cream Cheese Pie Dough (page 20), Whole Wheat Pie Dough (page 18), Cornmeal Pie Dough (page 19) or Flaky Pie Dough (page 15) for the All-Butter Pie Dough.

*Vegan Alternative:* Substitute Vegan Pie Dough (page 25) for the All-Butter Pie Dough and replace the unsalted butter in the streusel with vegan butter.

# Blueberry Sour Cream Pies

**Makes 24 pies**

*Folding fresh blueberries into a slightly tangy sour-cream custard makes this streusel-topped pie a richer, creamier cousin of classic blueberry pie. Served in a crunchy cornmeal crust, this is a refreshing recipe if you want to offer something unique without straying too far from tradition. Top these petite pies with a dollop of whipped cream or a tiny scoop of vanilla ice cream.*

## Tips

These pies are best eaten the same day they are baked.

The pies can be fully assembled (Steps 1 through 4) and frozen, tightly covered, in their tins for up to two days. Bake from frozen as directed.

- 4-inch (10 cm) round cutter
- Two 12-cup muffin tins

| | | |
|---|---|---|
| 1 | recipe Cornmeal Pie Dough (page 19) | 1 |

**Blueberry Filling**

| | | |
|---|---|---|
| 3/4 cup | packed light brown sugar | 175 mL |
| 3 tbsp | all-purpose flour | 45 mL |
| 1/4 tsp | ground cinnamon | 1 mL |
| 1/4 tsp | salt | 1 mL |
| 3/4 cup | sour cream | 175 mL |
| 1/4 cup | heavy or whipping (35%) cream | 60 mL |
| 2 | large egg yolks | 2 |
| 2 cups | blueberries | 500 mL |
| 1 | recipe Pecan Streusel Topping (see Variations, page 53) | 1 |
| | Whipped cream or vanilla ice cream, optional | |

1. On a lightly floured work surface, roll out dough to a thickness of $1/8$ inch (3 mm). Using cutter, cut into rounds and carefully fit into muffin cups (there will be some overlap). Reroll scraps as necessary.

2. Place tins in freezer for 30 minutes. Meanwhile, preheat oven to 375°F (190°C).

3. *Blueberry Filling:* In a large bowl, whisk together brown sugar, flour, cinnamon and salt. Add sour cream, heavy cream and egg yolks and mix to blend. Gently fold in blueberries.

4. Spoon 2 to $2^1/_2$ tbsp (30 to 37 mL) filling into each shell and top with $1^1/_2$ tbsp (22 mL) streusel.

5. Bake in center of preheated oven for 32 to 38 minutes, until crust and streusel are golden brown and filling is set. Cool in pans on wire racks for 15 minutes, then carefully remove from tins and transfer to racks to cool completely. Serve topped with whipped cream or ice cream, if desired.

## Variations

Substitute Flaky Pie Dough (page 15), All-Butter Pie Dough (page 16), Cream Cheese Pie Dough (page 20) or Toasted Coconut Tartlet Dough (page 22) for the Cornmeal Pie Dough.

# Fried Blackberry Pies

**Makes 12 to 16 pies**

- **GF Friendly**
- **Vegan Friendly**

---

*I keep this blackberry filling simple to highlight the flavor of the sweet fresh fruit, which contrasts beautifully with the crispy fried shell. Serve these juicy pies as a fun dessert at your next barbecue — along with a few napkins!*

---

## Tips

Be sure the filling is thoroughly cooled before filling the pies, or they will be difficult to seal properly. If you have time, refrigerate the filling until cold for better results.

The easiest way to zest or finely grate lemon peel is by using a Microplane or rasp grater, available at kitchen supply stores and many supermarkets. Avoid grating the white pith of the lemon, which can taste bitter.

- 5-inch (12.5 cm) round cutter
- Candy/deep-fry thermometer (see Tip, page 87)

### Blackberry Filling

| | | |
|---|---|---|
| 2½ cups | blackberries | 625 mL |
| ½ cup | granulated sugar | 125 mL |
| 2 tbsp | cornstarch | 30 mL |
| ¼ tsp | ground cinnamon | 1 mL |
| 2 tsp | finely grated lemon zest | 10 mL |
| 1 tbsp | freshly squeezed lemon juice | 15 mL |
| ½ cup | water | 125 mL |
| | | |
| 1 | recipe All-Butter Pie Dough (page 16) | 1 |
| 1 | large egg, lightly beaten with 1 tbsp (15 mL) water | 1 |

Canola or safflower oil
Confectioners' (icing) sugar, optional

1. *Blackberry Filling:* In a medium saucepan, toss blackberries with sugar, cornstarch and cinnamon. Stir in lemon zest and juice and water. Bring to a boil over medium heat, stirring, until blackberries have softened and mixture has thickened. Remove from heat and set aside to cool completely.

2. On a lightly floured work surface, roll out dough to slightly thicker than $\frac{1}{16}$ inch (2 mm). Using cutter, cut into rounds and place on baking sheets. Reroll scraps as necessary.

3. Brush surfaces with egg wash, then place about 2 tbsp (30 mL) cooled blackberry filling in center of each round. Fold in half, enclosing filling. Pinch edges together to seal, and crimp with the tines of a fork.

4. Place pies in freezer for 30 minutes.

5. In a deep skillet or Dutch oven, heat 2 inches (5 cm) oil until deep-fry thermometer registers 360°F (185°C). Fry pies in batches, turning once, until golden brown, 3 to 4 minutes total.

6. Transfer to a rack lined with paper towels to cool slightly. Dust with confectioners' sugar, if using, before serving.

## Tip

A deep-fry thermometer helps you to maintain the appropriate temperature (in this book, 360°F/185°C) of your oil, ensuring that your pies are properly cooked. These thermometers come in both digital and non-digital varieties. I prefer one that clips directly onto the side of the pot for easy reading. If you do not own a thermometer, the best way to test if your oil is ready for frying is to drop a small scrap of dough into the pot. If the dough fries on contact, the oil is ready.

## Variations

Substitute Cornmeal Pie Dough (page 19), Cream Cheese Pie Dough (page 20) or Hand Pie Dough (page 27) for the All-Butter Pie Dough.

*Vegan Alternative:* Substitute Vegan Pie Dough (page 25) for the All-Butter Pie Dough and replace the egg wash with water.

*Gluten-Free Alternative:* Substitute Gluten-Free Dough (page 24) for the All-Butter Pie Dough

## Make Ahead

The filling can be made up to two days in advance and refrigerated, covered.

The pies can be fully assembled (Steps 1 through 3) and frozen for up to one month. Freeze for at least 30 minutes on trays, then transfer to zip-top bags and seal. Fry from frozen as directed.

# Blackberry Sugarplum Cornmeal Pies

*This recipe was inspired by my friend Emily, who writes a blog called* Sugarplum. *I had never tried mixing blackberries and plums in a pie until I saw one of her irresistible-looking recipes. As these hand pies bake, the juicy deep purple filling bubbles through the holes in the crunchy cornmeal crust. Waiting for them to cool is the hardest part!*

## Tips

You will need about 7 large plums to make this recipe.

Look for fresh plums that have a rich color and are not overly soft, with punctures or bruises. Plums will continue to ripen after they are picked.

A zester, rasp grater or Microplane (a well-known make) is the easiest way to grate lemon zest. With its sharp teeth it successfully removes the flavorful zest from fruit while leaving the bitter white pith behind. You can also use this tool to grate whole nutmeg.

- 5-inch (12.5 cm) round cutter
- 2 baking sheets lined with parchment

| | | |
|---|---|---|
| 6 oz | fresh blackberries (about 1 cup/250 mL) | 175 g |
| 12 oz | plums, peeled and chopped | 375 g |
| 1/3 cup | granulated sugar | 75 mL |
| 1 1/2 tbsp | cornstarch | 22 mL |
| 1 tsp | finely grated lemon zest | 5 mL |
| 1 tsp | freshly squeezed lemon juice | 5 mL |
| 1/8 tsp | ground nutmeg | 0.5 mL |
| 1 | recipe Cornmeal Pie Dough (page 19) | 1 |
| 1 | large egg, lightly beaten with 1 tbsp (15 mL) water | 1 |
| | Coarse sugar | |

1. In a bowl, toss blackberries, plums, sugar, cornstarch, lemon zest and juice, and nutmeg. Set aside.

2. On a lightly floured surface, roll out dough to slightly thicker than $1/16$ inch (2 mm). Using cutter, cut into rounds and place on prepared baking sheets, spacing apart. Reroll scraps as necessary.

3. Brush edges of rounds with egg wash. Place about 2 tbsp (30 mL) filling in center of each circle. Fold in half, enclosing filling. Pinch edges together to seal, and crimp with the tines of a fork. Brush tops with egg wash and sprinkle with coarse sugar.

4. Place pies, on baking sheets, in freezer for 30 minutes. Meanwhile, position oven racks in upper and lower thirds of oven and preheat oven to 375°F (190°C).

5. Using tip of a sharp knife, cut 2 or 3 slits in top of each pie. Bake in preheated oven for 25 to 30 minutes, switching positions of baking sheets halfway through, until pies are golden brown. Cool for at least 5 minutes. Serve warm or at room temperature.

## Make Ahead

The pies can be fully assembled (Steps 1 through 3) and frozen for up to one month. Freeze for at least 30 minutes on trays, then transfer to zip-top bags and seal. Bake in preheated oven from frozen, as directed.

# Goat Cheese and Mixed Berry Hand Pies

**Makes 16 pies**

*I'm generally not a fan of cream cheese–based desserts, so whenever I can, I substitute soft goat cheese instead. These unique hand pies are sophisticated without being stuffy. Fresh, juicy berries balance out the creamy, tart goat cheese to make a pleasingly soft filling for the crisp sugar-coated crust.*

## Tips

The addition of salt enhances flavor in recipes. These recipes were all tested using natural fine kosher salt, but regular table salt can be substituted.

For step-by-step photographs of making hand pies, see page 35.

These pies are best baked and eaten the same day they are filled and shaped.

- 5-inch (12.5 cm) round cutter
- 2 baking sheets lined with parchment

| | | |
|---|---|---|
| 3½ oz | soft goat cheese (about ½ cup/125 mL) | 105 g |
| ¼ cup | heavy or whipping (35%) cream | 60 mL |
| 1 | large egg | 1 |
| ¼ cup | packed light brown sugar | 60 mL |
| 2 tbsp | all-purpose flour | 30 mL |
| ¼ tsp | salt (see Tips, left) | 1 mL |
| 1 cup | raspberries | 250 mL |
| 1 cup | blueberries | 250 mL |
| 1 | recipe Hand Pie Dough (page 27) | 1 |
| 1 | large egg, lightly beaten with 1 tbsp (15 mL) water | 1 |
| | Confectioners' (icing) sugar | |

1. In a bowl, mix goat cheese, cream, egg, brown sugar, flour and salt. Gently fold in berries.

2. On a lightly floured surface, roll out dough to slightly thicker than $\frac{1}{16}$ inch (2 mm). Using cutter, cut into rounds and place on prepared baking sheets, spacing apart. Reroll scraps as necessary.

3. Brush edges of rounds with egg wash. Place about $2\frac{1}{2}$ tbsp (37 mL) filling in center of each circle. Fold in half, enclosing filling. Pinch edges together to seal, and crimp with the tines of a fork. Brush tops with egg wash.

4. Place pies, on baking sheets, in freezer for 30 minutes. Meanwhile, position oven racks in upper and lower thirds of oven and preheat oven to 375°F (190°C).

5. Using tip of a knife, cut 2 or 3 slits in top of each pie. Bake in preheated oven for 25 to 30 minutes, switching positions of baking sheets halfway through, until puffed and golden brown. Cool on sheets set on wire racks for 10 minutes, then dust with confectioners' sugar.

## Variations

Substitute All-Butter Pie Dough (page 16) or Flaky Pie Dough (page 15) for the Hand Pie Dough.

# Lemon-Glazed Boysenberry Hand Pies

- **GF Friendly**
- **Vegan Friendly**

*Deep maroon boysenberries are a cross between blackberries and raspberries. They were originally grown in northern California by a man named Rudolph Boysen, but the vines were eventually moved south to Anaheim, where Knott's Berry Farm turned them into its now famous jam.*

## Tips

If you are using frozen boysenberries, thaw and drain them before using.

If you can't find boysenberries, use equal amounts of fresh raspberries and blackberries for your filling.

For step-by-step photographs of making hand pies, see page 35.

- 5-inch (12.5 cm) round cutter
- 2 baking sheets lined with parchment paper

**Filling**

| | | |
|---|---|---|
| 2 cups | boysenberries, fresh or frozen (see Tips, left) | 500 mL |
| 1/4 cup | granulated sugar | 60 mL |
| 2 tbsp | cornstarch | 30 mL |
| 1 tsp | finely grated lemon zest | 5 mL |
| 2 tsp | freshly squeezed lemon juice | 10 mL |
| 1/8 tsp | ground nutmeg | 0.5 mL |
| 1 | recipe Hand Pie Dough (page 27) | 1 |
| 1 | large egg, lightly beaten with 1 tbsp (15 mL) water | 1 |
| 1 | recipe Lemon Glaze (Variations, page 48) | 1 |

1. *Filling:* In a medium bowl, mix boysenberries, sugar, cornstarch, lemon zest and juice, and nutmeg. Set aside.

2. On a lightly floured surface, roll out dough to slightly thicker than $1/16$ inch (2 mm). Using cutter, cut into rounds and place on prepared baking sheets, spacing apart. Reroll scraps as necessary.

3. Brush edges of rounds with egg wash. Place about 2 tbsp (30 mL) boysenberry filling in center of each circle. Fold in half, enclosing filling. Pinch edges together to seal, and crimp with the tines of a fork. Brush tops with egg wash.

4. Place pies, on baking sheets, in freezer for 30 minutes. Meanwhile, position oven racks in upper and lower thirds of oven and preheat oven to 375°F (190°C).

5. Using tip of a knife, cut 2 or 3 slits in top of each pie. Bake in preheated oven for 22 to 28 minutes, switching positions of baking sheets halfway through, until pies are puffed and golden brown.

## Tip

A rolling pin is instrumental in achieving a uniform, smooth dough. Although most are made from either wood or marble, you can also purchase silicone or plastic rolling pins. My rolling pin of choice is the simple French version: long and slim, with tapered ends instead of handles. I feel that this model gives me the most control when rolling out dough.

6. Remove from oven and cool on baking sheets on wire racks for 10 minutes. Drizzle with lemon glaze. Let glaze set for 10 minutes before serving.

## Variations

Substitute Whole Wheat Pie Dough (page 18), Flaky Pie Dough (page 15) or All-Butter Pie Dough (page 16) for the Hand Pie Dough.

*Gluten-Free Alternative:* Substitute Gluten-Free Pie Dough (page 24) for the Hand Pie Dough.

*Vegan Alternative:* Substitute Vegan Pie Dough (page 25) for the Hand Pie Dough and replace the egg wash with water.

## Make Ahead

The pies can be fully assembled (Steps 1 through 3) and frozen for up to one month. Freeze for at least 30 minutes on trays, then transfer to zip-top bags and seal. Bake from frozen as directed.

# Berries and Cream Tartlets

● **GF Friendly**

*Classic French fruit tarts are as beautiful to look at as they are easy to make. They are traditionally prepared with vanilla pastry cream, but this version incorporates berry purée to add a pop of color and flavor to the filling. Warmed apricot jam gives the fruit topping a shiny coat for a simple and elegant presentation.*

## Tips

If using frozen berries (Step 4), thaw them before processing.

If you are using dried beans for blind baking, be aware that they can be reused many times. Store in a cool, dry place, tightly covered.

If you don't have a fine-mesh sieve for Step 4, line a strainer with cheesecloth instead.

For a simplified preparation, standard vanilla pastry cream without the purée mixed in can be used.

For step-by-step photographs of the blind-baking process, see page 33.

You can use any combination of fresh berries: raspberries, blackberries, blueberries, diced strawberries.

● 3½- to 4-inch (8.75 to 10 cm) round cutter
● Two 12-cup muffin tins
● Equipment for blind baking (see Tips, left)
● Food processor
● Fine-mesh sieve (see Tips, left)

| | | |
|---|---|---|
| 1 | recipe Sweet Tart Dough (page 17) | 1 |
| 1½ cups | blackberries or raspberries | 375 mL |
| 1 tbsp | granulated sugar | 15 mL |
| 1 tbsp | freshly squeezed lemon juice | 15 mL |
| 1 | recipe Vanilla Bean Pastry Cream (page 51) | 1 |
| ⅓ cup | apricot jam | 75 mL |
| 3 cups | fresh berries (see Tips, left) | 750 mL |

1. On a lightly floured work surface, roll out dough to a thickness of ⅛ inch (3 mm). Using cutter, cut into rounds and carefully fit into muffin cups (there will be some overlap). Reroll scraps as necessary.

2. Place tins in freezer for 30 minutes. Meanwhile, preheat oven to 350°F (180°C).

3. Blind-bake shells (see page 14 and Tips, left) in center of preheated oven for 10 minutes. Carefully remove weights and parchment; continue to bake until shells are golden brown, 5 to 8 minutes longer. Let cool in pans on racks for 10 minutes, then carefully remove from cups and transfer to rack to cool completely.

4. In food processor fitted with the metal blade, purée 1½ cups (375 mL) berries, sugar and lemon juice until smooth. Place sieve over a bowl and strain mixture, pressing with a wooden spoon. Discard solids.

5. In a bowl, mix ½ cup (125 mL) berry purée with pastry cream. Place about 2 tbsp (30 mL) in each shell.

6. In a small saucepan over medium-low heat, warm apricot jam. Place fresh berries in a large bowl and gently toss with warm jam to coat. Top each tart with 1½ to 2 tbsp (22 to 30 mL) glazed fruit. Refrigerate for up to 4 hours.

## Variations

Substitute Toasted Coconut Tartlet Dough (page 22) for the Sweet Tart Dough.

*Gluten-Free Alternative:* Substitute Gluten-Free Pie Dough (page 24) for the Sweet Tart Dough.

# Raspberry Nectarine Galettes

**Makes 16 galettes**

- **GF Friendly**
- **Vegan Friendly**

*A galette is a rustic free-form tart. Instead of being baked in a tin, the edges are simply folded around the filling, leaving the center exposed. These mini versions, combining the colorful duo of nectarines and raspberries, are about the size of an English muffin, making them as easy to eat as they are to prepare.*

## Tips

These galettes are best eaten the day they are prepared.

For step-by-step photographs of making galettes, see page 34.

If you are using my Gluten-Free Pie Dough (see Variations) you will find it to be quite forgiving and easy to work with because of the absence of gluten. When rolling out the dough, dust your work surface lightly with cornstarch, potato starch or rice flour in lieu of all-purpose flour.

- 5-inch (12.5 cm) round cutter
- 2 baking sheets lined with parchment

| | | |
|---|---|---|
| 2 lbs | nectarines, peeled and chopped | 1 kg |
| 1 cup | raspberries | 250 mL |
| $1/2$ cup | granulated sugar | 125 mL |
| 2 tbsp | cornstarch | 30 mL |
| $1/4$ tsp | ground cinnamon | 1 mL |
| $1/8$ tsp | salt | 0.5 mL |
| 2 tsp | freshly squeezed lemon juice | 10 mL |
| 1 | recipe All-Butter Pie Dough (page 16) | 1 |
| 1 | large egg, mixed with 1 tbsp (15 mL) water | 1 |
| | Coarse sugar for sprinkling | |

1. In a large bowl, mix nectarines, raspberries, sugar, cornstarch, cinnamon, salt and lemon juice.

2. On a lightly floured surface, roll out dough to a thickness of slightly more than $1/16$ inch (2 mm). Using cutter, cut into rounds and place on prepared baking sheets, spacing apart. Reroll scraps as necessary.

3. Brush egg wash around edges of rounds. Place about 2 tbsp (30 mL) filling in center of each round. Fold edges over filling so they overlap slightly but center is still exposed. Press firmly to seal. Brush top of dough with egg wash and sprinkle edges with coarse sugar.

4. Place galettes, on baking sheets, in freezer for 30 minutes. Meanwhile, position oven racks in upper and lower thirds of oven and preheat oven to 375°F (190°C).

5. Bake in preheated oven for 30 to 40 minutes, switching positions of baking sheets halfway through, until crust is golden brown. Let cool on sheets on wire racks for 15 minutes. Serve warm or at room temperature.

## Variations

Substitute Flaky Pie Dough (page 15) or Whole Wheat Pie Dough (page 18) for the All-Butter Pie Dough.

*Gluten-Free Alternative:* Substitute Gluten-Free Pie Dough (page 24) for the All-Butter Pie Dough.

*Vegan Alternative:* Substitute Vegan Pie Dough (page 25) for the All-Butter Pie Dough and replace the egg wash with water.

# Maple-Glazed Raspberry Streusel Breakfast Tarts

*These are a homemade, more sophisticated version of the store-bought breakfast toaster strudels I used to devour as a child. My favorite part was drizzling the sweet glaze over the warm, flaky pastry — a perfect contrast to the tart fruity filling inside.*

## Tips

Fresh or frozen raspberries will work in this recipe. Frozen raspberries can be added directly to the saucepan without thawing.

Because of its many, many layers of flour and butter, puff pastry does exactly as its name indicates: it puffs up when baked. Steam produced by the heated butter creates pockets of air and crisp, flaky layers that are perfect for these tartlets. Although you can find premade puff pastry in the frozen foods section of most grocery stores, I highly recommend that you take the time to try making your own, from the recipe I created just for this book. If you prefer to use frozen puff pastry, thaw it first.

● 2 baking sheets lined with parchment

### Filling

| | | |
|---|---|---|
| 2 cups | raspberries | 500 mL |
| 1 cup | granulated sugar | 250 mL |
| 1 tbsp | freshly squeezed lemon juice | 15 mL |

### Streusel

| | | |
|---|---|---|
| ½ cup | all-purpose flour | 125 mL |
| ½ cup | packed light brown sugar | 125 mL |
| ½ tsp | ground cinnamon | 2 mL |
| ¼ cup | unsalted butter, softened | 60 mL |
| 1 | recipe Shortcut Puff Pastry (page 29; see Tips, left) | 1 |
| 1 | large egg, lightly beaten with 1 tbsp (15 mL) water | 1 |
| 1 | recipe Maple Glaze (Variations, page 48) | 1 |

1. *Filling:* In a medium saucepan, combine raspberries, sugar and lemon juice. Bring to a boil over medium-high heat, mashing raspberries with a potato masher or the back of a spoon. Boil for 1 minute, stirring constantly, then reduce heat and simmer for 5 minutes, until mixture has thickened. Transfer to a bowl, cover and refrigerate until cold, about 2 hours.

2. *Streusel:* In a medium bowl, mix together flour, brown sugar, cinnamon and butter. Cover and refrigerate.

3. Divide puff pastry into quarters. Working with one quarter at a time, on a lightly floured surface, roll each out into a 13- by 9-inch (33 by 23 cm) rectangle. Cut into eight 4- by 3-inch (10 by 7.5 cm) rectangles (two rows of four), discarding scraps. Repeat with remaining dough.

4. Place four rectangles on prepared baking sheet and brush with egg wash. Place 2 tbsp (30 mL) raspberry filling in center of each rectangle. Top each with another rectangle. Pinch edges together to seal, and crimp with the tines of a fork. Repeat until all the dough and filling is used up.

5. Brush tops of pastries with egg wash and sprinkle with streusel, dividing equally and pressing it gently to adhere.

6. Place pastries, on baking sheets, in freezer for 30 minutes, until firm. Meanwhile, position oven racks in upper and lower thirds of oven and preheat oven to 350°F (180°C).

7. Bake in preheated oven until puffed and golden brown, about 25 to 30 minutes, switching positions of baking sheets halfway through. Let tarts cool on sheets on wire racks for 5 minutes, then drizzle with maple glaze. Serve warm.

## Variations
Substitute 2 lbs (1 kg) store-bought puff pastry, thawed, for 1 recipe Shortcut Puff Pastry.

Substitute 2 cups (500 mL) store-bought raspberry jam for the raspberry filling.

## Make Ahead
The raspberry filling and streusel topping can be prepared in advance and refrigerated, covered, for up to one week.

The tarts can be fully assembled (Steps 1 through 5) and frozen for up to one month. Freeze for at least 30 minutes on trays, then transfer to zip-top bags and seal. Bake from frozen as directed.

# Double-Crust Wyoming Huckleberry Pies

**Makes 16 pies**

● **Vegan Friendly**

*Jackson Hole, Wyoming, is one of my favorite places, so I try to visit there a few times every year. After a long day of hiking in Grand Teton National Park, my husband and I like to treat ourselves to a scoop of refreshing huckleberry ice cream, something we are not able to enjoy back home. Frozen huckleberries work perfectly in these pies, but if you are lucky enough to find fresh berries, by all means use them!*

## Tip

Huckleberry season runs from mid- to late July into August, so during this time you will be most likely to find them at farmers' markets and grocery stores.

● 3- and 4-inch (7.5 and 10 cm) round cutters
● Two 12-cup muffin tins, lightly greased

### Filling

| | | |
|---|---|---|
| 2 cups | fresh or frozen huckleberries (see Tips, left) | 500 mL |
| ½ cup | granulated sugar | 125 mL |
| ½ tsp | ground cinnamon | 2 mL |
| ¼ tsp | ground nutmeg | 1 mL |
| 1 tsp | freshly squeezed lemon juice | 5 mL |
| 3 tbsp | all-purpose flour | 45 mL |
| 1 | recipe All-Butter Pie Dough (page 16) | 1 |
| ¼ cup | cold unsalted butter, cut into 16 pieces | 60 mL |
| 1 | large egg, lightly beaten with 1 tbsp (15 mL) water | 1 |
| ⅓ cup | granulated sugar, mixed with ½ tsp (2 mL) ground cinnamon | 75 mL |

1. *Filling:* In large bowl, mix together huckleberries, sugar, cinnamon, nutmeg and lemon juice. Add flour and toss to coat. Set aside.

2. Divide dough into two pieces, one slightly larger than the other. On a lightly floured surface, roll out larger piece of dough to a thickness of ⅛ inch (3 mm).

3. Using 4-inch (10 cm) cutter, cut 16 rounds and carefully fit into muffin cups, flush with the tops. Reroll scraps as necessary. Fill each shell with about 2 tbsp (30 mL) huckleberry filling. Top each with 1 piece of butter.

4. On a lightly floured surface, roll out smaller piece of dough to ¹⁄₁₆ inch (2 mm). Using 3-inch (7.5 cm) cutter, cut 16 rounds, rerolling scraps as necessary.

5. Brush bottoms of smaller rounds with egg wash and carefully place on filled shells, pressing edges to seal tightly. Brush tops with egg wash and sprinkle with cinnamon sugar.

## Tip

The easiest way to remove tarts from muffin tins is to run a small, sharp knife or small offset spatula around the edges, loosening the sides. You should then be able to carefully lift out the tarts, guiding them with the knife or spatula.

6. Place tins in freezer for 30 minutes. Meanwhile, preheat oven to 400°F (200°C).

7. Using tip of a sharp knife, cut 3 small slits in top crusts. Bake on center rack in preheated oven for 12 minutes, then lower oven temperature to 350°F (180°C) and bake for 24 to 28 minutes, until tops are puffed and browned.

8. Cool pies in tins on wire racks for 15 minutes, then carefully transfer to racks to cool completely. Serve warm or at room temperature.

## Variation

*Vegan Alternative:* Substitute Vegan Pie Dough (page 25) for the All-Butter Pie Dough. Substitute vegan butter for the unsalted butter and replace the egg wash with water.

## Make Ahead

The pies can be fully assembled (Steps 1 through 5) and frozen for up to two weeks. Freeze in tins, tightly covered. Bake from frozen as directed.

# Port-Glazed Grape Tartlets

**Makes 24 tartlets**

- **GF Friendly**
- **Vegan Friendly**

*These mini tarts can be served as a simple but unique dessert or they can be topped with a small slice of blue cheese for a cocktail party. Port wine is reduced to a syrupy glaze that dresses up the deep purple Concord grape filling.*

## Tips

I prefer to use Concord grapes in this recipe because of their concentrated grape flavor and beautiful deep blue-purple color. But feel free to substitute an equal quantity of seedless red grapes.

The easiest way to remove tarts from muffin tins is to run a small, sharp knife or small offset spatula around the edges, loosening the sides. You should then be able to carefully lift out the tarts, guiding them with the knife or spatula.

These tarts are best eaten the day they are prepared.

- 4-inch (10 cm) round cutter
- Two 12-cup muffin tins, lightly greased

| | | |
|---|---|---|
| 1 | recipe All-Butter Pie Dough (page 16) | 1 |
| ¾ cup | port wine | 175 mL |
| ½ cup | granulated sugar | 125 mL |
| 2 tbsp | freshly squeezed lemon juice | 30 mL |
| 3 cups | seedless Concord grapes, divided (see Tips, left) | 750 mL |
| 2 tbsp | cornstarch | 30 mL |
| 3 tbsp | water | 45 mL |

1. On a lightly floured surface, roll out dough to a thickness of $1/8$ inch (3 mm). Using cutter, cut into rounds and carefully fit into muffin cups. Reroll scraps as necessary.

2. Place tins in freezer for 30 minutes. Meanwhile, preheat oven to 400°F (200°C).

3. In a large saucepan over medium-high heat, bring port, sugar and lemon juice to a boil, stirring frequently. Reduce heat and simmer for 10 minutes. Add $1^1/_2$ cups (375 mL) grapes to the saucepan, tossing to coat.

4. In a small bowl, whisk together cornstarch and water. Add cornstarch mixture to saucepan, stirring to blend. Continue to simmer until sauce has thickened, about 2 minutes. Remove pan from heat and add remaining $1^1/_2$ cups (375 mL) grapes; toss to coat. Set aside to cool completely.

5. Place 2 tbsp (30 mL) grape filling in each shell. Bake in center of preheated oven for 10 minutes. Lower temperature to 350°F (180°C) and bake until filling is bubbling and crust is golden brown, 18 to 23 minutes.

6. Cool tarts in pans on wire racks for 15 minutes, then carefully remove from tins and transfer to wire racks to cool completely.

## Variations

*Gluten-Free Alternative:* Substitute Gluten-Free Pie Dough (page 24) for the All-Butter Pie Dough.

*Vegan Alternative:* Substitute Vegan Pie Dough (page 25) for the All-Butter Pie Dough.

# Apples, Pears and Stone Fruit

# Caramel Apple Hand Pies

**Makes 12 pies**

*Who doesn't have fond memories of devouring a caramel apple as a child? Of course, with every caramel apple came a sticky face and hands, the not-so-pleasant side effects of this glorious treat. Problem solved! These little pies are a much neater version of the caramel apple on a stick. The addictive salted caramel sauce is neatly wrapped up inside a flaky, buttery crust.*

## Tips

Instead of drizzling the baked pies with caramel sauce, place the warmed sauce in a bowl for dipping!

An all-butter crust is my favorite variety because of its pure, rich flavor, its crisp yet tender texture and its beautiful golden color.

- 5-inch (12.5 cm) round cutter
- 2 baking sheets lined with parchment

### Filling

| | | |
|---|---|---|
| 2 tbsp | unsalted butter | 30 mL |
| 3 | Granny Smith apples, peeled and chopped | 3 |
| 1 tbsp | freshly squeezed lemon juice | 15 mL |
| 1/4 cup | packed light brown sugar | 60 mL |
| 2 tbsp | all-purpose flour | 30 mL |
| 1/4 tsp | ground cinnamon | 1 mL |
| 1/8 tsp | ground nutmeg | 0.5 mL |
| 1 | recipe All-Butter Pie Dough (page 16) | 1 |
| 1 | large egg, lightly beaten with 1 tbsp (15 mL) water | 1 |
| 1 | recipe Beth's Salted Caramel Sauce, cooled (page 52) | 1 |

1. *Filling:* In a medium skillet over medium heat, melt butter. Add apples and lemon juice and cook, stirring, until softened, 3 to 4 minutes. Drain and discard excess liquid. Transfer apples to a medium bowl. Set aside to cool completely.

2. In a small bowl, stir together brown sugar, flour, cinnamon and nutmeg. Add to apples and toss to blend.

3. On a lightly floured surface, roll out dough to slightly thicker than $1/16$ inch (2 mm). Using cutter, cut into rounds and place on prepared baking sheets, spacing apart. Reroll scraps as necessary.

4. Brush edges of rounds with egg wash. Place about 2 tbsp (30 mL) apple mixture in center of each round and top with 1 heaping tsp (6 mL) caramel sauce. Fold in half, enclosing filling. Pinch edges together to seal, and crimp with the tines of a fork.

5. Place pies, on baking sheets, in freezer for 30 minutes. Meanwhile, position oven racks in upper and lower thirds of oven and preheat oven to 375°F (190°C).

**Tip**

For step-by-step photographs of making hand pies, see page 35.

6. Using tip of a sharp knife, cut 2 or 3 slits in top of each pie. Bake in preheated oven for 25 to 30 minutes, switching positions of baking sheets halfway through, until pies are puffed and golden brown. Cool on sheets on wire racks for 5 minutes, then drizzle with remaining caramel sauce. Serve warm or at room temperature.

## Variations

Substitute Flaky Pie Dough (page 15), Whole Wheat Pie Dough (page 18), Cream Cheese Pie Dough (page 20), Hand Pie Dough (page 27) or Cornmeal Pie Dough (page 19) for the All-Butter Pie Dough.

Substitute other varieties of tart apples, such as Pippin or Cortland, for the Granny Smiths.

## Make Ahead

The pies can be fully assembled (Steps 1 through 4) and frozen for up to one month. Freeze for at least 30 minutes on trays, then transfer to zip-top bags and seal. Bake from frozen as directed.

# Fried Apple and Tart Cherry Pies

- - - - - - - - - - - - - - - - - - - - - - - - - - - - -

- **GF Friendly**
- **Vegan Friendly**

---

*This recipe was inspired by the apple pie that I make almost every year for Thanksgiving. Dried sour cherries create a surprising contrast, in both flavor and texture, to the generously spiced sweet apple filling. Sprinkled with cinnamon sugar and served warm, these pies are sure to make people thankful any day of the year!*

---

## Tips

Serve these pies for a special autumn weekend breakfast treat, as an alternative to cider doughnuts.

Tart apple varieties include Granny Smith, Cortland, Winesap and Pippin.

Sweet apple varieties include Gala, Fuji and Cameo.

- 5-inch (12.5 cm) round cutter
- Candy/deep-fry thermometer

**Filling**

| | | |
|---|---|---|
| ¼ cup | granulated sugar | 60 mL |
| ¼ cup | packed light brown sugar | 60 mL |
| 2 tbsp | cornstarch | 30 mL |
| 1 tsp | ground cinnamon | 5 mL |
| ¼ tsp | ground cardamom | 1 mL |
| ¼ tsp | ground nutmeg | 1 mL |
| 2 tbsp | unsalted butter | 30 mL |
| 1 | medium tart apple, peeled and chopped (see Tips, left) | 1 |
| 1 | medium sweet apple peeled and chopped (see Tips, left) | 1 |
| 2 tsp | freshly squeezed lemon juice | 10 mL |
| ¾ cup | water | 175 mL |
| ½ cup | coarsely chopped dried sour cherries | 125 mL |
| 1 | recipe All-Butter Pie Dough (page 16) | 1 |
| 1 | large egg, lightly beaten with 1 tbsp (15 mL) water | 1 |
| | Canola or safflower oil | |
| ½ cup | granulated sugar, mixed with ½ tsp (2 mL) ground cinnamon, optional | 125 mL |

1. *Filling:* In a small bowl, whisk together granulated and brown sugars, cornstarch, cinnamon, cardamom and nutmeg. Set aside.

2. In a medium skillet over medium-high heat, melt butter. Add apples and lemon juice; sauté until softened, about 3 to 4 minutes.

3. Reduce heat to medium and add sugar mixture, tossing to coat. Add water and dried cherries and cook, stirring, until thickened, about 3 minutes. Remove from heat and set aside to cool completely.

## Tips

If you are using my Gluten-Free Pie Dough (see Variations), you will find it to be quite forgiving and easy to work with because of the absence of gluten. When rolling out the dough, dust your work surface lightly with cornstarch, potato starch or rice flour in lieu of all-purpose flour.

A deep-fry thermometer helps you to maintain the appropriate temperature (in this book, 360°F/185°C) of your oil, ensuring that your pies are properly cooked. These thermometers come in both digital and non-digital varieties. I prefer one that clips directly onto the side of the pot for easy reading. If you do not own a thermometer, the best way to test if your oil is ready for frying is to drop a small scrap of dough into the pot. If the dough fries on contact, the oil is ready.

4. On a lightly floured surface, roll out dough to slightly thicker than $1/16$ inch (2 mm). Using cutter, cut into rounds and place on baking sheets, spacing apart. Reroll scraps as necessary.

5. Brush surfaces with egg wash. Place about 2 tbsp (30 mL) filling in center of each round. Fold in half, enclosing filling. Pinch edges together to seal, and crimp with the tines of a fork.

6. Place pies, on baking sheets, in freezer for 30 minutes.

7. In a deep skillet or Dutch oven, heat 2 inches (5 cm) oil until deep-fry thermometer registers 360°F (185°C). Fry pies in batches, turning once, until golden brown, 3 to 4 minutes in total. As completed, transfer to a rack lined with paper towels. Sprinkle with cinnamon sugar, if using, and let cool slightly before serving.

## Variations

Substitute Flaky Pie Dough (page 15) or Hand Pie Dough (page 27) for the All-Butter Pie Dough.

*Vegan Alternative:* Substitute Vegan Pie Dough (page 25) for the All-Butter Pie Dough and vegan butter for the unsalted butter. Replace the egg wash with water.

*Gluten-Free Alternative:* Substitute Gluten-Free Pie Dough (page 24) for the All-Butter Pie Dough.

## Make Ahead

The pies can be fully assembled (Steps 1 through 5) and frozen for up to two weeks. Freeze for at least 30 minutes on trays, then transfer to zip-top bags and seal. Fry from frozen as directed.

# Handheld Apfelstrudels

*My grandpa spent a lot of time in Germany, and as a result he loved all kinds of German food, including apple strudel. When I was learning to bake, one of my proudest moments was successfully making him a traditional* Apfelstrudel *from scratch. To this day, although my technique has improved, my recipe has stayed the same. Here is that recipe repackaged as a smaller, handheld strudel.*

## Tips

Granny Smith apples work well in this recipe.

Your phyllo sheets should be about 14 by 9 inches (35 by 23 cm). You can work with rectangles that approximate this size, but if the configuration of your phyllo sheet is dramatically different, roll it out or trim it to something that roughly conforms.

For step-by-step photographs of making phyllo packets (mini strudels), see page 38.

- Preheat oven to 350°F (180°C)
- Baking sheet lined with parchment
- Damp tea towel

### Filling

| | | |
|---|---|---|
| 2 tbsp | unsalted butter | 30 mL |
| 3 | large tart apples, peeled and chopped (see Tips, left) | 3 |
| 2 tsp | freshly squeezed lemon juice | 10 mL |
| ½ cup | fresh or dry bread crumbs | 125 mL |
| ¼ cup | granulated sugar | 60 mL |
| ½ tsp | ground cinnamon | 2 mL |
| ½ tsp | ground cardamom | 2 mL |
| ¼ cup | raisins | 60 mL |
| ⅔ cup | chopped lightly toasted hazelnuts | 150 mL |
| 24 | sheets phyllo pastry, thawed (see Tips, left) | 24 |
| ¾ cup | unsalted butter, melted | 175 mL |
| ¾ cup | granulated sugar, mixed with 1 tsp (5 mL) ground cinnamon | 175 mL |
| | Confectioners' (icing) sugar for sprinkling | |

1. *Filling:* In a large skillet over medium-high heat, melt butter. Add apples and lemon juice; sauté until softened, about 4 to 5 minutes.

2. Using a slotted spoon, transfer apples to a large bowl. Discard liquid in pan. Add bread crumbs, sugar, cinnamon, cardamom, raisins and hazelnuts to apples; stir to blend. Set aside to cool completely.

3. Place one sheet of phyllo on a clean work surface, short side facing you. (Cover remaining sheets with damp towel to prevent drying out.) Working quickly, brush sheet with melted butter and sprinkle with cinnamon sugar. Top with a second sheet of phyllo.

4. Place ¼ cup (60 mL) apple filling 1 inch (2.5 cm) from bottom edge of phyllo, leaving 3-inch (7.5 cm) borders on each side and about 10 inches (25 cm) at the top. Carefully fold both long sides over filling so they overlap completely, covering filling. You will now have a 3-inch (7.5 cm) by 14-inch (35 cm) rectangle.

## Tips

When working with thawed phyllo (Step 4), be sure to keep it covered with a damp clean tea towel. Until you brush it with the melted butter, it will dry out quickly when exposed to air.

These strudels are best eaten the same day they are baked.

5. Brush top surface of phyllo rectangle with melted butter and sprinkle with more cinnamon sugar. Fold up the 1-inch (2.5 cm) bottom edge to form a little packet for the filling, then fold the packet over and over until you reach the other end of the phyllo. Press the end to seal. Transfer packet to prepared baking sheet, seam side down. Brush top with butter and sprinkle with more cinnamon sugar. Repeat with remaining phyllo sheets and filling, making 12 packets in total.

6. Bake in center of preheated oven for 25 to 30 minutes, until phyllo is deep golden brown and crisp. Cool slightly, then sprinkle with confectioners' sugar. Serve warm or at room temperature.

## Make Ahead

The strudels can be fully assembled (Steps 1 through 5) and frozen for up to one month. Place in one layer in zip-top bags and freeze for at least 30 minutes. Bake from frozen as directed.

# Vermont Apple Cheddar Pies

**Makes 16 pies**

*My husband was raised in Vermont, a state as well-known for its cheese and maple syrup as it is for its beautiful fall foliage. In this recipe I incorporate both ingredients from the Green Mountain State to create a distinctively New England version of classic apple pie.*

## Tips

Select tart, firm apples such as the Granny Smith, Cortland, Winesap and Pippin varieties.

The pies can be fully assembled (Steps 1 through 4) and frozen for up to one month. Freeze for at least 30 minutes on trays, then transfer to zip-top bags and seal. Bake from frozen as directed.

- 5-inch (12.5 cm) round cutter
- 2 baking sheets lined with parchment

### Filling

| | | |
|---|---|---|
| 1 tbsp | unsalted butter | 15 mL |
| 3 | tart apples, peeled and chopped (see Tips, left) | 3 |
| ⅓ cup | granulated sugar | 75 mL |
| 2 tsp | freshly squeezed lemon juice | 10 mL |
| 3 tbsp | all-purpose flour | 45 mL |
| ½ tsp | ground cinnamon | 2 mL |
| ¼ tsp | ground nutmeg | 1 mL |
| 3 tbsp | pure maple syrup | 45 mL |
| 1 | recipe Savory Cheese Dough (page 23) | 1 |
| 1 | large egg, lightly beaten with 1 tbsp (15 mL) water | 1 |

1. *Filling:* In a medium skillet over medium heat, melt butter. Add apples, sugar and lemon juice and cook, stirring, until soft, about 4 to 5 minutes. Drain excess liquid from skillet and discard. Transfer apple mixture to a medium bowl.

2. Add flour, cinnamon, nutmeg and maple syrup and toss to blend. Set aside to cool completely.

3. On a lightly floured surface, roll out dough to slightly thicker than $1/16$ inch (2 mm). Using cutter, cut into rounds and place on prepared baking sheets, spacing apart. Reroll scraps as necessary.

4. Brush edges of rounds with egg wash. Place about 2 tbsp (30 mL) filling in center of each round. Fold in half, enclosing filling. Pinch edges together to seal, and crimp with the tines of a fork. Brush tops with egg wash.

5. Place pies, on baking sheets, in freezer for 30 minutes. Meanwhile, position oven racks in upper and lower thirds of oven and preheat oven to 375°F (190°C).

6. Using tip of a sharp knife, cut 2 or 3 slits in top of each pie. Bake in preheated oven for 25 to 30 minutes, switching positions of baking sheets halfway through, until puffed and golden brown and filling is bubbling. Let cool slightly. Serve warm or at room temperature.

# Spiced Pear and Hazelnut Streusel Pies

*Pears often play second fiddle to apples when it comes to pies, but their mildly delicate sweetness means they pair well (no pun intended!) with a variety of toppings and fillings.*

## Tips

Select firm, not overly ripe pears that hold their shape when baked. Bartlett, Bosc and Anjou varieties are all good choices.

The pies can be fully assembled (Steps 1 through 5) and frozen, tightly covered, in their tins for up to three days. Bake from frozen, as directed.

- 4-inch (10 cm) round cutter
- Two 12-cup muffin tins

| | | |
|---|---|---|
| 1 | recipe Flaky Pie Dough (page 15) | 1 |
| 2 tbsp | unsalted butter | 30 mL |
| 4 | pears, peeled and chopped (see Tips, left) | 4 |
| $\frac{1}{2}$ cup | packed light brown sugar | 125 mL |
| 1 tsp | ground cinnamon | 5 mL |
| 1 tsp | ground ginger | 5 mL |
| $\frac{1}{4}$ tsp | ground cloves | 1 mL |
| 1 tbsp | freshly squeezed lemon juice | 15 mL |
| 1 tsp | vanilla extract | 5 mL |
| $\frac{1}{4}$ cup | all-purpose flour | 60 mL |
| 1 | recipe Hazelnut Streusel Topping (see Variations, page 53) | 1 |

1. On a lightly floured surface, roll out dough to a thickness of $\frac{1}{8}$ inch (3 mm). Using cutter, cut into rounds and carefully fit into muffin cups (there will be some overlap). Reroll scraps as necessary.

2. Place tins in freezer for 30 minutes. Preheat oven to 350°F (180°C).

3. In a skillet over medium heat, melt butter. Add pears and cook, stirring, until softened, 3 to 4 minutes. Add brown sugar, cinnamon, ginger, cloves and lemon juice. Cook until liquid has almost completely disappeared, about 2 to 3 minutes. Stir in vanilla.

4. Transfer to a large bowl and toss with flour. Set aside to cool completely.

5. Place about 2 tbsp (30 mL) filling in each pie shell and top with about $1\frac{1}{2}$ tbsp (22 mL) streusel.

6. Bake in center of preheated oven for 28 to 33 minutes, until streusel is browned and filling is bubbling. Cool in pans on wire racks for 15 minutes, then carefully transfer to racks to cool completely.

## Variations

Substitute All-Butter Pie Dough (page 16) or Cream Cheese Pie Dough (page 20) for the Flaky Pie Dough.

# Autumn Harvest Pot Pies

● **Vegan Friendly**

*When most people think of pot pie, they likely envision a hearty savory meal. Why not make pot pies sweet as well? Here I've combined apples, pears and cranberries to create an autumn-inspired dessert version. While the pies are still warm, break through the crust and top with a scoop of ice cream — no bowl required!*

## Tip

Select firm, not overly ripe pears. Bartlett, Bosc and Anjou varieties are all good choices.

● 3- and 4½-inch (7.5 and 11.25 cm) round cutters
● Two 12-cup muffin tins, lightly greased

### Filling

| | | |
|---|---|---|
| 2 tbsp | unsalted butter | 30 mL |
| 2 | Granny Smith apples, peeled and chopped | 2 |
| 2 | pears, peeled and chopped (see Tip, left) | 2 |
| 1 tbsp | freshly squeezed lemon juice | 15 mL |
| ½ cup | fresh or thawed frozen cranberries, coarsely chopped | 125 mL |
| ¼ cup | dried cranberries | 60 mL |
| ½ cup | packed light brown sugar | 125 mL |
| ½ tsp | ground cinnamon | 2 mL |
| ¼ tsp | ground nutmeg | 1 mL |
| 3 tbsp | all-purpose flour | 45 mL |
| 1 | recipe All-Butter Pie Dough (page 16) | 1 |
| 1 | large egg, lightly beaten with 1 tbsp (15 mL) water | 1 |
| | Confectioners' (icing) sugar for sprinkling | |

1. *Filling:* In a large skillet over medium-high heat, melt butter. Add apples, pears and lemon juice; sauté until softened, about 4 to 5 minutes.

2. Transfer to a large bowl. Add fresh and dried cranberries, brown sugar, cinnamon and nutmeg. Add flour and toss to coat. Set aside to cool completely.

3. Divide dough into two pieces, one slightly larger than the other. On a lightly floured work surface, roll out larger piece of dough to a thickness of ⅛ inch (3 mm).

4. Using 4½-inch (11.25 cm) cutter, cut 16 rounds and carefully fit into muffin cups (they should stand a bit taller than edges of cups). Reroll scraps as necessary. Fill each shell with a heaping ¼ cup (60 mL) of filling.

5. On a lightly floured surface, roll out smaller piece of dough to a thickness of ¹⁄₁₆ inch (2 mm). Using 3-inch (7.5 cm) cutter, cut 16 rounds, rerolling scraps as necessary.

## Tips

The easiest way to remove tarts from muffin tins is to run a small, sharp knife or small offset spatula around the edges, loosening the sides. You should then be able to carefully lift out the tarts, guiding them with the knife or spatula.

Wire baking racks are important to have on hand for the cooling process. After pies have finished baking, either set the muffin tin on the rack or transfer the pies from the baking sheet to the rack. This lets the air circulate around the pies, cooling them evenly.

Expect a longer baking time (6 to 10 minutes) if you need to use 2 muffin tins because they are too large to fit on one rack.

6. Brush bottoms of smaller rounds with egg wash and carefully place over filled shells, pressing edges to seal tightly. Brush tops with egg wash.

7. Place tins in freezer for 30 minutes. Meanwhile, preheat oven to 375°F (190°C).

8. Using tip of a sharp knife, cut 3 slits in top crusts. Bake on center rack in preheated oven for 30 to 35 minutes, until tops are golden brown and filling is bubbling through holes.

9. Cool pies in tins on wire racks for 15 minutes, then carefully transfer to racks to cool completely. Sprinkle with confectioners' sugar. Serve warm or at room temperature.

## Variations

Substitute Flaky Pie Dough (page 15) or Whole Wheat Pie Dough (page 18) for the All-Butter Pie Dough.

*Vegan Alternative:* Substitute Vegan Pie Dough (page 25) for the All-Butter Pie Dough and vegan butter for the unsalted butter. Replace the egg wash with water.

## Make Ahead

The pies can be fully assembled (Steps 1 through 6) and frozen, tightly covered, in their tins for up to three days. Bake from frozen, as directed.

# Brown Butter Custard Pear Tarts

*I've always said that someone should bottle the aroma of brown butter and turn it into a perfume. Its intoxicating nutty scent draws people into the kitchen from all corners of the house. Although these tarts are petite, the combination of custardy brown butter filling, pears, vanilla and a dash of brandy is rich enough to satisfy any sweet tooth.*

## Tips

Use the dried discarded vanilla pod to make vanilla sugar. Submerge it in an airtight canister containing granulated sugar for about one week. Your sugar will smell delicious!

For easiest rolling, roll your dough, including scraps, between two sheets of plastic wrap. That way, you do not need to add flour to keep the dough from sticking to your work surface.

- 4-inch (10 cm) round cutter
- Two 12-cup muffin tins, lightly greased

| | | |
|---|---|---|
| ⅓ cup | unsalted butter | 75 mL |
| ½ | vanilla bean, split, seeds scraped out and reserved | ½ |
| 1 | recipe All-Butter Pie Dough (page 16) | 1 |
| ¼ cup | packed light brown sugar | 60 mL |
| ¼ cup | granulated sugar | 60 mL |
| ¼ cup | all-purpose flour | 60 mL |
| ¼ tsp | ground cinnamon | 1 mL |
| ¼ tsp | ground allspice | 1 mL |
| ⅛ tsp | salt | 0.5 mL |
| 1 | large egg | 1 |
| 2 | large egg yolks | 2 |
| 1 tbsp | brandy | 15 mL |
| 2 | large Anjou or Bartlett pears, peeled and diced | 2 |

1. In a medium saucepan over medium-high heat, melt butter with vanilla pod and seeds. Cook over medium heat until butter is deep golden brown and has a nutty aroma, 4 to 5 minutes. Remove from heat and set aside to cool.

2. On a lightly floured surface, roll out dough to a thickness of ⅛ inch (3 mm). Using cutter, cut into rounds and carefully fit into muffin cups (there will be some overlap). Reroll scraps as necessary.

3. Place tins in freezer for 30 minutes. Preheat oven to 400°F (200°C).

4. In a large bowl, whisk together brown and granulated sugars, flour, cinnamon, allspice and salt. Remove vanilla pod from butter mixture and discard (see Tips, left). Add butter mixture to bowl. Add egg and yolks and stir to blend. Add brandy, then fold in pears. Divide filling among chilled shells, placing about 2 tbsp (30 mL) in each.

## Tips

A dough scraper is very useful to have when making these recipes. During the rolling process, it collects the little bits for rerolling and it cleans up the pastry board very efficiently. It also simplifies picking up the cut rounds; you just slide the scraper underneath. Even if they are sticking a bit, they will detach without tearing.

Expect a longer baking time (6 to 10 minutes) if you need to use 2 muffin tins because they are too large to fit on one rack.

5. Bake in center of preheated oven for 12 minutes, then lower oven temperature to 350°F (180°C) and bake for 13 to 18 minutes, until filling is puffed and browned. Cool in tins set on wire racks, then carefully remove from tins. Serve warm or at room temperature.

## Variations

Substitute Flaky Pie Dough (page 15), Cream Cheese Pie Dough (page 20) or Toasted Coconut Tartlet Dough (page 22) for the All-Butter Pie Dough.

## Make Ahead

The pies can be fully assembled (Steps 1 through 4) and frozen, tightly covered, in their tins for up to three days. Bake from frozen, as directed.

# Southern Fried Peach Pies

- **GF Friendly**
- **Vegan Friendly**

*The first time I tried a fried pie was shortly after we moved to Texas from New Jersey (talk about culture shock!). I thought I had died and gone to heaven. The contrast between the crisp, glaze-coated shell and the juicy, lightly spiced peach filling was unlike any peach pie I had ever tasted. Right then and there I decided I would love living in the South!*

## Tip

Be sure the filling is thoroughly cooled before filling the pies, or they will be difficult to seal properly. If you have time, refrigerate the filling until cold for better results.

- 5-inch (12.5 cm) round cutter
- Candy/deep-fry thermometer

### Peach Filling

| | | |
|---|---|---|
| 2½ lbs | peaches, peeled and chopped | 625 g |
| ⅓ cup | packed light brown sugar | 75 mL |
| 1 tbsp | unsalted butter | 15 mL |
| 1 tsp | ground cinnamon | 5 mL |
| 1 tsp | ground ginger | 5 mL |
| ¼ tsp | ground nutmeg | 1 mL |
| 1 | recipe All-Butter Pie Dough (page 16) | 1 |
| 1 | large egg, lightly beaten with 1 tbsp (15 mL) water | 1 |
| | Canola or safflower oil | |
| 1 | recipe Vanilla Glaze (page 48), optional | 1 |
| | Confectioners' (icing) sugar, optional | |

1. *Peach Filling:* In a medium saucepan, combine peaches, brown sugar, butter, cinnamon, ginger and nutmeg. Bring to a boil over medium-high heat. Reduce heat and simmer until peaches have broken down and mixture has thickened, about 15 to 20 minutes. Remove from heat and set aside to cool completely.

2. On a lightly floured surface, roll out dough to slightly thicker than $1/16$ inch (2 mm). Using cutter, cut into rounds and place on baking sheets. Reroll scraps as necessary.

3. Brush surfaces with the egg wash, then place about 2 tbsp (30 mL) cooled filling in center of each round. Fold in half, enclosing filling. Pinch edges together to seal, and crimp with the tines of a fork.

4. Place pies, on baking sheets, in freezer for 30 minutes.

5. In a deep skillet or Dutch oven, heat 2 inches (5 cm) oil until deep-fry thermometer registers 360°F (185°C). Fry pies in batches, turning once, until golden brown, 3 to 4 minutes in total.

## Tip

A deep-fry thermometer helps you to maintain the appropriate temperature (in this book, 360°F/185°C) of your oil, ensuring that your pies are properly cooked. These thermometers come in both digital and non-digital varieties. I prefer one that clips directly onto the side of the pot for easy reading. If you do not own a thermometer, the best way to test if your oil is ready for frying is to drop a small scrap of dough into the pot. If the dough fries on contact, the oil is ready.

6. Transfer to a rack lined with paper towels to cool slightly. Drizzle with vanilla glaze or dust with confectioners' sugar before serving.

## Variations

Substitute Cream Cheese Pie Dough (page 20), Hand Pie Dough (page 27) or Cornmeal Pie Dough (page 19) for the All-Butter Pie Dough.

*Gluten-Free Alternative:* Substitute Gluten-Free Pie Dough (page 24) for the All-Butter Pie Dough.

*Vegan Alternative:* Substitute Vegan Pie Dough (page 25) for the All-Butter Pie Dough and vegan butter for the unsalted butter. Replace the egg wash with water. Use the vegan version of Vanilla Glaze (see Variations, page 48).

## Make Ahead

The peach filling can be made up to two days in advance and refrigerated, covered.

The pies can be assembled and frozen, stored in zip-top bags, for up to one month. Complete Steps 1 through 4, then transfer to bags and seal. Fry from frozen, as directed.

# Mini Peach Lattice Pies

**Makes 16 pies**

- **GF Friendly**
- **Vegan Friendly**

*There's something about a lattice-topped pie that impresses everyone. Although the process of creating a woven crust may seem daunting, a little bit of practice and a few simple steps will elevate you to expert pie-maker status among your peers. These juicy spiced peach pies are a delicious way to practice your technique!*

## Tips

When looking for fresh peaches, choose fruit that is fragrant, unblemished and not too firm. For convenience, you can use frozen peaches. Thaw enough to permit chopping.

For easiest rolling, roll your dough, including scraps, between two sheets of plastic wrap. That way, you do not need to add flour to keep the dough from sticking to your work surface.

- 3- and 4-inch (7.5 and 10 cm) round cutters
- Two 12-cup muffin tins, greased
- Pizza/pastry cutter

### Filling

| | | |
|---|---|---|
| 2½ lbs | peaches, peeled and chopped | 1.25 kg |
| 6 tbsp | granulated sugar | 90 mL |
| 2 tbsp | cornstarch | 30 mL |
| ½ tsp | ground cinnamon | 2 mL |
| ¼ tsp | ground cardamom | 1 mL |
| 2 tbsp | freshly squeezed lemon juice | 30 mL |
| 1 tsp | vanilla extract | 5 mL |
| 1 | recipe All-Butter Pie Dough (page 16) | 1 |
| 1 | large egg, lightly beaten with 1 tbsp (15 mL) water | 1 |
| ½ cup | granulated sugar, mixed with ½ tsp (2 mL) ground cinnamon | 125 mL |

1. *Filling:* In a large bowl, combine peaches, sugar, cornstarch, cinnamon, cardamom, lemon juice and vanilla.

2. Divide dough into two pieces, one slightly larger than the other. On a lightly floured surface, roll out larger piece of dough to a thickness of $\frac{1}{8}$ inch (3 mm).

3. Using 4-inch (10 cm) cutter, cut 16 rounds and carefully fit into muffin cups (they will stand a bit higher than edges of cups). Reroll scraps as necessary. Fill each cup with about 2 tbsp (30 mL) peach filling.

4. On a lightly floured surface, roll out smaller piece of dough to a thickness of $\frac{1}{8}$ inch (3 mm). Using 3-inch (7.5 cm) cutter, cut out 16 rounds, rerolling scraps as necessary. These will be the top crusts. Place on a baking sheet and, using pizza cutter or a paring knife, cut each round into 8 equal strips.

5. Brush edges of strips with egg wash. Arrange strips in lattice pattern (see page 122) on tops of pies, pressing to adhere. Brush lattices with egg wash and sprinkle with cinnamon sugar.

## Tip

For step-by-step photos of making a lattice crust, see page 36.

6. Place pies in freezer for 30 minutes. Meanwhile, preheat oven to 400°F (200°C).

7. Bake on center rack of preheated oven for 10 minutes. Lower oven temperature to 350°F (180°C) and bake for 30 minutes more, until crust is browned and pies are bubbling. Cool completely in tins on racks. Carefully remove from tins by running a sharp knife around the sides. Serve at room temperature.

## Variations

*Gluten-Free Alternative:* Substitute Gluten-Free Pie Dough (page 24) for the All-Butter Pie Dough.

*Vegan Alternative:* Substitute Vegan Pie Dough (page 25) for the All-Butter Pie Dough and vegan butter for the unsalted butter. Replace the egg wash with water.

## Make Ahead

The pies can be fully assembled with the lattice crusts and frozen, tightly covered in their tins, for up to two days. Bake from frozen as directed.

# Roasted Peaches and Cream Tartlets

*Roasting fruit at a high temperature brings out its natural sweetness and adds a mild caramel flavor. These tarts mix juicy roasted peaches with a creamy brown sugar custard filling — a perfect summer treat when peaches are at their peak.*

## Tips

These pies are best eaten the same day they are baked.

The easiest way to remove tarts from muffin tins is to run a small, sharp knife or small offset spatula around the edges, loosening the sides. You should then be able to carefully lift out the tarts, guiding them with the knife or spatula.

The pie shells (Step 3) can be shaped and frozen, tightly covered in their tins, for up to one week.

- Preheat oven to 400°F (200°C)
- Rimmed baking sheet lined with parchment
- 4-inch (10 cm) round cutter
- Two 12-cup muffin tins, lightly greased

| | | |
|---|---|---|
| 6 | ripe peaches, peeled and quartered | 6 |
| ¼ cup | granulated sugar | 60 mL |
| 1 | recipe Cream Cheese Pie Dough (page 20) | 1 |
| ¾ cup | packed light brown sugar | 175 mL |
| 6 tbsp | all-purpose flour | 90 mL |
| ¾ tsp | ground cinnamon | 3 mL |
| ¾ tsp | ground cardamom | 3 mL |
| ¼ tsp | salt | 1 mL |
| 6 | large egg yolks | 6 |
| 1 cup | heavy or whipping (35%) cream | 250 mL |
| 1 tbsp | vanilla extract | 15 mL |

1. On prepared baking sheet, toss peaches with granulated sugar. Roast in preheated oven for 30 to 40 minutes, stirring once, until softened and lightly browned. Remove from oven and set aside to cool completely. Chop coarsely and set aside.

2. On a lightly floured work surface, roll out dough to a thickness of $1/8$ inch (3 mm). Using cutter, cut into rounds and carefully fit into muffin cups. Reroll scraps.

3. Place tins in freezer for 30 minutes.

4. In a bowl, whisk together brown sugar, flour, spices and salt. Add egg yolks, cream and vanilla; whisk.

5. Place peaches in shells, dividing equally. Top each with about $1^1/_2$ tbsp (22 mL) custard mixture.

6. Bake on center rack of preheated oven for 12 minutes, then lower oven temperature to 350°F (180°C) and bake for 15 to 20 minutes, until custard is set and pale golden in color. Cool tarts completely in tins set on wire racks, then remove carefully and serve.

## Variations

Substitute Flaky Pie Dough (page 15), All-Butter Pie Dough (page 16) or Toasted Coconut Tartlet Dough (page 22) for the Cream Cheese Pie Dough.

# Apricot Frangipane Tartlets

**Makes 24 tartlets**

*Frangipane, the ground almond filling used in these tartlets, rises up around the apricot halves during the baking process. Everyone will think you spent hours preparing these beautiful bite-sized desserts, but using canned apricots means they come together in a snap!*

## Tips

For easiest rolling, roll your dough, including scraps, between two sheets of plastic wrap. That way, you do not need to add flour to keep the dough from sticking to your work surface.

These pies are best eaten the same day they are baked.

Try to find apricots canned in juice as opposed to light or heavy syrup, which will make the filling too sweet.

The pie shells (Steps 1 and 2) can be shaped and frozen, tightly covered in their tins, for up to one week.

• 4-inch (10 cm) round cutter
• Two 12-cup muffin tins
• Food processor

| 1 | recipe All-Butter Pie Dough (page 16) | 1 |
|---|---|---|

**Frangipane**

| 1 cup | sliced almonds | 250 mL |
|---|---|---|
| ½ cup | granulated sugar | 125 mL |
| 3 tbsp | all-purpose flour | 45 mL |
| ½ cup | unsalted butter, melted | 125 mL |
| 3 | large eggs | 3 |
| 1 tsp | vanilla extract | 5 mL |
| ½ tsp | almond extract | 2 mL |
| 24 | canned apricot halves, drained (see Tips, left) | 24 |
| | Confectioners' (icing) sugar for sprinkling | |

1. On a lightly floured surface, roll out dough to a thickness of $1/8$ inch (3 mm). Using cutter, cut into rounds and carefully fit into muffin cups. Reroll scraps as necessary.

2. Place tins in freezer for 30 minutes. Meanwhile, preheat oven to 350°F (180°C).

3. *Frangipane:* In food processor fitted with the metal blade, process almonds, sugar and flour until finely ground. Add butter, eggs and vanilla and almond extracts. Process until blended, stopping to scrape down sides of bowl as necessary.

4. Spoon about $1^1/_2$ tbsp (22 mL) frangipane into each chilled shell. Place one apricot half, cut side up, on top of filling in each shell, pressing in gently.

5. Bake in center of preheated oven for 33 to 38 minutes, until frangipane is puffed and golden brown. Cool tarts completely in tins set on wire racks, then carefully unmold. Sprinkle with confectioners' sugar before serving.

## Variations

Substitute Flaky Pie Dough (page 15), Cornmeal Pie Dough (page 19) or Toasted Coconut Tartlet Dough (page 22) for the All-Butter Pie Dough.

# Fried Apricot and Cranberry Pies

**Makes 12 to 16 pies**

- **GF Friendly**
- **Vegan Friendly**

*Instead of fresh fruit, the filling for these pies is made from dried apricots simmered in water. This produces a more pronounced apricot flavor and a vibrant orange color. Dried cranberries add a tart contrast.*

## Tips

A deep-fry thermometer helps you to maintain the appropriate temperature (in this book, 360°F/185°C) of your oil, ensuring that your pies are properly cooked. These thermometers come in both digital and non-digital varieties. I prefer one that clips directly onto the side of the pot for easy reading. If you do not own a thermometer, the best way to test if your oil is ready for frying is to drop a small scrap of dough into the pot. If the dough fries on contact, the oil is ready.

- 5-inch (12.5 cm) round cutter
- Candy/deep-fry thermometer

### Filling

| | | |
|---|---|---|
| 12 oz | dried apricots, chopped | 375 g |
| 1/2 cup | packed light brown sugar | 125 mL |
| 1 1/2 cups | water | 375 mL |
| 1 tbsp | unsalted butter | 15 mL |
| 1/2 tsp | ground cinnamon | 2 mL |
| 1/4 tsp | ground allspice | 1 mL |
| 1 tsp | freshly squeezed lemon juice | 5 mL |
| 1/2 cup | dried cranberries | 125 mL |
| 1 | recipe All-Butter Pie Dough (page 16) | 1 |
| 1 | large egg, lightly beaten with 1 tbsp (15 mL) water | 1 |
| | Canola or safflower oil | |
| | Confectioners' sugar for dusting, optional | |

1. *Filling:* In a medium saucepan over medium-high heat, bring apricots, brown sugar, water, butter, cinnamon, allspice and lemon juice to a boil. Reduce heat and simmer for 20 minutes. Add cranberries and continue to simmer until apricots have broken down and all the water has evaporated. Remove from heat and set aside to cool completely.

2. On a lightly floured surface, roll out dough to slightly thicker than $1/16$ inch (2 mm). Using cutter, cut into rounds and place on baking sheets. Reroll scraps as necessary.

3. Brush surfaces with egg wash. Place about 2 tbsp (30 mL) cooled apricot filling in center of each round. Fold in half, enclosing filling. Pinch edges together to seal, and crimp with the tines of a fork.

4. Place pies, on baking sheets, in freezer for 30 minutes.

## Tip

Dried apricots retain their bright orange color thanks to the addition of sulfur dioxide. Some natural foods and specialty food stores sell unsulfured dried apricots, which are browner in color.

5. In a deep skillet or Dutch oven, heat 2 inches (5 cm) oil until deep-fry thermometer registers 360°F (182°C). Fry pies in batches, turning once, until golden brown, 3 to 4 minutes total.

6. Transfer pies to a rack lined with paper towels to cool slightly. Dust with confectioners' sugar, if using, before serving.

## Variations

Substitute Flaky Pie Dough (page 15) or Hand Pie Dough (page 27) for the All-Butter Pie Dough.

*Gluten-Free Alternative:* Substitute Gluten-Free Pie Dough (page 24) for the All-Butter Pie Dough.

*Vegan Alternative:* Substitute Vegan Pie Dough (page 25) for the All-Butter Pie Dough and vegan butter for the unsalted butter. Replace the egg wash with water.

## Make Ahead

The filling can be made in advance and refrigerated, covered, for up to one week.

The pies can be fully assembled (Steps 1 through 3) and frozen for up to one month. Freeze for at least 30 minutes on trays, then transfer to zip-top bags and seal. Fry from frozen, as directed.

# Double Cherry Lattice Pies

- **GF Friendly**
- **Vegan Friendly**

*These pretty little pies are the perfect combination of sweet and tart because they use both juicy fresh cherries and sour dried cherries in the filling. A dash of almond extract provides an extra layer of unexpected flavor.*

## Tips

Because of the filling, these pies have a tendency to stick to their molds. Take extra care when greasing the tins.

For step-by-step photographs of making a lattice crust, see page 36.

- 3- and 4-inch (7.5 and 10 cm) round cutters
- Two 12-cup muffin tins, greased
- Pizza/pastry cutter (see Tips, page 121)

### Filling

| | | |
|---|---|---|
| 2 cups | quartered pitted fresh cherries | 500 mL |
| ⅔ cup | granulated sugar | 150 mL |
| 2 tbsp | cornstarch | 30 mL |
| 1 tbsp | freshly squeezed lemon juice | 15 mL |
| 1 tsp | vanilla extract | 5 mL |
| ½ tsp | almond extract | 2 mL |
| ½ cup | dried sour cherries | 125 mL |
| 1 | recipe All-Butter Pie Dough (page 16) | 1 |
| 1 | large egg, lightly beaten with 1 tbsp (15 mL) water | 1 |
| | Coarse sugar for sprinkling | |

1. *Filling:* In a large bowl, combine fresh cherries, sugar, cornstarch, lemon juice and vanilla and almond extracts. Stir in dried cherries. Set aside.

2. Divide dough into two pieces, one slightly larger than the other. On a lightly floured surface, roll out larger piece to a thickness of ⅛ inch (3 mm).

3. Using 4-inch (10 cm) cutter, cut 16 rounds and carefully fit into muffin cups (they will stand a bit taller than edges of cups). Reroll scraps as necessary. Fill each cup with about 2 tbsp (30 mL) reserved cherry filling.

4. On a lightly floured surface, roll out smaller piece of dough to a thickness of ⅛ inch (3 mm). Using 3-inch (7.5 cm) cutter, cut out 16 rounds, rerolling scraps as necessary. These will be the top crusts. Place on a baking sheet and, using pizza cutter or a paring knife, cut each round into 8 equal strips.

5. Brush edges of strips with egg wash. Arrange strips in a lattice pattern (page 122) on top of pies, pressing to adhere. Brush lattices with egg wash and sprinkle with coarse sugar.

6. Place pies in freezer for 30 minutes. Meanwhile, preheat oven to 425°F (220°C).

## Tip

A pastry cutter is a useful piece of kitchen equipment. Not only is it helpful for cutting strips of dough to make a lattice crust, it is useful for cutting squares or rectangles of dough for treats such as pocket pies. If you don't have one, a small, sharp knife makes a good substitute.

**7.** Bake on center rack of preheated oven for 10 minutes. Lower oven temperature to 350°F (180°C) and bake for 15 to 20 minutes more, until crust is browned and pies are bubbling. Cool pies completely in tins on wire racks. Carefully remove from tins by running a sharp knife around the sides. Serve at room temperature.

## Variations

Substitute Cream Cheese Pie Dough (page 20) for the All-Butter Pie Dough.

*Gluten-Free Alternative:* Substitute Gluten-Free Pie Dough (page 24) for the All-Butter Pie Dough.

*Vegan Alternative:* Substitute Vegan Pie Dough (page 25) for the All-Butter Pie Dough and replace the egg wash with water.

## Make Ahead

The pies can be completely assembled (Steps 1 through 5) and frozen, tightly covered in their tins, for up to two days. Bake from frozen, as directed.

# Lattice Crust

In addition to the recipes for which it is specified, a lattice crust makes a nice finish for open-faced mini fruit tarts.

1. Divide the dough into two pieces, one slightly larger than the other. Roll out the larger piece and cut bottom crusts as directed by the recipe. After you have filled your pie, on a lightly floured surface, roll out the remaining dough to a thickness of $1/_8$ inch (3 mm).

2. Transfer dough to a baking sheet. Using a round cutter slightly larger than the diameter of the pies (usually 3 to $3^1/_2$ inches/7.5 to 8.75 cm), cut out as many rounds as you have pies. Transfer rounds to a baking sheet, as completed. Reroll scraps as necessary.

3. Using a sharp knife or pastry cutter, cut each round into 8 strips of equal width. (If the dough becomes too soft to cut neatly, chill on baking sheet for 15 minutes to firm it up.) Number the strips from left to right.

4. Working with one pie at a time, place strips 1, 3, 5 and 7 (in that order) vertically across the pie, spacing apart.

5. Fold back strips 3 and 7 from top of pie. Take strip 2 from the baking sheet and lay it horizontally across strips 1 and 5, just above where strips 3 and 7 are folded back. Straighten strips 3 and 7, laying them on top of strip 2.

6. Fold back strips 1 and 5 from top of pie, to point where they meet strip 2. Lay strip 4 across pie, parallel to strip 2 but spaced apart, and lying on top of strips 3 and 7. Straighten strips 1 and 5, laying them across strip 4.

7. Fold back strips 3 and 7 from bottom of pie, to point where they meet strip 4. Lay strip 6 across pie, on top of strips 1 and 5 and parallel to strip 4. Straighten strips 3 and 7 so they lie on top of strip 6.

8. Fold back strips 1 and 5 from bottom of the pie, to the point where they meet strip 6. Lay strip 8 across pie, on top of strips 3 and 7 and parallel to strip 6. Straighten strips 1 and 5 so they lie on top of strip 8.

9. Press ends of strips into bottom crust to adhere. Brush tops of strips with egg wash. Place pies in freezer for 30 minutes, then bake according to recipe instructions.

# Citrus and Tropical Fruit Pies

# Shaker Lemon Mini Pies

*Thinly sliced whole lemons (rind included!) are the star ingredient in this traditional pie from the Ohio Shaker community, a religious sect today known mostly for their contributions to music and their beautiful handcrafted furniture. For best results, start the filling one day in advance so that the sour lemon slices have plenty of time to marinate in sugar, creating the signature marmalade-like filling.*

## Tips

Meyer lemons are larger, hybrid lemons that are sweeter and not as acidic tasting as regular lemons.

If you don't have a mandoline slicer, use a very sharp knife to slice the lemons as thinly as possible.

A dough scraper is very useful to have when making these recipes. During the rolling process, it collects the little bits for rerolling and it cleans up the pastry board very efficiently. It also simplifies picking up the cut rounds; you just slide the scraper underneath. Even if they are sticking a bit, they will detach without tearing.

- Mandoline (see Tips, left)
- 3- and 4-inch (7.5 and 10 cm) round cutters
- Two 12-cup muffin tins, lightly greased

| | | |
|---|---|---|
| 2 | large lemons (preferably Meyer lemons; see Tips, left) | 2 |
| 1⅓ cups | granulated sugar | 325 mL |
| 3 | large eggs | 3 |
| 3 tbsp | all-purpose flour | 45 mL |
| 3 tbsp | unsalted butter, melted | 45 mL |
| ⅛ tsp | salt | 0.5 mL |
| 1 | recipe All-Butter Pie Dough (page 16) | 1 |
| 1 | large egg, lightly beaten with 1 tbsp (15 mL) water | 1 |
| | Granulated sugar for sprinkling | |

1. Using mandoline, slice lemons into very thin rounds. Remove and discard seeds. In a medium bowl, toss lemon slices with sugar until evenly coated. Set aside at room temperature for at least 6 hours or overnight.

2. In a large bowl, whisk eggs with flour. Whisk in melted butter and salt, until smooth. Stir in reserved lemon mixture.

3. Divide dough into two pieces, one slightly larger than the other. On a lightly floured surface, roll out larger piece of dough to a thickness of ⅛ inch (3 mm).

4. Using 4-inch (10 cm) cutter, cut 16 rounds and carefully fit into muffin cups, flush with the tops. Reroll scraps as necessary. Fill each shell with about 2 tbsp (30 mL) lemon filling.

5. On lightly floured surface, roll out smaller piece of dough to ⅛ inch (3 mm). Using 3-inch (7.5 cm) cutter, cut 16 rounds, rerolling scraps as necessary.

6. Brush bottoms of smaller rounds with egg wash and carefully place on filled shells, pressing edges to seal tightly. Brush tops with egg wash and sprinkle with sugar.

7. Place tins in freezer for 30 minutes. Meanwhile, preheat oven to 400°F (200°C).

**Tip**

For easiest rolling, roll your dough, including scraps, between two sheets of plastic wrap. That way, you do not need to add flour to keep the dough from sticking to your work surface.

8. Using tip of a sharp knife, cut 3 small slits in top crusts. Bake on center rack in preheated oven for 12 minutes, then lower oven temperature to 350°F (180°C) and bake for 15 to 20 minutes more, until tops are puffed and browned.

9. Cool pies in tins on wire racks for 15 minutes, then carefully remove from pans and transfer to racks to cool completely. Serve at room temperature or chilled.

## Make Ahead

The pies can be fully assembled and frozen, tightly covered in their tins, for up to three days. Bake from frozen as directed.

# Orange Chess Pies

There are as many theories about the origin of this pie's name as there are variations of the recipe. Because of its simplicity, some say the name was derived from Southerners who referred to it as "jes' pie" (just pie). Cornmeal is the unique ingredient in the filling, and it is commonly included in most chess pie recipes.

## Tips

These pies are best eaten within a day or two of being baked.

For easiest rolling, roll your dough, including scraps, between two sheets of plastic wrap. That way, you do not need to add flour to keep the dough from sticking to your work surface.

- 4-inch (10 cm) round cutter
- Two 12-cup muffin tins

| | | |
|---|---|---|
| 1 | recipe Flaky Pie Dough (page 15) | 1 |
| 1½ cups | granulated sugar | 375 mL |
| 2 tbsp | cornmeal | 30 mL |
| 1½ tbsp | all-purpose flour | 22 mL |
| ¼ tsp | salt | 1 mL |
| ½ cup | unsalted butter, melted | 125 mL |
| 3 tbsp | evaporated milk | 45 mL |
| 1 tbsp | finely grated orange zest | 15 mL |
| 3 | large eggs | 3 |
| 1½ tsp | cider vinegar | 7 mL |
| 1 tsp | vanilla extract | 5 mL |

1. On a lightly floured work surface, roll out dough to a thickness of $1/8$ inch (3 mm). Using cutter, cut into rounds and carefully fit into muffin cups (there will be some overlap). Reroll scraps as necessary.

2. Place tins in freezer for 30 minutes. Meanwhile, preheat oven to 350°F (180°C).

3. In a large bowl, whisk together sugar, cornmeal, flour, salt, butter, evaporated milk and orange zest. Whisk in eggs, one at a time, whisking well after each addition. Whisk in vinegar and vanilla. Place about 2 tbsp (30 mL) filling in each pie shell.

4. Bake in center of preheated oven for 30 to 35 minutes, until tops of pies are puffed and browned. Cool pies for 10 minutes in pans on wire racks, then carefully remove from pans and transfer to racks to cool completely.

## Variations

Substitute Cornmeal Pie Dough (page 19), All-Butter Pie Dough (page 16) or Toasted Coconut Tartlet Dough (page 22) for the Flaky Pie Dough.

## Make Ahead

The pie shells can be shaped and frozen, tightly covered in their tins, for up to one week.

# Streusel-Topped Pineapple Rum Galettes

**Makes 16 galettes**

*Warning: the Hawaiian-inspired flavor of these palm-sized free-form tarts may cause some people to do the hula! Featuring buttery macadamia nut streusel sitting atop juicy pineapple, brown sugar and rum, these will earn you the title "Big Kahuna of Pies."*

## Tips

When purchasing fresh pineapple, look for firm fruit with green leaves and a fresh scent. Using a sharp knife, trim the pineapple and remove the outer rind. Slice the fruit into 1/2-inch (1 cm) rings and remove the core from each ring. Discard cores, then chop the flesh into 1/2-inch (1 cm) pieces.

The pies can be fully assembled (Steps 1 through 3) and frozen for up to three days. Freeze for at least 30 minutes on trays, then place in a single layer in zip-top bags. Bake from frozen, as directed.

- 5-inch (12.5 cm) round cutter
- 2 baking sheets lined with parchment

| | | |
|---|---|---|
| 3 tbsp | unsalted butter | 45 mL |
| 1/4 cup | packed light brown sugar | 60 mL |
| 2 tbsp | dark rum | 30 mL |
| 1/4 tsp | salt | 1 mL |
| 2 cups | drained fresh or canned pineapple pieces | 500 mL |
| 3 tbsp | all-purpose flour | 45 mL |
| 1 | recipe All-Butter Pie Dough (page 16) | 1 |
| 1 | large egg, mixed with 1 tbsp (15 mL) water | 1 |
| 1 | recipe Macadamia Nut Streusel Topping | 1 |

1. In a medium saucepan over medium heat, melt butter. Add brown sugar, rum and salt. Bring to a simmer, stirring constantly, and cook for 1 minute. Remove from heat. Add pineapple and toss to coat. Mix in flour. Set aside to cool completely.

2. On a lightly floured work surface, roll out dough to slightly thicker than $1/16$ inch (2 mm). Using cutter, cut into rounds and place on prepared baking sheets, spacing apart. Reroll scraps as necessary.

3. Brush edges of rounds with egg wash. Place 2 tbsp (30 mL) filling in center of each round. Fold edges over filling so they overlap slightly but center is still exposed. Press firmly to seal. Press about $1^1/2$ tbsp (22 mL) streusel onto exposed center. Brush top of dough with egg wash.

4. Place galettes in freezer for 30 minutes. Meanwhile, position oven racks in upper and lower thirds of oven and preheat oven to 375°F (190°C).

5. Bake in preheated oven for 25 to 30 minutes, switching positions of baking sheets halfway through, until crust and streusel are golden brown and filling is bubbly. Let cool on baking sheets on wire racks for at least 10 minutes before serving.

## Variations

Substitute Flaky Pie Dough (page 15), Cream Cheese Pie Dough (page 20) or Toasted Coconut Tartlet Dough (page 22) for the All-Butter Dough.

# Piña Colada Hand Pies

**Makes 16 pies**

- **GF Friendly**

*If you close your eyes and take a bite of these tropically themed hand pies, you are suddenly whisked away to an island retreat, no passport required! Served chilled, the custardy pineapple-coconut filling's flavor really shines. Bon voyage!*

## Tips

Look for canned crushed pineapple packaged in its own juice, not in heavy syrup.

Cream of coconut is used in desserts and beverages such as piña coladas. It is thick and sweet. Do not confuse it with coconut cream or coconut milk.

For step-by-step photographs of making hand pies, see page 35.

- 5-inch (12.5 cm) round cutter
- 2 baking sheets lined with parchment

| | | |
|---|---|---|
| 1 cup | cream of coconut (see Tips, left) | 250 mL |
| 1/2 cup | heavy or whipping (35%) cream | 125 mL |
| 4 | large egg yolks | 4 |
| 1 tbsp | dark rum | 15 mL |
| 1 tsp | vanilla extract | 5 mL |
| 1 cup | lightly toasted sweetened shredded coconut (see Tip, page 129) | 250 mL |
| 1 | can (8 oz/250 g) crushed pineapple, well drained | 1 |
| 1 | recipe Hand Pie Dough (page 27) | 1 |
| 1 | large egg, lightly beaten with 1 tbsp (15 mL) water | 1 |
| 1 | recipe Coconut Glaze (see Variations, page 48) | 1 |

1. In a medium saucepan, combine coconut cream, heavy cream and egg yolks, whisking to blend. Set saucepan over medium-low heat and cook slowly, whisking constantly, until thickened, about 13 to 15 minutes.

2. Remove from heat and stir in rum, vanilla, coconut and pineapple. Set aside to cool completely, then cover and refrigerate until cold, about 2 hours.

3. On a lightly floured surface, roll out dough to slightly thicker than $1/16$ inch (2 mm). Using cutter, cut into rounds and place on prepared baking sheets, spacing apart. Reroll scraps as necessary.

4. Brush edges of rounds with egg wash. Place 2 to $2^1/_2$ tbsp (30 to 37 mL) filling in center of each round. Fold in half, enclosing filling. Pinch edges together to seal, and crimp with the tines of a fork. Brush tops with egg wash.

5. Place pies, on baking sheets, in freezer for 30 minutes. Meanwhile, position oven racks in upper and lower thirds of oven and preheat oven to 375°F (190°C).

## Tip

To toast coconut, spread it in an even layer in a baking pan. Place pan in preheated 300°F (150°F) oven and toast, stirring every 5 minutes, until coconut is lightly golden, about 15 to 20 minutes.

6. Using tip of a sharp knife, cut 2 or 3 slits in top of each pie. Bake in preheated oven for 23 to 28 minutes, switching positions of baking sheets halfway through, until pies are puffed and browned. Cool for 10 minutes on sheets on wire racks, then drizzle with coconut glaze. Let glaze set for 10 minutes before serving.

## Variations

Substitute Flaky Pie Dough (page 15) or All-Butter Pie Dough (page 16) for the Hand Pie Dough.

*Gluten-Free Alternative:* Substitute Gluten-Free Pie Dough (page 24) for the Hand Pie Dough.

## Make Ahead

The pies can be fully assembled (Steps 1 through 4) and frozen for up to one month. Freeze for at least 30 minutes on trays, then transfer to zip-top bags and seal. Bake from frozen as directed.

# Mango Apricot Mini Pocket Pies

**Makes 16 pies**

- **GF Friendly**
- **Vegan Friendly**

*In these three-bite pockets, fresh mango and apricot, simmered to a jam-like consistency, create a tart filling that is beautifully complemented by a sweet coconut glaze.*

## Tip

For easiest rolling, roll your dough, including scraps, between two sheets of plastic wrap. That way, you do not need to add flour to keep the dough from sticking to your work surface.

- 3½-inch (8.75 cm) round cutter
- Food processor
- 2 baking sheets lined with parchment

| | | |
|---|---|---|
| 1 | large mango, peeled and chopped (see Tip, page 131) | 1 |
| 1 cup | diced fresh or drained canned apricots | 250 mL |
| ½ cup | granulated sugar | 125 mL |
| 2 tsp | freshly squeezed lemon juice | 10 mL |
| 1 tbsp | unsalted butter | 15 mL |
| 1 | recipe Pocket Pie Dough (page 26) | 1 |
| 1 | large egg, lightly beaten with 1 tbsp (15 mL) water | 1 |
| 1 | recipe Coconut Glaze (see Variations, page 48) | 1 |

1. In a medium saucepan over medium heat, bring mango, apricots, sugar and lemon juice to a boil, stirring constantly. Reduce heat and simmer until thickened and fruit has broken down, about 20 to 25 minutes. Add butter and stir until melted.

2. Transfer to food processor fitted with the metal blade and pulse until almost smooth. Transfer to a medium bowl and set aside to cool completely.

3. Divide dough into halves. On a lightly floured surface, roll out one half to a thickness of slightly more than $\frac{1}{16}$ inch (2 mm). Using cutter, cut into rounds and place on prepared baking sheets, spacing apart. Reroll scraps as necessary.

4. Brush surfaces with egg wash and place about 1 tbsp (15 mL) filling in center of each round.

5. On lightly floured surface, roll out remaining dough. Using cutter, cut out rounds, rerolling scraps as necessary. Place on top of filling, pressing edges together to seal, and crimp with the tines of a fork. Brush tops with egg wash.

6. Place tarts, on baking sheets, in freezer for 30 minutes. Meanwhile, position oven racks in upper and lower thirds of oven and preheat oven to 375°F (190°C).

## Tip

Ripe mangos should be soft to the touch, with a sweet smell. To ripen mangos more quickly, store them in a brown paper bag at room temperature.

7. When you're ready to bake, pierce tops several times with the tip of a sharp knife or a toothpick. Bake in preheated oven for 20 to 25 minutes, switching positions of baking sheets halfway through, until tarts are puffed and golden brown and filling is bubbling.

8. Let cool on baking sheets on wire racks for 10 minutes, then drizzle with coconut glaze. Let glaze set, then serve warm or at room temperature.

## Variations

*Gluten-Free Alternative:* Substitute Gluten-Free Pie Dough (page 24) for the Pocket Pie Dough.

*Vegan Alternative:* Substitute Vegan Pie Dough (page 25) for the Pocket Pie Dough and vegan butter for the unsalted butter. Replace the egg wash with water.

## Make Ahead

The tarts can be fully assembled (Steps 1 through 5) and frozen for up to two weeks. Freeze for at least 30 minutes on trays, then transfer to zip-top bags and seal. Bake from frozen, as directed.

The fruit filling can be prepared and refrigerated, tightly covered, for up to one week.

# Tropical Fruit Tartlets

## Makes 16 tartlets

*Delicate toasted coconut shells filled with creamy coconut custard set the tropical foundation for these brightly colored tartlets. Use the fruit suggested here or create your own combination — papayas, bananas, guavas or passion fruit are delicious alternatives.*

## Tips

Used canned full-fat (not "light") coconut milk, which is usually found in the baking or Asian foods section of most grocery stores. Full-fat coconut milk will yield a richer texture for the filling.

For step-by-step photographs of the blind baking process, see page 33.

A dough scraper is very useful to have when making these recipes. During the rolling process, it collects the little bits for rerolling and it cleans up the pastry board very efficiently. It also simplifies picking up the cut rounds; you just slide the scraper underneath. Even if they are sticking a bit, they will detach without tearing.

- 4-inch (10 cm) round cutter
- Two 12-cup muffin tins
- Pie weights or dried beans
- Parchment paper
- Food processor

| | | |
|---|---|---|
| 1 | recipe Toasted Coconut Tartlet Dough (page 22) | 1 |

### Coconut Custard

| | | |
|---|---|---|
| 1/2 cup | granulated sugar | 125 mL |
| 2 tbsp | cornstarch | 30 mL |
| 1 | large egg | 1 |
| 3 | large egg yolks | 3 |
| 1 3/4 cups | unsweetened coconut milk, divided (see Tips, left) | 425 mL |
| 1 tbsp | vanilla extract | 15 mL |
| 3/4 tsp | coconut extract | 3 mL |
| 1/3 cup | apricot jam | 75 mL |
| 2/3 cup | diced kiwifruit | 150 mL |
| 2/3 cup | diced mango | 150 mL |
| 2/3 cup | diced pineapple | 150 mL |

1. On a lightly floured work surface, roll out dough to a thickness of $1/8$ inch (3 mm). Using cutter, cut into rounds and carefully fit into muffin cups (there will be some overlap). Reroll scraps as necessary.

2. Place tins in freezer for 30 minutes. Meanwhile, preheat oven to 350°F (180°C).

3. Blind-bake shells (see page 14 and Tips, left) on center rack in preheated oven for 12 minutes. Carefully remove weights and parchment and continue to bake until shells are golden brown, 7 to 9 minutes. Cool tartlets completely in tins on wire racks.

4. *Coconut Custard:* In a medium bowl, whisk together sugar and cornstarch. Whisk in egg, egg yolks and $1/2$ cup (125 mL) coconut milk and continue whisking until smooth.

## Tip

These tartlets are best eaten the day they are assembled. The fresh fruit should be glazed with jam and placed on top of the custard shortly before serving.

5. In a large saucepan, bring remaining $1^1/_4$ cups (300 mL) coconut milk to a simmer. Whisking constantly, gradually add hot coconut milk to egg mixture; whisk until fully incorporated and smooth. Return mixture to saucepan and whisk over medium-low heat until thickened, about 4 to 5 minutes. Remove pan from heat and whisk in vanilla and coconut extracts. Spoon about 2 tbsp (30 mL) custard into each prepared shell. Refrigerate until cold, then carefully remove tarts from muffin tins.

6. In a small saucepan over medium-low heat, warm apricot jam until nicely runny. In a large bowl, combine kiwi, mango and pineapple. Add warm jam and toss gently to coat. Top each tart with 2 tbsp (30 mL) glazed fruit. Serve tarts shortly after assembling.

## Variations

Substitute Flaky Pie Dough (page 15) or All-Butter Pie Dough (page 16) for the Toasted Coconut Tartlet Dough.

Create your own combination of tropical fruits, making sure that the total volume is 2 cups (500 mL).

## Make Ahead

The pie shells can be formed and frozen in tins, covered, for up to one week. Blind-bake from frozen.

# Cuban Guava and Cream Cheese Turnovers

**Makes 16 turnovers**

*The filling in these simple guava pastries, known in Cuba as* pastelitos de guayaba, *is made from a mixture of sweetened cream cheese and guava paste. This flavorful candied guava purée can be found in Mexican or Latin American markets and in some well-stocked grocery stores.*

## Tips

Pair thin slices of leftover guava paste with sharp Cheddar or manchego cheese for a simple hors d'oeuvre.

A pizza cutter or pastry wheel is a nice tool to have on hand when cutting dough into rectangles or squares for pocket pies or turnovers, as well as for making a lattice crust.

- Preheat oven to 400°F (200°C)
- Electric mixer
- Pizza/pastry cutter
- 2 baking sheets lined with parchment

| | | |
|---|---|---|
| 8 oz | softened cream cheese | 250 g |
| ¼ cup | packed light brown sugar | 60 mL |
| 2 tbsp | heavy or whipping (35%) cream | 30 mL |
| 1 tsp | vanilla extract | 5 mL |
| 1 | recipe Shortcut Puff Pastry (page 29) | 1 |
| 1 | large egg, lightly beaten with 1 tbsp (15 mL) water | 1 |
| 8 oz | guava paste, cut into 16 thin slices | 250 g |
| 1 | recipe Vanilla Glaze (page 48) | 1 |

1. In a bowl, using electric mixer at medium speed, beat cream cheese, brown sugar and cream until light and fluffy, about 2 minutes. Beat in vanilla.

2. Divide puff pastry in half. On a lightly floured surface, roll one half into a 16- by 8-inch (40 by 20 cm) rectangle. Using a knife or pizza cutter, cut into six 4-inch (10 cm) squares. Repeat with remaining half.

3. Brush edges of squares with egg wash. Place one slice of guava paste in center of each square. Top with 1 tbsp (15 mL) cream cheese mixture. Fold squares in half diagonally, enclosing filling. Pinch edges together to seal, and crimp with the tines of a fork. Brush tops with egg wash.

4. Meanwhile, position oven racks in upper and lower thirds of oven and preheat oven to 400°F (200°C).

5. Bake turnovers in preheated oven until puffed and deep golden brown, 20 to 25 minutes, switching positions of baking sheets halfway through. Let pies cool on sheets on wire racks for 5 minutes, then drizzle with vanilla glaze. Let glaze set for 5 minutes and serve warm.

## Variation

Substitute store-bought puff pastry for the Shortcut Puff Pastry.

# Key Lime Tartlets with Gingersnap Crust

------------------------------------------------

*Although he is not a dessert person, my husband can't resist a piece of Key lime pie if he sees it on a dessert menu. I created these mini versions, supported by cupcake liners to keep the shells intact, so he could take them to work for a midday treat.*

## Tips

To make gingersnap crumbs, process gingersnap cookies in a food processor until finely ground. You'll need about 12 oz (375 g) gingersnap cookies to make 2¼ cups (550 mL) crumbs.

To toast pecans, spread them in a single layer on a baking sheet. Bake in a preheated 350°F (180°C) oven until lightly browned and fragrant, 8 to 10 minutes.

Using the bottom of a shot glass is an easy way to tightly pack the crumbs so they retain their shape while baking. Moistening the glass or your fingers keeps the crumbs from sticking.

Keep tarts chilled and serve within a day or two of baking. Garnish just before serving.

- **Preheat oven to 325°F (160°C)**
- **Food processor**
- **Two 12-cup muffin tins with paper liners**

| | | |
|---|---|---|
| 2¼ cups | gingersnap cookie crumbs (see Tips, left) | 550 mL |
| ¾ cup | lightly toasted pecans (see Tips, left) | 175 mL |
| ⅔ cup | unsalted butter, melted | 150 mL |
| 5 | large egg yolks | 5 |
| 1 | can (14 oz/440 g) sweetened condensed milk | 1 |
| 1 tbsp | finely grated Key lime zest | 15 mL |
| ⅔ cup | freshly squeezed Key lime juice | 150 mL |
| | Lightly sweetened whipped cream | |

1. In food processor fitted with the metal blade, process crumbs and pecans until finely ground. Drizzle butter over mixture and pulse until evenly moistened.

2. Press mixture into bottoms and sides of prepared muffin cups to form a thick crust (¼ inch/0.5 cm). Using a shot glass or moistened fingers, pack down crust.

3. Bake in center of preheated oven for 10 to 13 minutes, until edges are golden brown. If crusts start to lose their shape during baking, quickly reshape with a shot glass or the back of a moistened metal spoon. Cool in pans on racks for 10 minutes.

4. Increase oven temperature to 350°F (180°C).

5. In a medium bowl, whisk together egg yolks, condensed milk and lime zest and juice. Pour filling into shells, filling almost to the top. Bake in preheated oven for 14 to 16 minutes, until edges are set but center is still a bit jiggly. Cool completely in tins on wire racks. When cool, transfer tins to refrigerator and chill until cold, for at least 2 hours or up to 2 days. Garnish with whipped cream just before serving.

## Variation

Bake crusts (Step 3) for 13 to 15 minutes, until bottoms are golden brown. Fill shells with Lime Curd (Variations, page 47). Do not bake the filling (Steps 4 and 5); refrigerate immediately after filling.

# Brandied Chewy Date-Nut Pies

**Makes 24 pies**

● **GF Friendly**

*These chewy bites remind me of the very sweet, dense and rich date squares my mom used to make for us when we were kids (without the brandy, of course!). These pies travel well, making them great for a hostess gift or bake sale.*

## Tips

For easy preparation, look for pitted dates that are already chopped. If the dates are not soft, rehydrate them in warm water and drain well before adding to the filling.

If you don't own round cutters in the appropriate sizes, look for lids of the same size from prepared foods.

● 4-inch (10 cm) round cutter
● Two 12-cup muffin tins, lightly greased

| | | |
|---|---|---|
| 1 | recipe All-Butter Pie Dough (page 16) | 1 |
| 3 | large eggs | 3 |
| ½ cup | packed dark brown sugar | 125 mL |
| ¼ cup | light corn syrup | 60 mL |
| ¼ cup | dark corn syrup | 60 mL |
| ¼ cup | unsalted butter, melted | 60 mL |
| 1 tbsp | brandy | 15 mL |
| 1 tsp | vanilla extract | 5 mL |
| ¼ tsp | salt | 1 mL |
| 1 cup | chopped pitted dried dates (see Tips, left) | 250 mL |
| 1 cup | chopped walnuts | 250 mL |

1. On a lightly floured surface, roll out dough to a thickness of $1/8$ inch (3 mm). Using cutter, cut into rounds and carefully fit into muffin cups. Reroll scraps as necessary.

2. Place tins in freezer for 30 minutes. Meanwhile, preheat oven to 400°F (200°C).

3. In a large bowl, whisk together eggs, brown sugar, light and dark corn syrup, melted butter, brandy, vanilla and salt. Stir in dates and walnuts.

4. Spoon 2 to $2^{1}/_2$ tbsp (30 to 37 mL) filling into each chilled shell.

5. Bake in center of preheated oven for 10 minutes. Lower oven temperature to 350°F (180°C) and bake for 15 to 20 minutes more, until tops are puffed and browned.

6. Cool in pans on wire racks for 15 minutes, then carefully remove from tins and transfer to racks to cool completely.

## Variation

*Gluten-Free Alternative:* Substitute Gluten-Free Pie Dough (page 24) for the All-Butter Pie Dough.

## Make Ahead

The baked pies can be stored at room temperature, covered, for two to three days.

# Caramel and Custard-Filled Pies

# Crème Brûlée Tartlets

**Makes 24 tartlets**

● **GF Friendly**

*One of the best restaurant desserts I have ever eaten was a "Mini Crème Brûlée Tasting." It came with not one but five bite-size crème brûlée tartlets, all different flavors. This recipe was inspired by the simplest of the selection: a classic vanilla custard accented with a refreshing hint of orange.*

## Tips

For easiest rolling, roll your dough, including scraps, between two sheets of plastic wrap. That way, you do not need to add flour to keep the dough from sticking to your work surface.

For step-by-step photographs of the blind-baking process, see page 33.

● 3½-inch (8.75 cm) round cutter
● Two 12-cup muffin tins
● Kitchen torch, optional (see Tips, page 139)

| | | |
|---|---|---|
| 1 | recipe Sweet Tart Dough (page 17) | 1 |
| **Filling** | | |
| 6 | large egg yolks | 6 |
| 1½ cups | heavy or whipping (35%) cream | 375 mL |
| ¾ cup | whole milk | 175 mL |
| 6 tbsp | granulated sugar | 90 mL |
| 2 tsp | finely grated orange zest | 10 mL |
| 1 | vanilla bean, split, seeds scraped out and reserved | 1 |
| Pinch | salt | Pinch |

Granulated sugar for caramelizing

1. On a lightly floured surface, roll out dough to a thickness of $1/8$ inch (3 mm). Using cutter, cut into rounds and carefully fit into muffin cups. Reroll scraps as necessary.

2. Place tins in freezer for 30 minutes. Meanwhile, preheat oven to 350°F (180°C).

3. Blind-bake shells (see page 14 and Tips, left) in center of preheated oven for 15 minutes. Carefully remove weights and parchment and set aside to cool. Lower oven temperature to 300°F (150°C).

4. *Filling:* In a large bowl, whisk together egg yolks, cream, milk, sugar, orange zest, vanilla seeds and salt.

5. Spoon filling into cooled crusts to about three-quarters full. Bake in preheated oven for 23 to 28 minutes, until edges of filling are set but center is still a bit jiggly. Cool to room temperature in pans on wire racks, then carefully unmold and transfer to a baking sheet. Place in refrigerator to chill for at least 2 hours.

## Tips

If you don't have a kitchen torch, place the sugared tartlets under the broiler for a few minutes. Watch carefully to ensure the crusts do not burn.

The easiest way to remove tarts from muffin tins is to run a small, sharp knife or small offset spatula around the edges, loosening the sides. You should then be able to carefully lift out the tarts, guiding them with the knife or spatula.

6. Just before serving, sprinkle surface of each tartlet with an even coating of sugar. Using a kitchen torch, caramelize the sugar, avoiding the crust to prevent burning it (see Tips, left).

## Variations

Substitute All-Butter Pie Dough (page 16), Toasted Coconut Tartlet Dough (page 22) or Cream Cheese Pie Dough (page 20) for the Sweet Tart Dough.

*Gluten-Free Alternative:* Substitute Gluten-Free Pie Dough (page 24) for the Sweet Tart Dough.

## Make Ahead

The pies can be baked, removed from the tins and chilled for up to one day before caramelizing.

# Coconut Custard Tartlets

● **GF Friendly**

*Coconut lovers rejoice — this is the recipe of your dreams! These tarts have a double punch of coconut, because their creamy custard filling is baked inside a buttery toasted coconut crust.*

## Tips

Coconut chips are unsweetened large-flake pieces of dried coconut. Look for them in the bulk foods section of grocery stores or natural foods stores.

If you want to gild the lily, top each tartlet with a dollop of lightly sweetened whipped cream just before serving.

Wire baking racks are important to have on hand for the cooling process. After pies have finished baking, either set the muffin tin on the rack or transfer the pies from the baking sheet to the rack. This lets the air circulate around the pies, cooling them evenly.

● **4-inch (10 cm) round cutter**
● **Two 12-cup muffin tins**

| | | |
|---|---|---|
| 1 | recipe Toasted Coconut Tartlet Dough (page 22) | 1 |
| 2 | large eggs | 2 |
| $\frac{1}{3}$ cup | granulated sugar | 75 mL |
| $\frac{1}{4}$ tsp | salt | 1 mL |
| 1 cup | whole milk | 250 mL |
| $\frac{1}{4}$ cup | heavy or whipping (35%) cream | 60 mL |
| 1 tsp | vanilla extract | 5 mL |
| $\frac{1}{2}$ tsp | coconut extract | 2 mL |
| $1\frac{1}{4}$ cups | sweetened flaked coconut | 300 mL |
| | Toasted coconut chips, optional | |

1. On a lightly floured surface, roll out dough to a thickness of $\frac{1}{8}$ inch (3 mm). Using cutter, cut into rounds and carefully fit into muffin cups. Reroll scraps.

2. Place tins in freezer for 30 minutes. Meanwhile, preheat oven to 350°F (180°C).

3. In a medium saucepan, whisk together eggs, sugar, salt, milk and cream. Cook over medium-low heat, stirring constantly, until thickened, 6 to 8 minutes. Stir in vanilla and coconut extracts and flaked coconut. Set aside to cool slightly.

4. Spoon 2 to 3 tbsp (30 to 45 mL) filling into each shell, filling about three-quarters full. Bake in center of preheated oven until filling is set, puffed and lightly golden, 30 to 35 minutes. Cool in tins on wire racks for 15 minutes, then carefully unmold and transfer to racks to cool completely.

## Variations

Substitute Flaky Pie Dough (page 15), Cream Cheese Pie Dough (page 20) or All-Butter Pie Dough (page 16) for the Toasted Coconut Tartlet Dough.

*Gluten-Free Alternative:* Substitute Gluten-Free Pie Dough (page 24) for the All-Butter Pie Dough.

## Make Ahead

Once baked, the pies can be refrigerated or kept covered at room temperature for up to four days.

Strawberry Basil Hand Pies (page 80)

Lemon Meringue Tartlets (page 60),
Southern Fried Peach Pies (page 112)
and Campfire S'mores Pies (page 178)

Streusel-Topped Pineapple Rum Galettes (page 127)

Tropical Fruit Tartlets (page 132) and
Key Lime Tartlets with Gingersnap Crust (page 135)

Crème Brûlée Tartlets (page 138) and
Boston Cream Whoopie Pies (page 148)

Blueberry Lemon Pie Pops (page 162) and
Chocolate-Covered Cherry Pie Pops (page 188)

Chocolate Mocha Pecan Tarts (page 201)

Frozen Chocolate Mint Grasshopper Pies (page 206)

Pumpkin Pies with Spiced Walnut Streusel (page 222)

Chicken, Brie and Apple Turnovers (page 238)

Pork Empanadas with Salsa Verde (page 250)

Corn, Bacon, and Tomato Tarts (page 268)
and Caramel Apple Hand Pies (page 100)

# Southern Banana Pudding Pies

*When I was a child, whenever my mother made banana pudding, I thought she had created some sort of labor-intensive masterpiece. Little did I know it was just layers of pudding, vanilla wafers and bananas — simple, but extraordinarily delicious! These handheld versions of the comfort-food classic create the same layers in a wafer-coated crust. Drizzled with caramel sauce, they are indeed a masterpiece.*

## Tips

Nilla is a popular brand of vanilla wafers that is widely available.

To ensure that the vanilla wafers rolled into the crust are finely crushed, grind them in a food processor or mini-chopper for 10 to 15 seconds.

For step-by-step photographs of the process of making hand pies, see page 35.

● 5-inch (12.5 cm) round cutter
● 2 baking sheets lined with parchment

| | | |
|---|---|---|
| 1 cup | finely crushed vanilla wafer cookies (see Tips, left) | 250 mL |
| 1 | recipe Flaky Pie Dough (page 15) | 1 |
| 1 | large egg, lightly beaten with 1 tbsp (15 mL) water | 1 |
| 2 cups | Vanilla Bean Pastry Cream (page 51) | 500 mL |
| 16 | vanilla wafer cookies | 16 |
| 2 | bananas, sliced crosswise ¼ inch (0.5 cm) thick | 2 |
| 1 | recipe Beth's Salted Caramel Sauce (page 52), optional | 1 |
| | Confectioners' (icing) sugar, optional | |

1. On a lightly floured work surface, scatter a handful of crushed cookies. Place dough on surface and roll out to slightly thicker than $1/16$ inch (2 mm), embedding cookie crumbs in dough. Reroll scraps, scattering additional crumbs as necessary. Using cutter, cut into rounds and transfer to prepared baking sheets.

2. Brush edges with egg wash. Place about $1^1/_2$ tbsp (22 mL) pastry cream in center of each circle. Break a vanilla wafer in half and place on top of the cream; add 2 to 3 slices banana. Fold in half, enclosing filling. Pinch edges to seal, and crimp with a fork.

3. Place pies in freezer for 30 minutes. Meanwhile, position oven racks in upper and lower thirds of oven and preheat oven to 375°F (190°C).

4. Using tip of a sharp knife, cut 3 slits in top of each pie. Bake in preheated oven for 25 to 30 minutes, switching positions of baking sheets halfway through, until golden brown. Cool on sheets on racks for 10 minutes, then drizzle with caramel sauce, if using. Dust with confectioners' sugar, if using, and serve warm.

## Variations

In place of (or in addition to!) the salted caramel sauce, drizzle the baked pies with Chocolate Glaze (page 49) or Rich Chocolate Ganache (page 46).

Substitute Hand Pie Dough (page 27) or All-Butter Pie Dough (page 26) for the Flaky Pie Dough.

# English Banoffee Pies

● **GF Friendly**

*This traditional English dessert is made from three main ingredients: bananas and toffee (hence the name banoffee) and sweetened whipped cream. Store-bought toffee sauce can certainly be used, but it's much more fun to make your own, using a can of sweetened condensed milk.*

## Tips

When simmering the sweetened condensed milk, take extra care to ensure that the water level does not dip below the top of the can — or you might end up with a mess on your ceiling!

For step-by-step photographs of the blind-baking process, see page 33.

● 4-inch (10 cm) round cutter
● Two 12-cup muffin tins
● Pie weights or dried beans
● Parchment paper
● Electric mixer

### Toffee Sauce

| | | |
|---|---|---|
| 1 | can (14 oz/440 g) sweetened condensed milk | 440 g |

### Pies

| | | |
|---|---|---|
| 1 | recipe All-Butter Pie Dough (page 16) | 1 |
| 1 cup | heavy or whipping (35%) cream | 250 mL |
| 2 tbsp | granulated sugar | 30 mL |
| 3 | bananas, diced | 3 |

1. *Toffee Sauce:* Place unopened can of condensed milk in a large saucepan and add water to cover. Bring to a boil, reduce heat and simmer for 3 hours, adding more water as necessary to maintain level above top of can. Remove from heat and set aside for 30 minutes. Remove can from hot water and set aside on a wire rack for 10 minutes. Carefully open can and pour creamy toffee into a bowl.

2. *Pies:* On a lightly floured surface, roll out dough to a thickness of $1/8$ inch (3 mm). Using cutter, cut into rounds and carefully fit into muffin cups (there will be some overlap). Reroll scraps as necessary.

3. Place tins in freezer for 30 minutes. Meanwhile, preheat oven to 350°F (180°C).

4. Blind-bake shells (see page 14 and Tips, left) in center of preheated oven for 12 minutes. Carefully remove weights and parchment and continue to bake until shells are golden brown, 5 to 7 minutes longer. Let cool in pans on wire racks for 10 minutes, then carefully transfer shells to racks to cool completely.

5. Spoon about 1 tbsp (15 mL) toffee into each cooled pie shell. Refrigerate for 20 minutes, until toffee has set.

## Tip

The easiest way to remove tarts from muffin tins is to run a small, sharp knife or small offset spatula around the edges, loosening the sides. You should then be able to carefully lift out the tarts, guiding them with the knife or spatula.

6. Using electric mixer at high speed, beat cream until soft peaks form. Add sugar and continue to beat until firm peaks form.

7. Remove shells from refrigerator. Top toffee with a layer of banana, followed by a layer of whipped cream. Garnish with additional banana and a drizzle of toffee sauce. Serve immediately.

## Variations

Substitute Flaky Pie Dough (page 15) for the All-Butter Pie Dough.

*Gluten-Free Alternative:* Substitute Gluten-Free Pie Dough (page 24) for the All-Butter Pie Dough.

## Make Ahead

The toffee sauce can be prepared up to one week in advance. Cover tightly and refrigerate until ready to use.

# N'awlins Bananas Foster Hand Pies

• **GF Friendly**

*New Orleans — often pronounced "N'awlins" — is one of the most hedonistic food cities in the world. It is known as much for its generously seasoned Cajun cuisine as it is for over-the-top sweets. Bananas Foster was created in 1951 at Brennan's, one of that city's best-known restaurants. Since then, this decadent flambéed dessert has become a favorite worldwide.*

## Tips

If you don't feel comfortable about igniting the sauce by tilting the pan, or if you have an electric stove, you can use a stick flame such as a barbecue lighter.

For step-by-step photographs of the process of making hand pies, see page 35.

• **5-inch (12.5 cm) round cutter**
• **2 baking sheets lined with parchment**

| | | |
|---|---|---|
| 2 | large bananas, chopped | 2 |
| 3 tbsp | unsalted butter | 45 mL |
| 1/3 cup | packed dark brown sugar | 75 mL |
| 2 tsp | finely grated orange zest | 10 mL |
| 1/2 tsp | ground cinnamon | 2 mL |
| 1/4 tsp | ground nutmeg | 1 mL |
| 1 tbsp | vanilla extract | 15 mL |
| 3 tbsp | dark rum | 45 mL |
| 1/3 cup | chopped pecans, lightly toasted | 75 mL |
| 1 | recipe Hand Pie Dough (page 27) | 1 |
| 1 | large egg, lightly beaten with 1 tbsp (15 mL) water | 1 |
| 1 | recipe Beth's Salted Caramel Sauce (page 52) | 1 |
| | Confectioners' (icing) sugar | |

1. Place bananas in a medium bowl and set aside.

2. In a medium skillet over low heat, melt butter. Add brown sugar, orange zest, cinnamon and nutmeg; stir until sugar dissolves. Add vanilla and bring to a simmer. Add rum and carefully ignite by tilting pan toward burner (only if you have a gas stove; see Tips, left). Continue to cook until flames subside and sauce reaches a syrupy consistency. Pour over reserved bananas and toss well. Stir in pecans and set aside to cool completely.

3. On a lightly floured surface, roll out dough to slightly thicker than $1/16$ inch (2 mm). Using cutter, cut into rounds and place on prepared baking sheets, spacing apart. Reroll scraps as necessary.

4. Brush edges of rounds with egg wash. Place about 2 tbsp (30 mL) banana filling in center of each circle. Top with 1 tsp (5 mL) caramel sauce. Fold in half, enclosing filling. Pinch edges together to seal, and crimp with the tines of a fork. Brush tops of pies with egg wash.

## Tips

A dough scraper is very useful to have when making these recipes. During the rolling process, it collects the little bits for rerolling and it cleans up the pastry board very efficiently. It also simplifies picking up the cut rounds; you just slide the scraper underneath. Even if they are sticking a bit, they will detach without tearing.

Allow the pies to rest a short time before serving so they are cool enough to hold in your hand.

5. Place pies, on baking sheets, in freezer for 30 minutes. Meanwhile, position oven racks in upper and lower thirds of oven and preheat oven to 375°F (190°C).

6. Using tip of a sharp knife, cut 2 or 3 slits in top of each pie. Bake in preheated oven for 25 to 30 minutes, switching positions of baking sheets halfway through, until pies are puffed and golden brown. Let cool for 10 minutes on sheets in pan on wire racks, then drizzle with additional caramel sauce. Dust with confectioners' sugar and serve warm.

## Variations

Substitute Flaky Pie Dough (page 15) or All-Butter Pie Dough (page 16) for the Hand Pie Dough.

*Gluten-Free Alternative:* Substitute Gluten-Free Pie Dough (page 24) for the Hand Pie Dough.

## Make Ahead

The pies can be fully assembled (Steps 1 through 4) and frozen for up to one month. Freeze for at least 30 minutes on trays, then transfer to zip-top bags and seal. Bake as directed.

# Butterscotch Pudding Pies

● **GF Friendly**

*Is there any dessert more comforting than butterscotch pudding? Each rich and creamy bite is like a warm hug from Mom. For the ultimate butterscotch flavor, use dark brown sugar — and a healthy splash of Scotch!*

## Tips

For step-by-step photographs of the blind-baking process, see page 33.

The easiest way to remove tarts from muffin tins is to run a small, sharp knife or small offset spatula around the edges, loosening the sides. You should then be able to carefully lift out the tarts, guiding them with the knife or spatula.

Wire baking racks are important to have on hand for the cooling process. After pies have finished baking, either set the muffin tin on the rack or transfer the pies from the baking sheet to the rack. This lets the air circulate around the pies, cooling them evenly.

● 4-inch (10 cm) round cutter
● Two 12-cup muffin tins
● Pie weights or dried beans
● Parchment paper

| | | |
|---|---|---|
| 1 | recipe All-Butter Pie Dough (page 16) | 1 |

**Butterscotch Pudding**

| | | |
|---|---|---|
| 3 tbsp | cornstarch | 45 mL |
| 3 | large egg yolks | 3 |
| 2 cups | whole milk, divided | 500 mL |
| 3 tbsp | unsalted butter, in pieces | 45 mL |
| 1 cup | packed dark brown sugar (see Tip, page 147) | 250 mL |
| ¼ tsp | salt | 1 mL |
| 2 tbsp | Scotch or other whisky | 30 mL |
| 2 tsp | vanilla extract | 10 mL |
| | Lightly sweetened whipped cream, optional | |

1. On a lightly floured surface, roll out dough to a thickness of $1/8$ inch (3 mm). Using cutter, cut into rounds and carefully fit into muffin cups (there will be some overlap). Reroll scraps as necessary.

2. Place tins in freezer for 30 minutes. Meanwhile, preheat oven to 350°F (180°C).

3. Blind-bake shells (see page 14 and Tips, left) in center of preheated oven for 10 minutes. Carefully remove weights and parchment and continue to bake until shells are golden brown, 5 to 8 minutes longer. Let cool in pans on wire racks for 10 minutes, then carefully remove from cups (see Tips, left) and transfer to racks to cool completely.

4. *Butterscotch Pudding:* In a large bowl, whisk cornstarch with egg yolks and $1/2$ cup (125 mL) milk. Set aside.

5. In a large saucepan over medium heat, melt butter. Whisk in brown sugar and salt. Gradually add remaining $1^1/2$ cups (375 mL) milk, whisking constantly until smooth, and bring to a simmer.

## Tip

Because of its higher molasses content, dark brown sugar helps butterscotch pudding achieve a rich taste and color. If possible, don't substitute light brown sugar.

6. Whisking constantly, slowly add hot milk mixture to egg mixture. Return to saucepan and cook over medium-low heat until thickened, about 8 minutes. Remove from heat and stir in whisky and vanilla.

7. Pour pudding into tart shells, dividing equally. Chill until set, at least 2 hours or up to 2 days. Garnish with whipped cream, if using, and serve.

## Variations

Substitute Flaky Pie Dough (page 15) or Whole Wheat Pie Dough (page 18) for the All-Butter Pie Dough.

*Gluten-Free Alternative:* Substitute Gluten-Free Pie Dough (page 24) for the All-Butter Pie Dough.

# Boston Cream Whoopie Pies

---

*Based on their appearance, most people would label these desserts not as pies but as sandwich cookies. Once known as a traditional Amish and New England sweet (it's the state treat of Maine), whoopie pies can now be found almost anywhere, in a variety of flavors too long to list.*

## Tip

If you don't have a pastry bag, fill a zip-top bag with dough and snip off one corner. Pipe dough onto baking sheet in 1½-inch (4 cm) rounds.

- Preheat oven to 375°F (190°C)
- Electric mixer
- Pastry bag fitted with ½-inch (1 cm) tip
- 2 baking sheets lined with parchment

| | | |
|---|---|---|
| 2½ cups | all-purpose flour | 625 mL |
| 1½ tsp | baking powder | 7 mL |
| ¼ tsp | salt | 1 mL |
| ½ cup | unsalted butter, at room temperature | 125 mL |
| 1 cup | granulated sugar | 250 mL |
| 1 | large egg | 1 |
| 1 | large egg yolk | 1 |
| ½ cup | full-fat sour cream | 125 mL |
| ½ cup | whole milk | 125 mL |
| 1 tbsp | vanilla extract | 15 mL |
| 1½ cups | Vanilla Bean Pastry Cream (page 51) | 375 mL |
| 1 | recipe Chocolate Glaze (page 49) | 1 |

1. In a large bowl, whisk flour, baking powder and salt.

2. In another bowl, using electric mixer at medium speed, beat butter and sugar until light and fluffy, about 3 minutes. Add egg and egg yolk and beat for 2 minutes. Reduce speed to low. Add a third of the flour mixture to bowl, then add sour cream; mix until combined. Add another third of flour mixture, then milk; mix to combine. Add final third of flour mixture, then vanilla; mix until just combined.

3. Transfer batter to pastry bag. On prepared baking sheets, pipe into rounds 1½ inches (4 cm) in diameter, spacing apart. Bake on center rack of preheated oven for 10 to 13 minutes, until cookies spring back when lightly pressed. Cool on baking sheets for 10 minutes, then transfer to wire racks to cool completely.

4. Divide cookies into two equal batches. Spread about 1 tbsp (15 mL) pastry cream on flat sides of one batch. Top with second batch, pressing to adhere flat sides together. Drizzle chocolate glaze over tops of pies. (Or, dip half of each pie in glaze.) Let glaze set before serving.

---

## Variation

Substitute Rich Chocolate Ganache (page 46) for the Chocolate Glaze.

---

# Maple Sugar Buttermilk Tarts

*I found a recipe for buttermilk pie when searching through my grandmother's old tin recipe box. Wanting to give the flavor a bit more depth without changing her recipe too much, I simply swapped out the white sugar for rich maple sugar.*

## Tips

Maple sugar comes from the sap of the sugar maple tree. It is the crystallized product that remains when the sap is boiled and almost all of the water has been removed. Look for it in specialty markets or natural foods stores.

The easiest way to remove tarts from muffin tins is to run a small, sharp knife or small offset spatula around the edges, loosening the sides. You should then be able to carefully lift out the tarts, guiding them with the knife or spatula.

- 4-inch (10 cm) round cutter
- Two 12-cup muffin tins

| 1 | recipe All-Butter Pie Dough (page 16) | 1 |
|---|---|---|
| **Filling** | | |
| 1½ cups | maple sugar | 375 mL |
| 2 tbsp | all-purpose flour | 30 mL |
| ¼ tsp | baking soda | 1 mL |
| ½ cup | unsalted butter, melted | 125 mL |
| 4 | large eggs | 4 |
| 1 cup | buttermilk | 250 mL |
| 1 tsp | vanilla | 5 mL |

1. On a lightly floured work surface, roll out dough to a thickness of ⅛ inch (3 mm). Using cutter, cut into rounds and carefully fit into muffin cups (there will be some overlap). Reroll scraps as necessary.

2. Place tins in freezer for 30 minutes. Meanwhile, preheat oven to 350°F (180°C).

3. *Filling:* In a large bowl, whisk together maple sugar, flour and baking soda. Whisk in melted butter. Whisk in eggs, one at a time, whisking well after each addition. Whisk in buttermilk and vanilla.

4. Pour filling into chilled pie shells, filling each about two-thirds full.

5. Bake in center of preheated oven for 30 to 35 minutes, until tops have browned and filling is set. Let cool in tins on wire racks for 15 minutes, then carefully remove from cups and transfer to racks to cool completely. Serve at room temperature or refrigerate for up to 2 days.

## Make Ahead

The pies can be stored, covered, at room temperature or chilled for up to two days.

# Shoo-Fly Tartlets

Similar to English treacle tarts with a spiced streusel topping, these Pennsylvania Dutch pies take their name from their gooey molasses bottom layer — so sweet you will need to shoo away the flies before serving!

---

## Tips

Don't worry if the spiced topping starts to sink to the bottom of the tartlets when sprinkled on top. It will rise back up during the baking process.

The pies can be baked and stored at room temperature, covered, for two to three days. The flavors actually improve over time.

Expect a longer baking time (6 to 10 minutes) if you need to use 2 muffin tins because they are too large to fit on one rack.

- 4-inch (10 cm) round cutter
- Two 12-cup muffin tins
- Food processor

| 1 | recipe Cornmeal Pie Dough (page 19) | 1 |
|---|---|---|
| **Filling** | | |
| 1 cup | all-purpose flour | 250 mL |
| ⅔ cup | packed light brown sugar | 150 mL |
| 1 tsp | ground ginger | 5 mL |
| ½ tsp | ground cinnamon | 2 mL |
| ¼ tsp | ground nutmeg | 1 mL |
| ¼ tsp | ground cloves | 1 mL |
| 3 tbsp | cold unsalted butter, cubed | 45 mL |
| 1 tsp | baking soda | 5 mL |
| 1½ cups | boiling water | 375 mL |
| 1½ cups | dark (cooking) molasses | 375 mL |
| 2 | large eggs | 2 |

1. On a lightly floured work surface, roll out dough to a thickness of ⅛ inch (3 mm). Using cutter, cut into rounds and carefully fit into muffin cups (there will be some overlap). Reroll scraps as necessary.

2. Place tins in freezer for 30 minutes. Meanwhile, preheat oven to 400°F (200°C).

3. *Filling:* In food processor fitted with the metal blade, pulse flour, brown sugar, ginger, cinnamon, nutmeg and cloves. Add butter and pulse until coarse crumbs form. Set aside.

4. Place baking soda in a large bowl. Slowly add boiling water, whisking constantly. Whisk in molasses and eggs.

5. Place about 2 tbsp (30 mL) molasses filling in each chilled pie shell. Top each with 1 tbsp (15 mL) flour mixture.

6. Bake in center of preheated oven for 10 minutes. Lower oven temperature to 350°F (180°C) and bake for 15 to 20 minutes more, until tops are puffed and slightly cracked. Let cool completely in pans on wire racks, then carefully remove from cups and serve.

# Italian Cannoli Hand Pies

**Makes 16 pies**

● **GF Friendly**

---

*I once spent an afternoon wandering around the north end of Boston with my friend Laurie and her daughter Lily, in a quest for the perfect cannoli. When we finally found the bakery, the reward was well worth the effort: sweet ricotta custard dotted with chocolate chips, wrapped in a crisp fried pastry shell. We ended up purchasing an even dozen.*

---

## Tips

Cannoli shells are traditionally open-ended cylinders that are formed around a metal tube and fried before filling. These pies are filled, then fried.

Although these pies are best prepared the day they are filled, they can be fully assembled (Steps 1 through 3) and frozen for up to one month. Freeze for at least 30 minutes on trays, then transfer to zip-top bags and seal. Fry from frozen, as directed.

● 5-inch (12.5 cm) round cutter
● 2 baking sheets lined with parchment paper
● Candy/deep-fry thermometer

### Filling

| | | |
|---|---|---|
| 1½ cups | whole-milk ricotta cheese | 375 mL |
| 2 tsp | finely grated orange zest | 10 mL |
| 1 cup | confectioners' (icing) sugar | 250 mL |
| 2 tsp | vanilla extract | 10 mL |
| ½ cup | semisweet mini chocolate chips | 125 mL |
| 1 | recipe Hand Pie Dough (page 27) | 1 |
| 1 | large egg, lightly beaten with 1 tbsp (15 mL) water | 1 |
| | Canola or safflower oil for frying | |
| | Confectioners' (icing) sugar for dusting | |

1. *Filling:* In a medium bowl, mix together ricotta, orange zest, sugar and vanilla. Mix in chocolate chips.

2. On a lightly floured surface, roll out dough to slightly thicker than $1/16$ inch (2 mm). Using cutter, cut into rounds and place on prepared baking sheets, spacing apart. Reroll scraps as necessary.

3. Brush edges of rounds with egg wash. Place about 2 tbsp (30 mL) filling in center of each round. Fold in half, enclosing filling. Pinch edges together to seal, and crimp with the tines of a fork.

4. Place pies, on baking sheets, in freezer for 30 minutes.

5. In a deep skillet or Dutch oven, heat 2 inches (5 cm) oil until deep-fry thermometer registers 360°F (185°C). Fry pies in batches, turning once, until golden brown, 3 to 4 minutes in total.

6. Transfer to a rack lined with paper towels to cool slightly. Dust with confectioners' sugar before serving.

---

## Variations

Substitute Flaky Pie Dough (page 15) or All-Butter Pie Dough (page 16) for the Hand Pie Dough.

*Gluten-Free Alternative:* Substitute Gluten-Free Pie Dough (page 24) for the Hand Pie Dough.

# Rum Raisin Custard Pies

● **GF Friendly**

*Ice cream has always been my weakness, especially the rum raisin flavor, which is the inspiration for these "adults only" tarts. Soaking the raisins in rum has a double purpose: it plumps up the raisins and ensures that rum is included in each and every bite!*

## Tips

For maximum rum flavor, let the raisins soak at room temperature for at least 6 hours or overnight.

If you don't own round cutters in the appropriate sizes, look for lids of the same size from prepared foods.

● 4-inch (10 cm) round cutter
● Two 12-cup muffin tins, lightly greased
● Pie weights or dried beans
● Parchment paper

| | | |
|---|---|---|
| 1 cup | dark raisins | 250 mL |
| ¼ cup | dark rum | 60 mL |
| 1 | recipe All-Butter Pie Dough (page 16) | 1 |
| 1 | large egg | 1 |
| 3 | large egg yolks | 3 |
| ¾ cup | granulated sugar | 175 mL |
| ½ tsp | ground cinnamon | 2 mL |
| 1½ cups | heavy or whipping (35%) cream | 375 mL |
| ¾ cup | whole milk | 175 mL |
| 1 tbsp | unsalted butter | 15 mL |
| | Lightly sweetened whipped cream for serving | |

1. In a small saucepan over medium heat, bring raisins and rum to a simmer. Remove from heat and set aside to soak for 2 hours (see Tips, left). Drain, reserving raisins and 2 tbsp (30 mL) of the soaking liquid separately.

2. On a lightly floured work surface, roll out dough to a thickness of $1/8$ inch (3 mm). Using cutter, cut into rounds and carefully fit into muffin cups. Reroll scraps as necessary.

3. Place tins in freezer for 30 minutes. Meanwhile, preheat oven to 375°F (190°C).

4. In a large bowl, whisk together egg, egg yolks, sugar and cinnamon.

5. In a medium saucepan over medium heat, bring cream and milk to a simmer. Whisking constantly, gradually pour hot cream mixture into egg mixture; whisk until smooth. Return to saucepan and cook over medium-low heat, stirring constantly, until mixture becomes thick enough to coat the back of a spoon, about 8 minutes. Stir in butter and reserved raisin soaking liquid. Set aside.

## Tips

For step-by-step photographs of the blind baking process, see page 33.

The easiest way to remove tarts from muffin tins is to run a small, sharp knife or small offset spatula around the edges, loosening the sides. You should then be able to carefully lift out the tarts, guiding them with the knife or spatula.

Wire baking racks are important to have on hand for the cooling process. After pies have finished baking, either set the muffin tin on the rack or transfer the pies from the baking sheet to the rack. This lets the air circulate around the pies, cooling them evenly.

6. Blind-bake shells (page 14 and Tips, left) on center rack of preheated oven for 15 minutes. Carefully remove weights and parchment. Lower oven temperature to 325°F (160°C).

7. Place 2 tsp (10 mL) soaked raisins in each pie shell. Top with about 2 tbsp (30 mL) custard. Return tarts to oven and bake for 15 to 20 minutes, until centers are set. Cool completely in tins on wire racks, then carefully unmold and transfer to serving plates. Garnish with whipped cream and serve immediately, or refrigerate for up to 2 days.

## Variations

Substitute Flaky Pie Dough (page 15) or Toasted Coconut Tartlet Dough (page 22) for the All-Butter Pie Dough.

*Gluten-Free Alternative:* Substitute Gluten-Free Pie Dough (page 24) for the All-Butter Pie Dough.

## Make Ahead

Once baked and cooled, these pies can be covered and chilled for up to two days.

# Peanut Butter Pudding Tarts

• **GF Friendly**

*I eat at least a little bit of peanut butter every day, which is one of the reasons I decided to call my food blog* Peanut Butter and Julie! *Usually I mix it into a banana smoothie or spread it on whole-grain toast with some strawberry preserves, but I also enjoy it in desserts. Anyone who is a fan of salty-sweet flavors will enjoy these smooth and creamy pudding-filled pies.*

## Tip

This recipe was tested using so-called regular store-bought peanut butter as opposed to "natural" peanut butter. Regular peanut butter is creamy and thick at room temperature. Natural peanut butter has a thinner texture and tends to separate from the peanut oils at room temperature.

- 4-inch (10 cm) round cutter
- Two 12-cup muffin tins
- Pie weights or dried beans
- Parchment paper

| | | |
|---|---|---|
| 1 | recipe All-Butter Pie Dough (page 16) | 1 |

**Filling**

| | | |
|---|---|---|
| ²⁄₃ cup | creamy peanut butter, at room temperature (see Tips, left) | 150 mL |
| ½ cup | confectioners' (icing) sugar | 125 mL |
| ⅓ cup | packed light brown sugar | 75 mL |
| 3 tbsp | cornstarch | 45 mL |
| ¼ tsp | salt | 1 mL |
| 5 | large egg yolks | 5 |
| 1½ cups | whole milk | 375 mL |
| ½ cup | heavy or whipping (35%) cream | 125 mL |
| 2 tsp | vanilla extract | 10 mL |
| ½ cup | chopped lightly salted peanuts | 125 mL |
| | Lightly sweetened whipped cream, optional | |

1. On a lightly floured work surface, roll out dough to a thickness of ⅛ inch (3 mm). Using cutter, cut into rounds and carefully fit into muffin cups (there will be some overlap). Reroll scraps as necessary.

2. Place tins in freezer for 30 minutes. Meanwhile, preheat oven to 375°F (190°C).

3. Blind-bake shells (page 14) in center of preheated oven for 12 minutes. Carefully remove pie weights and parchment. Continue to bake until shells are golden brown, 5 to 8 minutes. Let cool completely in tins on wire racks.

4. *Filling:* In a medium bowl, stir together peanut butter and confectioners' sugar. Set aside.

5. In a medium saucepan, whisk together brown sugar, cornstarch, salt and egg yolks. Slowly add milk, whisking constantly until smooth. Whisk in cream.

6. Place saucepan over medium heat and bring mixture to a simmer, whisking constantly. Continue to cook and whisk until mixture thickens, about 2 minutes. Remove pan from heat and add peanut butter mixture, whisking until smooth. Whisk in vanilla.

## Tip

The easiest way to remove tarts from muffin tins is to run a small, sharp knife or small offset spatula around the edges, loosening the sides. You should then be able to carefully lift out the tarts , guiding them with the knife or spatula.

7. Divide warm custard evenly among cooled pie shells. Sprinkle with chopped peanuts and refrigerate until custard has set, at least 1 hour or up to 2 days.

8. When ready to serve, carefully remove pies from tins and transfer to serving plates. Top each pie with a dollop of whipped cream, if using.

## Variations

Substitute Flaky Pie Dough (page 15) or Dark Chocolate Pie Dough (page 21) for the All-Butter Pie Dough.

*Gluten-Free Alternative:* Substitute Gluten-Free Pie Dough (page 24) for the Flaky Pie Dough.

## Make Ahead

The pie shells can be formed and frozen in their tins, covered, for up to one week.

The shells can be baked and stored at room temperature, tightly covered, for up to three days.

# Gooey Maple Butter Tarts

**Makes 24 tarts**

● **GF Friendly**

*I was unfamiliar with butter tarts until recently. This quintessential Canadian dessert has a simple filling: butter, sugar, eggs, sometimes cream, golden raisins and — in this case — maple syrup. The result is a crisp topping over a pleasantly soft and gooey center.*

## Tips

The insides of these gooey tarts are supposed to be soft, so be careful that they don't overbake.

The easiest way to remove tarts from muffin tins is to run a small, sharp knife or small offset spatula around the edges, loosening the sides. You should then be able to carefully lift out the tarts, guiding them with the knife or spatula.

● 3½-inch (8.75 cm) round cutter
● Two 12-cup muffin tins

| | | |
|---|---|---|
| 1 | recipe All-Butter Pie Dough (page 16) | 1 |
| **Filling** | | |
| 9 tbsp | unsalted butter, melted | 135 mL |
| ¾ cup | packed light brown sugar | 175 mL |
| 6 tbsp | pure maple syrup | 90 mL |
| 3 tbsp | heavy or whipping (35%) cream | 45 mL |
| 2 | large eggs | 2 |
| ½ cup | golden raisins | 125 mL |
| ¼ tsp | salt | 1 mL |

1. On a lightly floured work surface, roll out dough to a thickness of $1/8$ inch (3 mm). Using cutter, cut into rounds and carefully fit into muffin cups. Reroll scraps as necessary.

2. Place tins in freezer for 30 minutes. Meanwhile, preheat oven to 375°F (190°C).

3. *Filling:* In a medium bowl, whisk together butter, brown sugar, maple syrup, cream and eggs. Stir in raisins and salt. Spoon about $1^1/_2$ tbsp (22 mL) filling into each shell. Bake in center of preheated oven for 15 to 20 minutes, until tops are browned, bubbling and just starting to set.

4. Cool pies in tins set on wire racks for 15 minutes, then carefully remove from tins and transfer to racks to cool completely. Serve at room temperature or refrigerate (see Make Ahead, below).

## Variations

Substitute Flaky Pie Dough (page 15) for the All-Butter Pie Dough.

*Gluten-Free Alternative:* Substitute Gluten-Free Pie Dough (page 24) for the All-Butter Pie Dough.

## Make Ahead

Once the tarts are baked and cooled, they can be stored, covered, at room temperature or in the refrigerator for up to three days.

# Honeyed Pine Nut Tarts

**Makes 24 tarts**

● **GF Friendly**

*When my brother Jay spent a summer abroad in Italy, he developed a love for pine nuts. After he returned, my mother and I were inundated with requests for fresh pesto and traditional Italian pignoli cookies. Packed as they are with toasted pine nuts, I have a feeling that these tarts will receive Jay's seal of approval.*

## Tips

Pine nuts can burn very easily, so be careful when toasting them. The easiest way to do this is in a dry skillet over medium-low heat. Shake the skillet often to ensure even browning. When the nuts are fragrant and lightly browned, take the pan off the heat and transfer the nuts to a plate to cool.

Once their container is opened, store pine nuts in the refrigerator or freezer, tightly sealed, so they do not become rancid.

The baked tarts can be stored at room temperature, covered, for up to three days.

● 4-inch (10 cm) round cutter
● Two 12-cup muffin tins, lightly greased

| | | |
|---|---|---|
| 1 | recipe All-Butter Pie Dough (page 16) | 1 |
| **Filling** | | |
| 6 tbsp | unsalted butter | 90 mL |
| ½ cup | packed dark brown sugar | 125 mL |
| ½ cup | liquid honey | 125 mL |
| 1 tsp | finely grated orange zest | 5 mL |
| ½ cup | heavy or whipping (35%) cream | 125 mL |
| 2 | large eggs | 2 |
| 1 cup | lightly toasted pine nuts (see Tips, left) | 250 mL |

1. On a lightly floured surface, roll out dough to a thickness of $1/8$ inch (3 mm). Using cutter, cut into rounds and carefully fit into muffin cups (there will be some overlap). Reroll scraps as necessary.

2. Place tins in freezer for 30 minutes. Meanwhile, preheat oven to 350°F (180°C).

3. *Filling:* In a medium saucepan over medium-high heat, cook butter until it melts and turns deep golden brown with a nutty aroma, 4 to 5 minutes. Add sugar, honey and orange zest. Cook over medium-high heat, stirring constantly, until sugar has dissolved. Boil for 2 minutes without stirring, then remove from heat. Standing well back (because mixture will sputter), stir in cream, whisking until smooth. Set aside to cool for 10 minutes, then stir in eggs and pine nuts.

4. Spoon about 2 tbsp (30 mL) filling into each chilled cup. Bake in center of preheated oven for 25 to 30 minutes, until filling is set around the edges but still a bit jiggly in the center. Cool tarts completely in tins set on wire racks, then carefully remove. Serve immediately or cover and store at room temperature for up to 3 days.

## Variations

Substitute Flaky Pie Dough (page 15) or Whole Wheat Pie Dough (page 18) for the All-Butter Pie Dough.

*Gluten-Free Alternative:* Substitute Gluten-Free Pie Dough (page 24) for the All-Butter Pie Dough.

# Maple Caramel Nut Tarts

● **GF Friendly**

---

*Once, when making traditional pecan squares, I discovered that not only was I out of honey, I didn't have enough pecans. I decided to substitute maple syrup for the honey and blend two kinds of nuts; then I tossed in dried cranberries to cut the sweetness. The results confirmed that sometimes it pays to stray from tradition.*

---

## Tips

Look for Grade B maple syrup for baking, as opposed to "Fancy" or Grade A. Not only does it lend a deeper maple flavor, it's usually less expensive.

Once baked, the tarts can be stored, covered, at room temperature or in the refrigerator, for four to five days.

● 4-inch (10 cm) round cutter
● Two 12-cup muffin tins, lightly greased

| | | |
|---|---|---|
| 1 | recipe All-Butter Pie Dough (page 16) | 1 |

**Filling**

| | | |
|---|---|---|
| ½ cup | unsalted butter, in pieces | 125 mL |
| ¾ cup | pure maple syrup (see Tip, left) | 175 mL |
| ¾ cup | packed light brown sugar | 175 mL |
| ¼ cup | heavy or whipping (35%) cream | 60 mL |
| 2 | large eggs | 2 |
| 1 cup | chopped walnuts | 250 mL |
| 1 cup | chopped pecans | 250 mL |
| ½ cup | coarsely chopped dried cranberries | 125 mL |

1. On a lightly floured surface, roll out dough to a thickness of ⅛ inch (3 mm). Using cutter, cut into rounds and carefully fit into muffin cups (there will be some overlap). Reroll scraps as necessary.

2. Place tins in freezer for 30 minutes. Meanwhile, preheat oven to 400°F (200°C).

3. *Filling:* In a large saucepan over medium heat, melt butter with maple syrup and brown sugar, stirring until sugar has dissolved. Bring to a boil and boil for 2 minutes. Remove from heat and stir in cream. Set aside to cool slightly.

4. When mixture has cooled, quickly beat in eggs, one at a time. Mix in walnuts, pecans and cranberries. Spoon into chilled shells, filling about three-quarters full.

5. Bake in center of preheated oven for 10 minutes, then lower temperature to 350°F (180°C) and bake for 18 to 23 minutes longer, until filling is set.

6. Cool tarts completely in tins placed on wire racks, then carefully unmold. Serve at room temperature or refrigerate for up to 5 days.

---

## Variations

Substitute Flaky Pie Dough (page 15) or Cream Cheese Pie Dough (page 20) for the All-Butter Pie Dough.

*Gluten-Free Alternative:* Substitute Gluten-Free Pie Dough (page 24) for the All-Butter Pie Dough.

---

# Pies for Kids of All Ages

# Tart Apple Pie Pops

- **GF Friendly**
- **Vegan Friendly**

*If you have a budding baker in the house, making these spiced apple pie pops can be a fun afternoon project. The smaller dough rounds are easy to work with, and the finished product is perfect for taking to school and sharing with friends!*

## Tips

Lollipop sticks can be found in the candy-making section of craft stores and in the baking aisle of well-stocked grocery stores.

For step-by-step photographs of making pie pops, see page 44.

- 3- and 3½-inch (7.5 and 8.75 cm) round cutters
- 24 wooden or paper lollipop sticks (see Tips, left)
- 2 baking sheets lined with parchment

### Filling

| | | |
|---|---|---|
| 3 tbsp | unsalted butter | 45 mL |
| 3 | tart apples, such as Granny Smith, peeled and chopped | 3 |
| 2 tsp | freshly squeezed lemon juice | 10 mL |
| 6 tbsp | granulated sugar | 90 mL |
| 1 tsp | ground cinnamon | 5 mL |
| ¼ tsp | ground allspice | 1 mL |
| ¼ tsp | ground nutmeg | 1 mL |
| 1½ tbsp | cornstarch | 22 mL |
| ½ cup | freshly squeezed orange juice or apple juice | 125 mL |
| | | |
| 1 | recipe All-Butter Pie Dough (page 16) | 1 |
| 1 | large egg, lightly beaten with 1 tbsp (15 mL) water | 1 |
| ½ cup | granulated sugar, mixed with ½ tsp (2 mL) ground cinnamon | 125 mL |

1. *Filling:* In a medium skillet over medium heat, melt butter. Add apples and lemon juice and cook, stirring, until apples have softened, 4 to 5 minutes.

2. In a small bowl, whisk together sugar, cinnamon, allspice, nutmeg and cornstarch. Add to apples, stirring to mix. Add orange juice and cook over medium heat, stirring occasionally, until mixture has thickened, 1 to 2 minutes. Remove from heat and set aside to cool completely.

3. Divide dough into two pieces, one slightly larger than the other. On a lightly floured surface, roll out smaller piece to slightly thicker than $\frac{1}{16}$ inch (2 mm). Cut out as many 3-inch (7.5 cm) rounds as possible. Carefully transfer to prepared baking sheet, spacing apart. Reroll scraps as necessary and continue cutting until you have 24 rounds.

4. Press the end of a lollipop stick into the bottom 1 inch (2.5 cm) of each round.

## Tip

The recipes in this book were tested with unsalted butter. Its lack of salt (used as a preservative) means a shorter time spent on grocery store shelves, resulting in higher-quality flavor. Using unsalted butter also allows you to control the amount of salt in your recipe. If you feel like splurging, opt for European-style butter, which has higher butterfat content and less moisture. Butter freezes well for up to six months.

5. Roll out larger piece of dough to slightly thicker than $1/16$ inch (2 mm). Using $3^1/_2$-inch (8.75 cm) cutter, cut out 24 rounds, rerolling scraps as necessary.

6. Brush smaller rounds with egg wash and place a generous 1 tbsp (15 mL) apple filling in center of each. Top each with a larger round, pinching together firmly around edges to stick and seal. Crimp with the tines of a fork.

7. Brush tops with egg wash and sprinkle with cinnamon sugar.

8. Place pie pops, on baking sheets, in freezer for 30 minutes. Meanwhile, position oven racks in upper and lower thirds of oven and preheat oven to 375°F (190°C).

9. When ready to bake, poke 3 or 4 small holes in each top crust with tip of a knife. Bake in preheated oven for 25 to 30 minutes, switching positions of baking sheets halfway through, until pops are puffed and golden brown. Let cool slightly before serving.

### Variations

Substitute Flaky Pie Dough (page 15), Cream Cheese Pie Dough (page 20) or Whole Wheat Pie Dough (page 18) for the All-Butter Pie Dough.

*Gluten-Free Alternative:* Substitute Gluten-Free Pie Dough (page 24) for the All-Butter Pie Dough.

*Vegan Alternative:* Substitute Vegan Pie Dough (page 25) for the All-Butter Pie Dough and vegan butter for the unsalted butter. Replace the egg wash with water.

### Make Ahead

Once the pops are assembled, they can be frozen for up to one month. Freeze for at least 30 minutes on baking sheets, then transfer to airtight containers or sealed zip-top bags. Bake from frozen, as directed.

# Blueberry Lemon Pie Pops

------------------------------------------------

**Makes 24 pops**

- **GF Friendly**
- **Vegan Friendly**

*Blueberry and lemon is one of my favorite flavor combinations. Sweet, juicy blueberries serve as the perfect contrast to tart, lip-puckering lemons. These pie pops pack a double punch of lemony goodness — once in the blueberry filling and once in the glaze. Make them as a fun dessert for kids at your next summer barbecue. (On second thought, the adults will probably want them too!)*

## Tips

The blueberry filling should not be prepared too far in advance, as the mixture will develop too much liquid. Frozen blueberries may be used if they have been thawed and drained.

For step-by-step photographs of making pie pops, see page 44.

- 3- and 3½-inch (7.5 and 8.75 cm) round cutters
- 24 wooden or paper lollipop sticks
- 2 baking sheets lined with parchment

### Blueberry Filling

| | | |
|---|---|---|
| 2 cups | blueberries (see Tips, left) | 500 mL |
| ½ cup | granulated sugar | 125 mL |
| 2 tsp | finely grated lemon zest | 10 mL |
| 2 tbsp | freshly squeezed lemon juice | 30 mL |
| 2 tbsp | cornstarch | 30 mL |
| ½ tsp | ground cinnamon | 5 mL |
| 1 | recipe All-Butter Pie Dough (page 16) | 1 |
| 1 | large egg, lightly beaten with 1 tbsp (15 mL) water | 1 |
| 1 | recipe Lemon Glaze (see Variations, page 48) | 1 |

1. *Blueberry Filling:* In a medium bowl, mix together blueberries, sugar, lemon zest and juice, cornstarch and cinnamon. Set aside.

2. Divide the dough into two pieces, one slightly larger than the other. On a lightly floured work surface, roll out smaller piece to slightly thicker than $1/16$ inch (2 mm). Cut as many 3-inch (7.5 cm) rounds as possible. Carefully transfer to prepared baking sheet, spacing apart. Reroll scraps as necessary and continue cutting until you have 24 rounds.

3. Press the end of a lollipop stick into the bottom 1 inch (2.5 cm) of each round.

4. Roll out larger piece of dough to slightly thicker than $1/16$ inch (2 mm). Using 3½-inch (8.75 cm) cutter, cut 24 rounds, rerolling scraps as necessary.

5. Brush smaller rounds with egg wash and place a generous 1 tbsp (15 mL) blueberry filling in center of each. Top each with a larger round, pinching together firmly around edges to adhere and seal. Crimp edges with the tines of a fork.

6. Place pie pops, on baking sheets, in freezer for 30 minutes. Meanwhile, position oven racks in upper and lower thirds of oven and preheat oven to 375°F (190°C).

## Tip

If you are using my Gluten-Free Pie Dough (see Variations) you will find it quite forgiving and easy to work with because of the absence of gluten. When rolling out the dough, dust your work surface lightly with either cornstarch, potato starch or rice flour in lieu of all-purpose flour.

7. When ready to bake, using the tip of a knife, poke 3 or 4 small holes in each top crust. Bake in preheated oven for 22 to 27 minutes, switching positions of baking sheets halfway through, until tops are puffed and golden brown. Let cool on baking sheets for 5 minutes, then drizzle with lemon glaze. Let glaze set for 10 minutes before serving.

## Variations

Substitute Flaky Pie Dough (page 15), Cream Cheese Pie Dough (page 20) or Hand Pie Dough (page 27) for the All-Butter Pie Dough.

*Gluten-Free Alternative:* Substitute Gluten-Free Pie Dough (page 24) for the All-Butter Pie Dough.

*Vegan Alternative:* Substitute Vegan Pie Dough (page 25) for the All-Butter Pie Dough. Substitute water for the egg wash.

## Make Ahead

Once the pops are assembled, they can be frozen for up to one month. Freeze for at least 30 minutes on baking sheets, then transfer to airtight containers or sealed zip-top bags. Bake from frozen, as directed.

# Brown Sugar Cinnamon Pocket Pies

**Makes 12 pies**

*When I was growing up, Saturday mornings meant two things: cartoons and Pop-Tarts. These handheld toaster pies were reserved for special weekend treats — so much better than plain old cereal! My brother and I each had our favorite flavors: mine was filled with brown sugar and cinnamon and topped with a creamy cinnamon glaze. I've recreated this childhood treat, doubling the sweet filling, which bubbles up while baking. Turns out they're not just for kids!*

## Tips

This filling likes to bubble up when baking, so make sure the edges are tightly sealed.

● Pizza/pastry cutter
● 2 baking sheets lined with parchment

| | | |
|---|---|---|
| 1 cup | packed light brown sugar | 250 mL |
| ¼ cup | unsalted butter, melted | 60 mL |
| ¼ cup | sweetened condensed milk | 60 mL |
| ¼ cup | all-purpose flour | 60 mL |
| 2 tbsp | corn syrup | 30 mL |
| 1 tbsp | vanilla extract | 15 mL |
| 1 tbsp | ground cinnamon | 15 mL |
| ¼ tsp | salt | 1 mL |
| 1 | recipe Pocket Pie Dough (page 26) | 1 |
| 1 | large egg, lightly beaten with 1 tbsp (15 mL) water | 1 |
| 1 | recipe Cinnamon Glaze (see Variations, page 48) | 1 |

1. In a medium bowl, mix together brown sugar, butter, condensed milk, flour, corn syrup, vanilla, cinnamon and salt.

2. Divide dough into halves. On a lightly floured surface, roll out one half into a 13-inch (33 cm) square, slightly thicker than $^1/_{16}$ inch (2 mm). Using a paring knife or pizza cutter, trim dough to a 12-inch (30 cm) square, discarding scraps. Cut square into 12 rectangles, 3 by 4 inches (7.5 by 10 cm) each. Transfer to prepared baking sheet, spacing apart.

3. Brush surfaces with egg wash. Place $1^1/_2$ tbsp (22 mL) brown sugar filling in center of each.

4. With remaining dough, repeat Step 2, creating 12 more rectangles. Place on top of filling, pressing edges together to seal. Crimp with the tines of a fork.

5. Place pocket pies, on baking sheets, in freezer for 30 minutes. Meanwhile, position oven racks in upper and lower thirds of oven and preheat oven to 350°F (180°C).

## Tips

For simplified shaping, form the pocket pies by using 4-inch (10 cm) rounds instead of rectangles (see Step 4, page 82). Reroll scraps as necessary when cutting out circles.

For easiest rolling, roll your dough, including scraps, between two sheets of plastic wrap. That way, you do not need to add flour to keep the dough from sticking to your work surface.

6. When ready to bake, pierce tops several times with tip of a sharp knife or a toothpick. Bake in preheated oven for 28 to 33 minutes, switching positions of baking sheets halfway through, until pies are puffed and golden brown. Let cool on sheets on wire racks for 10 minutes, then drizzle with cinnamon glaze. Let glaze set for 5 minutes before serving.

## Variation

Instead of using the cinnamon glaze, brush the tops of the pies with egg wash and sprinkle with cinnamon sugar before baking.

## Make Ahead

The pies can be fully assembled (Steps 1 through 4) and frozen for up to one month. Freeze for at least 30 minutes on baking sheets, then transfer to zip-top bags to freeze completely. Bake in preheated oven from frozen, as directed.

The filling can be made up to two days in advance and refrigerated, tightly covered.

# Peanut Butter and Jelly Pocket Pies

----------------------------------------------------

- **GF Friendly**
- **Vegan Friendly**

---

*It's hard to think of a flavor combination more classic than peanut butter and jelly. These portable treats take the lunchbox classic to a whole new level, enveloping fresh strawberry jam filling in a buttery crust smothered with creamy peanut butter glaze. Who says you can't improve on a classic?*

---

## Tip

For simplified shaping, form the pocket pies by using 4-inch (10 cm) rounds instead of rectangles (see Step 4, page 82). Reroll scraps as necessary when cutting out rounds.

- Pizza/pastry cutter
- 2 baking sheets lined with parchment

### Strawberry Filling

| | | |
|---|---|---|
| 2½ cups | sliced hulled strawberries | 625 mL |
| 1½ cups | granulated sugar | 375 mL |
| 1 tbsp | freshly squeezed lemon juice | 15 mL |
| 1 | recipe Pocket Pie Dough (page 26) | 1 |
| 1 | large egg, lightly beaten with 1 tbsp (15 mL) water | 1 |

### Peanut Butter Glaze

| | | |
|---|---|---|
| ⅓ cup | creamy peanut butter, at room temperature | 75 mL |
| 1¼ cups | confectioners' (icing) sugar, sifted | 300 mL |
| 1 tsp | vanilla extract | 5 mL |
| 4 tbsp | whole milk (approx.) | 60 mL |
| ½ cup | lightly salted peanuts, chopped | 125 mL |

1. *Strawberry Filling:* In a medium saucepan, combine strawberries, granulated sugar and lemon juice. Bring to a boil over medium-high heat, mashing strawberries with a potato masher or the back of a spoon until broken down. Reduce heat and simmer until thickened, 15 to 20 minutes. Remove from heat, cover and refrigerate until cold.

2. Divide dough into halves. On a lightly floured surface, roll out one half into a 13-inch (33 cm) square, slightly thicker than ¹/₁₆ inch (2 mm). Using a paring knife or pizza cutter, trim dough to a 12-inch (30 cm) square, discarding scraps. Cut the square into 12 rectangles, 3 by 4 inches (7.5 by 10 cm) each. Transfer to prepared baking sheets, spacing apart.

3. Brush surfaces with egg wash. Place about 1½ tbsp (22 mL) strawberry filling in center of each rectangle.

4. Using remaining dough, repeat Step 2, creating 12 more rectangles. Place on top of strawberry filling, pressing edges together to seal. Crimp with the tines of a fork.

----------------------------------------------------

## Tips

To make the glaze, start by adding 3 tbsp (45 mL) milk. Add the remaining milk 1 tsp (5 mL) at a time until you achieve a thick but spreadable glaze.

Time after time when making pies, I've found myself running into the garage or my upstairs office in search of a measuring tape or ruler. I finally had the sense to purchase one for using in the kitchen. A measuring tape comes in handy for almost every recipe, whether you are sizing cutters or rolling out dough to a specified size and shape.

5. Place pies, on baking sheets, in freezer for 30 minutes. Meanwhile, position oven racks in upper and lower thirds of oven and preheat oven to 350°F (180°C).

6. When ready to bake, pierce tops several times with tip of a sharp knife or a toothpick. Bake in preheated oven for 28 to 33 minutes, switching positions of baking sheets halfway through, until pies are puffed and golden brown. Let cool on sheets on wire racks for 10 minutes.

7. *Peanut Butter Glaze:* Meanwhile, in a small bowl, mix together peanut butter, confectioners' sugar, vanilla and enough of the milk to make a thick but spreadable glaze (see Tips, left). Spread glaze over warm pies and sprinkle with chopped peanuts. Serve warm or at room temperature.

## Variations

To simplify preparation, substitute store-bought strawberry jam for the strawberry filling.

*Vegan Alternative:* Substitute Vegan Pie Dough (page 25) for the Pocket Pie Dough. Replace the milk with full-fat coconut milk and substitute water for the egg wash.

*Gluten-Free Alternative:* Substitute Gluten-Free Dough (page 24) for the Pocket Pie Dough.

## Make Ahead

The pies can be fully assembled (Steps 1 through 4) and frozen for up to one month. Freeze for at least 30 minutes on baking sheets, then transfer to zip-top bags to freeze completely. Bake from frozen, as directed.

The strawberry filling can be refrigerated, covered, for up to one week.

# Cinna-Monkey Pie Pops

● **GF Friendly**

*When I owned a neighborhood bakery, we had a popular item on the kids' menu called the Cinna-Monkey. It was a toasted panini sandwich containing ripe bananas, peanut butter, honey and cinnamon. We soon learned that adults liked the sandwich just as much as children did. I think everyone will love this version on a stick!*

## Tips

For best results, select bananas that are ripe but still firm.

Lollipop sticks can be found in the candy-making section of craft stores and in the baking aisle of well-stocked grocery stores.

For step-by-step photographs of making pie pops, see page 44.

● 3- and 3½-inch (7.5 and 8.75 cm) round cutters
● 24 wooden or paper lollipop sticks
● 2 baking sheets lined with parchment

### Peanut Butter Filling

| 6 oz | peanut butter baking chips | 175 g |
|------|---------------------------|-------|
| ½ cup | heavy or whipping (35%) cream | 125 mL |
| 3 tbsp | creamy peanut butter | 45 mL |
| 1 tbsp | vanilla extract | 15 mL |
| ¼ tsp | ground cinnamon | 1 mL |

### Banana Filling

| 3 tbsp | unsalted butter | 45 mL |
|------|---------------------------|-------|
| 3 tbsp | packed light brown sugar | 45 mL |
| ⅛ tsp | salt | 0.5 mL |
| 2 | bananas, diced (see Tips, left) | 2 |
| 1 | recipe All-Butter Pie Dough (page 16) | 1 |
| 1 | large egg, lightly beaten with 1 tbsp (15 mL) water | 1 |
| 1 | recipe Honey Glaze (see Variations, page 48) | 1 |
| | Chopped peanuts, optional | |

1. *Peanut Butter Filling:* In a medium bowl, on Medium power, microwave peanut butter chips and cream in 15-second bursts, stirring after each, until chips soften. Whisk in peanut butter, vanilla and cinnamon; whisk until smooth. Set aside to cool to room temperature.

2. *Banana Filling:* In a small saucepan over medium heat, stir butter and brown sugar until butter has melted and mixture is smooth. Stir in salt and simmer for 2 to 3 minutes, stirring occasionally, until thickened. Add bananas and toss to coat. Remove from heat and set aside to cool completely.

3. Divide dough into two pieces, one slightly larger than the other. On a lightly floured surface, roll out smaller piece to slightly thicker than ¹⁄₁₆ inch (2 mm). Cut out as many 3-inch (7.5 cm) rounds as you can. Carefully transfer to prepared baking sheets, spacing apart. Reroll scraps as necessary until you have 24 rounds.

**Tip**

Once you start using parchment paper, you will never want to go back to silicone liners or greased baking sheets. Disposable, heat-resistant and nonstick, parchment will make your pie-baking life much, much easier! Use it to line baking sheets or tart shells when blind-baking. When you have finished baking, simply throw out the used parchment. It makes for extremely easy clean-up.

4. Press the end of a lollipop stick into the bottom 1 inch (2.5 cm) of each round.

5. Roll out larger piece of dough to slightly thicker than $1/_{16}$ inch (2 mm) and, using $3^1/_2$-inch (8.75 cm) cutter, cut 24 rounds, rerolling scraps as necessary.

6. Brush smaller rounds with egg wash. Place 2 tsp (10 mL) banana filling in center of each round. Top with 2 tsp (10 mL) peanut butter filling. Top each with a larger round, pinching edges together firmly to stick and seal. Crimp with the tines of a fork.

7. Place pie pops, on baking sheets, in freezer for 30 minutes. Meanwhile, position oven racks in upper and lower thirds of oven and preheat oven to 375°F (190°C).

8. When ready to bake, poke 3 or 4 small holes in each top crust with tip of a knife. Bake in preheated oven for 22 to 27 minutes, switching positions of baking sheets halfway through, until pops are puffed and golden brown. Let cool on sheets for 5 minutes, then drizzle with honey glaze and sprinkle with chopped peanuts. Let glaze set 10 minutes before serving.

## Variations

Substitute Flaky Pie Dough (page 15), Cream Cheese Pie Dough (page 20), Hand Pie Dough (page 27) or Whole Wheat Pie Dough (page 18) for the All-Butter Dough.

*Gluten-Free Alternative:* Substitute Gluten-Free Pie Dough (page 24) for the All-Butter Pie Dough.

## Make Ahead

Once the pops are assembled, they can be frozen for up to one month. Freeze for at least 30 minutes on baking sheets, then transfer to airtight containers or sealed zip-top bags. Bake from frozen, as directed.

# Double Strawberry Pie Pops

- - - - - - - - - - - - - - - - - - - - - - - - - - - - - - - - - - - - - - -

**Makes 24 pops**

- **GF Friendly**
- **Vegan Friendly**

---

*These pops combine jammy-tasting, slightly chewy dried strawberries with diced juicy fresh strawberries, resulting in an intensely flavored and multi-textured fruit filling.*

---

## Tips

Look for dried strawberries in the bulk or dried fruit section of natural or specialty foods stores or well-stocked supermarkets.

For step-by-step photographs of making pie pops, see page 44.

- 3-inch (7.5 cm) round cutter
- 24 wooden or paper lollipop sticks
- 2 baking sheets lined with parchment

### Strawberry Filling

| | | |
|---|---|---|
| 1 cup | dried strawberries, chopped (see Tip, left) | 250 mL |
| 1 cup | water | 250 mL |
| 1/4 cup | granulated sugar | 60 mL |
| 2 tbsp | freshly squeezed lemon juice | 30 mL |
| 1/8 tsp | ground cinnamon | 0.5 mL |
| 1 cup | diced hulled fresh strawberries | 250 mL |
| 1 tbsp | cornstarch | 15 mL |
| | | |
| 1 | recipe All-Butter Pie Dough (page 16) | 1 |
| 1 | large egg, lightly beaten with 1 tbsp (15 mL) water | 1 |
| | Coarse sugar for sprinkling | |

1. *Strawberry Filling:* In a medium saucepan over medium-high heat, bring dried strawberries, water, sugar, lemon juice and cinnamon to a boil, stirring constantly. Reduce heat and simmer, stirring occasionally, until water has evaporated and mixture has thickened, 15 to 20 minutes.

2. In a small bowl, toss fresh strawberries and cornstarch. Add to dried strawberry mixture and stir well. Set aside to cool completely.

3. Divide dough into halves. On a lightly floured surface, roll out one half to a thickness of slightly more than $1/16$ inch (2 mm). Using cutter, cut into rounds and carefully transfer to prepared baking sheets, spacing apart. Reroll scraps as necessary until you have 24 rounds.

4. Press the end of a lollipop stick into the bottom 1 inch (2.5 cm) of each round.

5. Roll out remaining half of the dough to slightly thicker than $1/16$ inch (2 mm). Cut 24 more rounds, rerolling scraps as necessary.

## Tip

If you are making Vegan Pie Dough (see Variations), you will be using vegan butter rather than the unsalted butter called for in most recipes. Vegan butter is designed to function in the same way as dairy-based butter, without using any animal products. Although the ingredients can vary depending on the manufacturer, most vegan butters use vegetable oils as their base. Earth Balance makes an excellent product that was used for testing these recipes; it can be found in most grocery stores.

6. Brush rounds holding lollipop sticks with egg wash and place 1 tbsp (15 mL) strawberry filling in center of each. Top with remaining rounds, pressing together firmly around edges to stick and seal. Crimp with the tines of a fork.

7. Brush tops with egg wash and sprinkle with coarse sugar.

8. Place pops on baking sheets in freezer for 30 minutes. Meanwhile, position oven racks in upper and lower thirds of oven and preheat oven to 375°F (190°C).

9. When ready to bake, poke 3 or 4 small holes in each top crust with tip of a sharp knife. Bake in preheated oven for 22 to 27 minutes, switching positions of baking sheets halfway through, until tops are puffed. Let cool slightly on baking sheets before serving.

## Variations

Substitute 1 recipe Flaky Pie Dough (page 15), Cream Cheese Pie Dough (page 20) or Hand Pie Dough (page 27) for the All-Butter Pie Dough.

*Gluten-Free Alternative:* Substitute Gluten-Free Pie Dough (page 24) for the All-Butter Pie Dough.

*Vegan Alternative:* Substitute Vegan Pie Dough (page 25) for the All-Butter Pie Dough (see Tip, left). Substitute water for the egg wash.

## Make Ahead

Once the pops are assembled, they can be frozen for up to one month. Freeze for at least 30 minutes on baking sheets, then transfer to airtight containers or sealed zip-top bags. Bake from frozen, as directed.

# Chocolate Chip Cookie Hand Pies

*I can't think of any children (or adults, for that matter) who wouldn't leap at the chance to enjoy a warm chocolate chip cookie fresh from the oven. What if that soft cookie dough center was surrounded by a flaky, buttery crust? Those leaps just might turn into back flips!*

## Tips

Because this filling has a much lower amount of leavening (baking soda), substituting store-bought cookie dough will not work for this recipe.

For step-by-step photographs of the process of making hand pies, see page 35.

- Electric mixer
- 4½-inch (11.25 cm) round cutter
- 2 baking sheets lined with parchment

### Cookie Dough

| | | |
|---|---|---|
| 1¼ cups | all-purpose flour | 300 mL |
| ¼ cup | large-flake (old-fashioned) rolled oats | 60 mL |
| ⅛ tsp | baking soda | 0.5 mL |
| ¼ tsp | ground cinnamon | 1 mL |
| ¼ tsp | ground ginger | 1 mL |
| ⅛ tsp | ground nutmeg | 0.5 mL |
| ¼ tsp | salt | 1 mL |
| ½ cup | unsalted butter, softened | 125 mL |
| ½ cup | packed light brown sugar | 125 mL |
| ¼ cup | granulated sugar | 60 mL |
| 1 | large egg | 1 |
| 2 tsp | vanilla extract | 10 mL |
| ¾ cup | semisweet chocolate chips | 175 mL |
| 1½ | recipes Hand Pie Dough (page 27; see Tips, left) | 1½ |
| 1 | large egg, lightly beaten with 1 tbsp (15 mL) water | 1 |
| | Confectioners' sugar for dusting | |

1. *Cookie Dough:* In a large bowl, whisk together flour, oats, baking soda, cinnamon, ginger, nutmeg and salt.

2. In a bowl, using electric mixer at medium speed, beat butter, brown sugar and granulated sugar until light and fluffy, about 2 minutes. Add egg and vanilla, beating until well combined. Add flour mixture and mix until combined. Stir in chocolate chips. Set aside.

3. On a lightly floured surface, roll out dough to slightly thicker than $1/16$ inch (2 mm). Using cutter, cut into rounds and place on prepared baking sheets, spacing apart. Reroll scraps as necessary.

## Tip

This recipe will leave you with some extra filling. You can either make a second half-batch of dough to make additional pies (recommended) or you can bake the cookie dough into chocolate chip cookies (16 to 20 minutes at 350°F/180°C) for flat but still yummy treats.

4. Brush edges of rounds with egg wash. Place 1 tbsp (15 mL) cookie dough filling in center of each circle. Fold circles in half, enclosing filling. Pinch edges together to seal, and crimp with the tines of a fork. Brush tops with egg wash.

5. Place pies on baking sheets in freezer for 30 minutes. Position oven racks in upper and lower thirds of oven and preheat oven to 375°F (190°C).

6. Using tip of a sharp knife, cut 2 or 3 slits in top of each pie. Bake in preheated over for 14 to 18 minutes, switching positions of baking sheets halfway through, until pies are puffed and golden brown. Cool for 5 minutes on sheets on wire racks, then sprinkle with confectioners' sugar. Serve warm or at room temperature.

### Variations

Substitute Flaky Pie Dough (page 15), Cream Cheese Pie Dough (page 20) or All-Butter Pie Dough (page 16) for the Hand Pie Dough.

### Make Ahead

The pies can be fully assembled (Steps 1 through 4) and frozen for up to one month. Freeze for at least 30 minutes on baking sheets, then transfer to zip-top bags and seal. Bake from frozen, as directed.

# Spiced Pumpkin Pie Pops

● **GF Friendly**

*When I was a child, after Thanksgiving dinner was finished, the last thing I wanted to do was sit around while the adults sipped their coffee and ate dessert. These pumpkin pie pops would have been a dream come true. I could have taken my dessert with me and excused myself to go play!*

## Tips

Don't have a round cutter? No problem! Use a drinking glass or the top of a small bowl to cut out the shapes instead.

For step-by-step photographs of making pie pops, see page 44.

● 3-inch (7.5 cm) round cutter (see Tips, left)
● 24 wooden or paper lollipop sticks
● 2 baking sheets lined with parchment

### Pumpkin Filling

| | | |
|---|---|---|
| 1 cup | canned pumpkin purée | 250 mL |
| ½ cup | packed light brown sugar | 125 mL |
| ½ cup | heavy or whipping (35%) cream | 125 mL |
| 1 | large egg | 1 |
| 1 tbsp | dark (cooking) molasses | 15 mL |
| ½ tsp | ground cinnamon | 2 mL |
| ¼ tsp | ground ginger | 1 mL |
| ⅛ tsp | ground nutmeg | 0.5 mL |
| ⅛ tsp | ground cloves | 0.5 mL |
| ⅛ tsp | salt | 0.5 mL |
| | | |
| 1 | recipe Flaky Pie Dough (page 15) | 1 |
| 1 | large egg, lightly beaten with 1 tbsp (15 mL) water | 1 |
| 1 | recipe Cinnamon Glaze (see Variations, page 48) | 1 |

1. *Pumpkin Filling:* In a medium bowl, stir together pumpkin purée, brown sugar, cream, egg, molasses, cinnamon, ginger, nutmeg, cloves and salt.

2. Divide dough into halves. On a lightly floured surface, roll out one half to a thickness of slightly more than $1/16$ inch (2 mm). Cut out as many 3-inch (7.5 cm) rounds as possible and carefully transfer to prepared baking sheet, spacing apart. Reroll scraps as necessary and continue cutting out until you have 24 rounds.

3. Press the end of a lollipop stick into the bottom 1 inch (2.5 cm) of each round.

4. Roll out remaining dough and cut 24 rounds, rerolling scraps as necessary.

5. Brush surfaces of rounds holding lollipop sticks with egg wash and place 1 tbsp (15 mL) pumpkin filling in center of each. Working quickly, top each with one of the remaining rounds. Pinch edges together firmly to stick and seal. Crimp with the tines of a fork.

## Tips

A dough scraper is very useful to have when making these recipes. During the rolling process, it collects the little bits for rerolling and it cleans up the pastry board very efficiently. It also simplifies picking up the cut rounds; you just slide the scraper underneath. Even if they are sticking a bit, they will detach without tearing.

Lollipop sticks can be found in the candy-making section of craft stores and in the baking aisle of well-stocked grocery stores.

6. Place pops on baking sheets in freezer for 30 minutes. Meanwhile, position oven racks in upper and lower thirds of oven and preheat oven to 375°F (190°C).

7. When ready to bake, using the tip of a knife, poke 3 or 4 small holes in each top crust. Bake in preheated oven for 22 to 27 minutes, switching positions of baking sheets halfway through, until tops are puffed and golden brown. Let cool on baking sheets for 5 minutes, then drizzle with cinnamon glaze. Let glaze set for 10 minutes before serving.

## Variations

Substitute All-Butter Pie Dough (page 16), Cream Cheese Pie Dough (page 20), Hand Pie Dough (page 27) or Whole Wheat Pie Dough (page 18) for the Flaky Pie Dough.

*Gluten-Free Alternative:* Substitute Gluten-Free Pie Dough (page 24) for the Flaky Pie Dough.

## Make Ahead

Once the pops are assembled, they can be frozen for up to one month. Freeze for at least 30 minutes on baking sheets, then transfer to airtight containers or sealed zip-top bags. Bake from frozen, as directed.

The pumpkin filling can be mixed and refrigerated, covered, one day in advance.

# Cookies-and-Cream Pies

---

*Although there is some disagreement as to the exact date and location it was invented, cookies-and-cream ice cream first skyrocketed to popularity when I was a small child. Nowadays you'll find it as the inspiration for everything from cupcakes to cereal — so why not mini pies?*

## Tips

Instead of using a food processor, you can crush the chocolate wafer cookies by placing them in a large zip-top bag and going over it with a rolling pin.

Don't have a round cutter? No problem! Use a drinking glass or the top of a small bowl to cut out the shapes instead.

- Food processor
- 5-inch (12.5 cm) round cutter
- 2 baking sheets lined with parchment

### Cookies-and-Cream Filling

| | | |
|---|---|---|
| ½ cup | granulated sugar | 125 mL |
| 3 tbsp | cornstarch | 45 mL |
| ⅛ tsp | salt | 0.5 mL |
| 1 cup | whole milk | 250 mL |
| 1 cup | heavy or whipping (35%) cream | 250 mL |
| 1 tbsp | unsalted butter | 15 mL |
| 1 tsp | vanilla extract | 5 mL |
| 1 cup | crushed chocolate sandwich cookies (such as Oreos) | 250 mL |
| 1½ cups | chocolate wafer cookies | 375 mL |
| 1 | recipe Dark Chocolate Pie Dough (page 21) | 1 |
| 1 | large egg, lightly beaten with 1 tbsp (15 mL) water | 1 |

1. *Cookies-and-Cream Filling:* In a medium saucepan, whisk together sugar, cornstarch and salt. Whisking constantly, slowly add milk; whisk until smooth. Whisk in cream.

2. Set saucepan over medium heat. Whisking constantly, bring to a simmer and cook until thick, about 5 minutes. Whisk in butter until melted. Whisk in vanilla. Remove from heat and set aside to cool completely.

3. Fold crushed sandwich cookies into cooled mixture.

4. In food processor fitted with the metal blade, process chocolate wafer cookies until finely ground. Scatter a lightly floured work surface with a handful of cookie crumbs. Roll out dough to slightly thicker than ¹⁄₁₆ inch (2 mm), embedding cookie crumbs in dough. Using cutter, cut into rounds and place on prepared baking sheets, spacing apart. Reroll scraps, scattering additional crumbs as necessary.

---

5. Brush edges of rounds with egg wash. Place about 2 tbsp (30 mL) filling in center of each circle. Fold in half, enclosing filling. Pinch edges together to seal and crimp with the tines of a fork. Brush tops with egg wash.

6. Place pies, on baking sheets, in freezer for 30 minutes. Meanwhile, position oven racks in upper and lower thirds of oven and preheat oven to 375°F (190°C).

7. Using tip of a knife, cut 2 or 3 slits in top of each pie. Bake in preheated oven for 23 to 28 minutes, switching positions of baking sheets halfway through, until pies are puffed and browned. Cool completely on sheets on wire racks.

## Make Ahead

The pies can be fully assembled (Steps 1 through 5) and frozen for up to three days. Freeze for at least 30 minutes on trays, then transfer to zip-top bags and seal. Bake from frozen, as directed.

# Campfire S'mores Pies

---

*Some desserts you just never outgrow. Take s'mores, for example. They're the quintessential kid's dessert: simple, sweet and ooey-gooey. This is a petite version of the campfire classic — still bursting with chocolate and toasted marshmallow goodness, but sophisticated enough for you to serve at your next grown-up party.*

---

**Tips**

These two-bite treats are best eaten shortly after preparation. The graham cracker pie dough requires a bit more TLC than other varieties, but the results are well worth the effort.

To simplify, use instant chocolate pudding mix to make the filling.

For step-by-step photographs of the blind-baking process, see page 33.

- 3½-inch (8.75 cm) round cutter
- Two 12-cup muffin tins
- Pie weights or dried beans
- Kitchen torch, optional

| 1 | recipe Graham Cracker Pie Dough (page 28) | 1 |

**Chocolate Pudding**

| 2 cups | whole milk, divided | 500 mL |
| ¼ cup | granulated sugar | 60 mL |
| 2 tbsp | unsweetened cocoa powder | 30 mL |
| 2 tbsp | cornstarch | 30 mL |
| 2 | large egg yolks | 2 |
| ¼ tsp | salt | 2 mL |
| 4 oz | semisweet or bittersweet chocolate, chopped | 125 g |
| 1 tsp | pure vanilla extract | 5 mL |
| 2 cups | miniature marshmallows | 500 mL |

1. On a generously floured surface (see Tips, page 179), roll out dough to ⅛ inch (2 mm) thickness. Using cutter, cut out rounds and carefully fit into muffin cups (they will come only halfway up the sides). Reroll scraps as necessary.

2. Place tins in freezer for 30 minutes. Meanwhile, preheat oven to 350°F (180°C).

3. Blind-bake shells (page 14 and Tips, left) on center rack in preheated oven for 8 minutes. Carefully remove parchment and weights; bake for 5 to 8 minutes longer, until browned around the edges. Cool completely in tins on wire racks, then carefully transfer to a baking sheet.

4. *Chocolate Pudding:* In a medium bowl, whisk together ½ cup (125 mL) milk, sugar, cocoa powder, cornstarch, egg yolks and salt.

5. In a medium saucepan, bring remaining 1½ cups (375 mL) milk to a simmer. In a slow, steady stream, pour hot milk into egg mixture, whisking constantly. Return mixture to saucepan and cook over low heat, whisking constantly, until thickened, 2 to 3 minutes. Remove from heat.

## Tips

The easiest way to remove pies from muffin tins is to run a small, sharp knife or small offset spatula around the edges, loosening the sides. You should then be able to carefully lift out the pies, guiding them with the knife or spatula.

Graham cracker dough is particularly sticky. Extra flour prevents it from sticking to the work surface.

**6.** Add chopped chocolate and vanilla; whisk until melted and smooth. Set aside until pudding cools to lukewarm, then place about 2 tbsp (30 mL) pudding in each pie shell. Refrigerate, covered, until cold, about 2 hours or up to 1 day.

**7.** Place a layer of mini marshmallows on top of pudding in each shell, dividing equally and covering surface. Using kitchen torch, lightly brown marshmallows (alternatively, place under a preheated broiler for 1 minute). Serve immediately.

## Variation

For an even more decadent dessert, replace the pudding with 1 tbsp (15 mL) Rich Chocolate Ganache (page 46).

## Make Ahead

The pie shells and pudding can be prepared one day in advance. The baked shells can be stored at room temperature, covered, and the cooked pudding should be transferred to a bowl, covered and refrigerated.

# Frozen Creamsicle Pies

---

*When I was growing up, during the summer, whenever I heard the ice-cream truck coming down the street, I begged my mother for change to buy a special frozen treat. Although I constantly promised myself I would try something new, I always opted for the same item: a vanilla-and-orange-flavored Creamsicle. These mini frozen pies are a replica of my favorite childhood treat — with the added bonus of a drip-catching vanilla wafer crust!*

## Tips

Once frozen and unmolded, these pies will keep well in the freezer, tightly covered, for up to four days.

For step-by-step photographs of the blind baking process, see page 33.

If you prefer, substitute Sweet Tart Dough (page 17), Toasted Coconut Tartlet Dough (page 22) or Cream Cheese Pie Dough (page 20) for the All-Butter Pie Dough.

- 3½- to 4-inch (8.75 to 10 cm) round cutter
- Two 12-cup muffin tins
- Pie weights or dried beans
- Parchment paper

| | | |
|---|---|---|
| 1½ cups | finely crushed vanilla wafer cookies | 375 mL |
| 1 | recipe All-Butter Pie Dough (page 16) | 1 |

**Filling**

| | | |
|---|---|---|
| 4 | large egg yolks | 4 |
| 2½ tbsp | cornstarch | 37 mL |
| ⅓ cup | granulated sugar | 75 mL |
| 1¾ cups | half-and-half (10%) cream | 425 mL |
| | Finely grated zest of 1 orange | |
| ⅔ cup | finely chopped white chocolate | 150 mL |
| ½ cup | freshly squeezed orange juice | 125 mL |
| 2 tsp | vanilla extract | 10 mL |

1. Scatter lightly floured work surface with a handful of cookie crumbs. Place dough on top and roll out to ⅛ inch (3 mm) thick, embedding the cookie crumbs in the crust. Cut into rounds and carefully fit into muffin cups (there will be some overlap). Reroll scraps, scattering additional crumbs as necessary.

2. Place tins in freezer for 30 minutes. Meanwhile, preheat oven to 350°F (180°C).

3. Blind-bake shells (page 14 and Tips, left) on center rack in preheated oven for 12 minutes. Carefully remove weights and parchment; bake for 7 to 10 minutes longer, until shells are golden brown. Cool completely in pans on wire racks.

4. *Filling:* In a large bowl, whisk together egg yolks, cornstarch and sugar. In a saucepan, bring cream and orange zest to a simmer. Whisking constantly, slowly add to egg mixture; whisk until smooth. Return to saucepan and whisk constantly over medium-low heat until thickened, 3 to 4 minutes. Add white chocolate and whisk until melted. Remove from heat. Whisk in orange juice and vanilla.

5. Spoon 2 tbsp (30 mL) filling into each shell. Transfer tins to freezer for at least 4 hours, until frozen, or, tightly covered, up to 4 days. Carefully unmold and serve.

# Carrot Cake Pies with Cream Cheese Crust

**Makes 24 pies**

*Carrot cake cupcakes are extremely popular but, topped with cream cheese frosting, they don't travel neatly in a lunchbox or brown paper bag. Opt instead for these portable pies: moist spiced carrot cake filling tucked tidily inside a tangy cream cheese crust.*

## Tips

The easiest way to shred carrots is to use a food processor fitted with the shredding disk, but you can also use a box grater.

Once baked, these pies can be frozen, sealed in a zip-top bag, for up to one week. Thaw at room temperature.

- 4-inch (10 cm) round cutter
- Two 12-cup muffin tins

| 1 | recipe Cream Cheese Pie Dough (page 20) | 1 |
|---|---|---|
| **Filling** | | |
| 1½ cups | shredded carrots (see Tips, left) | 375 mL |
| ½ cup | all-purpose flour | 125 mL |
| ½ cup | unsalted butter, melted | 125 mL |
| 2 | large eggs | 2 |
| ½ cup | granulated sugar | 125 mL |
| ½ cup | packed light brown sugar | 125 mL |
| 1 tsp | ground cinnamon | 5 mL |
| ½ tsp | ground ginger | 2 mL |
| ¼ tsp | ground cardamom | 1 mL |
| ¼ tsp | ground nutmeg | 1 mL |
| ¼ tsp | salt | 1 mL |
| 1 tsp | vanilla extract | 5 mL |
| ⅓ cup | golden raisins, optional | 75 mL |
| | Confectioners' (icing) sugar for dusting, optional | |

1. On a lightly floured work surface, roll out dough to a thickness of ⅛ inch (3 mm). Using cutter, cut into rounds and carefully fit into muffin cups (there may be some overlap). Reroll scraps as necessary.

2. Place tins in freezer for 30 minutes. Preheat oven to 350°F (180°C).

3. *Filling:* In a large bowl, toss carrots with flour to coat. Add butter and eggs, mixing to blend. Mix in granulated and brown sugars, cinnamon, ginger, cardamom, nutmeg, salt, vanilla and raisins, if using.

4. Spoon about 2 tbsp (30 mL) filling into each chilled shell. Bake in center of preheated oven for 23 to 28 minutes, until tops are puffed and set.

5. Cool pies in tins on wire racks for 10 minutes, then carefully transfer to racks to cool completely. Dust with confectioners' sugar, if using.

# Orange Fig Pie Pops

**Makes 24 pops**

- **GF Friendly**
- **Vegan Friendly**

*I used to love Fig Newton cookies, either as an afternoon snack (always with milk!) or as part of my school lunch. Now I've grown to love dried figs, whether I chop them for salads, turn them into jam or eat them straight out of the bag. These pops are my interpretation of a Fig Newton on a stick, topped with a sweet orange glaze. The glass of milk is optional, but recommended.*

## Tips

The majority of dried figs are one of two varieties. Mission figs are dark, moist and chewy, while Calimyrna figs are dryer and less sweet, with a thicker skin. Both will work in this recipe.

For step-by-step photographs of making pie pops, see page 44.

- 3-inch (7.5 cm) round cutter
- 24 wooden or paper lollipop sticks
- 2 baking sheets lined with parchment

### Fig Filling

| | | |
|---|---|---|
| 1½ cups | chopped dried figs (see Tips, left) | 375 mL |
| ¾ cup | water | 175 mL |
| 6 tbsp | granulated sugar | 90 mL |
| ¾ cup | freshly squeezed orange juice | 175 mL |
| 1 tbsp | finely grated orange zest | 15 mL |
| ½ tsp | ground cinnamon | 2 mL |
| | | |
| 1 | recipe All-Butter Pie Dough (page 16) | 1 |
| 1 | large egg, lightly beaten with 1 tbsp (15 mL) water | 1 |
| 1 | recipe Orange Glaze (see Variations, page 48) | 1 |

1. *Fig Filling:* In a medium saucepan over medium heat, bring figs, water, sugar, orange juice and zest, and cinnamon to a boil, stirring constantly. Reduce heat and simmer, stirring occasionally, until water has evaporated and mixture has thickened, about 20 to 25 minutes. Remove from heat and set aside to cool completely.

2. Divide dough into halves. On a lightly floured surface, roll out one half to slightly thicker than $1/16$ inch (2 mm). Cut as many 3-inch (7.5 cm) rounds as possible. Carefully transfer to prepared baking sheets, spacing apart. Reroll scraps as necessary and continue cutting until you have 24 rounds.

3. Press the end of a lollipop stick into the bottom 1 inch (2.5 cm) of each round.

4. Roll out remaining dough to slightly thicker than $1/16$ inch (2 mm). Cut 24 rounds, rerolling scraps as necessary.

5. Brush surfaces of rounds holding lollipop sticks with egg wash and place 1 tbsp (15 mL) fig filling in center of each. Top with remaining rounds, pressing edges together to stick and seal. Crimp with the tines of a fork.

## Tip

Lollipop sticks can be found in the candy-making section of craft stores and in the baking aisle of well-stocked grocery stores.

6. Place pops, on baking sheets, in freezer for 30 minutes. Meanwhile, position oven racks in upper and lower thirds of oven and preheat oven to 375°F (190°C).

7. When ready to bake, poke 3 or 4 small holes in each top crust with tip of a knife. Bake in preheated oven for 20 to 25 minutes, switching positions of baking sheets halfway through, until tarts are puffed and golden brown. Let cool on baking sheets for 5 minutes, then drizzle with orange glaze. Let glaze set for 10 minutes before serving.

## Variations

Substitute Flaky Pie Dough (page 15), Cream Cheese Pie Dough (page 20), Hand Pie Dough (page 27) or Whole Wheat Pie Dough (page 18) for the All-Butter Pie Dough.

*Gluten-Free Alternative:* Substitute Gluten-Free Pie Dough (page 24) for the All-Butter Pie Dough.

*Vegan Alternative:* Substitute 1 recipe Vegan Pie Dough (page 25) for the All-Butter Pie Dough. Substitute water for the egg wash.

## Make Ahead

Once the pops are assembled, they can be frozen for up to one month. Freeze for at least 30 minutes on baking sheets, then transfer to airtight containers or sealed zip-top bags. Bake from frozen, as directed.

The fig filling can be mixed and refrigerated, covered, for up to one week.

# Sweet 'n' Salty Peanut Turtle Pies

- - - - - - - - - - - - - - - - - - - - - - - - - - - - - - - - - - - - - - - - - - -

**Makes 16 pies**

● **GF Friendly**

*Every once in a while when I was tagging along with my mom to the grocery store, she would allow me to select something sweet from the bulk candy bins. I often picked the peanut turtle clusters. Not only were they bigger than most of the other candy, but turtles guaranteed three of my favorite ingredients — dark chocolate, sweet caramel and salty peanuts — in every bite.*

## Tips

The recipes in this book were tested with unsalted butter. Its lack of salt (used as a preservative) means a shorter time spent on grocery store shelves, resulting in higher-quality flavor. Using unsalted butter also allows you to control the amount of salt in your recipe. If you feel like splurging, opt for European-style butter, which has higher butterfat content and less moisture. Butter freezes well for up to six months. Do not substitute margarine for butter in these recipes, as it will significantly alter the result.

● 4-inch (10 cm) round cutter
● Two 12-cup muffin tins
● Pie weights or dried beans
● Parchment paper

| | | |
|---|---|---|
| 1 | recipe All-Butter Pie Dough (page 16) | 1 |
| **Filling** | | |
| ½ cup | sweetened condensed milk | 125 mL |
| ½ cup | packed light brown sugar | 125 mL |
| 2 tbsp | corn syrup | 30 mL |
| 6 tbsp | unsalted butter | 90 mL |
| ¼ tsp | salt | 1 mL |
| 1 tsp | vanilla extract | 5 mL |
| 1 cup | coarsely chopped lightly salted peanuts | 250 mL |
| **Chocolate Layer** | | |
| 1 cup | chopped bittersweet chocolate | 250 mL |
| ½ cup | sweetened condensed milk | 125 mL |
| 2 tbsp | unsalted butter | 30 mL |
| 2 | large egg yolks | 2 |
| | Lightly salted whole peanuts, optional | |

1. On a lightly floured work surface, roll out dough to a thickness of $\frac{1}{8}$ inch (3 mm). Using cutter, cut into rounds and carefully fit into muffin cups (there will be some overlap). Reroll scraps as necessary.

2. Place tins in freezer for 30 minutes. Meanwhile, preheat oven to 350°F (180°C).

3. Blind-bake shells (page 14 and Tips, page 185) on center rack in preheated oven for 10 minutes. Carefully remove weights and parchment; bake 7 to 10 minutes longer, until golden brown. Cool in tins on wire racks for 10 minutes, then carefully transfer to racks to cool completely.

4. *Filling:* In a medium saucepan over medium heat, bring condensed milk, brown sugar, corn syrup and butter to a boil, whisking constantly. Continue to cook and whisk for 4 minutes, until mixture thickens. Remove from heat and stir in salt and vanilla. Whisk for 2 minutes, allowing mixture to thicken slightly.

For step-by-step photographs of the blind-baking process, see page 33.

Store these pies in a covered container in the refrigerator between layers of waxed or parchment paper.

5. Place about $1^{1}/_{2}$ tbsp (22 mL) filling in each pie shell and sprinkle with 1 tbsp (15 mL) chopped peanuts. Chill until set, about 30 minutes.

6. *Chocolate Layer:* Meanwhile, in a medium saucepan over medium heat, combine chocolate, condensed milk and butter; whisk until smooth.

7. In a bowl, beat egg yolks. Add about $^{1}/_{2}$ cup (125 mL) hot chocolate mixture, whisking constantly. Transfer to saucepan and cook over medium-low heat for 2 to 3 minutes, until thickened.

8. Spoon chocolate mixture over cooled filling, smoothing with the back of the spoon. Top with a few whole peanuts, if using, and refrigerate until set, at least 1 hour or up to 5 days.

## Variations

Substitute Dark Chocolate Pie Dough (page 21) for the All-Butter Pie Dough.

*Gluten-Free Alternative:* Substitute Gluten-Free Pie Dough (page 24) for the All-Butter Pie Dough.

## Make Ahead

The assembled pies can be stored for up to five days in the refrigerator, tightly covered.

# Sticky Toffee Pudding Pies

**Makes 24 pies**

*My parents lived in London for a short time when my dad was a professor. Of course I took this opportunity to visit and to experience British cuisine. My favorite discovery was the appropriately named sticky toffee pudding: moist date cake infused with a rich, buttery toffee sauce that soaks in to create a pudding-like texture. It almost demands to be served with a scoop of vanilla ice cream!*

## Tips

For easiest rolling, roll your dough, including scraps, between two sheets of plastic wrap. That way, you do not need to add flour to keep the dough from sticking to your work surface.

For a different serving option, after topping with toffee sauce, place the pies under the broiler for a few minutes, watching carefully to ensure the crusts don't burn.

- **4-inch (10 cm) round cutter**
- **Two 12-cup muffin tins**
- **Electric mixer**

| | | |
|---|---|---|
| 1 | recipe All-Butter Pie Dough (page 16) | 1 |

**Filling**

| | | |
|---|---|---|
| 1¾ cups | chopped dates | 425 mL |
| 1½ cups | boiling water | 375 mL |
| 6 tbsp | unsalted butter, at room temperature | 90 mL |
| ¾ cup | packed light brown sugar | 175 mL |
| 2 | large eggs | 2 |
| ¾ cup | all-purpose flour | 175 mL |

**Toffee Sauce**

| | | |
|---|---|---|
| ½ cup | unsalted butter, in pieces | 125 mL |
| ½ cup | heavy or whipping (35%) cream | 125 mL |
| 1 cup | packed light brown sugar | 250 mL |

1. On a lightly floured work surface, roll out dough to a thickness of ⅛ inch (3 mm). Using cutter, cut into rounds and carefully fit into muffin cups (there will be some overlap). Reroll scraps as necessary.

2. Place tins in freezer for 30 minutes. Meanwhile, preheat oven to 350°F (180°C).

3. *Filling:* In a large bowl, combine dates and boiling water; set aside until water is absorbed.

4. In a large bowl, using electric mixer at medium speed, beat butter and brown sugar until light and fluffy. Add eggs, one at a time, beating well after each addition. Beat in flour. Fold in date mixture, using a rubber spatula.

5. Place 2 to 3 tbsp (30 to 45 mL) filling in each chilled pie shell. Bake on center rack of preheated oven for 20 to 25 minutes, until tops are puffed and set.

6. *Toffee Sauce:* Meanwhile, in a medium saucepan over medium heat, bring butter, cream and brown sugar to a boil, stirring constantly. Reduce heat to a low boil and cook, stirring frequently, until thickened, about 5 minutes. Remove from heat and set aside.

7. Cool pies in tins on wire racks for 5 minutes. Carefully transfer to racks set over baking sheets.

8. Using a toothpick, poke several holes in top of each pie. Spoon warm toffee sauce over pies, letting it soak in a bit before adding more. Serve warm (see Tips, left).

## Variation

Substitute Flaky Pie Dough (page 15) for the All-Butter Pie Dough.

## Make Ahead

The toffee sauce can be prepared up to three days in advance and rewarmed before topping the pies.

# Chocolate-Covered Cherry Pie Pops

*One of my favorite cookies to make is a dark chocolate cookie studded with chocolate chunks and dried sour cherries. I love how the tartness of the cherries contrasts with the deep, dark double dose of chocolate. These sophisticated pops wrap fresh cherries in a rich chocolate crust drizzled with bittersweet chocolate glaze — a chocolate-covered cherry on a stick!*

## Tips

Sweet cherries, such as the Bing and Rainier varieties, are generally available from May to August. Look for shiny, plump cherries with green stems and deep coloring.

For step-by-step photographs of making pie pops, see page 44.

- 3-inch (7.5 cm) round cutter
- 24 wooden or paper lollipop sticks
- 2 baking sheets lined with parchment

### Cherry Filling

| | | |
|---|---|---|
| 4 cups | fresh cherries, pitted and quartered (see Tip, left) | 1 L |
| ⅔ cup | granulated sugar | 150 mL |
| 2 tbsp | cornstarch | 30 mL |
| 1 tbsp | freshly squeezed lemon juice | 15 mL |
| 1 tsp | almond extract | 5 mL |
| 1 tsp | ground cinnamon | 5 mL |
| ¼ cup | water | 60 mL |
| 1 | recipe Dark Chocolate Pie Dough (page 21) | 1 |
| 1 | large egg, lightly beaten with 1 tbsp (15 mL) water | 1 |
| 1 | recipe Chocolate Glaze (page 49) | 1 |

1. *Cherry Filling:* In a medium saucepan over medium heat, combine cherries, sugar, cornstarch, lemon juice, almond extract and cinnamon, stirring to mix. Add water and bring to a boil. Reduce heat and simmer until thickened, stirring occasionally, about 5 minutes. Remove from heat and set aside to cool completely.

2. Divide dough into halves. On a lightly floured surface, roll out one half to a thickness of slightly more than $1/16$ inch (2 mm). Using cutter, cut into rounds and carefully transfer to prepared baking sheets, spacing apart. Reroll scraps as necessary, cutting out until you have 24 rounds.

3. Press the end of a lollipop stick into the bottom 1 inch (2.5 cm) of each round.

4. On a lightly floured surface, roll out remaining dough, cutting out 24 rounds and rerolling scraps as necessary.

**Tip**

Lollipop sticks can be found in the candy-making section of craft stores and in the baking aisle of well-stocked grocery stores.

5. Brush rounds holding lollipop sticks with egg wash and place 1 tbsp (15 mL) cherry filling in the center of each. Top each with a second round, pinching together firmly around the edges to stick and seal. Crimp with the tines of a fork.

6. Place pops, on baking sheets, in freezer for 30 minutes. Meanwhile, position oven racks in upper and lower thirds of oven and preheat oven to 375°F (190°C).

7. When ready to bake, using tip of a knife, poke 3 or 4 small holes in each top crust. Bake in preheated oven for 20 to 25 minutes, switching positions of baking sheets halfway through, until tops are puffed. Let cool on baking sheets for 10 minutes, then drizzle with chocolate glaze. Let glaze set for 10 minutes before serving.

## Variation

For a thicker coating, substitute Rich Chocolate Ganache (page 46) for the chocolate glaze.

## Make Ahead

Once the pops are assembled, they can be frozen for up to one month. Freeze for at least 30 minutes on baking sheets, then transfer to airtight containers or sealed zip-top bags. Bake from frozen, as directed.

The cherry filling can be mixed and refrigerated, covered, up to three days in advance.

# Chocolate Raspberry Pie Pops

*Chocolate and raspberries is my mom's favorite flavor combination, so this book would not be complete without at least one chocolate raspberry pie. This version, served on a stick, is perfect for people who want to get their chocolate-raspberry fix (ahem, Mom!) in just a few small bites.*

## Tips

If you are using frozen raspberries instead of fresh, there is no need to thaw them before adding them to the saucepan.

For step-by-step photographs of making pie pops, see page 44.

- 3-inch (7.5 cm) round cutter
- 24 wooden or paper lollipop sticks
- 2 baking sheets lined with parchment

### Raspberry Filling

| | | |
|---|---|---|
| 2 cups | fresh raspberries | 500 mL |
| 1 cup | granulated sugar | 250 mL |
| 1 tbsp | freshly squeezed lemon juice | 15 mL |
| 1 | recipe Dark Chocolate Pie Dough (page 21) | 1 |
| 1 | large egg, lightly beaten with 1 tbsp (15 mL) water | 1 |
| 1 | recipe Chocolate Glaze (page 49) | 1 |

1. *Raspberry Filling:* In a medium saucepan over medium-high heat, bring raspberries, sugar and lemon juice to a boil, mashing with a potato masher or the back of a spoon. Boil for 1 minute, stirring constantly, then reduce heat and simmer, stirring occasionally, until thickened, about 5 minutes. Transfer to a bowl, cover and refrigerate until cold.

2. Divide dough into halves. On a lightly floured surface, roll out one half to a thickness of slightly more than $1/16$ inch (2 mm). Cut out as many 3-inch (7.5 cm) rounds as possible and carefully transfer them to prepared baking sheets, spacing apart. Reroll scraps as necessary and continue cutting out until you have 24 rounds.

3. Press the end of a lollipop stick into the bottom 1 inch (2.5 cm) of each round.

4. Roll out remaining dough to slightly thicker than $1/16$ inch (2 mm). Cut out 24 more rounds, rerolling scraps as necessary.

5. Brush surfaces of rounds holding lollipop sticks with egg wash and place 1 tbsp (15 mL) raspberry filling in center of each. Top each with a second round, pinching together firmly around edges to stick and seal. Crimp with the tines of a fork.

6. Place pops, on baking sheets, in freezer for 30 minutes. Meanwhile, position oven racks in upper and lower thirds of oven and preheat oven to 375°F (190°C).

**Tip**

Lollipop sticks can be found in the candy-making section of craft stores and in the baking aisle of well-stocked grocery stores.

7. When ready to bake, poke 3 or 4 small holes in each top crust with the tip of a knife. Bake in preheated oven for 20 to 25 minutes, switching positions of baking sheets halfway through, until tops are puffed.

8. Let cool on baking sheets for 5 minutes, then drizzle with chocolate glaze. Let glaze set for 10 minutes before serving.

## Variation

For a thicker coating, substitute Rich Chocolate Ganache (page 46) for the chocolate glaze.

## Make Ahead

Once the pops are assembled, they can be frozen for up to one month. Freeze for at least 30 minutes on baking sheets, then transfer to airtight containers or sealed zip-top bags. Bake from frozen, as directed.

The raspberry filling can be stored in the refrigerator, covered, for up to one week.

# Oatmeal Raisin Cookie Pies

Makes 24 pies

*Nothing beats the spicy aroma of oatmeal raisin cookies in the oven — it makes the wait before they are cool enough to eat seem like hours. These mini pie versions of the classic cookie are golden on the outside but still soft and chewy in the center. If you feel like gilding the lily, drizzle them with Brown Butter Icing (page 50).*

## Tips

To soften hard brown sugar, place it in a microwave-safe bowl and cover with a damp paper towel. Cover bowl and microwave on High in 15-second bursts until sugar has softened.

Wire baking racks are important to have on hand for the cooling process. After pies have finished baking, either set the muffin tin on the rack or transfer the pies from the baking sheet to the rack. This lets the air circulate around the pies, cooling them evenly.

The pies can be fully assembled (Steps 1 through 5) and frozen, tightly wrapped in their tins, for up to two days. Bake from frozen, as directed.

- 4-inch (10 cm) round cutter
- Two 12-cup muffin tins

| | | |
|---|---|---|
| 1 | recipe Graham Cracker Pie Dough (page 28) | 1 |
| **Filling** | | |
| 1 cup | large-flake (old-fashioned) rolled oats | 250 mL |
| 2 tbsp | all-purpose flour | 30 mL |
| 1 ½ tsps | ground cinnamon | 7 mL |
| ½ tsp | each ground nutmeg, ginger, cloves and salt | 2 mL |
| 4 | large eggs | 4 |
| 1 cup | corn syrup | 250 mL |
| ½ cup | packed light brown sugar | 125 mL |
| ¼ cup | unsalted butter, melted | 60 mL |
| 1 tsp | vanilla extract | 5 mL |
| 1 cup | dark raisins | 250 mL |

1. On a lightly floured surface, roll out dough to a thickness of ⅛ inch (3 mm). Using cutter, cut into rounds and carefully fit into muffin cups. Reroll scraps.

2. Place tins in freezer while you prepare the filling.

3. *Filling:* In a large bowl, whisk together oats, flour, cinnamon, nutmeg, ginger, cloves and salt.

4. In a medium bowl, whisk together eggs, corn syrup, brown sugar, butter and vanilla. Add to oat mixture, mixing just until combined. Stir in raisins.

5. Place about 2 tbsp (30 mL) filling in each chilled pie shell. Place filled shells in freezer for 30 minutes. Meanwhile, preheat oven to 350°F (180°C).

6. Bake in center of preheated oven for 10 minutes; lower temperature to 325°F (160°C) and bake for 18 to 22 minutes, until top is browned and filling is just set.

7. Cool pies in pans on wire racks for 15 minutes, then carefully unmold and transfer to racks to cool.

## Variations

Substitute Flaky Pie Dough (page 15), Cream Cheese Pie Dough (page 20), Whole Wheat Pie Dough (page 18), Toasted Coconut Tartlet Dough (page 22) or All-Butter Pie Dough (page 16) for the Graham Cracker Pie Dough.

# Crazy about Chocolate Mini Pies

# Rich Chocolate Pudding Pies

*I used to love helping my mom make chocolate pudding. It was fascinating to watch the smooth liquid transform into silky-thick custard as I stood on a stool, carefully whisking it over the heat. Usually she would serve the pudding by itself in a bowl, but occasionally she would pour it into a pie shell to chill until it almost resembled rich fudge. Yum!*

## Tip

Espresso powder is my favorite "secret" ingredient to add to chocolate-based recipes. Just a small amount adds depth and richness to the chocolate flavor, usually without any trace of coffee-like notes. Not to be confused with instant coffee, instant espresso powder is intended for use in baking rather than for drinking. It can be found at some specialty food stores, well-stocked groceries or online retailers.

- 5-inch (12.5 cm) round cutter (see Tips, page 195)
- 2 baking sheets lined with parchment

### Chocolate Pudding

| | | |
|---|---|---|
| ⅓ cup | granulated sugar | 75 mL |
| 2 tbsp | cornstarch | 30 mL |
| ¼ cup | unsweetened cocoa powder | 60 mL |
| ½ tsp | instant espresso powder (see Tips, left) | 2 mL |
| ¼ tsp | salt | 1 mL |
| 1½ cups | whole milk | 375 mL |
| ½ cup | heavy or whipping (35%) cream | 125 mL |
| 5 oz | bittersweet chocolate, chopped | 150 g |
| 1 tbsp | unsalted butter | 15 mL |
| 1 tbsp | vanilla extract | 15 mL |
| 1 | recipe Hand Pie Dough (page 27) | 1 |
| 1 | large egg, lightly beaten with 1 tbsp (15 mL) water | 1 |
| | Confectioners' (icing) sugar for dusting | |

1. *Chocolate Pudding:* In a medium saucepan, whisk together sugar, cornstarch, cocoa, espresso powder and salt. Slowly add milk, whisking constantly until smooth. Whisk in cream.

2. Set saucepan over medium heat. Whisk constantly until mixture comes to a simmer and thickens, about 5 minutes. Add chocolate and butter, whisking until melted and smooth. Remove from heat and whisk in vanilla.

3. Transfer pudding to a bowl and cover with plastic wrap, pressing it down onto the surface. Refrigerate until cold and thickened, about 2 hours.

4. On a lightly floured surface, roll out dough to slightly thicker than $1/16$ inch (2 mm). Using cutter, cut into rounds and place on prepared baking sheets, spacing apart. Reroll scraps as necessary.

5. Brush edges of rounds with egg wash. Place 2 tbsp (30 mL) pudding in center of each round. Fold in half, enclosing filling. Pinch edges together to seal, and crimp with the tines of a fork. Brush tops with egg wash.

## Tips

Allow the pies to rest a while before serving so they are cool enough to hold in your hand!

Pressing plastic wrap onto the surface of the pudding prevents a skin from forming while it cools.

If you don't have a 5-inch (12.5 cm) cutter, use a container lid or small plate as a guide.

6. Place pies, on baking sheets, in freezer for 30 minutes. Meanwhile, position oven racks in upper and lower thirds of oven and preheat oven to 375°F (190°C).

7. Using tip of a knife, cut 2 or 3 slits in top of each pie. Bake in preheated oven for 20 to 25 minutes, switching positions of baking sheets halfway through, until puffed and browned. Let cool (see Tips, left) on sheets on wire racks for 10 minutes, then dust with confectioners' sugar.

## Make Ahead

The pies can be fully assembled (Steps 1 through 5) and frozen for up to three days. Freeze for at least 30 minutes on trays, then transfer to zip-top bags and seal. Bake from frozen, as directed.

# Chocolate Malt and Cherry Cream Pies

*I won a baking competition on the Food Network for my Double Chocolate Malt Shop Cupcakes with Cherry Vanilla Buttercream. The flavor combination of chocolate, malt and cherry was so well received that I decided to reinterpret it in these cream-filled pies.*

## Tips

Malted milk powder (Carnation is one brand) can usually be found in the cereal aisle of your grocery store.

The easiest way to remove tarts from muffin tins is to run a small, sharp knife or small offset spatula around the edges, loosening the sides. You should then be able to carefully lift out the tarts, guiding them with the knife or spatula.

For step-by-step photographs of the blind-baking process, see page 33.

- 4-inch (10 cm) round cutter
- Two 12-cup muffin tins
- Pie weights or dried beans
- Parchment paper

| | | |
|---|---|---|
| 1 | recipe Dark Chocolate Pie Dough (page 21) | 1 |
| 1/3 cup | granulated sugar | 75 mL |
| 2 1/2 tbsp | cornstarch | 37 mL |
| 1/2 cup | malted milk powder | 125 mL |
| 1/2 tsp | instant espresso powder, optional | 2 mL |
| 1/4 tsp | salt | 1 mL |
| 3 | large egg yolks | 3 |
| 1 cup | whole milk, divided | 250 mL |
| 1/2 cup | heavy or whipping (35%) cream | 125 mL |
| 4 oz | milk chocolate, chopped | 125 g |
| 1 tbsp | vanilla extract | 15 mL |
| 1 tbsp | unsalted butter | 15 mL |
| 2 tbsp | Kirsch or cherry liqueur | 30 mL |
| 1/2 cup | coarsely chopped malted milk balls | 125 mL |
| | Lightly sweetened whipped cream | |
| 24 | maraschino cherries | 24 |

1. On a lightly floured surface, roll out dough to a thickness of 1/8 inch (3 mm). Using cutter, cut into rounds and carefully fit into muffin cups (there will be some overlap). Reroll scraps as necessary.

2. Place tins in freezer for 30 minutes. Meanwhile, preheat oven to 350°F (180°C).

3. Blind-bake shells (page 14 and Tips, left) in center of preheated oven for 12 minutes. Carefully remove weights and parchment; continue to bake until shells are golden brown, 6 to 9 minutes longer. Let cool completely in pans on wire racks.

4. In a large bowl, whisk together sugar, cornstarch, malted milk powder, espresso powder (if using) and salt. Whisk in egg yolks and 1/2 cup (125 mL) milk, until smooth.

5. In a large saucepan over medium heat, bring remaining $1/2$ cup (125 mL) milk and cream to a simmer. Whisking constantly, gradually add to egg mixture; whisk until fully incorporated and smooth. Return to saucepan and whisk over medium-low heat until thickened, about 3 minutes. Add chocolate and whisk until melted and smooth. Remove pan from heat and whisk in vanilla, butter and Kirsch. Stir in malted milk balls.

6. Spoon pudding into baked shells. Refrigerate until chilled and set, at least 2 hours or up to 2 days. Carefully remove tarts from tins. Garnish each with a bit of whipped cream and a cherry before serving.

## Variations

Substitute bittersweet or semisweet chocolate for the milk chocolate in the filling.

## Make Ahead

The fully assembled pies can be chilled, covered, for up to two days. Garnish with the whipped cream and cherry just before serving.

# Mexican Chocolate Mousse Pies

**Makes 24 pies**

*These desserts might resemble everyday chocolate mousse pies, but their rich filling holds several surprises. Ground cinnamon, spicy cayenne pepper, dark espresso powder and coffee liqueur ensure that every one of your taste buds is satisfied.*

## Tips

Instead of using a food processor, crush chocolate wafer cookies by placing them in a large zip-top bag and breaking them up with a rolling pin.

For step-by-step photographs of the blind-baking process, see page 33.

- **4-inch (10 cm) round cutter**
- **Two 12-cup muffin tins**
- **Pie weights or dried beans**
- **Parchment paper**
- **Electric mixer**

| | | |
|---|---|---|
| 1½ cups | crushed chocolate wafer cookies | 375 mL |
| 1 | recipe Dark Chocolate Pie Dough (page 21) | 1 |
| 1½ cups | heavy or whipping (35%) cream, divided | 375 mL |
| ½ tsp | instant espresso powder | 2 mL |
| 6 oz | bittersweet or semisweet chocolate, chopped | 175 g |
| 2 tbsp | Kahlúa or other coffee-flavored liqueur | 30 mL |
| 1 tsp | vanilla extract | 5 mL |
| ¼ tsp | ground cinnamon | 1 mL |
| ¼ to ½ tsp | cayenne pepper (see Tip, page 199) | 1 to 2 mL |
| ⅛ tsp | salt | 0.5 mL |
| 2 tbsp | granulated sugar | 30 mL |
| | Lightly sweetened whipped cream, optional | |
| | Chocolate shavings, optional | |
| | Ground cinnamon for dusting, optional | |

1. Scatter a lightly floured work surface with a handful of cookie crumbs. Roll out dough to ⅛ inch (3 mm) thick, embedding cookie crumbs in dough. Using cutter, cut into rounds and carefully fit into muffin cups (there may be some overlap). Reroll scraps, scattering additional cookie crumbs as necessary.

2. Place tins in freezer for 30 minutes. Meanwhile, preheat oven to 350°F (180°C).

3. Blind-bake shells (page 14 and Tips, left) in center of preheated oven for 12 minutes. Carefully remove weights and parchment; continue to bake until the shells are browned and set, 6 to 9 minutes longer. Let cool completely in pans on wire racks.

## Tip

When adding the cayenne pepper, taste to test the amount of heat. Start with $\frac{1}{4}$ tsp (1 mL) and add more a bit at a time.

4. In a medium saucepan over medium heat, heat $\frac{1}{2}$ cup (125 mL) cream and espresso powder, stirring to dissolve the powder. When mixture comes to a simmer, remove from heat and add chocolate, stirring until melted and smooth. Add Kahlúa, vanilla, cinnamon, cayenne and salt, whisking until smooth. Set aside to cool completely.

5. Using electric mixer at medium speed, beat remaining 1 cup (250 mL) cream and sugar until stiff peaks form. Fold into chocolate mixture. Spoon mousse into prepared shells, smoothing tops. Chill until set, about 3 hours. Carefully remove pies from tins and garnish with additional whipped cream, shaved chocolate and cinnamon, if desired.

## Make Ahead

The pies can be fully assembled and chilled, covered, for three days. Garnish just before serving.

# Chocolate Orange Pies

**Makes 24 pies**

- **GF Friendly**

*When I owned a bakery, we sold a chocolate-orange sour cream crumb cake that just flew off the shelves. Orange zest and juice helped cut through the richness of the bittersweet chocolate. Here I've recreated that popular pairing in mini pies.*

## Tips

For a great two-bite sweet when you want something chocolatey, cut smaller rounds and fill with about 1½ tsp (7 mL) ganache.

Use freshly squeezed orange juice in place of the orange liqueur, if desired.

For step-by-step photographs of making hand pies, see page 35.

Glaze pies with Chocolate Glaze (page 49) instead of the orange glaze.

The pies can be fully assembled and frozen for up to one month. Freeze for at least 30 minutes on trays, then transfer to zip-top bags and seal. Bake from frozen, as directed.

- **4-inch (10 cm) round cutter**
- **2 baking sheets lined with parchment**

### Ganache

| | | |
|---|---|---|
| 8 oz | bittersweet chocolate, chopped | 250 g |
| ¾ cup | heavy or whipping (35%) cream | 175 mL |
| 1 tbsp | finely grated orange zest | 15 mL |
| 1 tbsp | orange-flavored liqueur (see Tips, left) | 15 mL |
| 1 | recipe All-Butter Pie Dough (page 16) | 1 |
| 1 | large egg, lightly beaten with 1 tbsp (15 mL) water | 1 |
| 1 | recipe Orange Glaze (see page 48) | 1 |

1. *Ganache:* Place chocolate in a medium heatproof bowl.

2. In a small saucepan over medium heat, bring cream and orange zest to a simmer. Pour hot cream over chocolate and set aside for 30 seconds. Stir until chocolate has melted and mixture is smooth. Stir in orange liqueur. Set aside to cool completely.

3. On a lightly floured surface, roll out dough to slightly thicker than ¹⁄₁₆ inch (2 mm). Cut into rounds and place on prepared baking sheets. Reroll scraps.

4. Brush edges of rounds with egg wash. Place 1 tbsp (15 mL) ganache in center of each round. Fold in half, enclosing filling. Pinch edges to seal, and crimp with the tines of a fork. Brush tops with egg wash.

5. Place pies, on baking sheets, in freezer for 30 minutes. Meanwhile, position oven racks in upper and lower thirds of oven and preheat oven to 350°F (180°C).

6. Using tip of a knife, cut a few slits in top of each pie. Bake in preheated oven for 22 to 27 minutes, switching positions of baking sheets halfway through, until pies are puffed and golden brown. Let cool on sheets on racks for 10 minutes, then drizzle with orange glaze. Let glaze set for at least 10 minutes before serving.

## Variations

Substitute Hand Pie Dough (page 27), Flaky Pie Dough (page 15) or Cream Cheese Pie Dough (page 20) for the All-Butter Pie Dough.

*Gluten-Free Alternative:* Substitute Gluten-Free Pie Dough (page 24) for the All-Butter Pie Dough.

# Chocolate Mocha Pecan Tarts

*Just small amounts of cocoa and espresso powder transform already rich pecan pie into a darker, more deeply flavored and certainly more decadent treat. At any dessert table, these tarts are sure to disappear quickly.*

## Tips

For best results, always sift cocoa powder before adding it to recipes, to avoid scattered clumps of bitter cocoa flavor in your pie filling.

Once they are baked, store these tarts at room temperature, covered, in layers separated by waxed paper.

These tarts tend to be sticky, so make sure the pans are evenly greased before baking.

The easiest way to remove tarts from muffin tins is to run a small, sharp knife or small offset spatula around the edges, loosening the sides. You should then be able to carefully lift out the tarts, guiding them with the knife or spatula.

- 3½-inch (8.75 cm) round cutter
- Two 12-cup muffin tins, greased

| 1 | recipe Dark Chocolate Pie Dough (page 21) | 1 |
|---|---|---|
| **Filling** | | |
| 3 tbsp | unsalted butter, melted | 45 mL |
| 3 tbsp | unsweetened cocoa powder | 45 mL |
| 3 tbsp | heavy or whipping (35%) cream | 45 mL |
| 2 tsp | instant espresso powder | 10 mL |
| ¾ cup | light corn syrup | 175 mL |
| ¾ cup | granulated sugar | 175 mL |
| 3 | large eggs | 3 |
| 1 tbsp | vanilla extract | 15 mL |
| ¼ tsp | salt | 1 mL |
| 1¼ cups | chopped pecans | 300 mL |

1. On a lightly floured surface, roll out dough to a thickness of ⅛ inch (3 mm). Using cutter, cut into rounds and fit into muffin cups. Reroll scraps as necessary.

2. Place tins in freezer for 30 minutes. Meanwhile, preheat oven to 350°F (180°C).

3. *Filling:* In a large bowl, whisk together butter, cocoa, cream and espresso powders until smooth. Add corn syrup, sugar, eggs, vanilla and salt, mixing until well combined. Stir in pecans.

4. Spoon filling into chilled shells until three-quarters full. Bake in center of preheated oven until filling is set, 22 to 27 minutes.

5. Cool pies completely in tins on wire racks for 15 minutes, then carefully remove from tins. Serve slightly warm or at room temperature.

## Make Ahead

The pies can be fully baked and stored at room temperature for three to four days.

# Double Chocolate Peanut Butter Hand Pies

*When my brother and I returned from Halloween trick-or-treating, we would dump our candy on the kitchen table and trade favorite varieties. His first choice was always my Reese's Peanut Butter Cups, which served as inspiration for these chocolate-glazed peanut butter hand pies.*

## Tips

Once you start using parchment paper, you will never want to go back to silicone liners or greased baking sheets. Disposable, heat-resistant and nonstick, parchment will make your pie-baking life much, much easier! Use it to line baking sheets or tart shells when blind-baking. When you have finished baking, simply throw out the used parchment. It makes for extremely easy clean-up.

Since these pies taste just as good at room temperature as they do warm from the oven, they are a great addition to a packed lunch or a bake sale.

For a thicker topping, substitute Rich Chocolate Ganache (page 46) for the chocolate glaze.

- 4-inch (10 cm) round cutter
- 2 baking sheets lined with parchment

### Filling

| | | |
|---|---|---|
| 1¼ cups | crunchy peanut butter, at room temperature | 300 mL |
| 1¼ cups | confectioners' (icing) sugar | 300 mL |
| 3 tbsp | unsalted butter, at room temperature | 45 mL |
| 2 tbsp | heavy or whipping (35%) cream | 30 mL |
| 2 tsp | vanilla extract | 10 mL |
| 1 | recipe Dark Chocolate Pie Dough (page 21) | 1 |
| 1 | large egg, lightly beaten with 1 tbsp (15 mL) water | 1 |
| 1 | recipe Chocolate Glaze (page 49) | 1 |
| | Chopped peanuts | |

1. *Filling:* In a large bowl, stir together peanut butter, confectioners' sugar, butter, cream and vanilla.

2. On a lightly floured surface, roll out dough to slightly thicker than $1/16$ inch (2 mm). Using cutter, cut into rounds and place on prepared baking sheets, spacing apart. Reroll scraps as necessary.

3. Brush edges of rounds with egg wash. Place a generous 1 tbsp (15 mL) filling in center of each. Fold in half, enclosing filling. Pinch edges to seal, and crimp with the tines of a fork. Brush tops with egg wash.

4. Place pies, on baking sheets, in freezer for 30 minutes. Meanwhile, position oven racks in upper and lower thirds of oven and preheat oven to 350°F (180°C).

5. Using tip of a sharp knife, cut 2 or 3 slits in top of each pie. Bake in preheated oven for 20 to 25 minutes, switching positions of baking sheets halfway through, until pies are puffed and golden brown. Let cool on sheets on wire racks for 15 minutes, then drizzle with chocolate glaze and sprinkle with chopped peanuts.

## Make Ahead

The pies can be assembled and frozen for up to one month. Freeze on trays, then transfer to zip-top bags and seal. Bake from frozen, as directed.

# Chocolate-Covered Coconut Almond Pies

**Makes 16 pies**

*Like my Double Chocolate Peanut Butter Hand Pies (page 202), this is another handheld treat inspired by candy. Although the chewy coconut center tastes great warm or at room temperature, these pies are really at their best chilled, when the ganache coating becomes fudgy and the coconut filling dense.*

## Tips

Use either blanched almonds or almonds with skins on, to suit your taste.

To serve these pies chilled, wait until the ganache topping has set fully. Place in layers in an airtight container, separated with waxed paper. Cover and refrigerate for up to four days.

If you don't have a 5-inch (12.5 cm) cutter, use a container lid or small plate as a guide.

The pies can be fully assembled and frozen for up to one month. Freeze for at least 30 minutes on trays, then transfer to zip-top bags and seal. Bake from frozen, as directed.

- 5-inch (12.5 cm) round cutter (see Tips, left)
- 2 baking sheets lined with parchment

| | | |
|---|---|---|
| ½ cup | sweetened condensed milk | 125 mL |
| ⅔ cup | confectioners' (icing) sugar | 150 mL |
| 2 cups | sweetened shredded coconut | 500 mL |
| 1 | large egg white | 1 |
| 2 tsp | vanilla extract | 10 mL |
| ⅛ tsp | salt | 0.5 mL |
| 1 | recipe Dark Chocolate Pie Dough (page 21) | 1 |
| 1 | large egg, lightly beaten with 1 tbsp (15 mL) water | 1 |
| 32 | whole almonds (see Tips, left) | 32 |
| 1 | recipe Rich Chocolate Ganache (page 46), warmed | 1 |

1. In a large bowl, stir together condensed milk, confectioners' sugar, coconut, egg white, vanilla and salt.

2. On a lightly floured surface, roll out dough to slightly thicker than $\frac{1}{16}$ inch (2 mm). Using cutter, cut into rounds and place on prepared baking sheets, spacing apart. Reroll scraps as necessary.

3. Brush edges of rounds with egg wash. Place about 2 tbsp (30 mL) coconut filling in center of each round. Press 2 almonds into filling, side by side. Fold rounds in half, enclosing filling. Pinch edges together to seal, and crimp with the tines of a fork. Brush tops with egg wash.

4. Place pies, on baking sheets, in freezer for 30 minutes. Meanwhile, position oven racks in upper and lower thirds of oven and preheat oven to 375°F (190°C).

5. Using tip of a sharp knife, cut 2 or 3 slits in top of each pie. Bake in preheated oven for 20 to 25 minutes, switching positions of baking sheets halfway through, until puffed and browned. Let cool on sheets on wire racks for 15 minutes, then dip top crust of each pie into warmed chocolate ganache. Place on wire racks until ganache has set and pies have cooled completely. Serve chilled (see Tips, left) or at room temperature.

# German Chocolate Hand Pies

Makes 16 pies

*You don't need to go to Germany in search of the cake that inspired this recipe! First created in the 1950s, it was originally called "German's Chocolate Cake" — named for Sam German, an American who developed the brand of sweet chocolate used in the dessert. In this version, the signature rich pecan-coconut filling is wrapped in a chocolate crust and drizzled with bittersweet chocolate ganache.*

## Tips

Serve these pies chilled or at room temperature. They may be stored in an airtight container, tightly covered, for four to five days.

For step-by-step photographs of making hand pies, see page 35.

- 5-inch (12.5 cm) round cutter (see Tip, page 205)
- 2 baking sheets lined with parchment

### Filling

| | | |
|---|---|---|
| 1 | can (7 oz/210 g) sweetened condensed milk | 1 |
| 5 tbsp | unsalted butter, in pieces | 75 mL |
| 1 tsp | vanilla extract | 5 mL |
| 2 | large egg yolks | 2 |
| 1¼ cups | sweetened shredded coconut | 300 mL |
| ¾ cup | chopped pecans | 175 mL |
| ½ cup | semisweet mini chocolate chips | 125 mL |
| 1 | recipe Dark Chocolate Pie Dough (page 21) | 1 |
| 1 | large egg, lightly beaten with 1 tbsp (15 mL) water | 1 |
| 1 | recipe Chocolate Ganache (page 46), warmed | 1 |

1. *Filling:* In a medium saucepan over medium-low heat, combine condensed milk, butter and vanilla, stirring until butter is melted.

2. In a medium bowl, whisk egg yolks. Whisking constantly, gradually add hot milk mixture. Return to saucepan and cook over medium-low heat, whisking constantly, until slightly thickened, 4 to 5 minutes. Remove from heat and stir in coconut and pecans. Set aside to cool completely, then stir in chocolate chips. Set aside.

3. On a lightly floured surface, roll out dough to slightly thicker than $1/16$ inch (2 mm). Using cutter, cut into rounds and place on prepared baking sheets, spacing apart. Reroll scraps as necessary.

4. Brush edges of rounds with egg wash. Place about 2 tbsp (30 mL) filling in center of each round. Fold in half, enclosing filling. Pinch edges together to seal, and crimp with the tines of a fork. Brush tops with egg wash.

5. Place pies, on baking sheets, in freezer for 30 minutes. Meanwhile, position oven racks in upper and lower thirds of oven and preheat oven to 375°F (190°C).

## Tip

If you don't have a 5-inch (12.5 cm) cutter, use a container lid or small plate as a guide.

6. Using tip of a sharp knife, cut 2 or 3 slits in top of each pie. Bake in preheated oven for 25 to 30 minutes, switching positions of baking sheets halfway through, until puffed and golden brown. Cool on sheets on wire racks for 15 minutes, then drizzle generously with warmed chocolate ganache. Cool completely.

## Variations

Sprinkle the ganache with additional chopped pecans or toasted coconut before it sets.

## Make Ahead

The pies can be fully assembled (Steps 1 through 4) and frozen for up to one month. Freeze for at least 30 minutes on trays, then transfer to zip-top bags and seal. Bake from frozen, as directed.

# Frozen Chocolate Mint Grasshopper Pies

**Makes 24 pies**

*When visiting New Hampshire, where we spent our summers, my family and I would often eat at a restaurant named Peter Christian's Tavern, where they served a decadent Grasshopper Brownie Chip Pie for dessert. This recipe is a cross between that special pie and my husband's favorite mint chocolate chip ice cream — sweet and refreshing at the same time.*

## Tips

Once the pies are frozen, they can be unmolded and placed in an airtight container in the freezer for up to five days.

For step-by-step photographs of the blind-baking process, see page 33.

- 3¹⁄₂- to 4-inch (8.75 to 10 cm) round cutter
- Two 12-cup muffin tins
- Pie weights or dried beans
- Parchment paper

| | | |
|---|---|---|
| 1¹⁄₂ cups | crushed chocolate wafer cookies | 375 mL |
| 1 | recipe Dark Chocolate Pie Dough (page 21) | 1 |

**Filling**

| | | |
|---|---|---|
| 4 | large egg yolks | 4 |
| 2¹⁄₂ tbsp | cornstarch | 37 mL |
| ¹⁄₃ cup | granulated sugar | 75 mL |
| 1 cup | whole milk, divided | 250 mL |
| ³⁄₄ cup | heavy or whipping (35%) cream | 175 mL |
| ²⁄₃ cup | chopped white chocolate | 150 mL |
| ¹⁄₄ cup | crème de menthe liqueur | 60 mL |
| 2 tbsp | white crème de cacao liqueur | 30 mL |
| ¹⁄₂ cup | finely chopped bittersweet chocolate | 125 mL |

1. On a lightly floured work surface, scatter ¹⁄₂ cup (125 mL) cookie crumbs. Place dough on surface and roll out to ¹⁄₈ inch (3 mm) thick, embedding cookie crumbs in dough. Using cutter, cut into rounds and carefully fit into muffin cups (there may be some overlap). Reroll scraps, scattering additional cookie crumbs on work surface as necessary.

2. Place tins in freezer for 30 minutes. Meanwhile, preheat oven to 350°F (180°C).

3. Blind-bake shells (page 14 and Tips, left) in center of preheated oven for 12 minutes. Carefully remove weights and parchment; continue to bake until the shells are browned and set, 6 to 9 minutes longer. Let cool completely in pans.

4. *Filling:* In a large bowl, whisk together egg yolks, cornstarch, sugar and ¹⁄₄ cup (60 mL) milk.

## Tip

If you would prefer a greener color for these pies and are not concerned about potential health issues related to the use of food coloring, whisk in a few drops of green food coloring along with the liqueurs.

5. In a medium saucepan, bring remaining milk and cream to a simmer. Whisking constantly, slowly add hot milk mixture to egg mixture; whisk until smooth. Return to saucepan and whisk constantly over medium-low heat until thickened, 3 to 4 minutes. Add white chocolate and whisk until melted. Remove from heat. Whisk in crème de menthe and crème de cacao. Cool completely, then whisk in bittersweet chocolate.

6. Spoon about 2 tbsp (30 mL) filling into baked shells, smoothing tops. Freeze pies for at least 4 hours, until very firm, or for up to 5 days, covered. Carefully unmold and serve (see Tips, page 206).

### Variations

Garnish the frozen pies with lightly sweetened whipped cream and additional shaved chocolate before serving.

Substitute mini chocolate chips for the chopped bittersweet chocolate.

### Make Ahead

Once frozen, pies can be stored, tightly covered, for up to five days.

# Chocolate Cappuccino Pocket Pies

*When I was a little girl, I couldn't imagine that I would ever drink coffee. I would tentatively try a sip from my mother's morning mug, then scrunch up my face at the bitter taste. Today I can't imagine starting my day without an extra-strong cappuccino, sometimes two. These treats are perfect for any coffee break, or served as a whimsical dessert. Who says pocket pies are only for kids?*

## Tip

The pies should be glazed shortly before serving. Store baked, unglazed tarts in an airtight container, either chilled or at room temperature, for up to three days.

- 4-inch (10 cm) round cutter
- 2 baking sheets lined with parchment

### Filling

| | | |
|---|---|---|
| 8 oz | white chocolate, chopped | 250 g |
| ¾ cup | heavy or whipping (35%) cream | 175 mL |
| 1 tbsp | instant espresso powder | 15 mL |
| 1 tsp | vanilla extract | 5 mL |
| 1 | recipe Pocket Pie Dough (page 26) | 1 |
| 1 | large egg, lightly beaten with 1 tbsp (15 mL) water | 1 |
| 1 | recipe Chocolate Glaze (page 49) | 1 |

1. *Filling:* Place chopped white chocolate in a medium heatproof bowl.

2. In a small saucepan over medium heat, bring cream and espresso powder to a simmer. Pour over white chocolate and let rest for 30 seconds. Stir until chocolate has melted and mixture is smooth. Stir in vanilla. Cover and refrigerate until cold.

3. Divide dough into halves. On a lightly floured surface, roll out one half to a thickness of slightly more than $1/16$ inch (2 mm). Using cutter, cut into rounds and place on prepared baking sheets, spacing apart. Reroll scraps as necessary.

4. On lightly floured surface, roll out remaining dough to a thickness slightly more than $1/16$ inch (2 mm). Using cutter, cut out rounds, rerolling scraps as necessary.

5. Brush surfaces of first set of rounds with egg wash and place 1 to $1^1/2$ tbsp (15 to 22 mL) chilled filling in center of each. Working quickly, place a round from the second set over the filling, pressing edges together to seal. Crimp edges with the tines of a fork. Repeat with remaining rounds. Brush tops with egg wash.

6. Place pocket pies on baking sheets in freezer for 30 minutes. Meanwhile, position oven racks in upper and lower thirds of oven and preheat oven to 375°F (190°C.)

## Tip

A rolling pin is instrumental in achieving a uniform, smooth dough. Although most are made from either wood or marble, you can also purchase silicone or plastic rolling pins. My rolling pin of choice is the simple French version: long and slim, with tapered ends instead of handles. I feel that this model gives me the most control when rolling out dough.

7. When ready to bake, pierce tops 3 or 4 times with tip of a sharp knife or a toothpick. Bake in preheated oven for 20 to 25 minutes, switching positions of baking sheets halfway through, until pies are puffed and golden brown. Let cool on sheets on wire racks for 10 minutes, then coat with chocolate glaze. Let glaze set for at least 15 minutes before serving.

## Variation

Substitute Dark Chocolate Pie Dough (page 21) for the Pocket Pie Dough.

## Make Ahead

The pies can be fully assembled (Steps 1 through 5) and frozen for up to one month. Freeze for at least 30 minutes on trays, then transfer to zip-top bags and seal. Bake from frozen and glaze as directed.

# Raspberry White Chocolate Mousse Tarts

**Makes 24 tarts**

● **GF Friendly**

*These beautiful, dainty tarts are perfect for a luncheon, bridal shower or, in my case, Mother's Day treat. My mom loves any dessert with raspberries in it, and this one features them twice: once in the smooth white chocolate mousse filling and once as a garnish on top.*

## Tip

Raspberry purée can be made from either fresh or thawed frozen raspberries. Place the raspberries in a food processor or blender and purée until smooth. Strain the mixture into a bowl using a fine-mesh sieve, pressing on the solids with a rubber spatula. Eight ounces (250 g) raspberries should yield about ½ cup (125 mL) purée.

For step-by-step photographs of the blind-baking process, see page 33.

● 3½- to 4-inch (8.75 to 10 cm) round cutter
● Two 12-cup muffin tins
● Pie weights or dried beans
● Parchment paper
● Electric mixer

| | | |
|---|---|---|
| 1 | recipe Sweet Tart Dough (page 17) | 1 |
| 2 tsp | unflavored gelatin | 10 mL |
| ¼ cup | framboise or raspberry liqueur, divided | 60 mL |
| 1½ cups | heavy or whipping (35%) cream, divided (see Tip, page 211) | 375 mL |
| 8 oz | white chocolate, chopped | 250 g |
| ½ cup | raspberry purée (see Tips, left) | 125 mL |
| | Lightly sweetened whipped cream, optional | |
| 24 | fresh raspberries | 24 |

1. On a lightly floured work surface, roll out dough to a thickness of ⅛ inch (3 mm). Using cutter, cut into rounds and carefully fit into muffin cups (there will be some overlap). Reroll scraps as necessary.

2. Place tins in freezer for 30 minutes. Meanwhile, preheat oven to 350°F (180°C).

3. Blind-bake shells (page 14 and Tips, left) in center of preheated oven for 12 minutes. Carefully remove weights and parchment; bake until shells are golden brown, 6 to 9 minutes longer. Let cool in pans on wire racks for 10 minutes, then carefully unmold and transfer to racks to cool completely.

4. In a medium saucepan, sprinkle gelatin over 2 tbsp (30 mL) framboise. Let soften for 5 minutes.

5. Add 1 cup (250 mL) cream to saucepan and stir over low heat until gelatin dissolves. Add white chocolate and stir until melted and smooth. Stir in raspberry purée and transfer to a medium bowl. Cover and refrigerate until cold.

6. Using electric mixer at high speed, whip remaining ½ cup (125 mL) cream until soft peaks form. Add remaining 2 tbsp (30 mL) framboise and whip until firm peaks form.

7. Fold whipped cream into raspberry mixture. Spoon raspberry mousse into tart shells, smoothing tops. Refrigerate for at least 2 hours or up to 1 day before serving. Garnish with lightly sweetened whipped cream, if using, and fresh raspberries.

## Variations

Substitute Toasted Coconut Tartlet Dough (page 22) for the Sweet Tart Dough.

*Gluten-Free Variation:* Substitute Gluten-Free Pie Dough (page 24) for the Sweet Tart Dough.

## Make Ahead

The tart shells can be blind-baked up to three days in advance and stored, tightly covered, at room temperature.

Fully assembled, these tarts can be stored, tightly covered, in the refrigerator for up to one day. Garnish with fresh raspberries just before serving.

# Rocky Road Brownie Pies

---

## Makes 24 pies

*When marshmallows are included as part of a brownie batter, they tend to melt and disappear during the baking process. These dense and rich brownie pies feature marshmallows as a top layer that is browned in the oven during the last few minutes of baking.*

---

## Tips

For best results, always sift cocoa powder before adding it to recipes, to avoid scattered clumps of bitter cocoa flavor in your pie filling.

Because the marshmallow topping is best when freshly browned, these pies are best served the day they are prepared.

The easiest way to remove pies from muffin tins is to run a small, sharp knife or small offset spatula around the edges, loosening the sides. You should then be able to carefully lift out the tarts, guiding them with the knife or spatula.

If you don't have a kitchen torch, place the marshmallow-topped pies (Step 6) under a preheated broiler for 1 minute.

- 4-inch (10 cm) round cutter
- Two 12-cup muffin tins
- Kitchen torch, optional (see Tips, left)

| | | |
|---|---|---|
| 1 | recipe Dark Chocolate Pie Dough (page 21) | 1 |

**Filling**

| | | |
|---|---|---|
| 6 oz | bittersweet chocolate, chopped | 175 g |
| ¾ cup | unsalted butter, in pieces | 175 mL |
| 3 | large eggs | 3 |
| 1½ cups | granulated sugar | 375 mL |
| 6 tbsp | all-purpose flour | 90 mL |
| ½ cup | unsweetened cocoa powder | 125 mL |
| ¼ tsp | salt | 1 mL |
| 2 cups | miniature marshmallows, divided | 500 mL |
| ⅔ cup | semisweet or bittersweet chocolate chips | 150 mL |
| ⅔ cup | chopped walnuts | 150 mL |

1. On a lightly floured surface, roll out dough to a thickness of $1/8$ inch (3 mm). Using cutter, cut into rounds and fit into muffin cups. Reroll scraps as necessary.

2. Place tins in freezer for 30 minutes. Meanwhile, preheat oven to 350°F (180°C).

3. *Filling:* In a medium saucepan over medium-low heat, melt butter and chocolate, stirring constantly until smooth. Remove pan from heat and quickly beat in eggs, one at a time, beating well after each addition. Stir in sugar.

4. Sift flour, cocoa and salt into a bowl, then add to chocolate mixture, stirring until just blended. Set aside to cool to room temperature. When cool, mix in $1/2$ cup (125 mL) marshmallows, chocolate chips and walnuts. Spoon 2 to 3 tbsp (30 to 45 mL) filling into each chilled shell.

5. Bake in center of preheated oven for 22 to 28 minutes, until tops are puffed and a toothpick inserted in the center comes out with moist crumbs attached. Remove from oven and place tins on wire racks to cool for 10 minutes.

6. Place about 1 tbsp (15 mL) mini marshmallows on top of each pie. Using a kitchen torch, lightly brown marshmallows. Cool completely, then carefully remove pies from tins.

# Holiday Pies

# Festive Cranberry Spice Pocket Pies

| | | |
|---|---|---|
| **Makes 16 pocket pies** | | |

● **Vegan Friendly**

*These not-too-sweet pockets contain a spiced mixture of fresh and dried cranberries, making them a unique addition to your holiday breakfast table. Serve them simply, dusted with confectioners' sugar, or give them a bit of extra pizzazz with a spiced cinnamon glaze.*

## Tips

Fresh cranberries keep very well in the freezer. Buy extra bags when they are in season so you can bake these pocket pies all year round!

For easiest rolling, roll your dough, including scraps, between two sheets of plastic wrap. That way, you do not need to add flour to keep the dough from sticking to your work surface.

● **4-inch (10 cm) round cutter**
● **2 baking sheets lined with parchment**

### Filling

| | | |
|---|---|---|
| 1½ cups | fresh or frozen cranberries, coarsely chopped (see Tips, left) | 375 mL |
| ½ cup | dried cranberries | 125 mL |
| ½ cup | granulated sugar | 125 mL |
| ¼ tsp | ground cinnamon | 1 mL |
| ⅛ tsp | ground allspice | 0.5 mL |
| 2 tbsp | unsalted butter, melted | 30 mL |
| 2 tbsp | all-purpose flour | 30 mL |
| 1 | recipe Pocket Pie Dough (page 26) | 1 |
| 1 | large egg, lightly beaten with 1 tbsp (15 mL) water | 1 |
| | Confectioners' (icing) sugar for dusting | |

1. *Filling:* In a large bowl, combine fresh and dried cranberries, sugar, cinnamon, allspice and butter. Add flour and toss to coat.

2. Divide dough into halves. On a lightly floured surface, roll out one half to a thickness of slightly more than $1/16$ inch (2 mm). Using cutter, cut into rounds and place on prepared baking sheets, spacing apart. Reroll scraps as necessary.

3. Brush surfaces of rounds with egg wash. Place about $1^1/_2$ tbsp (22 mL) filling in center of each round.

4. On a lightly floured surface, roll out remaining dough to a thickness of slightly more than $1/16$ inch (2 mm). Using cutter, cut out rounds, rerolling scraps as necessary. Place on top of filling, pressing edges together to seal, and crimp with the tines of a fork. Brush tops with egg wash.

5. Place pies, on baking sheets, in freezer for 30 minutes. Meanwhile, position oven racks in upper and lower thirds of oven and preheat oven to 375°F (190°C).

## Tips

A dough scraper is very useful to have when making these recipes. During the rolling process, it collects the little bits for rerolling and it cleans up the pastry board very efficiently. It also simplifies picking up the cut rounds; you just slide the scraper underneath. Even if they are sticking a bit, they will detach without tearing.

Wire baking racks are important to have on hand for the cooling process. After pies have finished baking, either set the muffin tin on the rack or transfer the pies from the baking sheet to the rack. This lets the air circulate around the pies, cooling them evenly.

6. When ready to bake, pierce tops several times with tip of a sharp knife or a toothpick. Bake in preheated oven for 25 to 30 minutes, switching positions of baking sheets halfway through, until tarts are puffed and golden brown and filling is bubbling. Let cool on sheets on wire racks for 10 minutes, then sprinkle with confectioners' sugar. Serve warm or at room temperature.

## Variations

Instead of using confectioners' sugar, top the baked and cooled pies with Vanilla Glaze (page 48) or one of its flavor variations. Cinnamon Glaze works especially well.

*Vegan Alternative:* Substitute Vegan Pie Dough (page 25) for the Pocket Pie Dough and vegan butter for the unsalted butter. Use water to replace the egg wash.

## Make Ahead

The pies can be fully assembled (Steps 1 through 4) and frozen for up to one month. Freeze completely on trays, then transfer to zip-top bags and seal. Bake from frozen, as directed.

# Maple Sweet Potato Pies

Makes 16 pies

● **GF Friendly**

---

*One of my favorite side dishes to make — not just for Thanksgiving but year-round — is a maple orange sweet potato salad. Because the three flavors complement each other so well, I knew they would work beautifully translated into a pie filling. The glaze flavor is up to you, depending on which ingredient you favor. Maple or orange? Try them both if you can't decide!*

## Tips

When shopping for sweet potatoes, choose ones that are uniform in size and firm. I prefer the sweeter red-skinned potatoes to other varieties.

You will need 2 medium to large sweet potatoes to yield the required amount for this recipe.

Before preheating the oven (step 4) position the oven racks in upper and lower thirds of the oven.

The pies can be fully assembled and frozen for up to one month. Freeze for at least 30 minutes on trays, then transfer to zip-top bags and seal. Bake from frozen, as directed.

● Food processor
● 5-inch (12.5 cm) round cutter
● 2 baking sheets lined with parchment

| | | |
|---|---|---|
| 1⅓ cups | mashed sweet potatoes (see Tips, left) | 325 mL |
| 6 tbsp | pure maple syrup | 90 mL |
| ¼ cup | heavy or whipping (35%) cream | 60 mL |
| 1 | large egg | 1 |
| 2 tsp | finely grated orange zest | 10 mL |
| ¼ tsp | ground cinnamon | 1 mL |
| ⅛ tsp | each ground nutmeg and salt | 0.5 mL |
| 1 | recipe Hand Pie Dough (page 27) | 1 |
| 1 | large egg, lightly beaten with 1 tbsp (15 mL) water | 1 |
| 1 | recipe Orange Glaze or Maple Glaze | 1 |

1. In food processor fitted with the metal blade, process sweet potatoes, maple syrup, cream, egg, orange zest, cinnamon, nutmeg and salt until smooth.

2. On a lightly floured surface, roll out dough to a thickness of about $1/16$ inch (2 mm). Cut into rounds and place on prepared baking sheets. Reroll scraps.

3. Brush edges with egg wash. Place 2 tbsp (30 mL) filling in center of each round. Fold in half, enclosing filling. Pinch edges together to seal, and crimp with the tines of a fork. Brush tops with egg wash.

4. Place pies, on baking sheets, in freezer for 30 minutes. Meanwhile, preheat oven to 375°F/190°C; (see Tips).

5. Using tip of a knife, cut 2 or 3 slits in top of each pie. Bake in preheated oven for 25 to 30 minutes, switching positions of baking sheets halfway through, until puffed and golden brown. Let cool on sheets on wire rack for 10 minutes, then drizzle with glaze. Let glaze set at least 10 minutes before serving.

## Variations

Substitute All-Butter Pie Dough, Flaky Pie Dough, Whole Wheat Pie Dough or Cream Cheese Pie Dough for the Hand Pie Dough.

*Gluten-Free Alternative:* Substitute Gluten-Free Pie Dough (page 24) for the Hand Pie Dough.

# Sweet Potato Praline Pies

● **GF Friendly**

*In the South, serving sweet potato pie for Thanksgiving is as traditional as serving turkey. These mini spiced custard versions feature a crunchy hazelnut praline topping and a dash of bourbon. They're guaranteed to turn even the biggest naysayer into a sweet potato fan!*

## Tips

While the shells are in the freezer, place rack in center position and preheat the oven to 350°F (180°C).

It's best not to store sweet potatoes in the refrigerator, which produces a tougher center. Instead, store them in a cool, dry, ventilated container for up to two weeks.

You will need 2 large sweet potatoes to yield the required amount for this recipe.

Once baked, store the pies chilled or at room temperature, tightly covered, for two to three days.

● 4-inch (10 cm) round cutter
● Two 12-cup muffin tins
● Food processor

| | | |
|---|---|---|
| 1 | recipe All-Butter Pie Dough (page 16) | 1 |

**Filling**

| | | |
|---|---|---|
| 1¾ cups | mashed sweet potatoes (see Tips, left) | 425 mL |
| ⅓ cup | packed light brown sugar | 75 mL |
| 1 tbsp | unsalted butter, at room temperature | 15 mL |
| 1 tbsp | bourbon | 15 mL |
| 1 tsp | vanilla extract | 5 mL |
| ½ tsp | ground cinnamon | 2 mL |
| ¼ tsp | each ground nutmeg and salt | 1 mL |
| 2 | large eggs | 2 |
| ½ cup | heavy or whipping (35%) cream | 125 mL |

**Praline**

| | | |
|---|---|---|
| 1⅓ cups | packed light brown sugar | 325 mL |
| 1½ cups | chopped pecans | 375 mL |
| ½ cup | unsalted butter, melted | 125 mL |

1. On a lightly floured surface, roll out dough to a thickness of ⅛ inch (3 mm). Cut into rounds and fit into muffin cups.

2. Place tins in freezer for 30 minutes (see Tips, left).

3. *Filling:* In food processor, process sweet potatoes, sugar, butter, bourbon, vanilla, spices and salt until smooth. Add eggs and cream; process until smooth.

4. *Praline:* In a medium bowl, mix together the brown sugar, pecans and melted butter. Set aside.

5. Divide filling among chilled pie shells and top with praline. Bake in preheated oven for 30 to 35 minutes, until praline is golden brown.

6. Cool in tins on wire racks for 15 minutes, then unmold and cool completely on wire racks.

## Variations

Substitute Flaky Pie Dough (page 15) or Whole Wheat Pie Dough (page 18) for the All-Butter.

*Gluten-Free Variation:* Substitute Gluten-Free Pie Dough (page 24) for the All-Butter Pie Dough.

# Holiday Eggnog Tartlets

- - - - - - - - - - - - - - - - - - - - - - - - - - - - - - - - - - - - -

● **GF Friendly**

*It's hard to attend a holiday
party without being tempted
by a generous cup (or two!)
of extremely rich, filling
eggnog. Change things up a
bit and serve these tiny tarts
instead. Their spiced, rum-
spiked custard filling can
satisfy that eggnog craving
in just a few bites, leaving
you with plenty of room to
sample other treats.*

## Tip

Once they are baked and
cooled, store the tartlets
for up to four days, tightly
covered, in the refrigerator.
Serve chilled or at room
temperature, topped
with lightly sweetened
whipped cream.

● 3$\frac{1}{2}$- to 4-inch (8.75 to 10 cm) round cutter
● Two 12-cup muffin tins, lightly greased

| | | |
|---|---|---|
| 1 | recipe All-Butter Pie Dough (page 16) | 1 |
| **Filling** | | |
| 6 | large egg yolks | 6 |
| $\frac{3}{4}$ cup | granulated sugar | 175 mL |
| 1$\frac{1}{2}$ cups | whole milk | 375 mL |
| $\frac{1}{2}$ cup | heavy or whipping (35%) cream | 125 mL |
| $\frac{3}{4}$ tsp | ground cinnamon | 3 mL |
| $\frac{3}{4}$ tsp | ground nutmeg | 3 mL |
| 3 tbsp | dark rum | 45 mL |
| | Lightly sweetened whipped cream, optional | |

1. On a lightly floured surface, roll out dough to a thickness of $\frac{1}{8}$ inch (3 mm). Using cutter, cut into rounds and carefully fit into muffin cups (there will be some overlap). Reroll scraps as necessary.

2. Place tins in freezer for 30 minutes. Meanwhile, preheat oven to 400°F (200°C).

3. *Filling:* In a large bowl, whisk together yolks and sugar until thick and pale yellow. Add milk, cream, cinnamon, nutmeg and rum, whisking until smooth.

4. Divide filling evenly among chilled crusts, using about 2 tbsp (30 mL) filling per shell.

5. Bake in center of preheated oven for 10 minutes. Lower oven temperature to 350°F (180°C) and bake until centers are set, 10 to 15 minutes longer. Cool completely in tins set on wire racks, then carefully remove tarts from tins and serve.

## Variations

Substitute Flaky Pie Dough (page 15), Toasted Coconut Tartlet Dough (page 22) or Cream Cheese Pie Dough (page 20) for the All-Butter Pie Dough.

*Gluten-Free Alternative:* Substitute Gluten-Free Pie Dough (page 24) for the All-Butter Pie Dough.

# Vegan Pumpkin Spice Pies

● **Vegan Friendly**

*Don't be surprised if even the non-vegans at your holiday table reach for one of these pies. Dense and custardy, this spiced filling tastes best chilled. The rustic vegan pie crust defies any theory that dairy-free desserts are impossible to enjoy.*

## Tips

For best results and the creamiest texture, opt for full-fat unsweetened coconut milk, found in the baking, dairy and/or health foods section of your grocery store.

When making Vegan Pie Dough you will use vegan butter rather than the unsalted butter called for in most recipes. Vegan butter is designed to function in the same way as dairy-based butter, without using any animal products. Although the ingredients can vary depending on the manufacturer, most vegan butters use vegetable oils as their base.

● 3½- to 4-inch (8.75 to 10 cm) round cutter
● Two 12-cup muffin tins

| | | |
|---|---|---|
| 1 | recipe Vegan Pie Dough (page 25) | 1 |

**Filling**

| | | |
|---|---|---|
| 2 cups | pumpkin purée | 500 mL |
| ½ cup | packed light brown sugar | 125 mL |
| ½ cup | unsweetened coconut milk (see Tips, left) | 125 mL |
| ¼ cup | cornstarch | 60 mL |
| ¼ cup | pure maple syrup | 60 mL |
| 2 tsp | ground cinnamon | 10 mL |
| 2 tsp | ground ginger | 10 mL |
| ½ tsp | ground allspice | 2 mL |
| ¼ tsp | ground cloves | 1 mL |
| ¼ tsp | salt | 1 mL |
| 2 tsp | vanilla extract | 10 mL |

1. On a lightly floured surface, roll out dough to a thickness of $\frac{1}{8}$ inch (3 mm). Using cutter, cut into rounds and carefully fit into muffin cups (there will be some overlap). Reroll scraps as necessary.

2. Place tins in freezer for 30 minutes. Meanwhile, preheat oven to 350°F (180°C).

3. *Filling:* In a large bowl, whisk together pumpkin, brown sugar, coconut milk, cornstarch, maple syrup, cinnamon, ginger, allspice, cloves, salt and vanilla.

4. Spoon filling into chilled shells, dividing evenly and filling almost to the top (it won't rise much). Bake in center of preheated oven for 20 to 25 minutes, until filling is set.

5. Cool pies in tins on wire racks for 10 minutes, then unmold and transfer to racks to cool completely. Serve at room temperature or chilled.

## Make Ahead

The pies can be fully baked and stored in the refrigerator, covered, for three to four days.

# Pear Streusel Tarts with Gingerbread Crust

*One of the first things I like to bake as the holiday season approaches is gingerbread. The aroma that fills the house while it is baking really puts me in a festive mood, preparing me for many hours in the kitchen. The crust for these streusel-topped pies is inspired by the flavors of gingerbread — a great match for the simple pear filling.*

## Tip

Select firm pears that hold their shape while baking, such as Bartlett, Bosc or Anjou.

- Food processor
- 4-inch (10 cm) round cutter
- Two 12-cup muffin tins

### Gingerbread Crust

| | | |
|---|---|---|
| 2¼ cups | all-purpose flour | 550 mL |
| ¾ cup | packed light brown sugar | 175 mL |
| 1½ tsp | ground ginger | 7 mL |
| 1½ tsp | ground cinnamon | 7 mL |
| ¼ tsp | ground cloves | 1 mL |
| ½ tsp | salt | 2 mL |
| ⅛ tsp | baking powder | 0.5 mL |
| ¾ cup | cold unsalted butter, cubed | 175 mL |
| 6 tbsp | cold buttermilk | 90 mL |
| 2 tbsp | dark (cooking) molasses | 30 mL |

### Pear Filling

| | | |
|---|---|---|
| 2 tbsp | unsalted butter | 30 mL |
| 4 | pears, peeled and diced | 4 |
| ½ cup | packed light brown sugar | 125 mL |
| 3 tbsp | cornstarch | 45 mL |
| ½ cup | golden raisins | 125 mL |

### Streusel

| | | |
|---|---|---|
| 1 cup | all-purpose flour | 250 mL |
| ¾ cup | packed light brown sugar | 175 mL |
| ½ cup | large-flake (old-fashioned) rolled oats | 125 mL |
| ½ cup | cold unsalted butter, cubed | 125 mL |

1. *Gingerbread Crust:* In food processor fitted with the metal blade, pulse flour, brown sugar, ginger, cinnamon, cloves, salt and baking powder. Scatter butter pieces over flour mixture and pulse several times, until butter is the size of small peas.

2. In a small bowl, whisk together buttermilk and molasses. While pulsing, gradually add to flour mixture, adding just enough so the dough holds together in moist clumps.

## Tip

The recipes in this book were tested with unsalted butter. Its lack of salt (used as a preservative) means a shorter time spent on grocery store shelves, resulting in higher-quality flavor. Using unsalted butter also allows you to control the amount of salt in your recipe. If you feel like splurging, opt for European-style butter, which has higher butterfat content and less moisture. Butter freezes well for up to six months. Do not substitute margarine for butter in these recipes, as it will significantly alter the product.

3. Transfer dough to a piece of plastic wrap and shape into a disk. Wrap tightly and chill until firm, at least 1 hour or up to 3 days.

4. On a lightly floured surface, roll out dough to a thickness of $1/8$ inch (3 mm). Using cutter, cut into rounds and carefully fit into muffin cups (there will be some overlap). Reroll scraps as necessary.

5. Place tins in freezer for 30 minutes. Meanwhile, preheat oven to 350°F (180°C).

6. *Pear Filling:* Meanwhile, in a medium skillet set over medium heat, melt butter. Add pears and cook, stirring gently, until softened, 3 to 4 minutes. Transfer to a medium bowl and toss with brown sugar and cornstarch. Stir in raisins. Set aside to cool completely.

7. *Streusel:* In a medium bowl, mix together flour, brown sugar and oats. Rub in the cold butter with your fingers until clumps form.

8. Place about 2 tbsp (30 mL) filling in each pie shell and top with about $1^1/_2$ tbsp (22 mL) streusel. Bake in center of preheated oven for 25 to 30 minutes, until streusel is browned and filling is bubbling. Cool in pans on wire racks for 15 minutes, then unmold and transfer to racks to cool completely.

## Make Ahead

The pies can be fully baked and stored, chilled or at room temperature, tightly covered, for three to four days.

# Pumpkin Pies with Spiced Walnut Streusel

*I prepare a large version of this pie every year that I host Thanksgiving or Christmas dinner. The streusel and filling are both heavy on the ginger, but it is balanced out by the creamy custard filling and a dollop of whipped cream on top. The flavors of the filling improve over time, so leftovers are encouraged!*

## Tips

The addition of salt enhances flavor in recipes. These recipes were all tested using natural fine kosher salt, but regular table salt can be substituted.

For easiest rolling, roll your dough, including scraps, between two sheets of plastic wrap. That way, you do not need to add flour to keep the dough from sticking to your work surface.

● 4-inch (10 cm) round cutter
● Two 12-cup muffin tins

| | | |
|---|---|---|
| 1 | recipe All-Butter Pie Dough (page 16) | 1 |
| **Filling** | | |
| 2 cups | canned pumpkin purée | 500 mL |
| 2 | large eggs | 2 |
| ²⁄₃ cup | packed light brown sugar | 150 mL |
| ¹⁄₂ cup | heavy or whipping (35%) cream | 125 mL |
| 1 tsp | ground cinnamon | 5 mL |
| 1 tsp | ground ginger | 5 ml |
| ¹⁄₂ tsp | allspice | 2 mL |
| ¹⁄₄ tsp | ground cloves | 1 mL |
| ¹⁄₄ tsp | salt | 1 mL |
| **Walnut Streusel** | | |
| 1¹⁄₂ cups | all-purpose flour | 375 mL |
| ³⁄₄ cup | packed light brown sugar | 175 mL |
| ³⁄₄ cup | chopped walnuts | 175 mL |
| 2 tsp | ground ginger | 10 mL |
| ³⁄₄ tsp | ground cinnamon | 3 mL |
| ¹⁄₈ tsp | salt | 0.5 mL |
| 6 oz | unsalted butter (12 tbsp/180 mL), at room temperature, cubed | 175 g |

1. On a lightly floured surface, roll out dough to a thickness of ¹⁄₈ inch (3 mm). Using cutter, cut into rounds and carefully fit into muffin cups (there will be some overlap). Reroll scraps as necessary.

2. Place tins in freezer for 30 minutes. Meanwhile, preheat oven to 375°F (190°C).

3. *Filling:* In a large bowl, whisk together pumpkin, eggs, brown sugar, cream, cinnamon, ginger, allspice, cloves and salt. Set aside.

4. *Walnut Streusel:* In a medium bowl, mix together flour, brown sugar, ginger, cinnamon and salt. Using your fingertips, rub in butter until small clumps form.

## Tips

Wire baking racks are important to have on hand for the cooling process. After pies have finished baking, either set the muffin tin on the rack or transfer the pies from the baking sheet to the rack. This lets the air circulate around the pies, cooling them evenly.

The baked pies can be fully cooled and stored at room temperature or in the refrigerator, covered, for three to four days.

5. Place about 2 tbsp (30 mL) filling in each pie shell. Top each pie with about $1^1/_2$ tbsp (22 mL) streusel.

6. Bake in center of preheated oven for 10 minutes. Lower temperature to 350°F (180°C) and bake for 15 to 20 minutes longer, until tops are puffed and streusel is golden brown.

7. Let pies cool in tins on wire racks for 15 minutes, then carefully unmold and transfer to racks to cool completely.

## Variations

Substitute Flaky Pie Dough (page 15), Cream Cheese Pie Dough (page 20) or Whole Wheat Pie Dough (page 18) for the All-Butter Pie Dough.

# Pumpkin Pecan Pies with Brown Butter Glaze

● **GF Friendly**

*These pies are brilliant! They solve the inevitable holiday dinner dilemma — you are quite full from dinner and have room for only one dessert. Which pie will it be, pumpkin or pecan? Combining both pies into one, glazed with an addictive brown butter icing, solves your problem.*

## Tips

For easiest rolling, roll your dough, including scraps, between two sheets of plastic wrap. That way, you do not need to add flour to keep the dough from sticking to your work surface.

A dough scraper is very useful to have when making these recipes. During the rolling process, it collects the little bits for rerolling and it cleans up the pastry board very efficiently. It also simplifies picking up the cut rounds; you just slide the scraper underneath. Even if they are sticking a bit, they will detach without tearing.

● **4-inch (10 cm) round cutter**
● **Two 12-cup muffin tins, lightly greased**

| | | |
|---|---|---|
| 1 | recipe All-Butter Pie Dough (page 16) | 1 |
| **Filling** | | |
| 1¼ cups | pumpkin purée | 300 mL |
| 1 cup | packed light brown sugar, divided | 250 mL |
| 4 | large eggs, divided | 4 |
| ¼ cup | heavy or whipping (35%) cream | 60 mL |
| ½ tsp | ground cinnamon | 2 mL |
| ½ tsp | ground ginger | 2 mL |
| ⅛ tsp | ground cloves | 0.5 mL |
| ¼ tsp | salt, divided | 1 mL |
| ½ cup | light corn syrup | 125 mL |
| 2 tbsp | butter, melted | 30 mL |
| 1 tsp | vanilla extract | 5 mL |
| 1¼ cups | chopped pecans | 300 mL |
| 1 | recipe Brown Butter Icing (page 50), warmed | 1 |

1. On a lightly floured surface, roll out dough to a thickness of ⅛ inch (3 mm). Using cutter, cut into rounds and carefully fit into muffin cups (there will be some overlap). Reroll scraps as necessary.

2. Place tins in freezer for 30 minutes. Meanwhile, preheat oven to 400°F (200°C).

3. *Filling:* In a large bowl, combine pumpkin, ½ cup (125 mL) brown sugar, 2 eggs, cream, cinnamon, ginger, cloves and ⅛ tsp (0.5 mL) salt.

4. In a separate large bowl, combine remaining brown sugar, eggs and salt with corn syrup, butter, vanilla and pecans.

5. Divide pumpkin mixture evenly among chilled tart shells. Top with pecan mixture.

## Tip

Brown butter, or *beurre noisette*, is made when butter is melted over low heat and allowed to separate into butterfat and milk solids. The milk solids naturally sink to the bottom of the pan and begin to brown, turning fragrant and nutty.

6. Bake in center of preheated oven for 10 minutes. Lower oven temperature to 350°F (180°C) and bake for 20 to 25 minutes longer, until tarts are puffed and set. Cool for 10 minutes in pans on wire racks, then carefully unmold and transfer to racks to cool completely.

7. Drizzle cooled tarts with warm Brown Butter Icing. Set aside to set for at least 10 minutes before serving.

## Variations

Substitute Flaky Pie Dough (page 15) or Cream Cheese Pie Dough (page 20) for the All-Butter Pie Dough.

*Gluten-Free Alternative:* Substitute Gluten-Free Pie Dough (page 24) for the All-Butter Pie Dough.

## Make Ahead

The pies can be baked (but not glazed) three days in advance and stored, covered, at room temperature.

# Chocolate Pumpkin Tartlets

*One year for Halloween I decided to try a chocolate and pumpkin swirled brownie recipe that I had seen in a magazine. I was a bit unsure about the chocolate and pumpkin combination, but I figured that I loved each flavor separately, so I would probably enjoy them together. I was right.*

## Tip

For best results, prepare these tarts one day in advance and refrigerate overnight so the flavors have a chance to develop. Serve chilled or at room temperature, garnished with lightly sweetened whipped cream.

- 3¹⁄₂- to 4-inch (8.75 to 10 cm) round cutter
- Two 12-cup muffin tins, lightly greased

| 1 | recipe Dark Chocolate Pie Dough (page 21) | 1 |
|---|---|---|
| **Filling** | | |
| ¾ cup | packed light brown sugar | 175 mL |
| 3 tbsp | unsweetened cocoa powder | 45 mL |
| 1 tsp | ground ginger | 5 mL |
| ¾ tsp | ground cinnamon | 3 mL |
| ¼ tsp | ground nutmeg | 1 mL |
| ⅛ tsp | ground cloves | 0.5 mL |
| ⅛ tsp | salt | 0.5 mL |
| 1¹⁄₂ cups | pumpkin purée | 375 mL |
| 3 | large eggs | 3 |
| ¹⁄₂ cup | heavy or whipping (35%) cream | 125 mL |
| 4 oz | semisweet chocolate, melted | 125 g |
| 1 tsp | vanilla extract | 5 mL |

1. On a lightly floured surface, roll out dough to a thickness of ¹⁄₈ inch (3 mm). Using cutter, cut into rounds and carefully fit into muffin cups (there will be some overlap). Reroll scraps as necessary.

2. Place tins in freezer for 30 minutes. Meanwhile, preheat oven to 400°F (200°C).

3. *Filling:* In a large bowl, whisk together brown sugar, cocoa, ginger, cinnamon, nutmeg, cloves and salt. Add pumpkin purée and stir to combine. Add eggs, cream, melted chocolate and vanilla; whisk to blend.

4. Spoon filling into chilled shells, dividing evenly and filling to about three-quarters full.

5. Bake in center of preheated oven for 10 minutes. Lower oven temperature to 350°F (180°C) and bake for 15 to 20 minutes longer, until tops are puffed but centers still jiggle slightly. Cool completely in pans on wire racks. Carefully unmold and transfer to a serving plate or, if you prefer to serve the pies chilled (see Tip, left), cover and refrigerate for up to 2 days.

## Make Ahead

The tarts can be fully baked and then refrigerated, covered, for two days.

# Texas Bourbon Pecan Pies

● **GF Friendly**

*Texans are known to be proud of their state, so it should come as no surprise that a pie featuring pecans, the official state nut, is on the table at holiday celebrations. While these tarts are small in size, their flavor, enhanced with a splash of bourbon, is as big as the Lone Star State itself.*

## Tips

Shelled pecans, sealed in a container, can be stored in the refrigerator for up to nine months and in the freezer for up to two years. Dry storage should not exceed two months.

The easiest way to remove tarts from muffin tins is to run a small, sharp knife or small offset spatula around the edges, loosening the sides. You should then be able to carefully lift out the tarts, guiding them with the knife or spatula.

The baked pies can be stored, covered, at room temperature for four to five days.

● 3$\frac{1}{2}$- to 4-inch (8.75 to 10 cm) round cutter
● Two 12-cup muffin tins

| 1 | recipe All-Butter Pie Dough (page 16) | 1 |
|---|---|---|
| **Filling** | | |
| 3 tbsp | unsalted butter, melted | 45 mL |
| $\frac{1}{4}$ cup | granulated sugar | 60 mL |
| $\frac{1}{4}$ cup | packed light brown sugar | 60 mL |
| $\frac{1}{2}$ cup | dark corn syrup | 125 mL |
| $\frac{1}{4}$ tsp | salt | 1 mL |
| 2 | large eggs | 2 |
| 1 to 2 tbsp | bourbon | 15 to 30 mL |
| 1 tsp | orange zest | 5 mL |
| 1 tsp | vanilla extract | 5 mL |
| 1 cup | chopped pecans | 250 mL |

1. On a lightly floured surface, roll out dough to a thickness of $\frac{1}{8}$ inch (3 mm). Using cutter, cut into rounds and carefully fit into muffin cups (there will be some overlap). Reroll scraps as necessary.

2. Place tins in freezer for 30 minutes. Meanwhile, preheat oven to 350°F (180°C).

3. *Filling:* In a medium saucepan over medium-high heat, bring butter, granulated and brown sugars, corn syrup and salt to a boil, stirring constantly. Boil for 1 minute, then remove from heat and set aside to cool for 10 minutes. Once cool, whisk in eggs, bourbon, orange zest, vanilla and pecans.

4. Spoon filling into chilled shells, until they are about three-quarters full. Bake in center of preheated oven until filling is set, 20 to 25 minutes.

5. Cool pies completely in tins on wire racks, about 15 minutes, then carefully unmold. Serve slightly warm or at room temperature.

## Variations

Substitute Flaky Pie Dough (page 15) or Cream Cheese Pie Dough (page 20) for the All-Butter Pie Dough.

*Gluten-Free Alternative:* Substitute Gluten-Free Pie Dough (page 24) for the All-Butter Pie Dough.

# Dried Fruit Mincemeat Hand Pies

---

## Makes 16 pies

• **Vegan Friendly**

*The original version of mincemeat pie, which dates back to the 16th century, did indeed contain mutton or beef. Although some modern recipes for mincemeat still include beef suet in the ingredients, most are simply a meatless combination of dried fruit, spices and brandy, making mincemeat similar to fruitcake ingredients.*

## Tips

For the most flavorful results, start this recipe several days in advance and let the mincemeat macerate in the refrigerator.

A zester, rasp grater or Microplane (a well-known make) is the easiest way to grate orange zest. With its sharp teeth it successfully removes the flavorful zest from fruit while leaving the bitter white pith behind. You can also use this tool to grate whole nutmeg.

- 5-inch (12.5 cm) round cutter
- 2 baking sheets lined with parchment

### Mincemeat

| | | |
|---|---|---|
| 1 | Granny Smith apple, chopped | 1 |
| ¼ cup | dark raisins | 60 mL |
| ¼ cup | golden raisins | 60 mL |
| ¼ cup | dried cranberries | 60 mL |
| ¼ cup | packed light brown sugar | 60 mL |
| ¼ cup | unsalted butter, melted | 60 mL |
| ¼ cup | brandy | 60 mL |
| 1 | orange, zested and juiced | 1 |
| ½ tsp | ground cinnamon | 2 mL |
| ¼ tsp | ground allspice | 1 mL |
| ¼ tsp | ground nutmeg | 1 mL |
| ⅛ tsp | ground cloves | 0.5 mL |
| ⅛ tsp | salt | 0.5 mL |
| 3 tbsp | all-purpose flour | 45 mL |
| | | |
| 1 | recipe Hand Pie Dough (page 27) | 1 |
| 1 | large egg, lightly beaten with 1 tbsp (15 mL) water | 1 |
| | Confectioners' (icing) sugar for dusting | |

1. *Mincemeat:* In a medium bowl, mix together apple, dark and golden raisins, cranberries, brown sugar, butter, brandy, orange zest and juice, cinnamon, allspice, nutmeg, cloves and salt.

2. Transfer mixture to a container, cover tightly, and refrigerate for at least 1 day or up to 5 days. Once mincemeat is chilled, add flour and toss well.

3. On a lightly floured surface, roll out dough to a thickness of about $1/16$ inch (2 mm). Using cutter, cut into rounds and place on prepared baking sheets, spacing apart. Reroll scraps as necessary.

## Tips

For step-by-step photographs of making hand pies, see page 35.

Wire baking racks are important to have on hand for the cooling process. After pies have finished baking, either set the muffin tin on the rack or transfer the pies from the baking sheet to the rack. This lets the air circulate around the pies, cooling them evenly.

**4.** Brush edges with egg wash. Place about 2 tbsp (30 mL) mincemeat in center of each round. Fold in half, enclosing filling. Pinch edges together to seal, and crimp with the tines of a fork. Brush tops with egg wash.

**5.** Place pies, on baking sheets, in freezer for 30 minutes. Meanwhile, position oven racks in upper and lower thirds of oven and preheat oven to 375°F (190°C).

**6.** Using tip of a knife, cut 2 or 3 slits in top of each pie. Bake in preheated oven for 20 to 25 minutes, switching positions of baking sheets halfway through, until puffed and browned. Cool on sheets on wire racks for 15 minutes, then dust with confectioners' sugar. Serve warm or at room temperature.

## Variations

Substitute Flaky Pie Dough (page 15), Cream Cheese Pie Dough (page 20) or All-Butter Pie Dough (page 16) for the Hand Pie Dough.

*Vegan Alternative:* Substitute Vegan Pie Dough (page 25) for the Hand Pie Dough and vegan butter for the unsalted butter. Use water instead of the egg wash.

## Make Ahead

The pies can be fully assembled (Steps 1 through 4) and frozen for up to one month. Freeze for at least 30 minutes on trays, then transfer to zip-top bags and seal. Bake from frozen, as directed.

# Raspberry Linzer Tartlets with Spiced Almond Crust

**Makes 16 tartlets**

*Linzer sandwich cookies are one of my favorite things to make for holiday cookie swaps and homemade gifts. Their flavor complexity comes not from the simple jam center but from the spiced ground almond crust. Cutting a small hole or shape in the top crust gives you a glimpse of the colorful fruit filling inside, a tart contrast to the cookie-like shell.*

## Tip

For easiest rolling, roll your dough, including scraps, between two sheets of plastic wrap. That way, you do not need to add flour to keep the dough from sticking to your work surface.

- Food processor
- Electric mixer
- 3- and 4-inch (7.5 and 10 cm) round cutters
- Two 12-cup muffin tins
- Pie weights or dried beans (see Tips, page 231)
- Parchment paper

### Linzer Crust

| | | |
|---|---|---|
| 1½ cups | lightly toasted sliced almonds | 375 mL |
| 1½ cups | all-purpose flour | 375 mL |
| ¾ tsp | ground cinnamon | 3 mL |
| ¼ tsp | ground allspice | 1 mL |
| ⅛ tsp | ground cloves | 0.5 mL |
| 2 tsp | finely grated orange zest | 10 mL |
| 6 oz | unsalted butter, softened | 175 g |
| ¼ cup | granulated sugar | 60 mL |
| 2 | large egg yolks | 2 |
| 2 tsp | vanilla extract | 10 mL |
| 1½ cups | raspberry jam | 375 mL |
| 1 tsp | freshly squeezed lemon juice | 5 mL |
| 1 | large egg, lightly beaten with 1 tbsp (15 mL) water | 1 |
| | Confectioners' (icing) sugar for dusting | |

1. *Linzer Crust:* In food processor fitted with the metal blade, process almonds until finely ground. Add flour, cinnamon, allspice, cloves and orange zest; pulse to combine.

2. In a bowl, using electric mixer, beat butter and sugar at medium-high speed until light and fluffy, about 2 minutes. Beat in egg yolks and vanilla. Add almond mixture, beating until combined.

3. Transfer dough to a large piece of plastic wrap and divide into two pieces, one slightly larger than the other. Shape into disks and wrap tightly in plastic. Chill until firm, at least 2 hours or up to 3 days.

## Tips

Pie weights are small, heavy objects that are used to weigh down a crust when it is being blind-baked, so that it doesn't pull away from the sides of the pan. Ceramic balls are the most popular variety, although stainless steel balls are common as well. Look for them in kitchen supply aisles or specialty kitchen stores.

For step-by-step photographs of the blind-baking process, see page 33.

4. On a generously floured surface, roll out larger piece of dough to a thickness of $\frac{1}{8}$ inch (3 mm). Using 4-inch (10 cm) cutter, cut into 16 rounds and carefully fit into muffin cups. Reroll scraps as necessary.

5. Place tins in freezer for 30 minutes. Meanwhile, preheat oven to 350°F (180°C).

6. Blind-bake shells (page 14 and Tips, left) in center of preheated oven for 12 minutes. Carefully remove weights and parchment. Return to oven and bake for 5 minutes longer, until browned. Cool completely in pans on wire racks.

7. In a bowl, mix raspberry jam and lemon juice. Divide evenly among cooled crusts.

8. On a lightly floured surface, roll out smaller piece of dough to slightly thicker than $\frac{1}{16}$ inch (2 mm). Using 3-inch (7.5 cm) cutter, cut 16 rounds, rerolling scraps as necessary. Cut a small shape (e.g., circle, heart) out of the center of each round.

9. Brush bottoms of top crusts with egg wash and carefully place over bottom crusts, pressing edges together to seal tightly. Brush tops with egg wash.

10. Place tins in freezer for 30 minutes. Maintain oven temperature at 350°F (180°C).

11. Bake in center of preheated oven for 15 to 20 minutes, until tops are golden brown. Cool completely in tins on wire racks, then carefully unmold and dust with confectioners' sugar.

## Make Ahead

Once the tarts are baked they can be stored at room temperature, covered and separated by layers by waxed paper, for three days.

# Hanukkah Rugelach Hand Pies

**Makes 16 pies**

*Rugelach, meaning "little twists," are traditional Jewish cookies made in the form of a crescent, similar to a croissant. Tangy cream cheese dough is rolled around a sweet filling that can include jam, dried fruit, nuts, cinnamon or chocolate. This recipe provides a twist on these twisted treats, enclosing the filling in a half-moon cream cheese crust sprinkled with cinnamon sugar.*

## Tip

If your raisins have been in storage for a while and are no longer plump, you can bring them back to life! Combine with ½ cup (125 mL) water or orange juice in a small saucepan and bring to a simmer. Remove from heat and set aside to soak for at least 30 minutes. Drain, discarding liquid, and proceed with the recipe.

The pies can be fully assembled and frozen for up to one month. Freeze for at least 30 minutes on trays, then transfer to zip-top bags and seal. Bake from frozen, as directed.

- Food processor
- 5-inch (12.5 cm) round cutter
- 2 baking sheets lined with parchment

### Filling

| | | |
|---|---|---|
| ½ cup | chopped walnuts or pecans | 125 mL |
| ½ cup | plump golden raisins (see Tips, left) | 125 mL |
| 2 tbsp | packed golden brown sugar | 30 mL |
| ½ cup | mini semisweet chocolate chips | 125 mL |

### Cinnamon Sugar

| | | |
|---|---|---|
| ½ cup | granulated sugar | 125 mL |
| ½ tsp | ground cinnamon | 2 mL |
| 1 | recipe Cream Cheese Pie Dough (page 20) | 1 |
| 1 | large egg, lightly beaten with 1 tbsp (15 mL) water | 1 |
| ⅔ cup | apricot or raspberry jam | 150 mL |

1. *Filling:* In food processor fitted with the metal blade, pulse walnuts, raisins and brown sugar 5 or 6 times, until coarsely chopped. Transfer to a medium bowl and stir in chocolate chips.

2. *Cinnamon Sugar:* In a small bowl, combine sugar and cinnamon. Set aside.

3. On a lightly floured surface, roll out dough to slightly thicker than $\frac{1}{16}$ inch (2 mm). Using cutter, cut into rounds and place on prepared baking sheets, spacing apart. Reroll scraps as necessary.

4. Brush edges of rounds with egg wash. Spread 2 tsp (10 mL) jam in center of each round and top with about $1\frac{1}{2}$ tbsp (22 mL) nut filling. Fold in half, enclosing filling. Pinch edges together to seal, and crimp with the tines of a fork. Brush tops with egg wash and sprinkle with cinnamon sugar.

5. Place pies, on baking sheets, in freezer for 30 minutes. Meanwhile, position oven racks in upper and lower thirds of oven and preheat oven to 375°F (190°C).

6. Using tip of a knife, cut 2 or 3 slits in top of each pie. Bake in preheated oven for 25 to 30 minutes, switching positions of baking sheets halfway through, until pies are puffed and golden brown. Serve warm or at room temperature.

# Lemon Coconut Macaroon Pies

• **GF Friendly**

*With their toasted coconut and almond flour shells and simple lemon curd filling, these beautiful, bright pies would be a welcome addition to Passover dinner or any other springtime celebration. The shells require a bit of extra patience to shape, but the results are well worth the effort.*

## Tip

Almond flour, or almond meal, is made from ground blanched almonds. Look for it in the natural foods section of your grocery store or make your own version by grinding almonds finely in a food processor. Once opened, bags of almond flour should be stored in a sealed container in the refrigerator or freezer.

● Preheat oven to 350°F (180°C)
● Two 12-cup muffin tins, greased
● Shot glass, optional

| | | |
|---|---|---|
| 6 cups | sweetened shredded coconut | 1.5 L |
| 6 | large egg whites | 6 |
| 1½ cups | granulated sugar | 375 mL |
| ¾ cup | almond flour (see Tip, left) | 175 mL |
| 1 tsp | vanilla extract | 5 mL |
| 2 cups | Lemon Curd (page 47) | 500 mL |
| | Lightly sweetened whipped cream | |

1. In large bowl, mix together coconut, egg whites, sugar, almond flour and vanilla (mixture should hold together when squeezed).

2. Dividing evenly, press mixture into bottom and sides of muffin cups to form a crust ¼ inch (0.5 cm) thick. Use a shot glass that has been run under water or moistened fingers to help form the crust without sticking.

3. Bake in center of preheated oven for 20 to 25 minutes, until edges are deep golden brown and bottoms have just started to brown. If crusts start to loose shape during baking, quickly reshape by using the glass, the back of a spoon or your fingers (be careful not to burn them!).

4. Cool shells completely in tins on wire racks, then carefully unmold and transfer to serving plate.

5. Fill with lemon curd and top with a dollop of whipped cream. Serve immediately.

## Make Ahead

Once baked, the unfilled tart shells can be stored in an airtight container for two days. In a humid environment, the shells should be used soon after baking.

# Derby Day Pies

*This elevated version of classic Southern pecan pie is served to celebrate the annual Kentucky Derby horse race at Churchill Downs. Adding walnuts instead of pecans, a generous amount of chocolate chips and the mandatory bourbon makes these buttery tartlets worthy of their own championship trophy.*

## Tips

Once the tarts are baked, they can be stored at room temperature or chilled, tightly covered, for four to five days.

The fully baked pies can also be cooled and frozen in sealed zip-top bags for up to two weeks. Thaw at room temperature.

● 4-inch (10 cm) round cutter
● Two 12-cup muffin tins

| | | |
|---|---|---|
| 1 | recipe All-Butter Pie Dough (page 16) | 1 |
| **Filling** | | |
| ¼ cup | all-purpose flour | 60 mL |
| ½ cup | packed light brown sugar | 125 mL |
| ½ cup | granulated sugar | 125 mL |
| ¼ tsp | salt | 1 mL |
| ½ cup | unsalted butter, melted | 125 mL |
| ½ cup | corn syrup | 125 mL |
| 3 | large eggs | 3 |
| 3 tbsp | bourbon | 45 mL |
| 1 cup | semisweet chocolate chips | 250 mL |
| 1 cup | chopped walnuts | 250 mL |
| 2 tsp | vanilla extract | 10 mL |

1. On a lightly floured work surface, roll out dough to a thickness of ⅛ inch (3 mm). Using cutter, cut into rounds and fit into muffin cups. Reroll scraps as necessary.

2. Place tins in freezer for 30 minutes. Meanwhile, preheat oven to 350°F (180°C).

3. *Filling:* In a large bowl, whisk together flour, brown and granulated sugars and salt. Add melted butter, corn syrup and eggs, whisking to combine. Stir in bourbon, chocolate chips, walnuts and vanilla.

4. Spoon 2 to 3 tbsp (30 to 45 mL) filling into each chilled shell. Bake in center of preheated oven for 20 to 25 minutes, until filling sets.

5. Cool in tins on wire racks for 15 minutes, then unmold and transfer to racks to cool completely. Serve at room temperature or chilled.

## Variations

Substitute Flaky Pie Dough (page 15), Cream Cheese Pie Dough (page 20), Dark Chocolate Pie Dough (page 21) or Whole Wheat Pie Dough (page 18) for the All-Butter Pie Dough.

# Meat and Seafood Pies

# Pesto Chicken Hand Pies

**Makes 12 pies**

● **GF Friendly**

*I have been making pesto chicken salad for years. It is one of my husband's favorite recipes, and it tastes fantastic as a sandwich between slices of toasted whole-grain bread. I knew it would be just as delicious as a handheld pie!*

## Tips

Add a halved sweet grape tomato or a few small slices of plum (Roma) tomato on top of the pesto chicken before sealing, for another layer of flavor and color.

To toast pine nuts, spread them in a single layer in a dry skillet over medium-low heat. Cook until browned, watching closely to prevent burning and shaking the skillet frequently to ensure even browning. Remove from heat and immediately transfer nuts to a plate to cool.

● Food processor
● 6-inch (15 cm) round cutter
● 2 baking sheets lined with parchment

### Filling

| | | |
|---|---|---:|
| 1 cup | packed fresh basil leaves | 250 mL |
| 1 cup | packed arugula | 250 mL |
| 5 | cloves garlic | 5 |
| ¾ cup | olive oil | 175 mL |
| ¼ cup | lightly toasted pine nuts (see Tips, left) | 60 mL |
| 1½ cups | freshly grated Parmesan cheese, divided | 375 mL |
| 2 tsp | freshly squeezed lemon juice | 10 mL |
| ¼ tsp | hot pepper flakes | 1 mL |
| 1 tsp | salt | 5 mL |
| 1 tsp | freshly ground black pepper | 5 mL |
| 3 cups | shredded roasted chicken breast | 750 mL |
| | | |
| 1 | recipe Flaky Pie Dough (page 15) | 1 |
| 1 | large egg, lightly beaten with 1 tbsp (15 mL) water | 1 |

1. *Filling:* In food processor fitted with the metal blade, pulse basil, arugula and garlic until finely chopped. With motor running, pour olive oil down feed tube in a steady stream. Add pine nuts, 1 cup (250 mL) Parmesan, lemon juice, hot pepper flakes, salt and pepper. Purée until smooth, stopping to scrape down sides of bowl as necessary.

2. In a large bowl, toss chicken with basil mixture until thoroughly coated.

3. On a lightly floured surface, roll out dough to slightly thicker than $1/16$ inch (2 mm). Using cutter, cut into rounds and place on prepared baking sheets, spacing apart. Reroll scraps as necessary.

4. Brush edges of rounds with egg wash. Place about $1/4$ cup (60 mL) filling in center of each. Sprinkle each mound with 2 tsp (10 mL) Parmesan. Fold rounds in half, enclosing filling. Pinch together edges to seal, and crimp with the tines of a fork. Brush tops with egg wash.

## Tips

When cutting large rounds, you can use the flat section of a two-piece tart pan as a template and the outer section as a cutter, being careful for sharp edges. If you don't have an appropriately-sized tart tin, a pot lid also makes a good guide.

For step-by-step photographs of making hand pies, see page 35.

5. Place pies, on baking sheets, in freezer for 30 minutes. Meanwhile, position oven racks in upper and lower thirds of oven and preheat oven to 375°F (190°C).

6. Using tip of a knife, cut 2 or 3 slits in top of each pie. Bake in preheated oven for 25 to 30 minutes, switching positions of baking sheets halfway through, until puffed and golden brown. Let cool on sheets on wire racks for 10 minutes before serving.

## Variations

Substitute Parmesan Pie Dough (see Variations, page 23) for the Flaky Pie Dough.

*Gluten-Free Alternative:* Substitute Gluten-Free Pie Dough (page 24) for the Flaky Pie Dough.

## Make Ahead

The pies can be assembled (Steps 1 through 4) and then frozen for up to one month. Freeze pies for at least 30 minutes on baking trays, then seal in zip-top bags. Bake from frozen, as directed.

# Chicken, Brie and Apple Turnovers

---

*I love coming up with new ways to cook and present chicken. This recipe, an autumn-inspired combination of chicken, apples, fresh sage and Brie wrapped in buttery puff pastry, is perfect for a brunch or a luncheon, served with a simple green salad.*

---

## Tips

The white rind of Brie is edible and is usually eaten along with the soft interior. If you don't wish to include the rind, you may trim and discard it before layering the cheese on the chicken filling.

For step-by-step photographs of making Shortcut Puff Pastry, see page 42.

- 2 baking sheets lined with parchment
- Pizza/pastry cutter, optional

**Filling**

| | | |
|---|---|---|
| 2 tbsp | unsalted butter | 30 mL |
| 1 | large shallot, minced | 1 |
| 1 | tart apple, peeled and chopped | 1 |
| 1 tbsp | chopped fresh sage | 15 mL |
| 1/8 tsp | ground nutmeg | 0.5 mL |
| | Salt and freshly ground black pepper | |
| 1 tbsp | all-purpose flour | 15 mL |
| 3/4 cup | apple cider | 175 mL |
| 1 tbsp | brandy, optional | 15 mL |
| 2 cups | shredded roasted chicken breast | 500 mL |
| 1/2 | recipe Shortcut Puff Pastry (page 29; see Tips, left) | 1/2 |
| 1 | large egg, lightly beaten with 1 tbsp (15 mL) water | 1 |
| 8 oz | soft Brie, sliced | 250 g |

1. *Filling:* In a large skillet, melt butter over medium-high heat. Add shallot and apple; sauté until softened, 4 to 5 minutes. Stir in sage and nutmeg; season to taste with salt and pepper.

2. Sprinkle flour over mixture, stirring to coat. Add cider, reduce heat and simmer until thickened. Stir in brandy, if using. Stir in chicken and simmer for 2 minutes. Remove from heat and set aside to cool completely.

3. Divide puff pastry in half. On a lightly floured surface, roll one half into a 15- by 10-inch (37.5 by 25 cm) rectangle. Using pizza cutter or a sharp knife, cut rectangle into six 5-inch (12.5 cm) squares. Repeat with remaining dough.

4. Brush edges of squares with egg wash. Place about 1/4 cup (60 mL) chicken mixture in center of each square. Top with 1 slice Brie. Fold squares in half diagonally, enclosing filling. Pinch together edges to seal, and crimp with the tines of a fork. Brush tops with egg wash.

## Tip

Wire baking racks are important to have on hand for the cooling process. After pies have finished baking, either set the muffin tin on the rack or transfer the pies from the baking sheet to the rack. This lets the air circulate around the pies, cooling them evenly.

5. Place pies, on baking sheets, in freezer for 30 minutes, until firm. Meanwhile, position oven racks in upper and lower thirds of oven and preheat oven to 375°F (190°C).

6. Bake in preheated oven for 25 to 30 minutes, switching positions of baking sheets halfway through, until puffed and deep golden brown. Let pies cool on sheets on wire racks for 5 minutes before serving.

## Variation

Substitute 1 lb (500 g) store-bought puff pastry, thawed, for $1/2$ recipe Shortcut Puff Pastry.

## Make Ahead

The turnovers can be assembled (Steps 1 through 4) and frozen for up to one month. Freeze pies for at least 30 minutes on baking trays, then seal in zip-top bags. Bake from frozen, as directed.

# Thai Chicken Pies with Spicy Peanut Sauce

• **GF Friendly**

*When I was in graduate school at Duke University, I used to go to a casual restaurant called Foster's Market at least three times a week, either for a quick breakfast or for one of their amazing sandwiches. Their Thai chicken wrap, served with spicy peanut sauce, was my very favorite sandwich and the inspiration for these crispy phyllo pies.*

## Tip

Look for phyllo dough that comes in one box containing two packs of smaller sheets (14 by 9 inches/23 by 35 cm) as opposed to one pack of larger sheets. You can work with rectangles that approximate this size, but if the configuration of your phyllo sheets is dramatically different, roll them out or trim to something that roughly conforms.

• Preheat oven to 375°F (190°C), placing racks in upper and lower thirds of oven
• 2 baking sheets lined with parchment
• Damp tea towel

### Filling

| | | |
|---|---|---|
| 1 tbsp | cornstarch | 15 mL |
| ¼ cup | low-sodium soy sauce | 60 mL |
| ¼ cup | rice wine vinegar | 60 mL |
| 3 tbsp | packed light brown sugar | 45 mL |
| 3 tbsp | freshly squeezed lime juice | 45 mL |
| 1 tbsp | dark sesame oil | 15 mL |
| 1 tbsp | fish sauce, optional | 15 mL |
| ⅛ tsp | hot pepper flakes | 0.5 mL |
| 1 tbsp | olive oil | 15 mL |
| ½ | yellow onion, chopped | ½ |
| ½ cup | chopped carrot | 125 mL |
| 2 tsp | chopped garlic | 10 mL |
| 1 tbsp | minced gingerroot | 15 mL |
| 1 cup | button or baby portobello mushrooms, chopped | 250 mL |
| 1 lb | lean ground chicken | 500 g |

### Peanut Sauce

| | | |
|---|---|---|
| ½ cup | creamy peanut butter | 125 mL |
| 2 tbsp | low-sodium soy sauce | 30 mL |
| 2 tbsp | rice wine vinegar | 30 mL |
| 2 tbsp | packed light brown sugar | 30 mL |
| 2 tbsp | freshly squeezed lime juice | 30 mL |
| 1 tbsp | dark sesame oil | 15 mL |
| ¼ tsp | hot pepper flakes | 1 mL |
| 24 | sheets phyllo dough, thawed (see Tips, left) | 24 |
| 1 cup | unsalted butter, melted | 250 mL |

1. *Filling:* In a medium bowl, whisk cornstarch with soy sauce until smooth. Add rice wine vinegar, brown sugar, lime juice, sesame oil, fish sauce (if using) and pepper flakes, whisking to blend.

## Tips

When working with thawed phyllo (Step 4), be sure to keep it covered with a damp clean tea towel. Until you brush it with melted butter, it will dry out quickly when exposed to air.

Phyllo dough is best kept frozen and thawed overnight in the refrigerator.

For step-by-step photographs of making phyllo packets, see page 38.

The pies can be assembled (Steps 1 through 6) and frozen for up to one month. Freeze pies completely on baking trays, then seal in zip-top bags. Bake from frozen, as directed.

If substituting any dough for the phyllo (Variations), cut out 6-inch (15 cm) rounds to enclose the filling. Bake in a preheated 375°F (190°C) oven for 25 to 30 minutes.

2. In a large skillet, heat oil over medium-high heat. Add onion and carrot and sauté until softened, about 4 minutes. Add garlic, ginger and mushrooms; sauté for 4 minutes, until mushrooms are softened. Add chicken and sauté, stirring occasionally, until cooked through, about 5 minutes. Add soy sauce mixture to skillet, reduce heat and simmer until thickened, about 5 minutes. Remove from heat and set aside to cool.

3. *Peanut Sauce:* In a medium bowl, combine peanut butter, soy sauce, rice wine vinegar, brown sugar, lime juice, sesame oil and pepper flakes, whisking to blend. Set aside.

4. Place 1 sheet phyllo on clean work surface, short side facing you. (Cover remaining sheets with damp towel to prevent drying out.) Brush sheet with melted butter and top with another sheet of phyllo.

5. Place $1/4$ cup (60 mL) chicken filling 1 inch (2.5 cm) from bottom edge of phyllo, leaving 3-inch (7.5 cm) borders on each side and about 10 inches (25 cm) at the top. Top chicken with 1 tbsp (15 mL) peanut sauce. Carefully fold both long sides over filling so they overlap completely, covering filling. You will now have a 3-inch (7.5 cm) by 14-inch (35 cm) rectangle.

6. Brush top surface of phyllo rectangle with melted butter. Fold up the 1-inch (2.5 cm) bottom edge to form a little packet for the filling, then fold packet over and over until you reach other end of phyllo. Press end to seal. Transfer packet to prepared baking sheet, seam side down. Brush top with butter. Repeat with remaining phyllo sheets and filling until you have 12 packets.

7. Bake in preheated oven for 22 to 28 minutes, switching positions of baking sheets halfway through, until phyllo is deep golden brown and crisp. Cool packets slightly on sheets on wire racks. Serve warm.

## Variations

Substitute Whole Wheat Pie Dough or Hand Pie Dough for the phyllo (see Tips, left).

*Gluten Free Variation:* Substitute Gluten-Free Pie Dough (page 24) for the phyllo and use gluten-free soy sauce.

# Chipotle Chicken Pockets

**Makes 12 pockets**

● **GF Friendly**

---

*Make a double batch of the spicy-sweet barbecue sauce for these pies, because you're going to want to put it on everything! Simply tossed with shredded chicken to fill yeasty pizza pockets, it's perfect for tailgating or watching a sporting event.*

---

## Tips

Fresh garlic bulbs should not be stored in the refrigerator, because its moisture tends to encourage the growth of mold. Store garlic bulbs in a ventilated dry location such as a mesh or wire basket or a small bowl.

This recipe will leave you with some extra filling. You can either make a second batch (or half-batch) of dough to make additional pies, or you can enjoy the filling on its own in a sandwich.

● **6-inch (15 cm) round cutter**
● **2 baking sheets lined with parchment**

### Spicy Barbecue Sauce

| | | |
|---|---|---|
| 1 tbsp | oil | 15 mL |
| ½ cup | chopped yellow onion | 125 mL |
| 1 tbsp | chopped fresh garlic | 15 mL |
| 1 | can (28 oz/794 g) crushed tomatoes | 1 |
| ½ cup | liquid honey | 125 mL |
| ½ cup | packed light brown sugar | 125 mL |
| 2 | chipotle chiles in adobo sauce, chopped | 2 |
| ½ cup | orange juice | 125 mL |
| ½ cup | cider vinegar | 125 mL |
| 2 tbsp | Worcestershire sauce | 30 mL |
| 1 tbsp | dry mustard powder | 15 mL |
| 1 tbsp | ground cumin | 15 mL |
| ½ tsp | salt | 2 mL |
| ½ tsp | freshly ground black pepper | 2 mL |
| 3½ cups | shredded roasted chicken breast | 875 mL |
| 1 | recipe Pizza/Calzone Dough (page 30) | 1 |
| 1 | large egg, lightly beaten with 1 tbsp (15 mL) water | 1 |
| 2 cups | shredded Monterey Jack cheese, optional | 500 mL |

1. *Spicy Barbecue Sauce:* In a large saucepan, heat oil over medium-high heat. Add onion and sauté for 5 minutes. Add garlic and sauté for 1 minute. Add crushed tomatoes, honey, brown sugar, chipotle peppers, orange juice, vinegar, Worcestershire sauce, mustard, cumin, salt and pepper; stir to mix. Bring to a boil, then reduce heat and simmer for 30 to 40 minutes, until sauce has reduced and thickened. Remove from heat and set aside to cool completely.

2. In a large bowl, toss chicken with enough sauce to generously coat. Set aside.

3. Divide dough into halves. On a lightly floured surface, roll out one half to slightly thicker than $1/16$ inch (2 mm). Using cutter, cut into rounds and place on prepared baking sheets, spacing apart. Reroll scraps as necessary. Repeat with remaining dough.

## Tips

Use the egg wash sparingly on the edges. They will be harder to seal if too wet. When crimping the edges, dip the fork in the egg wash if you have problems with it sticking to the dough.

Pizza/Calzone Dough is very springy. It doesn't hold its shape when rolled out as well as most other doughs.

4. Brush edges of rounds with egg wash (see Tips, left). Place about $1/4$ cup (60 mL) chicken filling in center of each round. Top with 2 tbsp (30 mL) cheese, if using. Fold rounds in half, enclosing filling then fold the edges over to create a double thickness. Pinch edges together to seal, and crimp with the tines of a fork. Brush tops with egg wash.

5. Place pockets, on baking sheets, in freezer for 30 minutes. Meanwhile, position oven racks in upper and lower thirds of oven and preheat oven to 375°F (190°C).

6. Bake in preheated oven for 35 to 45 minutes, switching positions of baking sheets halfway through, until puffed and golden brown. Cool for 5 minutes on sheets set on wire racks. Serve with extra sauce for dipping, if desired.

### Variations

Substitute Whole Wheat Pie Dough (page 18), Hand Pie Dough (page 27) or Savory Cheese Dough (page 23) for the Pizza/Calzone Dough.

*Gluten-Free Alternative:* Substitute Gluten-Free Pie Dough (page 24) for Pizza/Calzone Dough.

### Make Ahead

The pockets can be assembled (Steps 1 through 4) and frozen for up to two weeks. Freeze pies for at least 30 minutes on baking trays, then seal in zip-top bags. Bake from frozen, as directed.

# Chicken Bisteeya Phyllo Pies

**Makes 16 pies**

● **GF Friendly**

*Bisteeya, also spelled bastilla, are Moroccan chicken- and almond-filled phyllo pies packed with layer upon layer of spices. These aromatic flaky pockets are crisp and sweet on the outside but exotically savory on the inside.*

## Tips

Because saffron is expensive, select it carefully. Saffron should be packaged in foil to protect from exposure to air or light. Larger amounts tend to be sold in tins or wooden boxes.

For step-by-step photographs of making phyllo packets, see page 38.

● Preheat oven to 375°F (190°C)
● Food processor
● 2 baking sheets lined with parchment
● Damp tea towel

| | | |
|---|---|---|
| 1½ cups | sliced almonds | 375 mL |
| 6 tbsp | confectioners' (icing) sugar | 90 mL |
| 1 tsp | ground cinnamon | 5 mL |
| 2 tbsp | unsalted butter | 30 mL |
| ½ | yellow onion, chopped | ½ |
| | Salt and freshly ground black pepper | |
| ⅛ tsp | saffron threads, optional (see Tips, left) | 0.5 mL |
| 1 tsp | ground cinnamon | 5 mL |
| 1 tsp | ground cumin | 5 mL |
| 1 tsp | ground turmeric | 5 mL |
| ½ tsp | ground ginger | 2 mL |
| ⅛ tsp | cayenne pepper | 0.5 mL |
| 2 tbsp | chopped fresh parsley | 30 mL |
| 2 tbsp | chopped fresh cilantro | 30 mL |
| 3 cups | shredded roasted chicken breast | 750 mL |
| 3 | large eggs, lightly beaten | 3 |
| 32 | sheets phyllo dough, thawed (see Tips, page 245) | 32 |
| 1 cup | unsalted butter, melted | 250 mL |

1. In food processor fitted with the metal blade, process almonds, confectioners' sugar and cinnamon until almonds are finely ground.

2. In a large skillet over medium-high heat, melt butter. Add onion and sauté until soft, 4 to 5 minutes. Season to taste with salt and pepper.

3. Add saffron (if using), cinnamon, cumin, turmeric, ginger, cayenne, parsley and cilantro. Add chicken and sauté until chicken is heated through. Add eggs and cook, stirring, until eggs are cooked. Remove from heat and set aside to cool.

4. Place 1 sheet of phyllo on a clean work surface, short side facing you (see Tips, page 245). Working quickly, brush with melted butter and sprinkle with almond mixture. Top with a second sheet of phyllo.

## Tips

Your phyllo sheets should be about 14 by 9 inches (35 by 23 cm). You can work with rectangles that approximate this size, but if the configuration of your phyllo sheets is dramatically different, roll them out or trim to something that roughly conforms.

When working with thawed phyllo (Step 4), be sure to keep it covered with a damp clean tea towel. Until you brush it with melted butter, it will dry out quickly when exposed to air.

5. Place $1/4$ cup (60 mL) chicken filling 1 inch (2.5 cm) from bottom edge of phyllo, leaving 3-inch (7.5 cm) borders on each side and about 10 inches (25 cm) at the top. Sprinkle chicken with about 1 tbsp (15 mL) almond mixture. Carefully fold both long sides of phyllo over filling so they overlap completely, covering filling. You will now have a 3-inch (7.5 cm) by 14-inch (35 cm) rectangle.

6. Brush top surface of phyllo rectangle with melted butter. Fold up the 1-inch (2.5 cm) bottom edge to form a little packet for the filling, then fold packet over and over until you reach other end of phyllo. Press end to seal. Transfer packet to prepared baking sheet, seam side down. Brush top with butter. Repeat with remaining phyllo sheets and filling, making 16 packets in total.

7. Bake in preheated oven for 22 to 28 minutes (longer if frozen; see Make Ahead), switching positions of baking sheets halfway through, until phyllo is deep golden brown and crisp. Cool slightly, then sprinkle with almond mixture. Serve warm.

## Variations

Substitute 6-inch (15 cm) rounds of Whole Wheat Pie Dough (page 18), Hand Pie Dough (page 27), Flaky Pie Dough (page 15) or All-Butter Pie Dough (page 16) for the phyllo sheets.

*Gluten-Free Alternative:* Substitute Gluten-Free Pie Dough (page 24) for the phyllo dough and cut into 6-inch (15 cm) rounds.

## Make Ahead

The pies can be assembled (Steps 1 through 6) and frozen for two to three days. Freeze for at least 30 minutes on baking trays, then seal in zip-top bags. Bake from frozen, as directed, for an additional 4 to 7 minutes.

# Spicy Turkey Shepherd's Pies

*Need a fresh idea for Thanksgiving leftovers? Make them almost unrecognizable with this Southwestern version of shepherd's pie. Shredded turkey, blended with a zesty mixture of vegetables and seasonings, is topped with smoky mashed potatoes and baked until bubbly.*

## Tips

For easiest rolling, roll your dough, including scraps, between two sheets of plastic wrap. That way, you do not need to add flour to keep the dough from sticking to your work surface.

The easiest way to remove tarts from muffin tins is to run a small, sharp knife or small offset spatula around the edges, loosening the sides. You should then be able to carefully lift out the tarts, guiding them with the knife or spatula.

- 4½-inch (11.25 cm) round cutter
- 12-cup muffin tin, greased
- Potato masher

| | | |
|---|---|---|
| 1 | recipe Cornmeal Pie Dough (page 19) | 1 |
| 1 tbsp | olive oil | 15 mL |
| 5 tbsp | unsalted butter, divided | 75 mL |
| ½ cup | thinly sliced shallots | 125 mL |
| 1 | rib celery, chopped | 1 |
| 1 | red bell pepper, seeded and chopped | 1 |
| 1 | jalapeño pepper, seeded and chopped | 1 |
| 2 tsp | minced garlic | 10 mL |
| 1 tbsp | chopped fresh thyme | 15 mL |
| ¼ tsp | hot pepper flakes | 1 mL |
| 2 tbsp | all-purpose flour | 30 mL |
| ⅓ cup | dry white wine | 75 mL |
| 1¼ cups | reduced-sodium chicken stock | 300 mL |
| 2 cups | shredded roasted turkey breast | 500 mL |
| | Salt and freshly ground black pepper | |
| 3 | medium russet potatoes, peeled and cut into 1-inch pieces | 3 |
| ¼ cup | whole milk | 60 mL |
| 1 tsp | smoked sweet paprika | 5 mL |

1. On a lightly floured work surface, roll out dough to a thickness of ⅛ inch (3 mm). Using cutter, cut 12 rounds and carefully fit into muffin cups (they should stand a bit taller than edges of cups). Reroll scraps as necessary.

2. Place tins in freezer for 30 minutes. Meanwhile, preheat oven to 375°F (190°C).

3. In a large skillet, heat oil and 2 tbsp (30 mL) butter over medium heat. Add shallots, celery, red pepper and jalapeño; sauté until tender, about 5 minutes. Add garlic, thyme and hot pepper flakes; sauté for 1 minute. Add flour and cook, stirring, for 1 minute. Add white wine and stir until it almost evaporates. Add chicken stock and bring to a boil, stirring until thickened. Reduce heat and add turkey, stirring to mix. Season to taste with salt and pepper. Remove from heat and set aside to cool completely.

## Tips

These pies are best eaten the day they are baked.

If using leftover mashed potatoes, simply add smoked paprika to taste and top the filled pie shells as directed.

4. In a medium saucepan, combine potatoes with cold water to cover. Bring to a boil over medium-high heat. Reduce heat and simmer until potatoes are tender, 15 to 20 minutes. Drain and return to saucepan. Add remaining 3 tbsp (45 mL) butter and milk and mash with potato masher to incorporate. Stir in paprika and season to taste with salt and pepper.

5. Fill each shell with a heaping $1/4$ cup (60 mL) turkey filling. Top with 3 to 4 tbsp (45 to 60 mL) mashed potatoes, spreading to completely cover surface. Bake in center of preheated oven for 30 to 35 minutes, until tops are golden brown and filling is bubbling. Cool pies in tins on wire racks for 10 minutes, then carefully unmold and transfer to serving plates. Serve warm.

## Variations

Substitute Savory Cheese Dough (page 23), Flaky Pie Dough (page 15) or Whole Wheat Pie Dough (page 18) for the Cornmeal Pie Dough.

Substitute an equal quantity of mashed sweet potatoes for the russet potatoes.

# Fried Turkey Tamale Pies

| | | |
|---|---|---|
| **Makes 32 pies** | | |

**● GF Friendly**

*Tamales are a Latin American invention in which a wide variety of fillings are wrapped in banana leaves and steamed or boiled. This version is fried in cornmeal dough, yielding a crunchy shell for the well-seasoned ground turkey and tomato filling.*

## Tips

Use either fresh or frozen corn in this recipe.

A deep-fry thermometer helps you to maintain the appropriate temperature (in this book, 360°F/185°C) of your oil, ensuring that your pies are properly cooked. These thermometers come in both digital and non-digital varieties. I prefer one that clips directly onto the side of the pot for easy reading. If you do not own a thermometer, the best way to test if your oil is ready for frying is to drop a small scrap of dough into the pot. If the dough fries on contact, the oil is ready.

If you don't own round cutters in the appropriate sizes, look for lids of the same size from prepared foods.

● 5-inch (12.5 cm) round cutter
● Candy/deep-fry thermometer

| | | |
|---|---|---|
| 1 tbsp | olive oil | 15 mL |
| ½ | yellow onion, chopped | ½ |
| ½ | chopped red bell pepper | ½ |
| 1 | jalapeño pepper, seeded and chopped | 1 |
| 2 tsp | minced garlic | 10 mL |
| 1 lb | lean ground turkey | 500 g |
| 1 tbsp | chili powder | 15 mL |
| 1 tsp | smoked sweet paprika | 5 mL |
| ½ tsp | ground cumin | 2 mL |
| ½ tsp | dried oregano | 2 mL |
| | Salt and freshly ground black pepper | |
| 1 | can (28 oz/794 g) crushed tomatoes | 1 |
| 2 tbsp | tomato paste | 30 mL |
| 2 tbsp | fine cornmeal | 30 mL |
| ½ cup | corn kernels (see Tips, left) | 125 mL |
| 2 cups | shredded Cheddar cheese | 500 mL |
| 2 | recipes Cornmeal Pie Dough (page 19) | 2 |
| 1 | large egg, lightly beaten with 1 tbsp (15 mL) water | 1 |
| | Canola or safflower oil | |

1. In a large skillet, heat oil over medium-high heat. Add onion, red pepper and jalapeño; sauté until softened, about 5 minutes. Add garlic and sauté for 1 minute. Add turkey and sauté, stirring occasionally, until meat is cooked through, about 5 minutes. Stir in chili powder, paprika, cumin and oregano. Season to taste with salt and pepper.

2. Add crushed tomatoes, tomato paste and cornmeal to pan. Bring to a boil, reduce heat and simmer until thickened, about 20 minutes. Stir in corn. Remove from heat and set aside to cool completely.

3. On a lightly floured surface, roll out dough to slightly thicker than $1/16$ inch (2 mm). Using cutter, cut into rounds and place on baking sheets lined with parchment, spacing apart. Reroll scraps as necessary.

## Tips

Smoked paprika is made from sweet red bell peppers that have been dried in the sun, then smoked over wood fires. It lends a vibrant, smoky flavor and bright color to dishes. Substitute regular sweet paprika if you cannot find the smoked variety.

For step-by-step photographs of making hand pies, see page 35.

**4.** Brush surfaces of rounds with egg wash. Place about 2 tbsp (30 mL) filling in center of each round. Sprinkle with cheese. Fold round in half, enclosing filling. Pinch edges together to seal, and crimp with the tines of a fork.

**5.** Place pies, on baking sheets, in freezer for 30 minutes.

**6.** In a deep skillet or Dutch oven, heat 2 inches (5 cm) oil until deep-fry thermometer registers 360°F (185°C). Fry pies in batches, turning once, until golden brown, 4 to 5 minutes in total. Transfer to wire racks lined with paper towels to cool slightly. Serve warm.

## Variation

*Gluten-Free Alternative:* Substitute 2 recipes Gluten-Free Pie Dough (page 24) for the Cornmeal Pie Dough.

## Make Ahead

The pies can be assembled (Steps 1 through 4) and frozen for up to one month. Freeze pies for at least 30 minutes on baking trays, then seal in zip-top bags. Fry from frozen, as directed.

# Pork Empanadas with Salsa Verde

| Makes 32 empanadas |
|---|

- **GF Friendly**

*The word* empanada *comes from the Portuguese or Spanish word* empanar, *which means "to wrap in bread." These petite pies are served either fried or baked, and they come packed with flavorful fillings both sweet and savory. This fried pork-filled version, served with a spicy tomatillo salsa verde for dipping, makes a great party appetizer.*

## Tips

Smoked paprika is made from sweet red bell peppers that have been dried in the sun, then smoked over wood fires. It lends a vibrant, smoky flavor and bright color to dishes. Substitute regular sweet paprika if you cannot find the smoked variety.

When purchasing tomatillos, choose the smaller ones, which tend to be sweeter. Tomatillos should be firm and their skin free of blemishes. The husk should be light brown and fresh looking, not shriveled and dry.

- Blender
- 5-inch (12.5 cm) round cutter
- Candy/deep-fry thermometer

### Filling

| 1 tbsp | olive oil | 15 mL |
|---|---|---|
| ½ | yellow onion, chopped | ½ |
| ½ | jalapeño pepper, seeded and chopped | ½ |
| 1 tbsp | minced garlic | 15 mL |
| 1 tsp | ground cumin | 5 mL |
| 1 tsp | ground coriander | 5 mL |
| 1 tsp | smoked paprika | 5 mL |
| 1 lb | ground pork | 500 g |
| ¼ cup | chopped fresh cilantro | 60 mL |
| ⅓ cup | golden raisins | 75 mL |
| ¼ cup | chopped green olives | 60 mL |
| | Salt and freshly ground black pepper | |

### Salsa Verde

| 2 cups | chopped tomatillos (see Tips, left) | 500 mL |
|---|---|---|
| ½ cup | chopped white onion | 125 mL |
| 2 tsp | minced garlic | 10 mL |
| 1 | serrano chile pepper, seeded and minced | 1 |
| ¼ cup | chopped fresh cilantro leaves | 60 mL |
| 2 tbsp | freshly squeezed lime juice | 30 mL |
| ½ tsp | salt | 2 mL |
| 2 | recipes All-Butter Pie Dough (page 16) | 2 |
| 1 | large egg, lightly beaten with 1 tbsp (15 mL) water | 1 |
| | Canola or safflower oil | |

1. *Filling:* In a large skillet, heat oil over medium-high heat. Add onion and jalapeño pepper; sauté until softened, about 5 minutes. Add garlic, cumin, coriander and paprika; sauté for 1 minute.

When cutting large rounds, you can use the flat section of a two-piece tart pan as a template and the outer section as a cutter, being careful of sharp edges. If you don't have an appropriately-sized tart tin, a pot lid also makes a good guide.

For step-by-step photographs of making hand pies, see page 35.

2. Add pork to skillet. Sauté, breaking up pork with a wooden spoon, until meat is cooked through, about 5 minutes. Stir in cilantro, raisins and olives. Season to taste with salt and pepper. Remove from heat and set aside to cool completely.

3. *Salsa Verde:* In blender, purée tomatillos, onion, garlic, serrano pepper, cilantro, lime juice and salt. Transfer mixture to a medium saucepan. Cook over medium-low heat, stirring occasionally, until slightly thickened. Remove from heat and set aside to cool.

4. On a lightly floured work surface, roll out dough to $1/8$ inch (3 mm) thick. Using cutter, cut into rounds and place on baking sheets. Reroll scraps as necessary.

5. Brush surfaces of rounds with egg wash. Place about 2 tbsp (30 mL) filling in center of each round; top with salsa verde. Fold rounds in half, enclosing filling. Pinch edges together to seal, and crimp with the tines of a fork.

6. Place pies, on baking sheets, in freezer for 30 minutes.

7. In a deep skillet or Dutch oven, heat 2 inches (5 cm) oil until deep-fry thermometer registers 360°F (185°C). Fry empanadas in batches, turning once, until golden brown, 3 to 4 minutes in total.

8. Transfer empanadas to a wire rack lined with paper towels to cool slightly. Serve warm.

## Variations

Substitute 2 recipes Cornmeal Pie Dough (page 19) or Hand Pie Dough (page 27) for the All-Butter Pie Dough.

*Gluten-Free Alternative:* Substitute 2 recipes Gluten-Free Pie Dough (page 24) for the All-Butter Pie Dough.

## Make Ahead

The empanadas can be assembled (Steps 1 through 5) and frozen for up to one month. Freeze pies for at least 30 minutes on baking trays, then seal in zip-top bags. Fry from frozen, as directed.

# Spiced Pork and Apple Hand Pies

**Makes 12 pies**

● **GF Friendly**

*This recipe was inspired by my favorite homemade sausage recipe, which is filled with a blend of sweet and savory seasonings and mixed with tart, juicy apples. Serve these comforting pies as a warm dinner on a particularly cold night.*

## Tips

When buying fresh sage, look for leaves that are aromatic, with no soft brown spots or dry edges. Store sage, wrapped in paper towels in a plastic bag, in the refrigerator for up to five days.

This recipe will leave you with some extra filling. You can either make a second batch (or half-batch) of dough to make additional pies or you can enjoy the filling on its own.

● 6-inch (15 cm) round cutter
● 2 baking sheets lined with parchment

**Filling**

| | | |
|---|---|---|
| 1 tbsp | unsalted butter | 15 mL |
| 1 | tart apple, peeled and chopped | 1 |
| 1 | sweet apple, peeled and chopped | 1 |
| 1 tbsp | extra-virgin olive oil | 15 mL |
| 1/2 cup | chopped yellow onion | 125 mL |
| 1 lb | ground pork | 500 g |
| 1 tbsp | chopped fresh thyme | 15 mL |
| 1 tbsp | chopped fresh sage (see Tips, left) | 15 mL |
| 1/2 tsp | ground cinnamon | 2 mL |
| 1/4 tsp | ground allspice | 1 mL |
| 1/8 tsp | ground cloves | 0.5 mL |
| 1/8 tsp | cayenne pepper | 0.5 mL |
| 1 tsp | salt | 5 mL |
| 1/2 tsp | freshly ground black pepper | 2 mL |
| 2 tbsp | pure maple syrup | 30 mL |
| 1 | recipe Hand Pie Dough (page 27, see Tips, left) | 1 |
| 1 | large egg, lightly beaten with 1 tbsp (15 mL) water | 1 |

1. *Filling:* In a large skillet over medium-high heat, melt butter. Add apples and sauté until softened, 4 to 5 minutes. Transfer to a medium bowl.

2. In same skillet, heat olive oil. Add onion and sauté for 4 minutes. Add pork, thyme, sage, cinnamon, allspice, cloves, cayenne, salt and pepper. Cook, breaking up pork with wooden spoon, until meat is cooked through, about 5 minutes. Remove from heat and drizzle with maple syrup, stirring to mix. Remove from heat and set aside to cool completely. Add apples, stirring to mix.

## Tips

When cutting large rounds, you can use the flat section of a two-piece tart pan as a template and the outer section as a cutter, being careful of sharp edges. If you don't have an appropriately-sized tart tin, a pot lid also makes a good guide.

For step-by-step photographs of making hand pies, see page 35.

3. On a lightly floured surface, roll out dough to slightly thicker than $1/16$ inch (2 mm). Using cutter, cut into rounds and place on prepared baking sheets, spacing apart. Reroll scraps as necessary.

4. Brush edges of rounds with egg wash. Place about $1/4$ cup (60 mL) pork filling in center of each. Fold in half, enclosing filling. Pinch edges together to seal, and crimp with the tines of a fork. Brush tops with egg wash.

5. Place pies, on baking sheets, in freezer for 30 minutes. Meanwhile, position oven racks in upper and lower thirds of oven and preheat oven to 375°F (190°C).

6. Using tip of a sharp knife, cut 2 or 3 slits in top of each pie. Bake in preheated oven for 30 to 35 minutes, switching positions of baking sheets halfway through, until pies are puffed and golden brown. Cool on sheets on wire racks for 5 minutes before serving.

## Variations

Substitute Whole Wheat Pie Dough (page 18), Flaky Pie Dough (page 15) or All-Butter Pie Dough (page 16) for the Hand Pie Dough.

*Gluten-Free Alternative:* Substitute Gluten-Free Pie Dough (page 24) for the Hand Pie Dough.

## Make Ahead

The pies can be assembled (Steps 1 through 4) and frozen for up to two weeks. Freeze pies for at least 30 minutes on baking trays, then seal in zip-top bags. Bake from frozen, as directed.

# Handheld Tourtières

● **GF Friendly**

I was not familiar with tourtière, a Quebec meat pie traditionally served on Christmas Eve, until recently. These double-crusted pies are similar to pot pies filled with finely diced pork, beef, game or veal. This simply prepared pork version is slowly simmered with spices, resulting in a very tender and flavorful filling beneath a flaky, buttery crust. Tourtière is usually served with chutney.

## Tips

An alternative to buying ground pork is to make your own. Cut pork shoulder, butt or loin into 1-inch (2.5 cm) cubes. Freeze cubes in one layer on a baking sheet for 20 minutes. Grind the pork by pulsing 8 to 10 times in a food processor until it looks coarsely ground.

The easiest way to remove tarts from muffin tins is to run a small, sharp knife or small offset spatula around the edges, loosening the sides. You should then be able to carefully lift out the tarts, guiding them with the knife or spatula.

● 3- and 4-inch (7.5 and 10 cm) round cutters
● 12-cup muffin tin, lightly greased

### Filling

| | | |
|---|---|---|
| 1 lb | ground pork (see Tips, left) | 500 g |
| 1 cup | reduced-sodium ready-to-use chicken stock | 250 mL |
| 1 cup | chopped yellow onion | 250 mL |
| 2 tsp | chopped fresh sage | 10 mL |
| 1 tsp | salt | 5 mL |
| $\frac{1}{2}$ tsp | freshly ground black pepper | 2 mL |
| $\frac{1}{2}$ tsp | ground cinnamon | 2 mL |
| $\frac{1}{4}$ tsp | ground allspice | 1 mL |
| $\frac{1}{4}$ tsp | ground cloves | 1 mL |
| 1 | dried bay leaf | 1 |
| 1 | recipe All-Butter Pie Dough (page 16) | 1 |
| $\frac{1}{4}$ cup | unsalted butter | 60 mL |
| 1 | large egg, lightly beaten with 1 tbsp (15 mL) water | 1 |

1. *Filling:* In a large saucepan over medium-high heat, bring pork and stock to a boil. Reduce heat and add onion, sage, salt, pepper, cinnamon, allspice, cloves and bay leaf. Cover and cook over low heat, stirring occasionally, for 30 minutes. Remove lid and cook until most of the liquid evaporates, 20 to 30 minutes more. Remove from heat and set aside to cool completely. Remove and discard bay leaf.

2. Divide dough into two pieces, one slightly larger than the other. On a lightly floured work surface, roll out larger piece to a thickness of $\frac{1}{8}$ inch (3 mm). Using 4-inch (10 cm) cutter, cut out 12 rounds and carefully fit into muffin cups. Reroll scraps as necessary. Fill each shell with about 3 tbsp (45 mL) filling.

3. On lightly floured surface, roll out smaller piece of dough to a thickness of $\frac{1}{8}$ inch (3 mm). Using 3-inch (7.5 cm) cutter, cut out 12 rounds, rerolling scraps as necessary.

## Tips

For easiest rolling, roll your dough, including scraps, between two sheets of plastic wrap. That way, you do not need to add flour to keep the dough from sticking to your work surface.

Wire baking racks are important to have on hand for the cooling process. After pies have finished baking, either set the muffin tin on the rack or transfer the pies from the baking sheet to the rack. This lets the air circulate around the pies, cooling them evenly.

4. Brush bottoms of smaller rounds with egg wash and carefully place over filled shells, pinching edges together to seal tightly. Brush tops with egg wash.

5. Place tins in freezer for 30 minutes. Meanwhile, preheat oven to 400°F (200°C).

6. Using tip of a sharp knife, cut 3 small slits in top crusts. Bake on center rack in preheated oven for 12 minutes, then lower temperature to 350°F (180°C) and bake for 22 to 28 minutes longer, until tops are puffed and browned.

7. Cool pies in tins on wire racks for 10 minutes, then carefully unmold and transfer to racks or serving plates. Serve warm.

## Variations

Substitute Whole Wheat Pie Dough (page 18) or Flaky Pie Dough (page 15) for the All-Butter Pie Dough.

*Gluten-Free Alternative:* Substitute Gluten-Free Pie Dough (page 24) for the All-Butter Pie Dough.

## Make Ahead

The pies can be fully assembled (Steps 1 through 4) and frozen, tightly wrapped in their tins, for up to two weeks. Bake from frozen, as directed.

# Mini Cheese and Sausage Calzones

*My husband is definitely a connoisseur of pizza, so I take it as a true compliment when he gobbles down the version I make at home. These mini calzones are a variation on his favorite pizza, filled with sweet Italian sausage, garlicky spinach and a creamy blend of cheeses. The simple tomato sauce can either be added to the inside or passed for dipping, which he prefers.*

## Tips

For a leaner alternative, use sweet Italian turkey sausage instead of pork sausage.

When cutting large rounds, you can use the flat section of a two-piece tart pan as a template and the outer section as a cutter, being watchful for sharp edges. If you don't have an appropriately-sized tart tin, a pot lid also makes a good guide.

- 6-inch (15 cm) round cutter
- 2 baking sheets lined with parchment

### Filling

| | | |
|---|---|---|
| 2 tbsp | extra-virgin olive oil | 30 mL |
| 12 oz | Italian sweet sausage, casings removed (see Tips, left) | 375 g |
| 2 tsp | chopped garlic | 10 mL |
| 5 oz | fresh spinach | 150 g |
| ¾ cup | whole-milk ricotta cheese | 175 mL |
| ¼ cup | freshly grated Parmesan cheese | 60 mL |
| 3 tbsp | chopped parsley | 45 mL |
| ¼ tsp | hot pepper flakes | 1 mL |
| | Salt and freshly ground black pepper | |
| 1 | recipe Pizza/Calzone Dough (page 30) | 1 |
| 1 | large egg, lightly beaten with 1 tbsp (15 mL) water | 1 |
| 1½ cups | shredded mozzarella cheese, optional | 375 mL |

### Sauce

| | | |
|---|---|---|
| 1 tbsp | extra-virgin olive oil | 15 mL |
| ½ | yellow onion, chopped | ½ |
| 2 tsp | chopped garlic | 10 mL |
| 1 | can (28 oz/794 g) crushed tomatoes (see Tips, left) | 1 |
| 3 tbsp | chopped parsley | 45 mL |
| ¼ tsp | hot pepper flakes | 1 mL |

1. In a large skillet, heat olive oil over medium heat. Add sausage and cook, breaking up with a wooden spoon, until browned. Transfer to paper towels to drain, reserving 1 tbsp (15 mL) oil in pan.

2. Add garlic to pan and sauté for 1 minute. Add spinach and sauté until wilted, 3 to 4 minutes.

3. In a large bowl, mix cooked sausage with ricotta, Parmesan, parsley and hot pepper flakes. Add spinach and season to taste with salt and pepper. Set aside to cool completely.

## Tips

If preferred, you can add about 2 tbsp (30 mL) sauce along with the filling before sealing the calzones. Pass extra sauce separately for dipping.

Use the egg wash sparingly on the edges. They are harder to seal if too wet. When crimping the edges, dip the fork in the egg wash if you have problems with it sticking to the dough.

4. Divide dough in half. On a lightly floured surface, roll one half to a thickness of $1/8$ inch (3 mm). Using cutter, cut into rounds and place on prepared baking sheets, spacing apart. Reroll scraps as necessary.

5. Brush rounds with egg wash (see Tip, left). Place about $1/4$ cup (60 mL) sausage filling in center of each round. Top with 2 tbsp (30 mL) mozzarella, if using. Fold rounds in half, enclosing filling then fold the edges over to create a double thickness. Pinch edges together to seal, and crimp with the tines of a fork. Brush tops with egg wash. Repeat process with remaining dough.

6. Place pies, on baking sheets, in freezer for 30 minutes. Meanwhile, position oven racks in upper and lower thirds of oven and preheat oven to 400°F (200°C).

7. *Sauce:* In a medium saucepan, heat olive oil over medium-high heat. Add onion and sauté until soft, about 4 minutes. Add garlic and sauté 1 minute more. Add crushed tomatoes, parsley and hot pepper flakes. Bring mixture to a boil and simmer until reduced and thickened, about 10 minutes.

8. Using the tip of a sharp knife, cut 3 slits in the top of each calzone. Bake in preheated oven for 35 to 45 minutes, switching positions of baking sheets halfway through, until puffed and golden brown. Let cool 5 minutes before serving with dipping sauce.

### Make Ahead

The calzones can be fully assembled (Steps 1 through 5) and frozen for up to one month. Freeze for at least 30 minutes on trays, then enclose in zip-top bags. Bake from frozen, as directed.

# Italian Sausage and Pepper Calzones

● **GF Friendly**

---

*The first time I went to a professional baseball game was also the first time I tried sausage and peppers. Slowly simmered in tomato sauce, the tender peppers and spicy sausage were nestled in a soft sandwich roll — portable, but still a bit messy to eat while watching the game. Perhaps the vendors should start selling this version, packed with a similar filling but more manageable in size, and certainly easier to eat!*

---

## Tip

When cooking with wine, it's not necessary to use an expensive bottle, but it's a good idea to use one that you will also enjoy drinking.

● **6-inch (15 cm) round cutter**
● **2 baking sheets lined with parchment**

### Filling

| | | |
|---|---|---|
| 2 tbsp | extra-virgin olive oil | 30 mL |
| 1 lb | Italian sausage or turkey sausage links | 500 g |
| 1 | yellow onion, thinly sliced | 1 |
| 1 | red pepper, thinly sliced | 1 |
| 1 | yellow pepper, thinly sliced | 1 |
| 2 | cloves garlic, chopped | 2 |
| 2 tsp | dried oregano | 10 mL |
| 1½ cups | crushed tomatoes | 375 mL |
| 3 tbsp | tomato paste | 45 mL |
| ½ cup | dry red wine (see Tip, left) | 125 mL |
| ¼ tsp | hot pepper flakes | 1 mL |
| ½ tsp | salt | 2 mL |
| ¼ tsp | freshly ground black pepper | 1 mL |
| 1 | recipe Pizza/Calzone Dough (page 30) | 1 |
| 1 | large egg, lightly beaten with 1 tbsp (15 mL) water | 1 |

1. *Filling:* In a large skillet, heat olive oil over medium heat. Add sausages and cook, turning occasionally, until browned on all sides, 8 to 10 minutes. Transfer to paper towels to drain. When cool enough to handle, cut into bite-size pieces.

2. Increase heat to medium-high. Add onion and peppers to pan and sauté until golden, about 6 minutes. Add garlic and oregano; sauté for 1 minute.

3. Add crushed tomatoes, tomato paste, wine, hot pepper flakes, salt and pepper to pan. Bring to a boil, then reduce heat. Add reserved sausage pieces and simmer, stirring occasionally, until sauce has thickened, 20 to 25 minutes. Remove from heat and set aside to cool completely.

## Tips

Pizza/Calzone Dough is very springy. It doesn't hold its shape when rolled out as well as most other doughs.

A pizza stone definitely falls into the "nice to have" rather than "need to have" category. However, using one to bake pies that use Pizza/Calzone Dough will result in a uniformly crisp crust. For best results, preheat the stone in the oven for at least 15 minutes before placing the calzones on it.

Use the egg wash sparingly on the edges. They are harder to seal if too wet. When crimping the edges, dip the fork in the egg wash if you have problems with it sticking to the dough.

This recipe will leave you with some extra filling. You can either make a second batch (or half-batch) of dough to make additional pies, or you can enjoy the filling on its own.

4. Divide dough into two pieces. On a lightly floured surface, roll one piece to a thickness of $1/8$ inch (3 mm). Using cutter, cut into rounds and place on prepared baking sheets, spacing apart. Reroll scraps as necessary.

5. Brush edges of rounds with egg wash (see Tips, left). Place about $1/4$ cup (60 mL) filling in center of each. Fold rounds in half, enclosing filling, then fold the edges over to create a double thickness. Pinch edges together to seal, and crimp with the tines of a fork. Brush tops with egg wash. Repeat with remaining dough.

6. Place pies, on baking sheets, in freezer for 30 minutes. Meanwhile, position oven racks in upper and lower thirds of oven and preheat oven to 400°F (200°C).

7. Using tip of a sharp knife, cut 3 slits in top of each pie. Bake in preheated oven for 35 to 45 minutes, switching positions of baking sheets halfway through, until puffed and golden brown. Let cool for 5 minutes on sheets on wire racks before serving.

## Variations

Substitute Savory Cheese Dough (page 23), Flaky Pie Dough (page 15) or Hand Pie Dough (page 27) for the Pizza/Calzone Dough.

*Gluten-Free Alternative:* Substitute Gluten-Free Pie Dough (page 24) for the Pizza/Calzone Dough.

## Make Ahead

The calzones can be assembled (Steps 1 through 5) and frozen for up to two weeks. Freeze pies for at least 30 minutes on baking trays, then seal in zip-top bags. Bake from frozen, as directed.

# Huevos Wrapcheros Hand Pies

● **GF Friendly**

*When you want to take breakfast-on-the-go to an entirely new level, hand your family these zesty, hearty pies as they head out the door. Spicy chorizo sausage and eggs are layered with pinto beans, cheese and a seasoned chili-tomato sauce – guaranteed fuel for an activity-filled morning.*

## Tip

Be sure to buy fresh chorizo sausage, which is sold soft in casings and must be cooked before consumption, and not dried cured chorizo, which can be sliced and eaten from the package.

● 6-inch (15 cm) round cutter
● 2 baking sheets lined with parchment

### Tomato Sauce

| | | |
|---|---|---|
| 1 tbsp | olive oil | 15 mL |
| ½ cup | chopped white onion | 125 mL |
| 1 tsp | minced garlic | 5 mL |
| ¼ cup | canned diced green chiles | 60 mL |
| 1 | can (15 oz/470 g) diced tomatoes, with juices | 1 |
| 1 tsp | ground cumin | 5 mL |
| 1 tsp | chili powder | 5 mL |
| 2 tbsp | chopped cilantro leaves | 30 mL |
| | Salt and freshly ground black pepper | |

### Chorizo Filling

| | | |
|---|---|---|
| 1 tbsp | olive oil | 15 mL |
| 6 oz | fresh chorizo sausage, casings removed (see Tip, left) | 175 g |
| 6 | large eggs, lightly beaten | 6 |
| ¾ cup | drained canned pinto beans | 175 mL |
| ¾ cup | shredded sharp Cheddar cheese | 175 mL |
| 1 | recipe Hand Pie Dough (page 27) | 1 |
| 1 | large egg, lightly beaten with 1 tbsp (15 mL) water | 1 |

1. *Tomato Sauce:* In a medium saucepan, heat olive oil over medium-high heat. Add onion and garlic; sauté until softened, about 5 minutes. Stir in chiles, tomatoes with juices, cumin and chili powder. Reduce heat and simmer, stirring occasionally, until thickened, about 15 minutes. Stir in cilantro and season to taste with salt and pepper. Remove from heat and set aside to cool completely.

2. *Chorizo Filling:* In a large skillet, heat olive oil over medium-high heat. Add chorizo and sauté, breaking up with a wooden spoon, until cooked through. Drain excess fat from pan.

## Tips

For easiest rolling, roll your dough, including scraps, between two sheets of plastic wrap. That way, you do not need to add flour to keep the dough from sticking to your work surface.

For step-by-step photographs of making hand pies, see page 35.

3. Add eggs to skillet and cook, stirring constantly, until they are set but not too dry. Season to taste with salt and pepper. Remove from heat and set aside to cool to room temperature.

4. On a lightly floured surface, roll out dough to slightly thicker than $1/16$ inch (2 mm). Using cutter, cut into rounds and place on prepared baking sheets, spacing apart. Reroll scraps as necessary.

5. Brush edges of rounds with egg wash. Place 2 tbsp (30 mL) chorizo mixture in center of each round. Top with 1 tbsp (15 mL) beans, 1 tbsp (15 mL) cheese and 1 tbsp (15 mL) tomato sauce. Fold rounds in half, enclosing filling. Pinch edges together to seal, and crimp with the tines of a fork. Brush tops with egg wash.

6. Place pies, on baking sheets, in freezer for 30 minutes. Meanwhile, position oven racks in upper and lower thirds of oven and preheat oven to 375°F (190°C).

7. Using tip of a sharp knife, cut 3 slits in top of each pie. Bake in preheated oven for 25 to 30 minutes, switching positions of baking sheets halfway through, until pies are puffed and golden brown. Let cool on sheets on wire racks for 5 minutes before serving. Pass extra sauce for dipping, if desired.

### Variations

Substitute black or refried beans for the pinto beans.

Substitute Whole Wheat Pie Dough (page 18), Savory Cheese Dough (page 23) or Flaky Pie Dough (page 15) for the Hand Pie Dough.

*Gluten-Free Alternative:* Substitute Gluten-Free Pie Dough (page 24) for the Hand Pie Dough.

### Make Ahead

The pies can be assembled (Steps 1 through 5) and frozen for up to three days. Freeze pies for at least 30 minutes on baking trays, then seal in zip-top bags. Bake from frozen, as directed.

# Croque Madame Breakfast Cups

*I took six years of French classes in middle school and high school. Occasionally our professeur would allow us to have a fun French food day, when we could bring in regional specialties and enjoy a feast. Back then my contributions consisted of things such as bakery croissants, but today I would most definitely prepare these cups, a play on the famous croque madame bistro sandwich.*

## Tips

These breakfast cups are best eaten immediately after baking.

For step-by-step photographs of making Shortcut Puff Pastry, see page 42.

- 12-cup muffin tin, lightly greased
- Pizza/pastry cutter

| | | |
|---|---|---|
| ½ | recipe Shortcut Puff Pastry (page 29) | ½ |

**Sauce**

| | | |
|---|---|---|
| 2 tbsp | unsalted butter | 30 mL |
| 2 tbsp | all-purpose flour | 30 mL |
| 1 cup | whole milk | 250 mL |
| ⅛ tsp | ground nutmeg | 0.5 mL |
| Pinch | cayenne pepper | Pinch |
| 2 tbsp | dry white wine | 30 mL |
| 1 tbsp | Dijon mustard | 15 mL |
| | Salt and freshly ground black pepper | |
| ¼ cup | shredded Gruyère cheese | 60 mL |

**Filling**

| | | |
|---|---|---|
| 6 tbsp | shredded Gruyère cheese | 90 mL |
| 6 tbsp | diced Black Forest ham | 90 mL |
| 12 | large eggs | 12 |
| 2 tbsp | chopped fresh parsley | 30 mL |

1. Divide puff pastry into halves. On a lightly floured surface, roll out one half into a 15- by 10-inch (37.5 by 25 cm) rectangle. Using pizza cutter or sharp knife, cut into six 5-inch (12.5 cm) squares. Fit each square into a muffin cup so corners rise above rims. Repeat with second piece of pastry.

2. Place tin in freezer for 30 minutes. Preheat oven to 400°F (200°C).

3. *Sauce:* In a medium saucepan over medium-low heat, melt butter. Add flour and cook, whisking constantly, for 2 minutes. Gradually whisk in milk, continuing to whisk until mixture comes to a boil. Reduce heat and whisk in nutmeg, cayenne, wine and mustard. Season to taste with salt and pepper. Simmer, whisking frequently, for 3 minutes. Add Gruyère and whisk until smooth. Remove from heat and set aside.

Because of its many, many layers of flour and butter, puff pastry does exactly as its name indicates: it puffs up when baked. Steam produced by the heated butter creates pockets of air and crisp, flaky layers that are perfect for turnovers, free-form tartlets and even pot pies. Although you can find premade puff pastry in the frozen foods section of most grocery stores, I highly recommend that you take the time to try the Shortcut Puff Pastry that I created just for this book.

4. *Filling:* In a small bowl, stir together Gruyère and ham. Place 1 tbsp (15 mL) in bottom of each shell. Top with 1 tbsp (15 mL) sauce. Carefully crack an egg on top of sauce.

5. Bake in center of preheated oven for 15 to 20 minutes, until pastry is browned and puffed and eggs are set.

6. Cool for 5 minutes in tin on a wire rack, then carefully unmold cups and transfer to serving plates. Sprinkle with parsley and serve warm. Drizzle with additional sauce, if desired.

## Make Ahead

The puff pastry shells can be formed and frozen in their tin, covered, for up to three days.

# Savory Pear, Prosciutto and Blue Cheese Tarts

**Makes 24 tarts**

● **GF Friendly**

*Occasionally, when I want to make a dinner that is easy to prepare but still full of flavor, I'll make simple flatbread pizzas, usually accompanied by a small salad. By far my favorite topping combination is a mixture of juicy pears, salty prosciutto and tangy blue cheese. Here I've repackaged these ingredients as tarts that will make a perfect passed appetizer at your next party.*

## Tip

When buying prosciutto, read the label for country of origin. Authentic (and the best-tasting!) prosciutto comes from Italy's Parma region; it will be labeled "Prosciutto di Parma."

● **4-inch (10 cm) round cutter**
● **Two 12-cup muffin tins, greased**

| 1 | recipe All-Butter Pie Dough (page 16) | 1 |
|---|---|---|
| **Filling** | | |
| 1 tbsp | unsalted butter | 15 mL |
| 1/2 | red onion, chopped | 1/2 |
| 2 cups | chopped peeled pears (Bartlett or Anjou) | 500 mL |
| 2 tsp | chopped fresh rosemary | 10 mL |
| 3 oz | thinly sliced prosciutto, chopped (see Tip, left) | 90 g |
| | Salt and freshly ground black pepper | |
| 1 1/2 cups | crumbled blue cheese | 375 mL |

1. On a lightly floured surface, roll out dough to a thickness of $1/8$ inch (3 mm). Using cutter, cut out 24 rounds and carefully fit into muffin cups, rerolling scraps as necessary.

2. Place tins in freezer for 30 minutes. Meanwhile, preheat oven to 400°F (200°C).

3. *Filling:* In a large skillet, melt butter over medium-high heat. Add onion and sauté for 2 minutes. Add pears and sauté until softened, about 3 to 4 minutes. Stir in rosemary and prosciutto and remove from heat. Season to taste with salt and pepper. Set aside to cool.

4. Place about 2 tbsp (30 mL) filling in each shell. Top with 1 tbsp (15 mL) blue cheese.

5. Bake on center rack in preheated oven for 10 minutes. Reduce oven temperature to 350°F (180°C) and bake for 20 to 25 minutes longer, until crust is golden and cheese is bubbling.

6. Cool tarts in tins on wire racks for 10 minutes, then carefully unmold and transfer to serving plates. Serve warm or at room temperature.

## Tip

The easiest way to remove pies from muffin tins is to run a small, sharp knife or small offset spatula around the edges, loosening the sides. You should then be able to carefully lift them out, guiding them with the knife or spatula.

## Variations

Substitute Whole Wheat Pie Dough (page 18) or Flaky Pie Dough (page 15) for the All-Butter Pie Dough.

*Gluten-Free Alternative:* Substitute Gluten-Free Pie Dough (page 24) for the All-Butter Pie Dough.

## Make Ahead

The tarts can be assembled (Steps 1 through 4) and chilled overnight, tightly covered, in their tins. Bake from frozen, as directed.

# Caramelized Cauliflower, Sage and Pancetta Turnovers

*If you know people who claim to dislike cauliflower, you can change their minds with one of these turnovers. Fresh sage, crisp pancetta, almonds and Parmesan season a roasted cauliflower filling — they'll most likely end up asking for seconds!*

## Tips

The easiest way to dice pancetta is to freeze ¼-inch (0.5 cm) slices for 30 minutes. This makes it firm enough to cut through without tearing.

When cutting large rounds, you can use the flat section of a two-piece tart pan as a template and the outer section as a cutter, being careful of sharp edges. If you don't have an appropriately-sized tart tin, a pot lid also makes a good guide.

You will need to bake this recipe in batches. While the first batch is baking, assemble and freeze the second batch.

- Preheat oven to 425°F (220°C)
- Rimmed baking sheet
- Food processor
- 5-inch (12.5 cm) round cutter
- 4 baking sheets lined with parchment

### Filling

| | | |
|---|---|---|
| 1 | head cauliflower, sliced ¼ inch (0.5 cm) thick | 1 |
| 2 tbsp | extra-virgin olive oil | 30 mL |
| | Salt and freshly ground black pepper | |
| 4 oz | diced pancetta (see Tip, left) | 125 g |
| 6 tbsp | panko bread crumbs | 90 mL |
| 6 tbsp | blanched whole almonds | 90 mL |
| 1 tbsp | chopped fresh sage | 15 mL |
| 2 tbsp | unsalted butter, melted | 30 mL |
| 1 cup | freshly grated Parmesan cheese | 250 mL |
| 2 | recipes Hand Pie Dough (page 27) | 2 |
| 1 | large egg, lightly beaten with 1 tbsp (15 mL) water | 1 |

1. *Filling:* On rimmed baking sheet, toss cauliflower with olive oil. Season to taste with salt and pepper; toss again. Roast in preheated oven for 30 to 40 minutes, stirring occasionally, until soft and lightly caramelized. Transfer to a large bowl and turn off oven.

2. In a large skillet over medium-low heat, cook pancetta until browned and crisp, 8 to 10 minutes. Drain on paper towels, then add to cauliflower.

3. In food processor fitted with the metal blade, process bread crumbs, almonds and sage until almonds are ground. Drizzle with melted butter and pulse until evenly coated. Add to cauliflower mixture along with Parmesan, tossing to blend.

## Tips

Once you start using parchment paper, you will never want to go back to silicone liners or greased baking sheets. Disposable, heat-resistant and nonstick, parchment will make your pie-baking life much, much easier! Use it to line baking sheets or tart shells when blind-baking. When you have finished baking, simply throw out the used parchment. It makes for extremely easy clean-up.

For step-by-step photographs of making hand pies, see page 35.

4. On a lightly floured surface, roll out dough to a thickness of $1/8$ inch (3 mm). Using cutter, cut into rounds and place on prepared baking sheets, spacing apart. Reroll scraps as necessary.

5. Brush surfaces of rounds with egg wash. Place about 2 tbsp (30 mL) filling in center of each. Fold rounds in half, enclosing filling. Pinch edges together to seal, and crimp with the tines of a fork. Brush tops with egg wash.

6. Place pies, on baking sheets, in freezer for 30 minutes. Meanwhile, position oven racks in upper and lower thirds of oven and preheat oven to 375°F (190°C).

7. Using tip of a sharp knife, cut 2 or 3 slits in top of each pie. Bake in preheated oven for 25 to 30 minutes, switching positions of baking sheets halfway through, until puffed and golden brown. Let cool on sheets on wire racks for 5 minutes before serving.

## Variations

Substitute Whole Wheat Pie Dough (page 18), Parmesan Cheese Dough (see Variations, page 23) or Flaky Pie Dough (page 15) for the Hand Pie Dough.

## Make Ahead

The pies can be assembled (Steps 1 through 5) and frozen for up to one month. Freeze pies for at least 30 minutes on baking trays, then seal in zip-top bags. Bake from frozen, as directed.

# Corn, Bacon and Tomato Tarts

● **GF Friendly**

*When we lived in New Jersey, ears of sweet farm-stand corn and ripe, juicy tomatoes made a nightly appearance on our dinner table during the summer. These colorful tarts mix those two Garden State staples with smoky bacon, tangy Cheddar and fresh basil, all cradled in a flaky puff pastry shell.*

## Tips

Here's an easy and tidy way to remove kernels from an ear of corn: Invert a smaller bowl inside a larger bowl. Stand ear of corn on smaller bowl and cut off kernels with a sharp serrated knife so they fall directly into the larger bowl.

Substitute 2 cups (500 mL) frozen corn for the fresh corn.

● **2 baking sheets lined with parchment**
● **Pizza/pastry cutter**

### Filling

| | | |
|---|---|---|
| 2 | slices thick-cut smoked bacon | 2 |
| ½ | yellow onion, chopped | ½ |
| 1 | clove garlic, minced | 1 |
| 2 | ears sweet corn, kernels removed (about 2 cups/500 mL; see Tips, left) | 2 |
| 1 cup | grape tomatoes, halved | 250 mL |
| ¼ cup | julienned fresh basil leaves (see Tips, page 269) | 60 mL |
| | Salt and freshly ground black pepper | |
| ½ | recipe Shortcut Puff Pastry (page 29) | ½ |
| 1 | large egg, lightly beaten with 1 tbsp (15 mL) water | 1 |
| 1 cup | shredded sharp (aged) Cheddar cheese | 250 mL |

1. *Filling:* In a large skillet over medium-high heat, fry bacon until crisp. Transfer to paper towels to drain. Pour off all but 1 tbsp (15 mL) fat from pan and lower heat to medium.

2. Add onion and garlic to pan and cook, stirring, until onion is softened, 5 to 6 minutes. Add corn and cook, stirring, until cooked through, 3 to 4 minutes. Add tomatoes and cook, stirring, for 2 minutes.

3. Crumble bacon into skillet. Stir in basil and season to taste with salt and pepper. Remove from heat and set aside.

4. On a lightly floured surface, roll out pastry into a 21- by 11-inch (53 by 29 cm) rectangle. Using a paring knife or pizza cutter, trim to 20 by 10 inches (50 by 25 cm), discarding scraps. Cut into eight 5-inch (12.5 cm) squares and transfer to prepared baking sheets.

5. Brush surfaces of squares with egg wash. Place about 2 tbsp (30 mL) cheese in center of each square and top with about ¼ cup (60 mL) filling.

## Tips

To julienne basil, start with large, clean, unbruised leaves. Stack them together like sheets of paper, then roll the stack into a cigar shape. Using a sharp knife, thinly slice across the roll. This technique is also referred to as chiffonade.

For step-by-step photographs of making Shortcut Puff Pastry, see page 42.

6. Fold up corners of each square around filling so points meet near center but do not touch. Press lightly to distribute filling evenly. Brush tops with egg wash.

7. Place tartlets, on baking sheets, in refrigerator or freezer for 30 minutes. Meanwhile, position oven racks in upper and lower thirds of oven and preheat oven to 400°F (200°C).

8. Bake in preheated oven for 25 to 30 minutes, switching positions of baking sheets halfway through, until golden brown and puffed. Serve warm.

## Variations

Substitute store-bought puff pastry for the Shortcut Puff Pastry.

Substitute 1 recipe Cornmeal Pie Dough (page 19) for the $1/2$ recipe Shortcut Puff Pastry.

*Gluten-Free Alternative:* Substitute 1 recipe Gluten-Free Pie Dough (page 24) for the $1/2$ recipe Shortcut Puff Pastry.

## Make Ahead

The filling can be prepared one day in advance and refrigerated, covered.

The tartlets can be fully assembled (Steps 1 through 6) and refrigerated on the baking sheets, covered, for up to four hours.

# "Tidy Joe" Hand Pies

**Makes 12 pies**

- **GF Friendly**

*Sloppy Joes have certainly earned their name. My mother used to make these hearty sandwiches on a regular basis, and on multiple occasions enjoying these tasty treats created stains on my clothes as well as on the tablecloth. Here is a tidier version that wraps the warm seasoned beef and tomato filling in a spill-proof shell.*

## Tips

This recipe makes a generous amount of filling. Leftover filling can be stored in the refrigerator, tightly sealed in a container, for five days. Use in sandwiches for a meal later in the week.

Tomato purée is a canned product that usually consists only of tomatoes, but it can also be found in a seasoned form. It is not as thick as tomato paste and it lacks some of the additional ingredients found in tomato sauce. In a pinch, substitute an equal quantity of tomato sauce.

- 6-inch (15 cm) round cutter
- 2 baking sheets lined with parchment

### Filling

| | | |
|---|---|---|
| 2 tbsp | extra-virgin olive oil | 30 mL |
| ½ | yellow onion, chopped | ½ |
| 1 | rib celery, chopped | 1 |
| ½ | red bell pepper, seeded and chopped | ½ |
| 2 tsp | minced garlic | 10 mL |
| 1 lb | lean ground beef | 500 g |
| ½ tsp | salt | 2 mL |
| ¼ tsp | freshly ground black pepper | 1 mL |
| 1 | can (14 oz/400 g) tomato purée (see Tips, left) | 1 |
| ¼ cup | ketchup | 60 mL |
| 1 tbsp | packed light brown sugar | 15 mL |
| 1 tbsp | cider vinegar | 15 mL |
| 1 tbsp | Worcestershire sauce | 15 mL |
| 1 tbsp | chili powder | 15 mL |
| 1 tsp | ground cumin | 5 mL |
| ¼ tsp | hot pepper flakes | 1 mL |
| 1 | recipe Pizza/Calzone Dough (page 30) | 1 |
| 1 | large egg, lightly beaten with 1 tbsp (15 mL) water | 1 |
| 2 cups | shredded Cheddar cheese, optional | 500 mL |

1. *Filling:* In a large skillet, heat olive oil over medium-high heat. Add onion, celery and bell pepper; sauté for 5 minutes. Add garlic and sauté for 1 minute. Add ground beef and sauté, breaking up with a wooden spoon, until meat is cooked through, about 5 minutes. Stir in salt and pepper.

2. Add tomato purée, ketchup, brown sugar, vinegar, Worcestershire, chili powder, cumin and hot pepper flakes. Bring to a boil, then reduce heat and simmer, stirring occasionally, until sauce has thickened, about 20 minutes. Remove from heat and set aside to cool completely.

3. Divide dough in half. On a lightly floured surface, roll one half to a thickness of $1/8$ inch (3 mm). Using cutter, cut into rounds and place on prepared baking sheets, spacing apart. Reroll scraps as necessary.

4. Brush edges of rounds with egg wash (see Tips, left). Place about $1/4$ cup (60 mL) filling in center of each round. Top with 2 tbsp (30 mL) cheese, if using. Fold rounds in half, enclosing filling, then fold the edges over to create a double thickness. Pinch edges together to seal, and crimp with the tines of a fork. Brush tops with egg wash.

5. Place pies, on baking sheets, in freezer for 30 minutes. Meanwhile, position oven racks in upper and lower thirds of oven and preheat oven to 375°F (190°C).

6. Using tip of a sharp knife, cut 3 slits in top of each pie. Bake in preheated oven for 35 to 45 minutes, switching positions of baking sheets halfway through, until pies are puffed and golden brown. Let pies cool on sheets on wire racks for 5 minutes before serving.

## Variations

Substitute Whole Wheat Pie Dough (page 18), Savory Cheese Dough (page 23), Flaky Pie Dough (page 15) or Hand Pie Dough (page 27) for the Pizza/Calzone Dough.

*Gluten-Free Alternative:* Substitute Gluten-Free Pie Dough (page 24) for the Pizza/Calzone Dough.

## Make Ahead

The pies can be assembled (Steps 1 through 4) and frozen for up to one month. Freeze pies for at least 30 minutes on baking trays, then seal in zip-top bags. Bake from frozen, as directed.

# Argentinean Beef Pies with Chimichurri Sauce

**Makes 12 pies**

● **GF Friendly**

*Chimichurri sauce usually accompanies grilled meat in Argentinean cooking. Made from a blend of herbs, garlic, vinegar and hot red pepper, this condiment works very well as a dipping sauce for these spicy South American–inspired beef pies.*

## Tips

If you want to make these pies several days in advance, eliminate the hard-cooked egg in the filling. Freeze the fully assembled pies on trays, then transfer to sealed zip-top bags for up to one month. Bake directly from frozen, as directed.

This recipe will leave you with some extra filling. You can either make a second batch (or half-batch) of dough to make additional pies, or you can enjoy the filling on its own.

● Food processor
● 6-inch (15 cm) round cutter
● 2 baking sheets lined with parchment

### Filling

| | | |
|---|---|---|
| 1 tbsp | extra-virgin olive oil | 15 mL |
| ½ | yellow onion, chopped | ½ |
| 1 tbsp | minced garlic | 15 mL |
| 1 lb | lean ground beef | 500 g |
| ¼ cup | chopped green onions | 60 mL |
| 2 tbsp | smoked sweet paprika | 30 mL |
| 1 tbsp | ground cumin | 15 mL |
| 2 tsp | dried oregano | 10 mL |
| | Salt and freshly ground black pepper | |
| ¼ cup | sliced green olives | 60 mL |
| ⅓ cup | chopped fresh cilantro leaves | 75 mL |
| 2 | hard-cooked eggs, chopped | 2 |

### Chimichurri Sauce

| | | |
|---|---|---|
| ½ cup | extra-virgin olive oil | 125 mL |
| ½ cup | red wine vinegar | 125 mL |
| ½ cup | chopped green onions | 125 mL |
| ½ cup | chopped parsley leaves | 125 mL |
| 2 tbsp | chopped garlic | 30 mL |
| ¼ tsp | hot pepper flakes | 1 mL |
| | | |
| 1 | recipe Hand Pie Dough (page 27; see Tips, left) | 1 |
| 1 | large egg, lightly beaten with 1 tbsp (15 mL) water | 1 |

1. *Filling:* In a large skillet, heat oil over medium-high heat. Add onion and sauté until softened, about 5 minutes. Add garlic and sauté for 1 minute. Add ground beef and sauté, stirring occasionally, until cooked through, about 5 minutes. Stir in green onions, paprika, cumin and oregano. Season to taste with salt and pepper. Remove from heat.

## Tips

When cutting large rounds, you can use the flat section of a two-piece tart pan as a template and the outer section as a cutter, being careful of sharp edges. If you don't have an appropriately-sized tart tin, a pot lid also makes a good guide.

For step-by-step photographs of making hand pies, see page 35.

2. Stir in olives, cilantro and egg. Set aside to cool completely.

3. *Chimichurri Sauce:* In food processor fitted with the metal blade, process olive oil, vinegar, green onions, parsley, garlic and hot pepper flakes until finely chopped and almost smooth, stopping to scrape down sides of bowl as necessary. Set aside.

4. On a lightly floured surface, roll out dough to slightly thicker than $1/16$ inch (2 mm). Using cutter, cut into rounds and place on prepared baking sheets, spacing apart. Reroll scraps as necessary.

5. Brush surfaces of rounds with egg wash. Place about 3 tbsp (45 mL) filling in center of each round. Drizzle with chimichurri sauce. Fold in half, enclosing filling. Pinch edges together to seal, and crimp with the tines of a fork. Brush tops with egg wash.

6. Place pies, on baking sheets, in freezer for 30 minutes. Meanwhile, position oven racks in upper and lower thirds of oven and preheat oven to 375°F (190°C).

7. Using tip of a sharp knife, cut 3 slits in top of each pie. Bake in preheated oven for 30 to 35 minutes, switching positions of baking sheets halfway through, until pies are golden brown and puffed. Cool for 5 minutes on sheets placed on wire racks. Serve warm, with remaining chimichurri sauce for dipping.

## Variations

Substitute Savory Cheese Dough (page 23) or Flaky Pie Dough (page 15) for the Hand Pie Dough.

*Gluten-Free Alternative:* Substitute Gluten-Free Pie Dough (page 24) for the Hand Pie Dough.

## Make Ahead

The pies can be assembled (Steps 1 through 5) one day in advance and refrigerated, covered, overnight. Bake as directed.

# Jamaican Beef Patties

Jamaican patties are savory
turnovers commonly eaten
not only in Jamaica but
all over the Caribbean.
Although these pastries
are traditionally filled
with ground beef, as in
this version, they can also
be made with chicken,
vegetables or seafood.

## Tips

When seeding and chopping
hot peppers such as
Scotch bonnet chiles, wear
disposable plastic gloves.
This will prevent the burning
capsaicin from getting on
your fingers and (painfully!)
transferring to other parts of
your body, such as your eyes.

If you can't find a Scotch
bonnet pepper, substitute
an equal quantity of
habanero chile.

- 6-inch (15 cm) round cutter
- 2 baking sheets lined with parchment

### Filling

| | | |
|---|---|---|
| 2 tbsp | butter | 30 mL |
| 1 | small yellow onion, chopped | 1 |
| 2 | green onions, chopped | 2 |
| 1 tsp | finely chopped Scotch bonnet chile pepper | 5 mL |
| 1 lb | lean ground beef | 500 g |
| 1 tbsp | chopped fresh thyme leaves | 15 mL |
| 2 tsp | smoked sweet paprika | 10 mL |
| 2 tsp | curry powder | 10 mL |
| 1/2 tsp | ground allspice | 2 mL |
| 1 tsp | salt | 5 mL |
| 1/4 tsp | freshly ground black pepper | 1 mL |
| 1 tbsp | tomato paste | 15 mL |
| 1/2 cup | panko bread crumbs | 125 mL |
| 1 cup | reduced-sodium beef stock | 250 mL |
| 1 | recipe Flaky Pie Dough (page 15) | 1 |
| 1 | large egg, lightly beaten with 1 tbsp (15 mL) water | 1 |

1. *Filling:* In a large skillet, melt butter over medium-high heat. Add yellow and green onions and chile pepper; sauté until softened, 3 to 4 minutes. Add ground beef, thyme, paprika, curry powder, allspice, salt and pepper; sauté until beef is browned, about 3 to 4 minutes.

2. Add tomato paste and bread crumbs, stirring to blend. Add beef stock, then cover and reduce heat. Simmer for 10 minutes or until liquid is absorbed. Remove from heat and set aside to cool completely.

3. On a lightly floured surface, roll out dough to slightly thicker than $1/16$ inch (2 mm). Using cutter, cut into rounds and place on prepared baking sheets, spacing apart. Reroll scraps as necessary.

4. Brush edges of rounds with egg wash. Place about $1/4$ cup (60 mL) filling in center of each round. Fold in half, enclosing filling. Pinch edges together to seal, and crimp with the tines of a fork. Brush tops with egg wash.

## Tips

When cutting large rounds, you can use the flat section of a two-piece tart pan as a template and the outer section as a cutter, being careful of sharp edges. If you don't have an appropriately-sized tart tin, a pot lid also makes a good guide.

For step-by-step photographs of making hand pies, see page 35.

5. Place patties, on baking sheets, in freezer for 30 minutes. Meanwhile, position oven racks in upper and lower thirds of oven and preheat oven to 375°F (190°C).

6. Using tip of a knife, cut 2 or 3 slits in top of each pie. Bake in preheated oven for 30 to 35 minutes, switching positions of baking sheets halfway through, until patties are puffed and golden brown. Serve warm.

## Variations

Substitute Hand Pie Dough (page 27), Whole Wheat Pie Dough (page 18) or All-Butter Pie Dough (page 16) for the Flaky Pie Dough.

## Make Ahead

The patties can be assembled and frozen for up to one month. Complete Steps 1 through 4, then freeze pies for at least 30 minutes on baking trays. Seal in zip-top bags. Bake from frozen, as directed.

# Indian-Spiced Lamb Samosas

---

## Makes 32 samosas

• **GF Friendly**

---

*It seems as though every culture has its own version of a savory mini pie. In India, samosas — small fried or baked pastries with fillings that often include potatoes, generous seasonings and lamb — fit the description. This recipe can be used to make smaller samosas, which are perfect for passed appetizers, or larger ones, for an exotic portable meal.*

## Tips

*Garam masala* translates as "hot spice" in Hindi. This mixture of spices is commonly used in Indian cooking and is readily available in most grocery store spice sections.

Fresh or frozen peas may be used in this recipe.

• 5-inch (12.5 cm) round cutter
• Candy/deep-fry thermometer

### Filling

| | | |
|---|---|---|
| 1 tbsp | extra-virgin olive oil | 15 mL |
| 1 tbsp | unsalted butter | 15 mL |
| ½ | yellow onion, chopped | ½ |
| 1 | medium russet potato, peeled and cubed | 1 |
| 1 tbsp | minced gingerroot | 15 mL |
| 1 | red or green chile pepper, seeded and minced | 1 |
| 2 | cloves garlic, minced | 2 |
| 1½ tsp | ground cumin | 7 mL |
| 1½ tsp | ground coriander | 7 mL |
| 1½ tsp | garam masala (see Tips, left) | 7 mL |
| ½ tsp | ground cinnamon | 2 mL |
| | Salt and freshly ground black pepper | |
| 1 lb | ground lamb or beef | 500 g |
| ⅓ cup | dry white wine | 75 mL |
| ¼ cup | reduced-sodium chicken stock | 60 mL |
| 2 tbsp | chopped fresh cilantro leaves | 30 mL |
| 1 tbsp | chopped mint leaves | 15 mL |
| ¼ cup | sweet green peas (see Tips, left) | 60 mL |
| 2 | recipes All-Butter Pie Dough (page 16) | 2 |
| 1 | large egg, lightly beaten with 1 tbsp (15 mL) water | 1 |
| | Canola or safflower oil | |

1. *Filling:* In a large skillet, heat oil and butter over medium-high heat. Add onion and potato; sauté until softened and lightly browned, about 4 to 5 minutes. Add ginger, chile pepper, garlic, cumin, coriander, garam masala, cinnamon, and salt and pepper to taste; sauté for 2 minutes.

2. Add ground lamb, wine and chicken stock. Reduce heat, cover and simmer, stirring occasionally, until meat has cooked through, 6 to 8 minutes. Stir in cilantro and mint. Simmer, uncovered, until liquid has evaporated, about 10 minutes. Remove from heat and stir in peas. Set aside to cool completely.

## Tips

To make larger samosas, use a 6-inch (15 cm) cutter and $1/4$ cup (60 mL) filling per round. Fry for the same amount of time (4 to 5 minutes) as the smaller versions.

A deep-fry thermometer helps you to maintain the appropriate temperature (in this book, 360°F/185°C) of your oil, ensuring that your pies are properly cooked. These thermometers come in both digital and non-digital varieties. I prefer one that clips directly onto the side of the pot for easy reading. If you do not own a thermometer, the best way to test if your oil is ready for frying is to drop a small scrap of dough into the pot. If the dough fries on contact, the oil is ready.

3. On a lightly floured surface, roll out dough to slightly thicker than $1/16$ inch (2 mm). Using cutter, cut into rounds and place on baking sheets. Reroll scraps as necessary.

4. Brush surfaces of rounds with egg wash. Place about 2 tbsp (30 mL) filling in center of each round. Fold in half, enclosing filling. Pinch edges together to seal, and crimp with the tines of a fork.

5. Place samosas, on baking sheets, in freezer for 30 minutes.

6. In a deep skillet or Dutch oven, heat 2 inches (5 cm) oil until deep-fry thermometer registers 360°F (185°C). Fry samosas in batches, turning once, until golden brown, 4 to 5 minutes in total.

7. Transfer to a wire rack lined with paper towels to cool slightly. Serve warm.

## Variations

Substitute 2 recipes Hand Pie Dough (page 35) for the All-Butter Pie Dough.

If you prefer, bake your samosas instead of frying them, at 375°F (190°C) for 25 to 30 minutes.

*Gluten-Free Alternative:* Substitute 2 recipes Gluten-Free Pie Dough (page 24) for the All-Butter Pie Dough.

## Make Ahead

The samosas can be assembled (Steps 1 through 4) and frozen for up to two weeks. Freeze for at least 30 minutes on baking trays, then seal in zip-top bags. Fry from frozen, as directed.

# Greek Lamb and Feta Phyllo Pies

Makes 16 pies

*I have yet to meet a Greek dish that I don't like. From its colorful array of fresh vegetables to the frequent inclusion of tangy, salty feta cheese, Greek cuisine tops my list of favorite foods from other cultures. Featuring ground lamb, fresh mint, vegetables and feta, these crispy phyllo packets enclose some of Greek food's greatest hits.*

## Tip

Fresh mint should be stored wrapped in a damp (not wet) paper towel and sealed in a plastic bag. Store in the refrigerator for up to two weeks.

- Preheat oven to 375°F (190°C), positioning racks in upper and lower thirds
- 2 baking sheets lined with parchment
- Damp tea towel

### Filling

| | | |
|---|---|---|
| 1 tbsp | olive oil | 15 mL |
| ½ | red onion, chopped | ½ |
| 1 tbsp | chopped garlic | 15 mL |
| 1 cup | diced zucchini | 250 mL |
| 1 lb | ground lamb or beef | 500 g |
| | Salt and freshly ground black pepper | |
| 1 | can (14 oz/440 g) diced tomatoes, drained | 1 |
| 2 tbsp | red wine vinegar | 30 mL |
| 2 tsp | dried oregano | 10 mL |
| 2 tbsp | chopped fresh parsley leaves | 30 mL |
| 2 tbsp | chopped fresh mint leaves | 30 mL |
| ⅓ cup | chopped pitted kalamata olives | 75 mL |
| 32 | sheets phyllo dough, thawed (see Tips, page 279) | 32 |
| 1 cup | unsalted butter, melted | 250 mL |
| 1 cup | crumbled feta cheese | 250 mL |

1. *Filling:* In a large skillet, heat oil over medium-high heat. Add onion and sauté until softened, about 4 minutes. Add garlic and zucchini and sauté for 2 minutes. Add lamb and sauté, stirring frequently, until meat is no longer pink, about 5 minutes. Season to taste with salt and pepper.

2. Add tomatoes, vinegar and oregano to pan; lower heat and simmer for 5 minutes. Stir in parsley, mint and olives. Remove from heat and set aside to cool to room temperature.

## Tips

Your phyllo sheets should be about 14 by 9 inches (35 by 23 cm). You can work with rectangles that approximate this size, but if the configuration of your phyllo sheet is dramatically different, roll it out or trim it to something that roughly conforms.

When working with thawed phyllo (Step 3), be sure to keep it covered with a damp clean tea towel. Until you brush it with melted butter, it will dry out quickly when exposed to air.

For step-by-step photographs of making phyllo packets, see page 38.

3. Place 1 sheet phyllo on a clean work surface, short side facing you. Working quickly, brush with melted butter and top with a second sheet of phyllo. (Cover remaining sheets with damp towel to prevent drying out.)

4. Place $\frac{1}{4}$ cup (60 mL) lamb filling 1 inch from bottom edge of phyllo, leaving 3-inch (7.5 cm) borders on each side and about 10 inches (25 cm) at the top. Place 1 tbsp (15 mL) crumbled feta on top of lamb. Carefully fold both long sides of phyllo over filling so they overlap completely, covering filling. You will now have a 3-inch (7.5 cm) by 14-inch (35 cm) rectangle.

5. Brush top surface of phyllo rectangle with melted butter. Fold up the 1-inch (2.5 cm) bottom edge to form a little packet for the filling, then fold the packet over and over until you reach the other end of the phyllo. Press the end to seal. Transfer packet to prepared baking sheet, seam side down. Brush top with butter. Repeat process with remaining phyllo sheets and filling, making 16 packets in total.

6. Bake in preheated oven for 20 to 25 minutes (slightly longer if frozen; see Make Ahead), switching positions of baking sheets halfway through, until phyllo is deep golden brown and crisp. Cool pockets slightly on sheets placed on wire racks. Serve warm.

## Make Ahead

The pies can be assembled (Steps 1 through 5) and frozen for up to one month. Freeze for at least 30 minutes on baking trays, then seal in zip-top bags. Bake from frozen, as directed, for an additional 4 to 7 minutes.

# Wild Salmon Pot Pies

*These elegant little pot pies, enclosed in buttery puff pastry, would make a perfect first course for your next dinner party. Because they are easy to bake straight from the freezer, you can spend time enjoying your guests rather than working in the kitchen.*

## Tip

When buying fresh salmon, look for deep pink steaks that spring back when pressed gently, with a mild as opposed to "fishy" aroma.

- 3- and 4½-inch (7.5 and 11.25 cm) round cutters
- Two 12-cup muffin tins, lightly greased

### Filling

| | | |
|---|---|---|
| 2 tbsp | unsalted butter | 30 mL |
| ½ | yellow onion, chopped | ½ |
| 1 | carrot, chopped | 1 |
| 1 | rib celery, chopped | 1 |
| 1½ cups | coarsely chopped trimmed white mushrooms | 375 mL |
| ½ cup | dry white wine | 125 mL |
| 1 lb | skinless wild salmon steaks, cut into 1-inch (2.5 cm) pieces | 500 g |
| ¼ cup | all-purpose flour | 60 mL |
| 1 cup | whole milk | 250 mL |
| 2 tbsp | chopped fresh dill fronds | 30 mL |
| | Salt and freshly ground black pepper | |
| ½ cup | frozen peas | 125 mL |
| 1 | recipe Shortcut Puff Pastry (page 29) | 1 |
| 1 | large egg, lightly beaten with 1 tbsp (15 mL) water | 1 |

1. *Filling:* In a large skillet over medium-high heat, melt butter. Add onion, carrot and celery; sauté until softened, about 6 minutes. Add mushrooms and sauté until tender, about 4 minutes.

2. Add wine to skillet and stir for 1 minute. Add salmon and sauté until almost cooked through, 3 to 4 minutes. Sprinkle flour over mixture and stir gently to coat without breaking up salmon. Slowly add milk, stirring to incorporate. Add dill and season to taste with salt and pepper. Reduce heat and simmer until sauce has thickened, 2 to 3 minutes. Stir in peas. Remove from heat and set aside to cool.

3. Divide puff pastry in two, one piece slightly larger than the other. On a lightly floured work surface, roll out larger piece of dough to a thickness of ⅛ inch (3 mm). Using 4½-inch (11.25 cm) cutter, cut 16 rounds and carefully fit into muffin cups. Reroll scraps as necessary.

## Tips

Because of its many, many layers of flour and butter, puff pastry does exactly as its name indicates: it puffs up when baked. Steam produced by the heated butter creates pockets of air and crisp, flaky layers that are perfect for turnovers, free-form tartlets and even pot pies. Although you can find premade puff pastry in the frozen foods section of most grocery stores, I highly recommend that you take the time to try the Shortcut Puff Pastry that I created just for this book. You'll be happy you did!

For step-by-step photographs of making Shortcut Puff Pastry, see page 42.

**4.** Fill each shell with a heaping $1/4$ cup (60 mL) filling and set aside.

**5.** On lightly floured surface, roll out smaller piece of dough to slightly thicker than $1/16$ inch (2 mm). Using 3-inch (7.5 cm) cutter, cut 16 rounds, rerolling scraps as necessary.

**6.** Brush bottoms of smaller rounds with egg wash and carefully place over filled shells, pressing edges together to seal tightly. Brush tops with egg wash.

**7.** Place tins in freezer for 30 minutes. Meanwhile, position oven racks in upper and lower thirds of oven and preheat oven to 400°F (200°C).

**8.** Using tip of a sharp knife, cut 3 slits in top crusts. Bake in preheated oven for 20 to 25 minutes (slightly longer if fully frozen; see Make Ahead), switching positions of baking sheets halfway through, until tops are puffed and golden and filling is bubbling through holes.

**9.** Cool pies in tins on wire racks for 5 minutes, then carefully unmold and transfer to serving plates. Serve warm.

## Variation

Substitute 2 lbs (1 kg) store-bought puff pastry for the Shortcut Puff Pastry.

## Make Ahead

The pies can be assembled (Steps 1 through 6) and frozen for up to two days. Freeze pies in tins, tightly wrapped. Bake from frozen, as directed, for an additional 5 to 10 minutes.

# New England Lobster Pot Pies

| | | |
|---|---|---|
| **Makes 16 pot pies** | | |

*Unless you live on the northeastern coast of North America, a meal that includes lobster is probably a rare occurrence. These mini pot pies are a great way to serve lobster because it won't break the bank. Mixed with plenty of vegetables and a smooth sherry sauce, this filling makes a little bit of lobster go a long way.*

## Tip

When boiling lobster, allow 12 minutes cooking time for the first pound (500 g), after the water returns to a boil, and 4 minutes for every additional pound. The lobster should be fully submerged in the water.

- 3- and 4½-inch (7.5 and 11.25 cm) round cutters
- Two 12-cup muffin tins, lightly greased

### Filling

| | | |
|---|---|---|
| ¼ cup | unsalted butter | 60 mL |
| 2 | large shallots, minced | 2 |
| 1 | bulb fennel, chopped | 1 |
| 1 | carrot, chopped | 1 |
| 2 tsp | minced garlic | 10 mL |
| 2 tsp | chopped fresh thyme | 10 mL |
| ¼ cup | all-purpose flour | 60 mL |
| ½ cup | dry sherry | 125 mL |
| 1 cup | ready-to-use fish stock or chicken stock | 250 mL |
| | Salt and freshly ground black pepper | |
| 3 tbsp | heavy or whipping (35%) cream | 45 mL |
| 2 cups | cooked lobster meat, cut into bite-size pieces (see Tip, left) | 500 mL |
| ½ cup | frozen sweet corn kernels | 125 mL |
| 1 | recipe All-Butter Pie Dough (page 16) | 1 |
| 1 | large egg, lightly beaten with 1 tbsp (15 mL) water | 1 |

1. *Filling:* In a large skillet over medium-high heat, melt butter. Add shallots, fennel and carrot; sauté until softened, about 8 minutes. Add garlic and thyme; sauté for 2 minutes.

2. Add flour to the skillet and stir constantly for 2 minutes. Slowly add sherry and stock, stirring constantly. Season to taste with salt and pepper; simmer until thickened, about 5 minutes. Add cream, lobster and corn; stir for 2 minutes. Remove from heat and set aside to cool.

3. Divide dough into two pieces, one slightly larger than the other. On a lightly floured surface, roll out larger piece of dough to a thickness of ⅛ inch (3 mm). Using 4½-inch (11.25 cm) cutter, cut 16 rounds and carefully fit into muffin cups (they should stand a bit taller than edges of the cups). Reroll scraps as necessary.

4. Fill each shell with a heaping ¼ cup (60 mL) lobster filling.

## Tips

For easiest rolling, roll your dough, including scraps, between two sheets of plastic wrap. That way, you do not need to add flour to keep the dough from sticking to your work surface.

Expect a longer baking time (6 to 10 minutes) if you need to use 2 muffin tins and they are too large to fit on one rack.

5. On a lightly floured surface, roll out smaller piece of dough to slightly thicker than $^1/_{16}$ inch (2 mm). Using 3-inch (7.5 cm) cutter, cut 16 rounds, rerolling scraps as necessary.

6. Brush bottoms of smaller rounds with egg wash and carefully place over filled shells, pressing edges together to seal tightly. Brush tops with egg wash.

7. Place tins in freezer for 30 minutes. Meanwhile, preheat oven to 375°F (190°C).

8. Using tip of a sharp knife, cut 3 slits in top crusts. Bake in center of preheated oven for 30 to 40 minutes (see Tips, left), until tops are golden brown and filling is bubbling. Cool pies in tins on wire racks for 10 minutes, then carefully unmold and transfer to serving plates. Serve warm.

## Variation

Substitute Flaky Pie Dough (page 15) for the All-Butter Pie Dough.

## Make Ahead

The pies can be assembled (Steps 1 through 6) and frozen for up to three days. Freeze pies in tins, tightly wrapped. Bake from frozen, as directed.

# Chicken and Shrimp Pot Stickers

*I don't think my dad
ever dines at a Chinese
restaurant or orders Chinese
takeout without getting
an order of pot stickers, so
I know he will ask me to
make this recipe the next
time he visits. These two-
bite dumplings have a crisp
browned bottom and a juicy,
well-seasoned filling. Serve
them alone or with a simple
homemade dipping sauce.*

## Tip

If you cannot find gyoza
wrappers at your grocery
store, cut 4-inch (10 cm)
rounds from egg roll
wrappers instead.

● Fine-mesh strainer

### Filling

| | | |
|---|---|---|
| 2 cups | finely chopped napa cabbage | 500 mL |
| 1 tsp | salt | 5 mL |
| 12 oz | ground chicken | 375 g |
| 4 oz | peeled, deveined shrimp, finely chopped | 125 g |
| 1 tbsp | minced peeled gingerroot | 15 mL |
| 1 tbsp | minced garlic | 15 mL |
| 2 | green onions, finely chopped | 2 |
| 2 tbsp | low-sodium soy sauce | 30 mL |
| 1 tbsp | mirin (see Tips, left) | 15 mL |
| 2 tsp | dark sesame oil | 10 mL |
| ¼ tsp | hot pepper flakes | 1 mL |
| 1 | egg, lightly beaten | 1 |
| 36 | 4-inch (10 cm) gyoza (pot sticker) wrappers | 36 |
| ¾ cup | canola or vegetable oil | 175 mL |

1. *Filling:* In fine-mesh strainer set over a large bowl, mix cabbage and salt; set aside for 30 minutes. Squeeze as much liquid from cabbage into bowl as possible; discard liquid.

2. Return cabbage to bowl. Add chicken, shrimp, ginger, garlic, green onions, soy sauce, mirin, sesame oil, hot pepper flakes and egg. Mix thoroughly.

3. Fill a small bowl with water. On a clean surface, lay out one gyoza wrapper. Place 1 tbsp (15 mL) filling in center and brush edges with water. Bring together opposite edges, enclosing filling in a half-moon shape. Form 4 to 6 small pleats along curved edge, pinching to seal completely. Stand dumpling upright, seam side up, and gently press down to flatten bottom. Place on a baking sheet and cover loosely with plastic wrap. Repeat with remaining wrappers and filling.

To serve pot stickers, make a simple dipping sauce with equal parts low-sodium soy sauce and unseasoned rice vinegar, finished with a splash of dark sesame oil. For heat, add a generous pinch of hot pepper flakes.

Mirin is a sweet rice wine found in the Asian food section of most grocery stores.

4. In a large skillet, heat $1/4$ cup (60 mL) oil over medium-high heat until it shimmers. Place as many dumplings as possible in the skillet, in a tight circular pattern, seam sides up. Fry until bottoms are light golden brown, about 2 minutes.

5. Reduce heat to medium and, standing well back (oil will splatter), add $1/4$ cup (60 mL) water to skillet. Cover and cook until liquid has evaporated and bottoms are crisp, 3 to 4 minutes. Transfer dumplings from skillet to a plate and keep warm. Repeat with remaining pot stickers. Serve warm, with dipping sauce, if desired (see Tips, left).

## Variation

Substitute an equal quantity of ground pork for the ground chicken.

## Make Ahead

The pot stickers can be prepared through Step 3, placed on baking sheets and frozen. Transfer frozen dumplings to zip-top bags and store for up to one month. Cook from frozen, as directed.

# Shrimp Empanadas

**Makes 16 empanadas**

● **GF Friendly**

*For such small packages, these empanadas hold an immense amount of flavor! I knew that these would be delicious when I kept returning for "just one more taste" of the filling — always a good sign. You can make these empanadas as smaller or larger pies (these are smaller) depending on how you plan to serve them. No matter what the size, they are certain to disappear quickly.*

## Tip

Although shrimp can be deveined after cooking, it's easier to do while they're raw. Run a deveiner or the tip of a small, sharp knife down the back of the shrimp and remove the dark vein.

● 5-inch (12.5 cm) round cutter
● Candy/deep-fry thermometer

**Filling**

| | | |
|---|---|---|
| 1 tbsp | extra-virgin olive oil | 15 mL |
| ½ | red onion, chopped | ½ |
| 1 | jalapeño pepper, seeded and chopped | 1 |
| 2 tsp | minced garlic | 10 mL |
| 1 tsp | ground cumin | 5 mL |
| 1 tsp | dried oregano | 5 mL |
| 1 tbsp | all-purpose flour | 15 mL |
| 1 cup | drained canned diced tomatoes | 250 mL |
| ½ cup | drained canned black beans | 125 mL |
| 8 oz | fresh or frozen shrimp, peeled, deveined and coarsely chopped (see Tip, left) | 250 g |
| 1 tbsp | freshly squeezed lime juice | 15 mL |
| 2 tbsp | chopped fresh cilantro leaves | 30 mL |
| | Salt and freshly ground black pepper. | |
| 1 | recipe All-Butter Pie Dough (page 16) | 1 |
| 1 | large egg, lightly beaten with 1 tbsp (15 mL) water | 1 |
| | Canola or safflower oil | |

1. *Filling:* In a large skillet, heat oil over medium-high heat. Add onion and jalapeño; sauté until softened, about 5 minutes. Add garlic, cumin and oregano; sauté for 1 minute. Sprinkle with flour and stir to coat. Add tomatoes, beans and shrimp to skillet. Reduce heat and simmer until shrimp are pink and mixture has thickened, about 5 minutes. Stir in lime juice and cilantro. Season to taste with salt and pepper. Remove from heat and set aside to cool completely.

2. On a lightly floured work surface, roll out dough to slightly thicker than $1/16$ inch (2 mm). Using cutter, cut into rounds and place on baking sheets, spacing apart. Reroll scraps as necessary.

3. Brush surfaces of rounds with egg wash. Place 2 to 3 tbsp (30 to 45 mL) filling in center of each round. Fold in half, enclosing filling. Pinch edges together to seal, and crimp with the tines of a fork.

## Tips

To make larger empanadas, use a 6-inch (15 cm) round cutter and $\frac{1}{4}$ cup (60 mL) filling each. Fry for 4 to 5 minutes, until golden brown.

For step-by-step photographs of making these hand pies, see page 35.

4. Place empanadas, on baking sheets, in freezer for 30 minutes.

5. In a deep skillet or Dutch oven, heat 2 inches (5 cm) oil until deep-fry thermometer registers 360°F (185°C). Fry empanadas in batches, turning once, until golden brown, 3 to 4 minutes in total.

6. Transfer to wire rack lined with paper towels to cool slightly. Serve warm.

## Variations

Substitute Hand Pie Dough (page 27) for the All-Butter Pie Dough.

The empanadas can be baked instead of fried, at 375°F (190°C) for 25 to 30 minutes.

*Gluten-Free Alternative:* Substitute Gluten-Free Pie Dough (page 24) for the All-Butter Pie Dough. Substitute 1 tbsp (15 mL) rice flour or cornstarch for the all-purpose flour in the filling.

## Make Ahead

The empanadas can be assembled (Steps 1 through 3) and frozen for up to one month. Freeze for at least 30 minutes on baking trays, then seal in zip-top bags. Bake from frozen, as directed.

# Carolina Crab Boil Quiches

**Makes 24 quiches**

● **GF Friendly**

*I spent one summer on the Outer Banks of North Carolina, where I experienced my first authentic crab boil, featuring red potatoes, sweet corn, freshly caught crab and the mandatory zesty seasoning. These mini quiches were inspired by the flavors of that experience. Feel free to adjust the seasoning to your preferred level of zest.*

## Tips

While shells are in the freezer, preheat oven to 375°F (190°C).

The quiches can be fully baked, cooled to room temperature and frozen for up to two weeks, sealed in a zip-top bag. Reheat at 350°F (180°C) on baking sheets, without defrosting, for 15 to 20 minutes or until heated through.

For step-by-step photographs of the blind-baking process, see page 33.

● 4-inch (10 cm) round cutter
● Two 12-cup muffin tins, lightly greased

| | | |
|---|---|---|
| 1 | recipe Flaky Pie Dough (page 15) | 1 |
| 2 tbsp | olive oil | 30 mL |
| 1 cup | diced (1/4 inch/0.5 cm) red potatoes | 250 mL |
| 1/2 | red onion, chopped | 1/2 |
| 2 | green onions, chopped | 2 |
| 1/2 cup | each whole milk and heavy cream | 125 mL |
| 3 | large eggs | 3 |
| 1/2 cup | shredded sharp (aged) Cheddar cheese | 125 mL |
| 1 1/2 cups | canned pasteurized lump crabmeat | 375 mL |
| 1 tsp | Old Bay or crab boil seasoning | 5 mL |
| | Salt and freshly ground black pepper | |

1. On a lightly floured work surface, roll out dough to a thickness of 1/8 inch (3 mm). Using cutter, cut into rounds and carefully fit into muffin cups (there will be some overlap). Reroll scraps as necessary.

2. Place tins in freezer for 30 minutes (see Tips, left).

3. In a large skillet, heat oil over medium-high heat. Add potatoes and onion; sauté for about 6 minutes, until lightly browned. Add green onions and sauté for 30 seconds. Remove from heat.

4. In a large bowl, whisk together milk, cream and eggs. Add potato mixture, cheese, crab and seasoning. Season to taste with salt and pepper; stir to blend.

5. Blind-bake shells (page 14 and Tips, left) in center of preheated oven for 12 minutes. Carefully remove parchment and weights; cool for 5 minutes. Lower oven temperature to 350°F (180°C).

6. Pour or spoon filling into warm shells, dividing equally. Bake in center of preheated oven for 30 to 35 minutes, until tops are puffed and set. Cool in tins on wire racks for 10 minutes, then carefully unmold. Serve warm or at room temperature.

## Variations

Substitute All-Butter Pie Dough (page 16) or Savory Cheese Dough (page 23) for Flaky Pie Dough.

*Gluten-Free Alternative:* Substitute 1 recipe Gluten-Free Pie Dough (page 24) for the Flaky Pie Dough.

# Vegetarian Savories

# Roasted Tomato, Basil and Mozzarella Pies

Makes 24 pies

● **GF Friendly**

*Caprese salad is becoming as common on restaurant menus as the Caesar salad. And why not? The combination of fragrant basil, thick slices of ripe tomato and fresh buffalo mozzarella is hard to beat. Roasting tomatoes with onions lends an extra touch of juicy sweetness to these Caprese salad–inspired pies.*

## Tips

Fresh mozzarella, usually stored in water, has a shorter shelf life than shredded mozzarella. It should generally be used within three to four days.

A dough scraper is very useful to have when making these recipes. During the rolling process, it collects the little bits for rerolling and it cleans up the pastry board very efficiently. It also simplifies picking up the cut rounds; you just slide the scraper underneath. Even if they are sticking a bit, they will detach without tearing.

● Preheat oven to 425°F (220°C)
● Rimmed baking sheet
● $4\frac{1}{2}$-inch (11.25 cm) round cutter
● 2 baking sheets lined with parchment

### Filling

| | | |
|---|---|---|
| 3 cups | grape tomatoes | 750 mL |
| 1 | yellow onion, thinly sliced | 1 |
| 3 tbsp | extra-virgin olive oil | 45 mL |
| 1 tsp | salt | 5 mL |
| $\frac{1}{2}$ tsp | freshly ground black pepper | 2 mL |
| $\frac{1}{2}$ cup | julienned fresh basil leaves | 125 mL |
| 1 | recipe All-Butter Pie Dough (page 16) | 1 |
| 1 | large egg, lightly beaten with 1 tbsp (15 mL) water | 1 |
| $1\frac{1}{2}$ cups | chopped fresh or shredded mozzarella (see Tips, left) | 375 mL |

1. On rimmed baking sheet, toss tomatoes and onion with olive oil. Sprinkle with salt and pepper. Roast in preheated oven for 30 to 35 minutes, stirring once, until tomatoes start to blister and onion is browned. Transfer to a large bowl and stir in basil. Set aside to cool completely. Turn off oven.

2. On a lightly floured surface, roll out dough to slightly thicker than $\frac{1}{16}$ inch (2 mm). Using cutter, cut into rounds and place on prepared baking sheets, spacing apart. Reroll scraps as necessary.

3. Brush edges of rounds with egg wash. Place about 1 tbsp (15 mL) tomato filling in center of each round. Top with 1 tbsp (15 mL) mozzarella. Fold rounds in half, enclosing filling. Pinch edges together to seal, and crimp with the tines of a fork. Brush tops with egg wash.

4. Place pies, on baking sheets, in freezer for 30 minutes. Position oven racks in upper and lower thirds of oven and preheat oven to 375°F (190°C).

## Tip

If you are using my Gluten-Free Pie Dough (see Variations, right) you will find that it is quite forgiving and easy to work with, because of the absence of gluten. When rolling out the dough, dust your work surface lightly with cornstarch, potato starch or rice flour in lieu of all-purpose flour.

5. Using tip of a sharp knife, cut 2 or 3 slits in top of each pie. Bake in preheated oven for 25 to 30 minutes, switching positions of baking sheets halfway through, until puffed and golden brown. Let cool on sheets on wire rack for 5 minutes before serving.

## Variations

Substitute Herbed Flaky Pie Dough (see Variation, page 15) or Hand Pie Dough (page 27) for the All-Butter Pie Dough.

*Gluten-Free Alternative:* Substitute Gluten-Free Pie Dough (page 24) for the All-Butter Pie Dough.

## Make Ahead

The pies can be assembled (Steps 1 through 3) and frozen for up to five days. Place in freezer for at least 30 minutes on baking trays, then seal in zip-top bags. Bake from frozen, as directed.

# Baked Brie and Tomato-Onion Jam Turnovers

*One of our favorite local restaurants features a baked Brie appetizer on their menu, wrapped in phyllo along with slow-roasted tomatoes, that my husband always orders. I can seldom resist reaching over for at least one bite of the buttery melting cheese. These are bite-size versions of that appetizer that incorporate a sweet-and-sour tomato jam.*

## Tips

Your phyllo sheets should be about 14 by 9 inches (35 by 23 cm). You can work with rectangles that approximate this size, but if the configuration of your phyllo sheet is dramatically different, roll it out or trim it to something that roughly conforms.

When working with thawed phyllo (Step 2), be sure to keep it covered with a damp clean tea towel. Until you brush it with melted butter, it will dry out quickly when exposed to air.

- Preheat oven to 375°F (190°C), positioning racks in upper and lower thirds
- 2 baking sheets lined with parchment
- Damp tea towel

### Tomato-Onion Jam

| | | |
|---|---|---:|
| 1 tbsp | unsalted butter | 15 mL |
| 1 | yellow onion, thinly sliced | 1 |
| 1/3 cup | granulated sugar | 75 mL |
| 2 cups | chopped plum (Roma) tomatoes | 500 mL |
| 2 tbsp | red wine vinegar | 30 mL |
| 1/2 tsp | salt | 2 mL |
| 1/2 tsp | ground ginger | 2 mL |
| 1/4 tsp | freshly ground black pepper | 1 mL |
| 1/4 tsp | ground cumin | 1 mL |
| 1/4 tsp | ground cinnamon | 1 mL |
| 1/8 tsp | ground cloves | 0.5 mL |
| 1/8 tsp | hot pepper flakes | 0.5 mL |
| 24 | sheets phyllo dough, thawed (see Tips, left) | 24 |
| 3/4 cup | unsalted butter, melted | 175 mL |
| 8 oz | Brie cheese, cut into 1-inch (2.5 cm) pieces | 250 g |

1. *Tomato-Onion Jam:* In a medium saucepan, melt butter over medium-high heat. Add onion and sauté until softened, 6 to 8 minutes. Add sugar, tomatoes, vinegar, salt, ginger, pepper, cumin, cinnamon, cloves and hot pepper flakes. Bring to a boil, stirring constantly. Reduce heat and simmer, stirring occasionally, until thickened to jam consistency, about 40 minutes. Transfer to a bowl and set aside to cool completely.

2. Place one sheet of phyllo on a clean work surface, short side facing you. Working quickly, brush with melted butter and fold in half lengthwise. Brush again with butter. (Cover remaining phyllo sheets with damp tea towel until ready to use.)

## Tips

For step-by-step photographs of making phyllo triangles, see page 40.

These turnovers are best baked the day they are assembled, and eaten soon after baking, while still warm.

3. Place one piece Brie on bottom left side of strip, leaving about a 1-inch (2.5 cm) border at the bottom. Top with about 1 tbsp (15 mL) tomato-onion jam. Fold bottom left corner over filling to form a triangle, then continue to fold triangles up the strip of phyllo to the top, as if you are folding a flag. Brush top of triangle with butter, pressing end to seal. Place triangle, seam side down, on prepared baking sheet. Repeat with remaining phyllo sheets, Brie and jam.

4. Bake in preheated oven for 20 to 25 minutes, switching positions of baking sheets halfway through, until phyllo is deep golden brown and crisp and cheese has melted. Cool slightly on sheets placed on wire racks. Serve warm.

# Sun-Dried Tomato Pesto and Goat Cheese Pies

● **GF Friendly**

*Marinated sun-dried tomatoes and toasted almonds bring an interesting twist to traditional pesto. Paired with soft, warm goat cheese, this simple and elegant bite is sure to become a new favorite.*

## Tips

This sun-dried tomato pesto is addictive! Use any leftovers as a sandwich spread or topping for bruschetta.

Once you start using parchment paper, you will never want to go back to silicone liners or greased baking sheets. Disposable, heat-resistant and nonstick, parchment will make your pie-baking life much, much easier! Use it to line baking sheets or tart shells when blind-baking. When you have finished baking, simply throw out the used parchment. It makes for extremely easy clean-up.

● Food processor
● 4½-inch (11.25 cm) round cutter
● 2 baking sheets lined with parchment

### Sun-Dried Tomato Pesto

| | | |
|---|---|---|
| ½ cup | packed fresh basil leaves | 125 mL |
| ½ cup | packed fresh parsley leaves | 125 mL |
| 2 tsp | minced garlic | 10 mL |
| ½ cup | extra-virgin olive oil | 125 mL |
| ½ cup | toasted almonds | 125 mL |
| 1 cup | julienned oil-packed sun-dried tomatoes, drained | 250 mL |
| ½ cup | freshly grated Parmesan cheese | 125 mL |
| ½ tsp | salt | 2 mL |
| ¼ tsp | freshly ground black pepper | 1 mL |
| ¼ tsp | hot pepper flakes | 1 mL |
| 1 | recipe Flaky Pie Dough (page 15) | 1 |
| 1 | large egg, lightly beaten with 1 tbsp (15 mL) water | 1 |
| 1 cup | crumbled soft goat cheese | 250 mL |

1. *Sun-Dried Tomato Pesto:* In food processor fitted with the metal blade, pulse basil, parsley and garlic until finely chopped. With the motor running, pour olive oil down the feed tube in a steady stream. Add almonds, sun-dried tomatoes, Parmesan, salt, pepper and hot pepper flakes. Purée until smooth, stopping to scrape down sides of bowl as necessary.

2. On a lightly floured surface, roll out dough to slightly thicker than ¹⁄₁₆ inch (2 mm). Using cutter, cut into rounds and place on prepared baking sheets, spacing apart. Reroll scraps as necessary.

3. Brush edges of rounds with egg wash. Place about 1 tbsp (15 mL) pesto in center of each round. Top with 2 tsp (10 mL) goat cheese. Fold rounds in half, enclosing filling. Pinch edges together to seal, and crimp with the tines of a fork. Brush tops with egg wash.

## Tips

Wire baking racks are important to have on hand for the cooling process. After pies have finished baking, either set the muffin tin on the rack or transfer the pies from the baking sheet to the rack. This lets the air circulate around the pies, cooling them evenly.

For step-by-step photographs of making hand pies, see page 35.

4. Place pies, on baking sheets, in freezer for 30 minutes. Meanwhile, position oven racks in upper and lower thirds of oven and preheat oven to 375°F (190°C).

5. Using tip of a sharp knife, cut 2 or 3 slits in top of each pie. Bake in preheated oven for 20 to 25 minutes, switching positions of baking sheets halfway through, until puffed and golden brown. Let cool on sheets on wire rack, for 5 minutes before serving.

## Variations

Substitute All-Butter Pie Dough (page 16) or Hand Pie Dough (page 27) for the Flaky Pie Dough.

*Gluten-Free Alternative:* Substitute Gluten-Free Pie Dough (page 24) for the Flaky Pie Dough.

## Make Ahead

The pies can be assembled and frozen for up to one month. Place in freezer for at least 30 minutes on baking trays, then seal in zip-top bags. Bake from frozen, as directed.

# Potato, Leek and Gorgonzola Tarts

*A tried-and-true side dish that I prepare when entertaining, especially during cooler weather, is a rich potato and leek gratin topped with a bubbling layer of tangy Gorgonzola cheese. These tarts are more compact versions that still contain all of the gratin's great flavors.*

## Tips

To clean leeks, trim off the root end close to the white base. Remove any coarse outer leaves and discard. Slice leeks down the center and rinse under cold running water to remove all dirt and sand between the leaves. Drain completely.

Expect a longer baking time (6 to 10 minutes) if you need to use 2 muffin tins and they are too large to fit on one rack.

- 4-inch (10 cm) round cutter
- Two 12-cup muffin tins, greased

| | | |
|---|---|---|
| 1 | recipe Flaky Pie Dough (page 15) | 1 |
| **Filling** | | |
| 1 tbsp | unsalted butter | 15 mL |
| 1 tbsp | extra-virgin olive oil | 15 mL |
| 1 | leek, sliced thinly (see Tips, left) | 1 |
| 2 cups | diced ($\frac{1}{4}$ inch/0.5 cm) red potatoes | 500 mL |
| 1 tbsp | chopped fresh thyme | 15 mL |
| | Salt and freshly ground black pepper | |
| 2 tbsp | all-purpose flour | 30 mL |
| $\frac{1}{4}$ cup | dry white wine | 60 mL |
| $1\frac{1}{2}$ cups | heavy or whipping (35%) cream | 375 mL |
| $1\frac{1}{2}$ cups | crumbled Gorgonzola cheese | 375 mL |

1. On a lightly floured surface, roll out dough to a thickness of $\frac{1}{8}$ inch (3 mm). Using cutter, cut 16 rounds and carefully fit into muffin cups. Reroll scraps as necessary.

2. Place tins in freezer for 30 minutes. Meanwhile, preheat oven to 400°F (200°C).

3. *Filling:* In a large skillet, heat butter and oil over medium-high heat. Add leek and sauté for 2 minutes. Add potatoes and thyme; sauté until potatoes are browned and tender, about 5 minutes. Season to taste with salt and pepper. Add flour and stir constantly for 1 minute. Add wine and stir until evaporated. Remove from heat and set aside to cool for 10 minutes.

4. Place about $1\frac{1}{2}$ tbsp (22 mL) filling in each chilled shell. Top with 1 tbsp (15 mL) cream and 1 tbsp (15 mL) Gorgonzola.

5. Bake in center of preheated oven for 10 minutes. Reduce oven temperature to 350°F (180°C) and bake for 20 to 25 minutes longer, until filling and cheese are bubbling. Cool pies in tins on wire racks for 10 minutes, then carefully unmold and transfer to serving plates. Serve warm or at room temperature.

## Tip

The easiest way to remove pies from muffin tins is to run a small, sharp knife or small offset spatula around the edges, loosening the sides. You should then be able to carefully lift out the pies, guiding them with the knife or spatula.

## Variation

Substitute All-Butter Pie Dough (page 16) for the Flaky Pie Dough.

## Make Ahead

The pies can be assembled (Steps 1 through 4) and refrigerated, covered, overnight. They can also be frozen in their tins, tightly wrapped, for up to five days. Bake as directed.

# Maple Orange Glazed Root Vegetable Galettes

**Makes 16 galettes**

- **GF Friendly**
- **Vegan Friendly**

*My in-laws live in Vermont, where they make their own maple syrup, so we always have plenty of that delectable treat in our pantry. One of my favorite ways to use it is as a glaze for pan-roasted root vegetables. In addition to its distinctive sweet flavor, the syrup adds a beautiful glossy sheen. These mini galettes make a unique side dish to accompany a simple roasted chicken or pork tenderloin.*

## Tips

When shopping for turnips, select dense, smaller varieties. The roots should be firm and the greens should be bright and fresh looking.

For easiest rolling, roll your dough, including scraps, between two sheets of plastic wrap. That way, you do not need to add flour to keep the dough from sticking to your work surface.

- 5-inch (12.5 cm) round cutter
- 2 baking sheets lined with parchment

### Filling

| | | |
|---|---|---|
| 2 tbsp | unsalted butter | 30 mL |
| 1½ cups | chopped peeled parsnips | 375 mL |
| 1½ cups | chopped peeled carrots | 375 mL |
| 1½ cups | chopped peeled turnips (see Tips, left) | 375 mL |
| 1 tbsp | chopped fresh thyme leaves | 15 mL |
| | Salt and freshly ground black pepper | |
| ½ cup | orange juice | 125 mL |
| ¼ cup | pure maple syrup | 60 mL |
| | | |
| 1 | recipe All-Butter Pie Dough (page 16) | 1 |
| 1 | large egg, mixed with 1 tbsp (15 mL) water | 1 |

1. *Filling:* In a large skillet, melt butter over medium-high heat. Add parsnips, carrots and turnips; sauté until browned, about 5 to 6 minutes. Stir in thyme and season to taste with salt and pepper. Add orange juice to the skillet. Reduce heat, cover and simmer until vegetables are tender, 4 to 5 minutes. Uncover and stir in maple syrup; simmer until liquid has reduced and vegetables are glazed.

2. On a lightly floured surface, roll out dough to slightly thicker than $1/16$ inch (2 mm). Using cutter, cut into rounds and place on prepared baking sheets, spacing apart. Reroll scraps as necessary.

3. Brush edges of rounds with egg wash. Place about 3 tbsp (45 mL) filling in center of each round, leaving a border of $1^1/4$ inches (3 cm) around it. Fold up edges of dough over edges of filling, pleating dough as necessary (center of filling should remain exposed). Brush sides and top of dough with egg wash.

4. Place galettes in freezer, on baking sheets, for 30 minutes. Meanwhile, position oven racks in upper and lower thirds of oven and preheat oven to 400°F (200°C).

## Tips

When cutting large rounds, you can use the flat section of a two-piece tart pan as a template and the outer section as a cutter, being careful of sharp edges. If you don't have an appropriately-sized tart tin, a pot lid also makes a good guide.

For step-by-step photographs of making galettes, see page 34.

5. Bake in preheated oven for 25 to 30 minutes, switching positions of baking sheets halfway through, until crust is golden brown. Cool on sheets placed on wire racks for at least 5 minutes before serving.

## Variations

Substitute Flaky Pie Dough (page 15) or Whole Wheat Pie Dough (page 18) for the All-Butter Pie Dough.

*Gluten-Free Alternative:* Substitute Gluten-Free Pie Dough (page 24) for the All-Butter Pie Dough.

*Vegan Alternative:* Substitute Vegan Pie Dough (page 25) for the All-Butter Pie Dough and vegan butter for the unsalted butter. Substitute water for the egg wash.

## Make Ahead

The galettes can be assembled and refrigerated, covered, for up to six hours. Bake as directed.

# Butternut Squash and Apple Turnovers

**Makes 12 turnovers**

- **GF Friendly**
- **Vegan Friendly**

*Whenever I find good
butternut squash at the
grocery store, I grab it.
It's one of my favorite
vegetables, and I turn it
into everything from a thick
and comforting soup to
moist breakfast muffins.
In these pies the squash
is simply diced and pan-
roasted with apples and
thyme. Sometimes I'll add
a crumble of blue cheese on
top, but it's certainly not
necessary.*

## Tips

Tart apples such as Granny
Smiths work best in
these pies.

Butternut squash should be
stored in a cool, dry place
rather than the refrigerator.

This recipe will leave you with
some extra filling. You can
either make a second batch
(or half-batch) of dough
to make additional pies or
you can enjoy the filling on
its own.

- 6-inch (15 cm) round cutter
- 2 baking sheets lined with parchment

### Filling

| | | |
|---|---|---:|
| 2 tbsp | unsalted butter | 30 mL |
| 1 tbsp | extra-virgin olive oil | 15 mL |
| 1 | yellow onion, chopped | 1 |
| 1 lb | butternut squash, peeled and cut into $\frac{1}{2}$-inch (1 cm) cubes | 500 g |
| 2 | apples, peeled and chopped (see Tips, left) | 2 |
| 2 tsp | chopped thyme leaves | 10 mL |
| 1 tsp | salt | 5 mL |
| $\frac{1}{2}$ tsp | freshly ground black pepper | 2 mL |
| 1 | recipe Hand Pie Dough (page 27; see Tips, left) | 1 |
| 1 | large egg, lightly beaten with 1 tbsp (15 mL) water | 1 |
| 1 cup | crumbled blue cheese, optional | 250 mL |

1. *Filling:* In a large skillet, melt butter with olive oil over medium-high heat. Add onion and squash; cook for 10 minutes, stirring occasionally. Add apples, thyme, salt and pepper. Cover and reduce heat. Cook until squash and apples are tender, about 6 to 8 minutes. Remove from heat and set aside to cool completely.

2. On a lightly floured surface, roll out dough to slightly thicker than $\frac{1}{16}$ inch (2 mm). Using cutter, cut into rounds and place on prepared baking sheets, spacing apart. Reroll scraps as necessary.

3. Brush edges of rounds with egg wash. Place about $\frac{1}{4}$ cup (60 mL) filling in center of each round and top with 1 tbsp (15 mL) blue cheese, if using. Fold in half, enclosing filling. Pinch edges together to seal, and crimp with the tines of a fork. Brush tops with egg wash.

4. Place pies, on baking sheets, in freezer for 30 minutes. Meanwhile, position oven racks in upper and lower thirds of oven and preheat oven to 375°F (190°C).

## Tips

When cutting large rounds, you can use the flat section of a two-piece tart pan as a template and the outer section as a cutter, being careful of sharp edges. If you don't have an appropriately-sized tart tin, a pot lid also makes a good guide.

For step-by-step photographs of making hand pies, see page 35.

5. Using tip of a sharp knife, cut 2 or 3 slits in top of each pie. Bake in preheated oven for 25 to 30 minutes, switching positions of baking sheets halfway through, until puffed and golden brown. Let cool on sheets on wire racks for 5 minutes before serving.

## Variations

Substitute Flaky Pie Dough (page 15) or Whole Wheat Pie Dough (page 18) for the Hand Pie Dough.

*Gluten-Free Alternative:* Substitute Gluten-Free Pie Dough (page 24) for the Hand Pie Dough.

*Vegan Alternative:* Substitute Vegan Pie Dough (page 25) for the Hand Pie Dough. Substitute water for the egg wash and use vegan butter instead of unsalted butter. Omit the blue cheese.

## Make Ahead

The turnovers can be assembled and frozen for up to one month. Place in the freezer on baking trays for at least 30 minutes, then seal in zip-top bags. Bake from frozen, as directed.

# Spicy Jamaican Black Bean and Sweet Potato Pies

- **GF Friendly**
- **Vegan Friendly**

*Spicy, distinctive and complex, Jamaican jerk seasoning is commonly used to marinate grilled chicken, fish or pork. In this recipe I paired it with two other ingredients often found in Caribbean cuisine: roasted sweet potatoes and black beans. These little pies will really wake up your taste buds!*

## Tip

If you prefer your food to be very spicy, opt for the Scotch bonnet pepper over the jalapeño. Scotch bonnets are chiles that are similar to habanero peppers, and they are often used in Caribbean cooking.

- Preheat oven to 400°F (200°C)
- Rimmed baking sheet
- Food processor
- 6-inch (15 cm) round cutter
- 2 baking sheets lined with parchment

### Filling

| | | |
|---|---|---|
| 2 cups | diced peeled sweet potatoes | 500 mL |
| 6 tbsp | extra-virgin olive oil, divided | 90 mL |
| | Salt and freshly ground black pepper | |
| ½ | yellow onion, chopped | ½ |
| 2 | green onions, chopped | 2 |
| 1 | Scotch bonnet or jalapeño pepper, seeded and chopped (see Tip, left) | 1 |
| 2 tbsp | freshly squeezed lime juice | 30 mL |
| 1 tbsp | low-sodium soy sauce | 15 mL |
| 2 tbsp | packed light brown sugar | 30 mL |
| 2 tsp | chopped fresh thyme leaves | 10 mL |
| 1 tsp | ground allspice | 5 mL |
| ½ tsp | ground cinnamon | 2 mL |
| ½ tsp | ground nutmeg | 2 mL |
| 1 | can (15 oz/470 g) black beans, drained | 1 |
| ¼ cup | chopped fresh cilantro leaves | 60 mL |
| 1 | recipe Flaky Pie Dough (page 15) | 1 |
| 1 | large egg, lightly beaten with 1 tbsp (15 mL) water | 1 |

1. *Filling:* On rimmed baking sheet, toss sweet potatoes with 2 tbsp (30 mL) olive oil and season to taste with salt and pepper. Roast in preheated oven, stirring occasionally, until tender, 25 to 35 minutes. Transfer to a large bowl and turn off oven.

2. In food processor fitted with the metal blade, purée onion, green onions, chile pepper, remaining ¼ cup (60 mL) olive oil, lime juice, soy sauce, brown sugar, thyme, allspice, cinnamon and nutmeg until smooth. Add to sweet potatoes, tossing to coat. Stir in beans and cilantro.

## Tips

When cutting large rounds, you can use the flat section of a two-piece tart pan as a template and the outer section as a cutter, being careful of sharp edges. If you don't have an appropriately-sized tart tin, a pot lid also makes a good guide.

For step-by-step photographs of making hand pies, see page 35.

3. On a lightly floured surface, roll out dough to slightly thicker than $1/16$ inch (2 mm). Using cutter, cut into rounds and place on prepared baking sheets, spacing apart. Reroll scraps as necessary.

4. Brush edges of rounds with egg wash. Place about $1/4$ cup (60 mL) filling in center of each round. Fold in half, enclosing filling. Pinch edges together to seal, and crimp with the tines of a fork. Brush tops with egg wash.

5. Place pies, on baking sheets, in freezer for 30 minutes. Meanwhile, position oven racks in upper and lower thirds of oven and preheat oven to 400°F (200°C).

6. Using tip of a knife, cut 2 or 3 slits in top of each pie. Bake in preheated oven for 25 to 30 minutes, switching positions of baking sheets halfway through, until puffed and golden brown. Let cool on sheets on wire racks for 5 minutes before serving.

## Variations

Substitute Hand Pie Dough (page 27) or Whole Wheat Pie Dough (page 18) for the Flaky Pie Dough.

*Gluten-Free Alternative:* Substitute Gluten-Free Pie Dough (page 24) for the Flaky Pie Dough. Substitute gluten-free soy sauce for the low-sodium soy sauce.

*Vegan Alternative:* Substitute Vegan Pie Dough (page 25) for the Flaky Pie Dough and water for the egg wash.

## Make Ahead

The pies can be assembled (Steps 1 through 4) and frozen for up to one month. Place in the freezer for at least 30 minutes on baking trays, then seal in zip-top bags. Bake from frozen, as directed.

# Moroccan Chickpea Hand Pies

- **GF Friendly**
- **Vegan Friendly**

*The filling for these pies is a variation on a vegetarian soup I make that is full of both flavor and protein. In addition to traditional Moroccan seasonings such as cumin and coriander, the interesting incorporation of peanut butter adds a subtle but noticeably smooth and toasty flavor.*

## Tips

An alternative to using canned chickpeas is to cook dried chickpeas. For this quantity you need 1 cup (250 mL) dried chickpeas. Cover with 3 cups (750 mL) water and set aside to soak overnight. Drain and transfer to a large saucepan. Add 3 cups (750 mL) fresh water, bring to a boil and simmer for approximately 1 hour or until tender. Drain and cool before using in the recipe.

This recipe will leave you with some extra filling. You can either make a second batch (or half-batch) of dough to make additional pies or you can enjoy the filling on its own.

- 6-inch (15 cm) round cutter
- 2 baking sheets lined with parchment

### Filling

| | | |
|---|---|---|
| 1 tbsp | olive oil | 15 mL |
| ½ | yellow onion, chopped | ½ |
| ½ | red bell pepper, seeded and chopped | ½ |
| 2 | carrots, chopped | 2 |
| 2 | cloves garlic, minced | 2 |
| 1 | can (14 oz/440 g) diced tomatoes, with juices | 1 |
| 1 | can (14 oz/440 g) chickpeas, drained (see Tips, left) | 1 |
| 2 tbsp | freshly squeezed lemon juice | 30 mL |
| 1 tsp | ground ginger | 5 mL |
| 1 tsp | ground cumin | 5 mL |
| 1 tsp | curry powder | 5 mL |
| 1 tsp | ground coriander | 5 mL |
| 1 tsp | chili powder | 5 mL |
| ½ tsp | salt | 2 mL |
| ½ tsp | freshly ground black pepper | 2 mL |
| ¼ cup | golden raisins | 60 mL |
| 2 tbsp | creamy peanut butter | 30 mL |
| 2 | recipes Hand Pie Dough (page 27; see Tips, left) | 2 |
| 1 | large egg, lightly beaten with 1 tbsp (15 mL) water | 1 |

1. *Filling:* In a large skillet, heat oil over medium-high heat. Add onion, bell pepper and carrots; sauté until softened, about 6 minutes. Add garlic and sauté for 1 minute. Add tomatoes with juices, chickpeas, lemon juice, ginger, cumin, curry powder, coriander, chili powder, salt and pepper. Bring to a boil, reduce heat and simmer, stirring occasionally, until thickened, 10 to 15 minutes.

2. Stir in raisins and peanut butter; simmer for 5 minutes. Remove from heat and set aside to cool completely.

When cutting large rounds, you can use the flat section of a two-piece tart pan as a template and the outer section as a cutter, being careful of sharp edges. If you don't have an appropriately-sized tart tin, a pot lid also makes a good guide.

For step-by-step photographs of making hand pies, see page 35.

3. On a lightly floured surface, roll out dough to slightly thicker than $1/16$ inch (2 mm). Using cutter, cut into rounds and place on prepared baking sheets, spacing apart. Reroll scraps as necessary.

4. Brush edges of rounds with egg wash. Place about $1/4$ cup (60 mL) filling in center of each round. Fold in half, enclosing filling. Pinch edges together to seal, and crimp with the tines of a fork. Brush tops with egg wash.

5. Place pies, on baking sheets, in freezer for 30 minutes. Meanwhile, position oven racks in upper and lower thirds of oven and preheat oven to 375°F (190°C).

6. Using tip of a sharp knife, cut 2 or 3 slits in top of each pie. Bake in preheated oven for 25 to 30 minutes, switching positions of baking sheets halfway through, until puffed and golden brown. Let cool on sheets on wire racks for 5 minutes before serving.

## Variations

Substitute 2 recipes Flaky Pie Dough (page 15) or Whole Wheat Pie Dough (page 18) for the Hand Pie Dough.

*Gluten-Free Alternative:* Substitute 2 recipes Gluten-Free Pie Dough (page 24) for the Hand Pie Dough.

*Vegan Alternative:* Substitute 2 recipes Vegan Pie Dough (page 25) for the Hand Pie Dough and water for the egg wash.

## Make Ahead

The pies can be assembled (Steps 1 through 4) and frozen for up to one month. Place in freezer for at least 30 minutes on baking trays, then seal in zip-top bags. Bake from frozen, as directed.

# Minestrone Pot Pies

- **GF Friendly**
- **Vegan Friendly**

*I don't know anyone who enjoys a hearty bowl of soup as much as my dad. He loves to eat it served with a big piece of fresh bread for dunking or, even better, in a bowl made of bread. I think these pot pies, chockfull of vegetables in a thick tomato sauce, will get his seal of approval.*

## Tip

Cannellini beans are often referred to as white kidney beans. If you cannot find them, use red kidney beans or garbanzo beans (chickpeas) in their place.

- 3- and 4½-inch (7.5 and 11.25 cm) round cutters
- Two 12-cup muffin tins, lightly greased

### Filling

| | | |
|---|---|---|
| 1 tbsp | butter | 15 mL |
| 1 tbsp | olive oil | 15 mL |
| ½ | red onion, chopped | ½ |
| 1 | carrot, chopped | 1 |
| 1 | rib celery, chopped | 1 |
| 1 tbsp | minced garlic | 15 mL |
| 1 cup | cubed peeled potato | 250 mL |
| 1 | bunch kale, trimmed and chopped | 1 |
| 1 tbsp | chopped fresh thyme | 15 mL |
| 1 | can (14 oz/440 g) can diced tomatoes, drained | 1 |
| 2 tbsp | tomato paste | 30 mL |
| ½ cup | dry white wine | 125 mL |
| 1 cup | chicken or vegetable stock | 250 mL |
| 1 cup | drained canned cannellini beans (see Tip, left) | 250 mL |
| 1½ cups | freshly grated Parmesan cheese, divided Salt and freshly ground black pepper | 375 mL |
| 1 | recipe Flaky Pie Dough (page 15) | 1 |
| 1 | large egg, lightly beaten with 1 tbsp (15 mL) water | 1 |

1. *Filling:* In a large skillet, heat butter and oil over medium-high heat. Add onion, carrot, celery and garlic; sauté until tender, about 5 minutes. Add potato, kale and thyme; sauté for 4 minutes. Add tomatoes and tomato paste, stirring to blend. Add white wine and chicken stock. Bring to a boil, reduce heat and simmer for 10 minutes. Add beans to skillet and simmer, stirring occasionally, until mixure has thickened, 15 to 20 minutes.

2. Add ³⁄₄ cup (175 mL) Parmesan and stir until melted. Season to taste with salt and pepper. Remove from heat and set aside to cool completely.

## Tips

Expect a longer baking time (6 to 10 minutes) if you need to use 2 muffin tins and they are too large to fit on one rack.

The easiest way to remove pies from muffin tins is to run a small, sharp knife or small offset spatula around the edges, loosening the sides. You should then be able to carefully lift out the pies, guiding them with the knife or spatula.

3. Divide dough into two pieces, one slightly larger than the other. On a lightly floured surface, roll out larger piece to a thickness of $1/8$ inch (3 mm). Using $4^1/_2$-inch (11.25 cm) cutter, cut 16 rounds and carefully fit into muffin cups (they should stand a bit taller than edges of cups). Reroll scraps as necessary.

4. Fill each shell with a heaping $1/4$ cup (60 mL) minestrone filling and top with additional Parmesan.

5. On lightly floured surface, roll out smaller piece of dough to slightly thicker than $1/16$ inch (2 mm). Using 3-inch (7.5 cm) cutter, cut 16 rounds, rerolling scraps as necessary.

6. Brush bottoms of smaller rounds with egg wash and carefully place on top of filled shells, pinching edges together to seal tightly. Brush tops with egg wash.

7. Place tins in freezer for 30 minutes. Meanwhile, preheat oven to 375°F (190°C).

8. Using tip of a sharp knife, cut 3 slits in top crusts. Bake on center rack of preheated oven for 30 to 40 minutes, until tops are golden brown and filling is bubbling through holes.

9. Cool pies in tins on wire racks for 10 minutes, then carefully unmold and transfer to serving plates. Serve warm.

### Variations

Substitute Parmesan Cheese Dough (see Variations, page 23) or Whole Wheat Pie Dough (page 18) for the Flaky Pie Dough.

*Gluten-Free Alternative:* Substitute Gluten-Free Pie Dough (page 24) for the Flaky Pie Dough.

*Vegan Alternative:* Substitute Vegan Pie Dough (page 25) for the Flaky Pie Dough. Eliminate the Parmesan cheese or replace with vegan cheese. Replace the butter with 1 tbsp (15 mL) oil and substitute water for the egg wash.

### Make Ahead

The pies can be assembled and frozen for up to five days. Place in the freezer in their tins, tightly wrapped. Bake from frozen, as directed.

# Wild Mushroom and Fresh Herb Tarts

| | | |
|---|---|---|
| **Makes 8 tarts** | | |

● **GF Friendly**

*My husband and I both love wild mushrooms, so I am always trying to create new ways to serve them for dinner. These flaky pies, made with puff pastry, were inspired by a wild mushroom and fontina pizza I made, which he devoured with gusto. Depending on how spicy you like your food, you can double the hot pepper flakes or omit them altogether.*

## Tips

Substitute 1 lb (500 g) store-bought puff pastry, thawed, for ½ recipe Shortcut Puff Pastry.

It is best to use fresh herbs in recipes, but this is not always possible. If you need to substitute dried herbs for fresh, use 1 tsp (5 mL) dried for every 1 tbsp (15 mL) fresh.

● Pizza/pastry cutter, optional
● 2 baking sheets lined with parchment

### Filling

| | | |
|---|---|---|
| 1 tbsp | olive oil | 15 mL |
| 9 oz | mixed wild mushrooms (such as shiitake, cremini and portobello) | 275 g |
| ¼ cup | dry white wine | 60 mL |
| 1 tbsp | chopped fresh thyme leaves | 15 mL |
| ¼ cup | chopped fresh Italian parsley leaves | 60 mL |
| ⅛ tsp | hot pepper flakes | 0.5 mL |
| | Salt and freshly ground black pepper | |
| ½ | recipe Shortcut Puff Pastry (page 29; see Tips, left) | ½ |
| 1 | large egg, lightly beaten with 1 tbsp (15 mL) water | 1 |
| 1 cup | shredded fontina cheese | 250 mL |
| ½ cup | freshly grated Parmesan cheese | 125 mL |

1. *Filling:* In a large skillet, heat oil over medium-high heat. Add mushrooms and sauté until softened and any accumulated liquid has evaporated, 8 to 10 minutes. Add wine and sauté until almost evaporated, 2 to 3 minutes. Stir in thyme, parsley and hot pepper flakes. Season to taste with salt and pepper and transfer to a bowl. Set aside to cool completely.

2. On a lightly floured surface, roll out pastry into a 21- by 11-inch (53 by 28 cm) rectangle. Using a sharp knife or pizza cutter, trim to an even 20 by 10 inches (50 by 25 cm), discarding scraps. Cut into eight 5-inch (12.5 cm) squares and transfer to prepared baking sheets.

3. Brush surfaces of squares with egg wash. Place about 2 tbsp (30 mL) fontina in center of each square. Top with about ¼ cup (60 mL) mushroom filling and 1 tbsp (15 mL) Parmesan.

## Tips

To produce a flaky crust, it is important that the puff pastry remain cool throughout the assembly process. If the pastry becomes too warm at any point, transfer it to a baking sheet and return it to the refrigerator for 20 minutes. Pick up the process where you left off.

For step-by-step photographs of making Shortcut Puff Pastry, see page 42.

4. Fold up corners of each square around filling so points meet near center but do not touch. Press lightly to distribute filling evenly. Brush tops with egg wash.

5. Place tarts, on baking sheets, in refrigerator or freezer and chill for 30 minutes. Meanwhile, position oven racks in upper and lower thirds of oven and preheat oven to 400°F (200°C).

6. Bake in preheated oven for 25 to 30 minutes, switching positions of baking sheets halfway through, until golden brown and puffed. Serve warm.

## Variations

Substitute 1 recipe Cornmeal Pie Dough (page 19) for the $1/2$ recipe Shortcut Puff Pastry.

*Gluten-Free Alternative:* Substitute 1 recipe Gluten-Free Pie Dough (page 24) for the $1/2$ recipe Shortcut Puff Pastry.

## Make Ahead

The mushroom filling can be prepared one day in advance, covered and refrigerated.

The assembled tarts can be prepared in advance and refrigerated for up to three hours.

# Ratatouille Turnovers

- **GF Friendly**
- **Vegan Friendly**

*The name of this traditional Provençal stewed vegetable dish is derived from the French verb* touiller, *which means "to toss." Colorful eggplant, peppers, red onions and zucchini are roasted and then, yes, tossed with tomatoes, basil and capers before being baked in flaky crusts.*

## Tips

When shopping for eggplant, choose ones that are firm and heavy for their size. The skin should be smooth and shiny, with a bright purple color, and free of discoloration, scars and bruises.

This recipe will leave you with some extra filling. You can either make a second batch (or half-batch) of dough to make additional pies or you can enjoy the filling on its own.

- Preheat oven to 450°F (230°C)
- Roasting pan
- 6-inch (15 cm) round cutter
- 2 baking sheets lined with parchment

### Filling

| | | |
|---|---|---|
| 1 | large eggplant, cut in 1-inch (2.5 cm) cubes | 1 |
| 1 | medium zucchini, chopped | 1 |
| 1 | red bell pepper, seeded and chopped | 1 |
| 1 | yellow onion, chopped | 1 |
| 1 tbsp | minced garlic | 15 mL |
| 3 tbsp | extra-virgin olive oil | 45 mL |
| 1 tbsp | herbes de Provence | 15 mL |
| 1 tsp | salt | 5 mL |
| ½ tsp | freshly ground black pepper | 2 mL |
| ¼ tsp | hot pepper flakes | 1 mL |
| 1½ cups | crushed tomatoes | 375 mL |
| ¼ cup | chopped fresh basil leaves | 60 mL |
| 3 tbsp | capers | 45 mL |
| | Salt and freshly ground black pepper | |
| | | |
| 1 | recipe Flaky Pie Dough (page 15) | 1 |
| 1 | large egg, lightly beaten with 1 tbsp (15 mL) water | 1 |
| ¾ cup | freshly grated Parmesan cheese | 175 mL |

1. *Filling:* In a large bowl, combine eggplant, zucchini, bell pepper, onion, garlic, olive oil, herbes de Provence, salt, pepper and hot pepper flakes. Toss well.

2. Spread out vegetables in roasting pan and roast in preheated oven until tender, stirring once, about 25 minutes. Add crushed tomatoes and stir well. Cover pan with foil and roast for 10 minutes more. Turn off oven. Transfer vegetables to a large bowl and stir in basil and capers. Season to taste with salt and pepper. Set aside to cool completely.

3. On a lightly floured surface, roll out dough to slightly thicker than $1/16$ inch (2 mm). Using cutter, cut into rounds and place on prepared baking sheets, spacing apart. Reroll scraps as necessary.

When cutting large rounds, you can use the flat section of a two-piece tart pan as a template and the outer section as a cutter, being careful of sharp edges. If you don't have an appropriately-sized tart tin, a pot lid also makes a good guide.

For step-by-step photographs of making these hand pies, see page 35.

4. Brush edges of rounds with egg wash. Place about $1/4$ cup (60 mL) filling in center of each round. Top with 1 tbsp (15 mL) Parmesan. Fold in half, enclosing filling. Pinch edges together to seal, and crimp with the tines of a fork. Brush tops with egg wash.

5. Place pies, on baking sheets, in freezer for 30 minutes. Meanwhile, position oven racks in upper and lower thirds of oven and preheat oven to 375°F (190°C).

6. Using tip of a sharp knife, cut 2 or 3 slits in top of each pie. Bake in preheated oven for 30 to 35 minutes, switching positions of baking sheets halfway through, until puffed and golden brown. Let cool on sheets on wire racks for 5 minutes before serving.

## Variations

Substitute Pizza/Calzone Dough (page 30), Savory Cheese Dough (page 23) or Hand Pie Dough (page 27) for the Flaky Pie Dough.

*Gluten-Free Alternative:* Substitute Gluten-Free Pie Dough (page 24) for the Flaky Pie Dough.

*Vegan Alternative:* Substitute Vegan Pie Dough (page 25) for the Flaky Pie Dough. Eliminate the Parmesan or replace with vegan cheese, and substitute water for the egg wash.

## Make Ahead

The turnovers can be assembled and frozen for up to one month. Place in freezer on baking trays for at least 30 minutes, then seal in zip-top bags. Bake from frozen, as directed.

# Roasted Vegetable Calzones

- **GF Friendly**
- **Vegan Friendly**

*While my husband prefers his pizza packed with sausage and cheese, I prefer mine loaded with an array of roasted fresh vegetables. Roasting vegetables is not only easy but brings out their natural sweetness and intensifies their flavor. These calzones can be enjoyed with or without cheese — they're fantastic either way.*

## Tip

Cremini mushrooms are a cross between white button mushrooms and portobellos, with an earthier flavor than button mushrooms. They are sometimes sold as "baby bella" mushrooms.

- Preheat oven to 400°F (200°C)
- Rimmed baking sheet
- 6-inch (15 cm) round cutter
- 2 baking sheets lined with parchment

### Filling

| | | |
|---|---|---|
| 1 | red onion, chopped | 1 |
| 1 | red bell pepper, seeded and chopped | 1 |
| 6 oz | cremini mushrooms, quartered | 175 g |
| 1 cup | grape tomatoes | 250 mL |
| 2 tsp | minced garlic | 10 mL |
| ¼ cup | extra-virgin olive oil | 60 mL |
| 1 tsp | salt | 5 mL |
| ½ tsp | freshly ground black pepper | 2 mL |
| ½ cup | chopped marinated artichoke hearts | 125 mL |
| ⅓ cup | chopped pitted kalamata olives | 75 mL |
| ¼ cup | chopped fresh basil leaves | 60 mL |
| 1 | recipe Pizza/Calzone Dough (page 30) | 1 |
| 1 | large egg, lightly beaten with 1 tbsp (15 mL) water | 1 |
| 1½ cups | shredded mozzarella cheese, optional | 375 mL |

1. *Filling:* On rimmed baking sheet, combine onion, bell pepper, mushrooms and tomatoes. Scatter garlic evenly overtop. Drizzle olive oil evenly overtop and sprinkle with salt and pepper. Toss well. Roast in preheated oven, stirring once, until vegetables are softened and browned, about 25 minutes. Remove from oven and set aside to cool completely. Turn off oven.

2. Transfer vegetables to a large bowl. Add artichokes, olives and basil; toss to mix.

3. Divide dough into halves. On a lightly floured surface, roll one piece to a thickness of ⅛ inch (3 mm). Using cutter, cut into rounds and place on prepared baking sheets, spacing apart. Reroll scraps as necessary. Repeat with second half of dough.

## Tips

Pizza/Calzone Dough is very springy. It doesn't hold its shape when rolled out as well as most other doughs.

Use the egg wash sparingly on the edges. They are harder to seal if too wet. When crimping the edges, dip the fork in the egg wash if you have problems with it sticking to the dough.

4. Brush edges of rounds with egg wash (see Tips, left). Place about $1/4$ cup (60 mL) vegetable filling in center of each round. Top with 2 tbsp (30 mL) mozzarella, if using. Fold rounds in half, enclosing filling, then fold the edges over to create a double thickness. Pinch edges together to seal, and crimp with the tines of a fork. Brush tops with egg wash.

5. Place pies, on baking sheets, in freezer for 30 minutes. Meanwhile, position oven racks in upper and lower thirds of oven and preheat oven to 400°F (200°C).

6. Using tip of a sharp knife, cut 3 small slits in top of each calzone. Bake in preheated oven for 35 to 45 minutes, switching positions of baking sheets halfway through, until puffed and golden brown. Let cool on sheets on wire racks for 5 minutes before serving.

## Variations

Substitute Whole Wheat Pie Dough (page 18), Hand Pie Dough (page 27) or Savory Cheese Dough (page 23) for the Pizza/Calzone Dough.

*Gluten-Free Alternative:* Substitute Gluten-Free Pie Dough (page 24) for the Pizza/Calzone Dough.

*Vegan Alternative:* Substitute Vegan Pie Dough (page 25) for the Pizza/Calzone Dough. Omit the mozzarella or use vegan cheese, and replace the egg wash with water.

## Make Ahead

The pies can be assembled and frozen for up to one month. Freeze for at least 30 minutes on baking trays, then seal in zip-top bags. Bake from frozen, as directed.

# Eggplant Caponata Pies

**Makes 16 pies**

- **GF Friendly**
- **Vegan Friendly**

*Caponata is a classic sweet-and-sour Sicilian dish that includes eggplant, briny capers, plump golden raisins and buttery pine nuts. There are many variations of this recipe. It often incorporates seafood and can be served as either a side dish or a main course. Here it fits perfectly into a crisp handheld crust.*

## Tip

Choose Italian (flat-leaf) parsley as opposed to the coarser curly variety often used as a garnish.

- 5- to 6-inch (12.5 to 15 cm) round cutter
- 2 baking sheets lined with parchment

### Filling

| | | |
|---|---|---|
| ¾ cup | olive oil | 175 mL |
| 1 | medium eggplant, peeled and cubed | 1 |
| 1 | red onion, chopped | 1 |
| 3 | cloves garlic, chopped | 3 |
| 1 | can (14 oz/440 g) diced tomatoes, with juices | 1 |
| 3 tbsp | tomato paste | 45 mL |
| ¼ cup | balsamic vinegar | 60 mL |
| 1 tbsp | granulated sugar | 15 mL |
| ¼ cup | capers | 60 mL |
| ¼ cup | golden raisins | 60 mL |
| ¼ cup | chopped parsley leaves (see Tip, left) | 60 mL |
| 2 tbsp | pine nuts | 30 mL |
| | Salt and freshly ground black pepper | |
| 1 | recipe Hand Pie Dough (page 27) | 1 |
| 1 | large egg, lightly beaten with 1 tbsp (15 mL) water | 1 |

1. *Filling:* In a large skillet, heat oil over medium-high heat. Add eggplant and sauté until browned, about 8 minutes. Transfer to a large bowl.

2. Add onion and garlic to skillet and sauté for 4 minutes. Add tomatoes, with juices, and tomato paste. Reduce heat and simmer, stirring occasionally, until thickened, about 10 minutes. Add vinegar, sugar, capers and raisins; stir well and simmer, stirring occasionally, for 10 minutes. Add to eggplant. Add parsley and pine nuts and toss to blend. Season to taste with salt and pepper. Set aside to cool completely.

3. On a lightly floured surface, roll out dough to slightly thicker than $1/16$ inch (2 mm). Using cutter, cut into rounds and place on prepared baking sheets, spacing apart. Reroll scraps as necessary.

## Tips

If you don't own round cutters in the appropriate sizes, look for lids of the same size from prepared foods.

For step-by-step photographs of making hand pies, see page 35.

4. Brush edges of rounds with egg wash. Place about $1/4$ cup (60 mL) filling in center of each round. Fold in half, enclosing filling. Pinch together edges to seal, and crimp with the tines of a fork. Brush tops with egg wash.

5. Place pies, on baking sheets, in freezer for 30 minutes. Meanwhile, position oven racks in upper and lower thirds of oven and preheat oven to 375°F (190°C).

6. Using tip of a sharp knife, cut 2 or 3 slits in top of each pie. Bake in preheated oven for 30 to 35 minutes, switching positions of baking sheets halfway through, until puffed and golden brown. Let cool on sheets on wire racks for 5 minutes before serving.

## Variations

Substitute Whole Wheat Pie Dough (page 18), Flaky Pie Dough (page 15) or Savory Cheese Dough (page 23) for the Hand Pie Dough.

*Gluten-Free Alternative:* Substitute Gluten-Free Pie Dough (page 24) for the Hand Pie Dough.

*Vegan Alternative:* Substitute Vegan Pie Dough (page 25) for the Hand Pie Dough and water for the egg wash.

## Make Ahead

The pies can be assembled (Steps 1 through 4) and frozen for up to one month. Freeze for at least 30 minutes on baking trays, then seal in zip-top bags. Bake from frozen, as directed.

# Port-Glazed Fig and Blue Cheese Pies

● **GF Friendly**

*Every year, as soon as fresh figs are in season, I buy them as quickly as we can eat them. Sometimes I will grill them wrapped in prosciutto, or include them, simply quartered, in a salad. One of my favorite recipes involves glazing figs in a port reduction and serving them as a topping for bruschetta, over which I sprinkle tangy blue cheese. If you love figs, you will love these pies.*

## Tip

Fresh figs should be used soon after they are purchased. They keep best at room temperature, but they will keep a bit longer in the refrigerator. However, chilling tends to take away from their full flavor.

● **5-inch (12.5 cm) round cutter**
● **2 baking sheets lined with parchment**

### Filling

| | | |
|---|---|---|
| 1¾ cups | ruby port | 425 mL |
| 16 | fresh black figs, stemmed and quartered (see Tip, left) | 16 |
| ½ cup | granulated sugar | 125 mL |
| 2 tsp | chopped fresh rosemary | 10 mL |
| 2 tbsp | freshly squeezed lemon juice | 30 mL |
| ¼ tsp | salt | 1 mL |
| ¼ tsp | freshly ground black pepper | 1 mL |
| 1 tbsp | unsalted butter | 15 mL |
| 1 | recipe Hand Pie Dough (page 27) | 1 |
| 1 | large egg, lightly beaten with 1 tbsp (15 mL) water | 1 |
| 1 cup | crumbled blue cheese | 250 mL |

1. *Filling:* In a large saucepan, combine port, figs, sugar, rosemary, lemon juice, salt and pepper. Bring to a boil over medium-high heat, stirring constantly to dissolve sugar. Reduce heat and simmer until liquid is reduced and becomes syrupy, about 25 minutes. Remove from heat and set aside to cool completely.

2. On a lightly floured surface, roll out dough to slightly thicker than $^1/_{16}$ inch (2 mm). Using cutter, cut into rounds and place on prepared baking sheets, spacing apart. Reroll scraps as necessary.

3. Brush edges of rounds with egg wash. Place 4 fig quarters in center of each round and top with 1 tbsp (15 mL) blue cheese. Fold in half, enclosing filling. Pinch edges together to seal, and crimp with the tines of a fork. Brush tops with egg wash.

4. Place pies, on baking sheets, in freezer for 30 minutes. Meanwhile, position oven racks in upper and lower thirds of oven and preheat oven to 375°F (190°C).

## Tips

Once you start using parchment paper, you will never want to go back to silicone liners or greased baking sheets. Disposable, heat-resistant and nonstick, parchment will make your pie-baking life much, much easier! Use it to line baking sheets or tart shells when blind-baking. When you have finished baking, simply throw out the used parchment. It makes for extremely easy clean-up.

For step-by-step photographs of making hand pies, see page 35.

5. Using tip of a sharp knife, cut 2 or 3 slits in top of each pie. Bake in preheated oven for 20 to 25 minutes, switching positions of baking sheets halfway through, until puffed and golden brown. Let pies cool on sheets on wire racks for 5 minutes before serving.

## Variations

Substitute Whole Wheat Pie Dough (page 18), Flaky Pie Dough (page 15) or Savory Cheese Dough (page 23) for the Hand Pie Dough.

*Gluten-Free Alternative:* Substitute Gluten-Free Pie Dough (page 24) for the Hand Pie Dough.

## Make Ahead

The pies can be assembled and frozen for up to one month. Freeze for at least 30 minutes on baking trays, then seal in zip-top bags. Bake from frozen, as directed.

# Caramelized Onion and Fresh Peach Pies

---

**Makes 12 pies**

- **GF Friendly**
- **Vegan Friendly**

---

*To me, it's a true sign that summer is at its peak when you can find peaches at their juiciest. These pies are proof that ingredients need not be complex in order to yield mouthwatering results. Vidalia onions are slowly caramelized until they are a rich golden brown, and then they are tossed with juicy ripe peaches — simple, sweet, spectacular!*

---

## Tip

Don't try to rush the cooking of caramelized onions. If you do, you will end up instead with browned sautéed onions, which have an entirely different flavor than sweet, melt-in-your-mouth caramelized onions.

- 5- or 6-inch (12.5 or 15 cm) round cutter
- 2 baking sheets lined with parchment
- Pastry brush

### Filling

| | | |
|---|---|---:|
| 1 tbsp | unsalted butter | 15 mL |
| 1 tbsp | extra-virgin olive oil | 15 mL |
| 1 | large Vidalia onion, sliced thinly | 1 |
| 1 tbsp | packed brown sugar | 15 mL |
| 2 tsp | chopped fresh thyme | 10 mL |
| 1 tsp | salt | 5 mL |
| ½ tsp | ground black pepper | 2 mL |
| 3 | ripe peaches, peeled and chopped | 3 |
| 1 | recipe All-Butter Pie Dough (page 16) | 1 |
| 1 | large egg, lightly beaten with 1 tbsp (15 mL) water | 1 |

1. *Filling:* In a large skillet, melt butter with olive oil over medium heat. Add onion and sauté, stirring frequently, for 10 minutes. Add brown sugar, thyme, salt and pepper. Sauté until onions are deep golden brown and caramelized, about 30 minutes. Transfer to a large bowl and set aside to cool completely. When cool, add peaches and toss to mix.

2. On a lightly floured surface, roll out dough to slightly thicker than ¹⁄₁₆ inch (2 mm). Using cutter, cut into rounds and place on prepared baking sheets, spacing apart. Reroll scraps as necessary.

3. Brush edges of rounds with egg wash. Place about ¼ cup (60 mL) filling in center of each round. Fold in half, enclosing filling. Pinch edges together to seal, and crimp with the tines of a fork. Brush tops with egg wash.

4. Place pies, on baking sheets, in freezer for 30 minutes. Meanwhile, position oven racks in upper and lower thirds of oven and preheat oven to 375°F (190°C).

## Tips

A dough scraper is very useful to have when making these recipes. During the rolling process, it collects the little bits for rerolling and it cleans up the pastry board very efficiently. It also simplifies picking up the cut rounds; you just slide the scraper underneath. Even if they are sticking a bit, they will detach without tearing.

For step-by-step photographs of making hand pies, see page 35.

5. Using the tip of a sharp knife, cut 2 or 3 slits in top of each pie. Bake in preheated oven for 28 to 33 minutes, switching positions of baking sheets halfway through, until puffed and golden brown. Let cool on sheets on wire racks for 5 minutes before serving.

## Variations

Substitute Whole Wheat Pie Dough (page 18), Flaky Pie Dough (page 15) or Cornmeal Pie Dough (page 19) for the All-Butter Pie Dough.

*Gluten-Free Alternative:* Substitute Gluten-Free Pie Dough (page 24) for the All-Butter Pie Dough.

*Vegan Alternative:* Substitute Vegan Pie Dough (page 25) for the All-Butter Pie Dough. Replace the egg wash with water and use vegan butter or 1 tbsp (15 mL) olive oil in place of the butter.

## Make Ahead

The pies can be assembled and frozen for up to one month. Freeze for at least 30 minutes on baking trays, then seal in zip-top bags. Bake from frozen, as directed.

# Mini Broccoli and Cheddar Crustless Quiches

*While these quiches might be missing crusts, they certainly aren't lacking in flavor. This recipe comes together in minutes — perfect when time is limited. They also make a protein-packed breakfast on the go. Grab one (or two!) on your way out the door.*

## Tip

If using frozen broccoli florets instead of fresh, heat in the microwave according to package instructions, and drain fully before adding to bowl. Otherwise the quiches will be watery.

- Preheat oven to 325°F (160°C)
- 12-cup muffin tin, greased

| | | |
|---|---|---|
| 1 tbsp | unsalted butter | 15 mL |
| ½ | yellow onion, chopped | ½ |
| 5 | large eggs | 5 |
| 1 cup | whole milk | 250 mL |
| 1 cup | steamed fresh or frozen broccoli florets, chopped | 250 mL |
| ⅔ cup | shredded Cheddar cheese | 150 mL |
| 2 tbsp | chopped fresh parsley leaves | 30 mL |
| 2 tbsp | chopped green onions | 30 mL |
| ½ tsp | salt | 2 mL |
| ½ tsp | ground black pepper | 2 mL |

1. In a medium skillet, melt butter over medium-high heat. Add onion and sauté until softened, about 5 minutes. Remove from heat and set aside.

2. In a large bowl, whisk together eggs and milk until well blended. Add broccoli, cheese, parsley, green onions, salt, pepper and reserved onion, stirring to mix.

3. Pour mixture into prepared muffin tins, filling almost to the top.

4. Bake in preheated oven for 25 to 30 minutes, until tops are puffed and set. Cool for 10 minutes, then carefully run a knife around edges and unmold. Serve warm or at room temperature.

### Make Ahead

The quiches can be fully baked, cooled to room temperature and frozen for up to two weeks, sealed in a zip-top bag. Reheat from frozen on baking sheets, at 350°F (180°C) for 15 to 20 minutes or until heated through.

**Library and Archives Canada Cataloguing in Publication**

Hession, Julie Anne
 175 best mini pie recipes / Julie Anne Hession.

Includes index.
ISBN 978-0-7788-0439-0

1. Pies.  2. Cookbooks.
I. Title.  II. Title: One hundred seventy-five best mini pie recipes.

TX773.H475 2013        641.86'52        C2012-907556-6

# Index